Pro Java M

Ovidiu Iliescu

Apress®

Pro Java ME Apps

ISBN-13 (pbk): 978-1-4302- 3327-5

ISBN-13 (electronic): 978-1-4302- 3328-2

President and Publisher: Paul Manning
Lead Editor: Steve Anglin
Development Editor: Douglas Pundick
Technical Reviewer: Carol Hamer
Editorial Board: Steve Anglin, Mark Beckner, Ewan Buckingham, Gary Cornell, Jonathan Gennick, Jonathan Hassell, Michelle Lowman, James Markham, Matthew Moodie, Jeff Olson, Jeffrey Pepper, Frank Pohlmann, Douglas Pundick, Ben Renow-Clarke, Dominic Shakeshaft, Matt Wade, Tom Welsh
Coordinating Editor: Adam Heath
Copy Editor: Mary Ann Fugate, Sharon Wilkey
Compositor: MacPS, LLC
Indexer: SPi Global
Artist: SPi Gobal
Cover Designer: Anna Ishchenko

Distributed to the book trade worldwide by Springer Science+Business Media, LLC., 233 Spring Street, 6th Floor, New York, NY 10013. Phone 1-800-SPRINGER, fax (201) 348-4505, e-mail orders-ny@springer-sbm.com, or visit www.springeronline.com.

For information on translations, please e-mail rights@apress.com, or visit www.apress.com.

Apress and friends of ED books may be purchased in bulk for academic, corporate, or promotional use. eBook versions and licenses are also available for most titles. For more information, reference our Special Bulk Sales–eBook Licensing web page at www.apress.com/bulk-sales.

The source code for this book is available to readers at www.apress.com. You will need to answer questions pertaining to this book in order to successfully download the code.

Mom, Dad, Grandpa – Thank you for everything. I love you.

Contents at a Glance

Contents

About the Author

Ovidiu Iliescu is a self-taught software developer; he started to write computer programs when he was 9 and now has almost 15 years of experience under his belt. After writing desktop applications and web-based applications, Ovidiu shifted his attention to the field of mobile development. With a passion for all things computer related, his main interests besides mobile software are computer graphics, algorithms and optimizations.

Ovidiu lives in Romania and has recently started his own software company, November Solutions, to turn his ideas into products – and maybe conquer the world. Currently, he is also working as a software developer for Enough Software and occasionally takes on interesting projects as a freelancer.

You can get in touch with Ovidiu by visiting his website at `www.ovidiuiliescu.com`.

About the Technical Reviewer

Carol Hamer received her Ph.D. in Number Theory from Rutgers, the State University of New Jersey. Since then, she has worked as a software engineer for twelve years in the U.S., France, and Switzerland, including three years working for In-Fusio Mobile Games.

Carol has written three books on mobile game programming: *J2ME Games with MIDP2*, *Creating Mobile Games*, and *Learn BlackBerry Games Development*, all from Apress.

Acknowledgments

Douglas Pundick and Carol Hamer have provided valuable help and suggestions for the book's content. Adam Heath has kept an watchful eye on things and has extended my deadlines more than once. Mary Ann Fugate and Sharon Wilkey have painstakingly copy edited the entire manuscript. Without them, this book could not exist. Thank you!

My friends and loved ones have been very supportive of me during the entire writing process. They have tolerated my busy schedule and my sometimes weary attitude. For this they have my gratitude.

Special thanks go out to Robert Virkus and to everyone at Enough Software for their support and for being an exceptionally awesome bunch of people.

Finally, a lot of people not mentioned here worked behind the scenes at Apress and at other companies to bring this book to light. Thank you!

Introduction

I find mobile phones to be amazing pieces of technology. They allow you to be almost anywhere in the world and still be able to reach your friends, loved ones, colleagues or business partners with a press of a button. If that wasn't enough, they have grown so powerful that they are now nothing short of pocket computers. Only a few decades ago the only place you could see a similar devices was a Star Trek movie – now they're reality.

Modern mobile phones run on a variety of software platforms, but by far the most popular one in terms of reach and market share is Java ME. This once feature-limited platform has grown and matured over the years along with the hardware supporting it; is now capable of delivering truly amazing applications that have the potential to reach hundreds of millions (if not billions) of people.

It is a bit disappointing, then, that the techniques developers use to write Java ME applications have not kept up with the times. Many developers, especially less experienced ones, tend to approach Java ME development in the same extremely conservative way that it was approached almost a decade ago, when the platform was in its infancy. Or, even worse, they treat Java ME like a desktop platform, with complete disregard to its nuances and to the fact that it is, in fact, a mobile platform designed to run on mobile devices. As a consequence, many Java ME applications fall short of their potential.

The book you are reading right now aims to correct this by presenting how modern Java ME application development should be approached – complete with all the important tips and techniques applicable to the platform today.

What is covered in this book

This book is somewhat different from other Java ME books, in that it is built around writing a complete and fully-functional Java ME application from scratch, using modern day development techniques. To this end, everything from writing an application framework to writing a UI module (complete with widgets and touch support) will be discussed – no important application component will be left uncovered.

Furthermore, you will get to see how all of these fit into the context of a real-world application and how individual application components interact and work together. Decisions made along the way will be explained, potential pitfalls will be highlighted and important advice stemming from hands-on experience will be given - all in an effort to create a comprehensive picture of what modern Java ME application development is all about.

Once the application is written, we will cover other aspects essential to Java ME development. Code optimization, application testing, advanced graphics, improving the user's experience and the proper Java ME developer's mindset will all be discussed.

Finally, we will take a look at Java ME's future in order to get a better understanding of where the platform is heading and a list of further research topics relevant to Java ME development will be given.

What you will need for this book

First of all, you should be familiar with Java ME development on at least an intermediate level. This is not a beginner's book – in fact, it is assumed that you have worked on at least one medium-sized Java ME application before.

Second, the target device for the source code presented in this book is the WTK emulator. For best results, it is recommended that you have both versions 2.5.2 and 3.0 installed. The WTK emulator has been chosen because of its ubiquitous nature and because it is pretty much the "reference implementation" for Java ME. However, the code is designed to be as portable as possible; running it on other emulators and on real devices should work just fine (but cannot be guaranteed).

It is also recommended that you run all the code presented and experiment with it. Java ME is all about subtleties, many of which have to be seen in action in order to be grasped. For obvious reasons, this is not possible with static code listings.

Let the fun begin

Java ME development, for me, is always a fun endeavor. While not always easy, it is almost never dull either; there's always some new challenge to overcome and something new to learn from overcoming it.

With this in mind, I hope that you will enjoy reading this book and that the information contained within will help make your life as a Java ME developer easier, more fun and more interesting.

## Chapter 1

Getting Started

Ten years ago, if you wanted to write software for mobile phones, you pretty much had only one option: Java ME (or, as it was known back then, J2ME). Things have changed in recent years, and a multitude of mobile platforms have appeared, each with its own strengths and weaknesses. Despite these newcomers, Java ME is still a strong platform for mobile development. The catch is that the quality bar is set pretty high these days, and in order to compete in the real world, your applications must be very competent from a technical standpoint. This book aims to teach you how to achieve just that.

First, however, you must understand where Java ME stands today.

Java ME, Smartphones, and Feature Phones

Some people think that Java ME has no place in a world where all the news is about iPhone and Android smartphones. This is simply not true. Java ME is still a great platform for mobile development. Let's look at why that is.

Java ME's Advantages

First, contrary to popular belief, Java ME *is* a viable option for smartphone software development. For one thing, Symbian is the most widespread smartphone operating system in use today and it has full support for Java ME. Blackberry devices also support Java ME. And there are even ways to get Java ME apps on Android and on the iPhone, using cross-platform conversion tools and emulators. Thus, Java ME is supported in one form or another by most smartphones in use today—and it can make use of their superior capabilities.

Moreover, while smartphones tend to get all the hype these days because of their cool new capabilities, it's worth noting that modern feature phones are starting to play in the same ballpark. Features like touchscreens, 3D accelerators, sensors (accelerometers for example), geo-location support, multitasking, large amounts of RAM, fast CPUs, and high-resolution screens are gradually starting to become common in the feature phone world too, in which Java ME is the uncontested king.

Furthermore, feature phone sales are still considerably higher than smartphone sales. For example, according to Wikipedia, feature phones have an 83% market share in the US as of 2010. This means that 83% of all US phones can't run Android or iPhone apps, but they *can* run Java ME apps, which makes Java ME the best platform if you want to achieve high market penetration.

Finally, Java ME is designed to be simple and modular. Everything but core features is defined and regulated by individual Java Specification Requests (JSRs): 3D support in JSR 184, PIM and file system support in JSR 75, sensor support in JSR 256, and so forth. This means two things. First, Java ME as a whole can evolve and improve while still maintaining backward compatibility. You will always be able to leverage your existing know-how and software base, since there will be no groundbreaking and compatibility-breaking changes along the way, only optional and incremental improvements that don't affect existing functionality. Second, you can tailor your applications to provide the exact feature set needed for any given target device, based on the functionality that particular device supports.

In the end, you get a platform that is supported in one form or another on the vast majority of phones in use today and that, unlike rival platforms, can run on low-end feature phones too, not just on state-of-the-art smartphones. Furthermore, the platform is flexible enough to allow you to use fancy features where available (such as 3D support and geo-location), so you're not limited to just the core Java ME features. So you see, Java ME is still an excellent candidate for developing your mobile applications.

Java ME's Disadvantages

Like all software platforms, Java ME has weaknesses as well as strengths. In order to provide a fair assessment, let's look at Java ME's most notable disadvantages—and how these can be mitigated.

The main problem with Java ME is that its core API is somewhat outdated and low-level by today's standards. Fortunately, plenty of third-party libraries out there, from UI libraries to utility libraries, can help alleviate this. This can even be considered an advantage, as you are free to choose whatever libraries and coding paradigms best suit your particular project, thus keeping your code base clean and to the point.

Java ME also suffers from device fragmentation (which is somewhat unavoidable considering the staggering number of devices that support Java ME). This was a huge problem in the early days; however, device support has become more standardized and tools have appeared to combat fragmentation. Today, fragmentation is still a problem, but to a much lesser degree, and there are plenty of resources you can use to resolve it. We will discuss fragmentation later in the book.

Java ME is also somewhat less tolerant than competing platforms. Having to work, in general, with fewer resources than other modern-day platforms means that problems like memory leaks and inefficient algorithms are much more likely to cause stability and performance issues. The best solution for this is to code defensively and to optimize your algorithms and your code—we'll discuss both topics later.

In addition, Java ME simply lacks support for some features. For example, system-wide notifications are unavailable, as is support for writing widgets and for low-level interactions with the hardware and with the operating system. The upcoming MIDP 3.0 standard will alleviate some of these problems, but until then Java ME applications have to be, for the most part, stand-alone and self-contained, with only limited access to certain operating system and hardware features.

> **NOTE:** There are ways to mix regular Java ME API calls with platform-specific API calls (this is frequently done in Blackberry applications), but the end result is not, strictly speaking, a Java ME application, so for bookkeeping purposes it doesn't count.

Finally, Java ME generally lacks the integration of an application store within the underlying platform, something both Android and iPhone have going for them. However, in recent years, Java ME application stores such as Nokia's Ovi Store and GetJar have become mainstream and well-known, so getting your software to your customers isn't a real problem anymore.

The Bottom Line

First, the bad: Java ME is not a universal solution from a technical point of view. I would not use it, for example, for writing an extremely sophisticated, state-of-the-art 3D game. I probably wouldn't use it if my application needed to target only the latest and greatest smartphones, as native applications are better suited for this. Finally, even if I wanted to, I couldn't use it for applications that require intimate interactions with the operating system or for writing widgets.

That being said, Java ME is well-suited for pretty much everything else, from business applications and regular games (even 3D ones) to applications that by their very nature require high market penetration, such as social networking clients and supporting applications for web-based services (for file transfer, web mail, etc.).

When you add in business factors, Java ME becomes a really strong contender: it's hard to argue against the world's most popular mobile platform, with literally billions of devices out there supporting it.

Overall, Java ME is still quite a robust platform. Though it has undergone changes and repositioning throughout the years, it remains a useful vehicle for building mobile applications.

Creating a Java ME Application

The best way to learn how to create a high-quality Java ME application is to actually create one, so the rest of this book will be dedicated to this endeavor. We'll start with the basics, such as the project's idea and goals, and progress toward a fully functional Java ME application.

As this is a technical book, we will focus primarily on technical aspects—everything else will be discussed only marginally.

> **NOTE:** Modern Java ME apps typically have thousands or tens of thousands of lines of code, but we will include in the book only the minimum amount of code necessary to illustrate the subject at hand. The full source code is available on the Apress web site.

The Idea for the Application

Every project starts with an idea. Since this book is a learning tool, our project should be something simple, fun, rewarding, and easy to understand, but at the same time it should be substantive enough to have the potential of becoming a Pro Java ME application.

Beginner programming books typically start with a "Hello, world" example, but we need something a little more complex. So for our project, we'll write a Java ME Twitter client. This makes sense because

- *Its complexity is just right*: A Twitter client is sufficiently complex to present a challenge and provide enough learning material for our purposes, yet simple enough to be presented and discussed within a reasonable number of pages.

- *It is straightforward*: Twitter provides a clean and simple API for accessing its services. Documentation and code examples are also readily available on the Internet.

- *It is fun*: The interactive nature of Twitter makes this a fun project. As we write the code, you will be able to easily see it in action at every step along the way, and show it to your friends and family for fame and feedback.

- *It teaches a lot of stuff*: To write a Twitter client, we will deal with everything from creating a UI to writing a networking layer and using persistent storage to save application settings.

- *It provides a good starting point for other applications*: Once the Twitter client is ready, you can modify it to support other Twitter-like services or even instant messaging protocols.

Goals, Features, Revenue Sources, and Target Devices

After settling on a particular idea, the tech and business teams should decide together what the project's goals and desired feature set are. The keyword here is "together"; compared to other more powerful mobile platforms, it is much more important for Java ME projects that the tech team have a say.

For example, if one business goal is to include DivX support in the application, the tech team should veto this because Java ME simply doesn't have enough horsepower for real-time DivX decoding. On the other hand, if the target is a native Symbian application or a native Android one, this goal could be achieved, though with difficulty.

It is also important for the tech team to know how the application is supposed to generate revenue, as this can affect the development process, sometimes significantly. For example, if the application is designed to generate revenue via integration with third-party services, like Amazon, this must be taken into consideration when designing the application's architecture and especially its networking module.

If, however, the primary source of revenue is direct sales, then the developers can include some form of copy protection, such as International Mobile Equipment Identity (IMEI) checks, in order to decrease piracy and increase sales. Or, if the application generates money indirectly by increasing the company's exposure and showcasing its products, the code must be thoroughly optimized and every ounce of performance must be squeezed out, so that users get the best possible experience.

These points are valid for all mobile platforms, of course, but Java ME projects must pay extra attention to them as they do not have the benefit of an integrated app store, plentiful (even excessive) resources, and extensive built-in networking capabilities like other mobile platforms.

The tech team also needs to be aware of the project's budget in terms of money, time, and manpower, and should have a definite say in how this budget is expended (again, much more so than with other platforms). For example, if the project doesn't have much money but does have enough manpower and time, the UI module could be built entirely in-house, as opposed to licensing a third-party library. While this decision has wide ramifications and must be given careful thought in the case of Java ME projects, it's usually not even a topic of discussion for Android or for the iPhone, as their native UI capabilities are more than sufficient for most projects.

Next, the target devices and features to be included for each device should be decided on. Java ME also differs from other mobile platforms in this respect, as the gamut of devices is very wide and there's a huge gap between high-end and low-end devices, which means you can't target all devices, nor can you typically include the same feature set on all the devices you target.

So determining your target devices is a very important step and this should be in tune with your business goals. For example, if your application is supposed to generate revenue via monthly subscriptions, it makes little sense to target low-end phones as their owners are less likely to spend money on subscriptions. Instead, you should target higher-end devices: this will allow you to include more features and polish, thus making your application more appealing. And since higher-end devices are more expensive, it generally follows that their owners are more likely to spend money on your service every month—if only because they typically have more money to spend.

Conversely, if your application is designed to make money for you by increasing the visibility of your company and your products, then you should target as many popular (in terms of units sold) and affordable devices as possible and settle on a feature set that works well on all of them, thus ensuring maximum exposure. The same is true for applications that rely on one-time sales to generate revenue: if you target a wider array of devices, the chances of making a sale increase accordingly. You can also decrease the purchase price in order to make your product more appealing to potential buyers (you'll earn less per sale, but you'll make more sales).

Sometimes the very nature of the application dictates the devices you can target. For example, touch-only devices make poor candidates for emulators because of their limited input capabilities.

The media formats an application can use depend on the media support of the target devices—and, unlike other mobile platforms, it's usually not feasible in Java ME to add support for non-native media types. This limits the quality and quantity of media you can use in your application, from the UI graphics to the sound effects, and also affects the build process.

For example, if all your target devices support SVG graphics and MP3 files, you can create a great-looking vector-based UI with your application and accompany it with high-quality audio effects, plus you can have a single build for all devices. However, if some of your devices do not support these formats, then for those devices you must render the vector graphics to bitmap formats like PNG and convert the MP3 sounds to WAV or AMR. This not only complicates the build process considerably, it also increases the size of the application JAR file, while actually decreasing media quality. And that's not all: some devices don't support all variations of a specific format, so besides choosing the proper media format, the correct encoding parameters must also be set. This means that, in the case of Java ME projects, the tech team should work closely with the media team to ensure that the media resources used are properly crafted and optimized for the target devices.

Identifying the Target Devices

Our Twitter client will be written to run on the WTK emulator. This decision was made so that as many people as possible can run the code, regardless of what devices they have at their disposal. This also means that the code can be written with "best practices" in mind, as targeting real devices frequently involves cutting corners and using little hacks and workarounds for device-specific problems.

However, real-life projects must run on real-life devices. With this in mind, as a matter of best practices, you should always try to run your projects (Twitter client included) on any and all devices at your disposal, even if they are not expressly supported. Do a little research, both theoretical and hands-on, about each device and try to identify its strengths and weaknesses with respect to the project at hand.

In the end, you should have a list of devices that can run your project fully and, for those devices that can run it only partially (typically because of bugs or performance issues), the reasons this happens as well as potential solutions. This "extra information" usually proves to be invaluable. For example, the fact that your application is GC-heavy may not be noticeable when your target devices are all high-end, but as soon as you run the code on mid-level or low-end devices, this quickly becomes apparent—and you can then start to address the problem, which would otherwise have gone unnoticed until it was too late.

A later chapter deals with the issues of device fragmentation and porting applications to other platforms and devices. You can use the information in that chapter to adapt the Twitter client to your specific device(s), if needed.

That being said, the code presented in this book has been written so that it is as device-independent as possible, in order to minimize or altogether eliminate the effort required to port it.

Identifying Java ME Technical Limitations

Writing software for mobile devices means taking into account various factors that are essentially non-issues in the desktop world, such as battery life, screen size, and network connectivity.

On top of that, mobile software in general and Java ME in particular have limitations of their own, which must be identified and dealt with accordingly. These can range from the obvious, like "you have only 1 MB of RAM available on device X," to the more obscure, like "object creation on device Y is too slow." Let's look at some of the most common Java ME technical limitations.

Device Fragmentation

Device fragmentation comes in two forms: hardware and software. Hardware fragmentation is to be expected, as not all devices can have the same specifications, and developers can plan and write their code according to the resources available at their disposal.

Software fragmentation, however, is a far greater problem, possibly the biggest problem affecting Java ME (and, to a lesser extent, other platforms, such as Android). Not all devices implement the Java ME API in the same way, and some of them even implement it wrongly. This can range from easy-to-spot-and-resolve issues like different keycodes on different devices, to blatant bugs that appear only in some circumstances and only on some devices, and which are hard to debug.

For example, on Blackberry devices, `drawRGB()` raises an `ArrayIndexOutOfBounds` exception when the (x,y) coordinates specified are negative (i.e., drawing starts outside of the screen area). As long as both coordinates are positive, this does not happen. This is hard to debug because the documentation says that the exception is only to be thrown "if the requested operation will attempt to access an element of `rgbData` whose index is either negative or beyond its length." As a developer, you are a lot more likely to think that the error appears because you specified the wrong parameters to `drawRGB()`, thus causing the code to reference an element outside of the array's bounds, than you are to believe that the error is caused by a buggy platform implementation—which is, in fact, the case.

Later in the book, we will discuss how to deal with both hardware and software fragmentation; the solutions are surprisingly similar.

Screen Pixel Density and Screen Size

The most important thing about pixel density is that, in conjunction with screen size and screen resolution, it affects how much information you can comfortably display on the screen at once. Let me explain: if a device has a 3-inch display with a 1024×768 resolution and a default font height of 10 pixels, you can have up to 76 rows of text on the screen at the same time. However, the text would be so small that it would be nearly impossible to read. This is also why no such device exists, to my knowledge.

Now consider the following two scenarios:

- A device with a 10-inch display featuring a 1024×768 resolution

- Another device with a 3-inch display, but with a resolution that's three times smaller (341×256)

In both of these scenarios, the text would be physically three times bigger than in the original scenario, and thus easier to read. For a clear comparison, look at Figure 1–1.

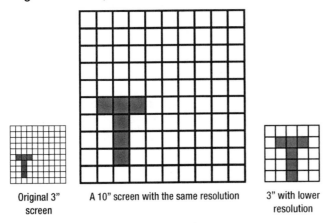

Original 3"   A 10" screen with the same resolution   3" with lower
screen   resolution

Figure 1–1. *Screen pixel density comparison*

Fixed-size graphics are similarly affected. Due to pixel density, a given sprite, button, or UI widget can look too small on one device and too big on another, even if the size in pixels is the same.

Screen size is even more important than screen density, because if the screen is big enough you can get away with a lower density: the image quality won't be as good, but you'll be able to read what's on the screen and that's what matters.

Another thing to keep in mind is that a UI design can be great on one device and lousy on another simply because the screen is physically too small for the design in question, regardless of the resolution. This means that some research and hands-on experience are needed to find a suitable UI design and size for any given target device.

While developers should be aware of these issues, it is mostly the design team that must make decisions in this area. As a general guideline, the vast majority of Java ME devices have a 320×240 screen resolution, with a screen size of 2.2–2.8 inches. Some newer Java ME devices with touchscreen support, for example, those coming from Nokia, have a screen size of 3.0–4.0 inches and higher resolutions, 480×360 in Nokia's case.

UI Design

Probably the biggest UI-related limitation of Java ME is that, for historical reasons, you can use the device's native widgets only to create simple-looking interfaces. Anything more complex is simply not possible natively, so you are forced to use your own GUI toolkit, or a third-party one—virtually all Pro Java ME applications use non-native GUI toolkits. This, of course, means your application's look and feel will probably be out of tune with the look and feel the user is accustomed to with native applications. This is not a problem for games or other multimedia applications, but for business applications it can be a minus, especially if one of the requirements is "native look and feel."

Another limitation of Java ME is that most users are accustomed to using the two softkeys for accessing the application's menu. However, some devices do not have softkeys. Blackberry devices, for example, do not have softkeys (instead they use the "menu" key), and some Java ME devices are touch-only. So right from the start we have three different methods of navigating the menus of an application. You can work around this either by having multiple builds and detecting the platform at runtime, or by designing and implementing your UI in such a way that it's possible to use all three methods seamlessly and independently.

Physical button placement can sometimes be an issue, or at least cause for frustration, because on some devices, especially those with accelerometers, the screen can be rotated and switched from portrait to landscape on the fly. Your application should not only be able to handle this, but it should also keep track of where the physical buttons on a device are located. This is especially important for softmenus. For example, Figure 1–2 shows what the correct softmenu placement and layout are when the application is in landscape mode, as well as an incorrect placement and layout for landscape mode. Notice that, in the correct layout, the softmenu options are right next to the softbutton, instead of at the bottom of the screen.

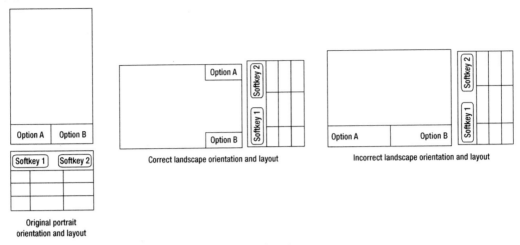

Figure 1–2. *How physical button position affects screen layout*

UI design should also attempt to take into account the screen characteristics mentioned earlier, like screen pixel density. On devices with high-density screens, it's often a good idea to make everything bigger (in pixels) so the application is easier to use. Since high-density screens are usually seen in higher-end devices, which have more processing power, you can use the extra pixels to add polish and fine touches to your UI, such as shadows and subtle animations, thus improving the user experience.

CPU and VM Characteristics

These characteristics are by far the ones that have the most influence over the speed of Java ME applications. First, let's talk about CPUs. As most mobile CPUs are ARM-based, we'll use them as a reference. For regular applications, anything in the 100–200MHz range should suffice these days. For computation-intensive applications or applications with lots of UI polish, you'll most likely need something in the 200–400MHz range, perhaps even more, to get a smooth user experience. Of course, these are ballpark figures and are affected by many factors, such as whether there are any background applications running and whether the CPU has Jazelle or ThumbEE support (ARM CPUs with Jazelle or ThumbEE support can run Java ME bytecode in hardware, thus providing a huge boost to performance).

Low-level functionality can sometimes be an important limitation. Some devices do not support floating point calculations natively, so instead they emulate them using integer arithmetic. This makes floating point operations on these devices extremely slow. It is also common that some mathematical operations, like addition, are faster than others, like division. On some devices, the difference is significant, so if your application relies heavily on these slower operations, it will be significantly slower than expected on the previously mentioned devices. Later in the book, we will see how to mitigate at least part of this problem by doing code optimization.

Even more important than CPU speed, especially for low-end devices, is VM (virtual machine) performance. Since Java ME is bytecode-interpreted, two devices with the same hardware specs but different VMs can vary wildly in terms of performance—so CPU speed alone is not a good performance indicator for Java ME. To figure out how well a given device will run your application, write small test applications that simulate the kind of loads that your real application is likely to have and measure their performance. To get an even better overview, gradually vary the "load factor" from 10% to 200%.

Memory-Related Performance

Obviously, the more memory you have at your disposal, the better. However, not all devices make all their free memory available to Java ME, so you should always take into consideration the actual Java ME memory available, not the device's declared memory capacity. Furthermore, especially on multitasking-capable devices, the actual amount of memory available at any given time can vary wildly. You should never assume that you'll always have the same amount of RAM at your disposal, and you should always code defensively to cope with this.

> **NOTE:** There are ways to work around memory issues—for example, simulating pagefiles using persistent storage mechanisms and splitting big loads into smaller and more manageable chunks. We will discuss these later in the book.

Second to memory size, what affects overall performance is the performance of the garbage collector, which is also related to VM performance (discussed previously). Java ME applications tend to create a lot of objects, and those objects have to be deleted at some point. When that happens, the garbage collector kicks in. Devices on the market today have a wide variety of garbage collectors, from those that do their job efficiently and unnoticed to those that take forever to run and freeze the entire application while they do so. Your application should be prepared to handle most of them, if not all, especially if it is a data-intensive application.

How fast object creation happens constitutes another important factor in the performance of any Java ME application. If your application manipulates a lot of objects, the speed at which these objects are created can critically limit the speed of your application, even more so than the garbage collector.

Battery Life

Battery life can vary widely from one device to another—and some projects even have specified a limit on how fast an application is allowed to drain a battery. So when you are developing a Java ME app, you need to try to maximize battery life.

The most effective way to conserve battery life is to throttle down your CPU usage and your network's access. This is not always easy, but it's important, particularly for applications that tend to run for long periods of time, like chat clients. Furthermore, throttling is frequently effective in prolonging battery life, provided it is implemented properly. We will learn more about this later in the book.

Network Variations

Most of the time, devices are connected via a 2G or 3G network, whose signal can drop at any time and whose speed can vary from extremely fast to very slow and back again in mere seconds. Pro Java ME applications have to take this into consideration.

For some applications, the number of dropped packets or the ping time is extremely important. If this is the case, the application must be able to detect problems in this area and notify the user of their existence.

Java ME also imposes a limit on the number of simultaneous connections an application can have. Though some devices support more, it is not a good idea to have more than two connections running at the same time.

Another thing to consider is how the data is sent. Sending data in smaller, discrete packages is usually better than sending it in larger chunks, as in some cases larger chunks can cause the application to stall while it waits for the data to be sent.

The format of the data is also important. Since data traffic costs money, using fewer bytes to send information saves money for the user and also makes your application more responsive, as it has less data to process. XML might be a well-known standard, but it is also extremely verbose. Consider using something more succinct, like JSON or a binary protocol.

Localization Issues

Localization is extremely important for Pro Java ME applications. To have the application interact with a user in his native language, using the formats for date and currency he is used to, is emblematic of high quality.

A crucial requirement for this, which is often overlooked, is to ensure that the target devices have proper support for the character set needed for a certain language. This is usually not a problem for Latin languages, but it can be one for non-Latin languages such as Greek. Character-set support for these languages is sometimes available only on certain country-specific firmware versions. This means that the text will look bad, full of placeholder characters, on devices that don't support the needed character set. The best workaround for this problem is to use bitmap fonts and embed the necessary character set directly into the application.

Equally important is the ability to support multiple date, time, currency, and number formats. Of these, proper date support is paramount. For example, some countries use DD/MM/YYYY instead of MM/DD/YYYY to specify dates, so a date like July 4, 2011 can be written either as 4/7/2011 or as 7/4/2011. Not handling these differences properly can cause confusion and frustration for users. As for number format support, consider the following example: to express the number 4 with three-decimal precision, some countries use "4.000" while others use "4,000". Using the wrong decimal separator can again cause confusion and frustration for users—if you are used to having a dot as a decimal separator instead of a comma, "4,000" might be interpreted as "four thousand."

Sometimes it's also necessary to localize graphics and other media. This can range from the obvious, like a country's flag, to the obscure, such as an icon that's perfectly acceptable in some cultures but offensive in others. While this is not usually a problem, you should be aware that it can happen.

Limited Access to Device Capabilities

An important set of limitations comes from the fact that Java ME is not usually able to access the full extent of a device's capabilities.

For example, some devices allow access only to certain parts of the file system but not to others, some devices provide support for accessing the user's phonebook while others do not, and so forth.

A good example is a phone's camera. The on-device camera can typically be accessed from Java ME, but frequently the maximum image size that can be captured is lower than the camera's actual maximum image size.

This means that you can't rely on the manufacturer's specifications and that you need to do some on-device testing in order to figure out what capabilities you can use and to what extent.

Regular Java ME Applications vs. Pro Java ME Applications

After you've identified the device limitations and dealt with all the other project management issues, development typically begins. Before we get to that, however, let's look at the most important differences between regular Java ME applications, the kind that you'd write as a hobby, and Pro Java ME applications, the kind we aim to create through the course of this book.

Pro Java ME Apps Are Smart

For example, they try to figure out the user's next action based on his previous ones. If the user has selected three e-mails and deleted each of them, the app could ask him "Do you want to delete this e-mail?" when a fourth is selected.

Pro Java ME apps also tend to handle special cases to enhance the user's experience to a much higher degree. While a regular application would be content to display something like "0 unread e-mail(s)" or "1 unread e-mail(s)" (using the same ambiguous template in both cases), pro apps would choose the appropriate template for each case, thus displaying "No unread e-mails," "One unread e-mail," and "2 unread e-mails" accordingly. This principle extends to other parts of the application as well—for example, choosing a different color scheme on the user's birthday.

High-quality Java ME applications are also very resource-conscious, adapting themselves on the fly to make the most of the resources available, be they scarce or plentiful.

Pro Java ME Apps Are Built Around a Custom Framework

Pro Java ME applications are invariably built around a custom framework. This framework is usually developed in-house to fit the specific project it will be used on and each framework is generally designed from scratch. This is done because the framework should always try to fit the specific needs of each project, in order to be as efficient and as easy to use as possible.

For example, the framework for a good Java ME HTML browser would be radically different from one for a Java ME e-mail client. The former would be geared toward handling UI layouts, with its structure, helper methods, and object hierarchy designed with this in mind, while the latter would be more focused on low-level client-server functionality and a lesser investment in UI-related features.

This is in contrast to other mobile platforms, such as Android, where resource abundance means that you can just combine both frameworks into a single one and use that single framework for both projects.

> **TIP:** If designing a new framework from scratch isn't feasible, you can start with an existing framework and add new features to it while removing unneeded ones. You should never reuse a framework as is unless the application you plan on writing is very similar to the one the framework was originally designed for.

Pro Java ME Apps Use Third-Party Libraries

Java ME is a mature technology with a proven track record, so it's no wonder it has a rich selection of libraries. You can find third-party libraries for anything from the GUI to database access. Furthermore, good Java ME libraries are built so that they transparently handle, at least partially, important Java ME issues such as device fragmentation and inconsistent APIs. This frees developers to focus on building the application, not on subduing the platform. For example, a good UI library knows how to handle the difference between Blackberry and regular Java ME devices, like the lack of softkeys on the Blackberry, and makes sure that the user sees a UI tailored to the platform he is running the application on.

It is thus no surprise that high-quality Java ME applications tend to use a lot of third-party libraries. They simply could not offer the same value and the same level of sophistication otherwise. And it's not just lone developers or small companies that use them; large companies use third-party libraries in their Java ME applications as well. The benefits in terms of time and money are simply too great to ignore, even for them.

This is in contrast to regular Java ME applications, which tend to use fewer third-party libraries, mostly for budgetary reasons.

Pro Java ME Apps Reuse Code

Code reuse has always been a touchy subject for Java ME, because of the widely different environments and circumstances Java ME applications have to run on. This means that much of the code you write for one project (or even for one device-specific build of a project) can't be used efficiently in another project.

However, top-notch Java ME apps tend to have a much higher code-reuse potential than regular Java ME apps. The important factors for this are heavy use of third-party libraries, code modularization, code flexibility (especially in terms of resource requirements), and use of proper abstractions. For example, a well-written HTML browser could be turned into a PDF viewer by taking its framework, UI library, and layout module, modifying them a bit, and using a PDFParser instead of an HTMLParser as an input source; the code would adapt itself to make the most of the resources available.

Contrast this with a less-than-stellar Java ME HTML browser where the layout module and the parser are intertwined, making repurposing them impossible, and which was written to meet only the specific resource requirements of parsing and rendering HTML. In fact, the potential for code reuse is often a good indicator of how well written and high-quality a Java ME application is—much more so than it is for other platforms.

Writing Flexible Java ME Applications

The key to the success of any Java ME application lies in its ability to run in multiple software and hardware environments. However, there's more to Java ME portability than just having your code run on a slew of different devices.

Portability also means that, regardless of the underlying hardware, your code runs great even in less-than-ideal circumstances—for example, when the battery is running low or when the device's CPU is decoding music in the background. Furthermore, as circumstances can change during runtime, sometimes several times in the course of a single run, your application has to be able to deal with these changes at a moment's notice.

This level of flexibility is not easy to achieve, as it involves a heavy dose of experience, skill, and sometimes luck. Fortunately, there are a few golden rules that Java ME developers should always strive to obey. In the following pages we'll go over the most important ones, such as coding defensively, shunning complexity, and avoiding making wrong assumptions about the platform and the environment.

> **NOTE:** Runtime flexibility is of lesser concern on other modern-day platforms, such as Android and iOS. Applications for these platforms not only have more resources at their disposal, they are also native, and thus have far better control over their environment and their resources than Java ME ones, which run totally constrained in their virtual machines.

Coding Defensively

This is the most important rule of mobile software development, particularly for Java ME, and will continue be so for the foreseeable future. To most developers, this translates to something like "check if you have enough disk space available on the device before attempting a write" or "read the device's screen resolution at runtime," but this is only the tip of the iceberg. Consider, for example, the code snippet in Listing 1–1.

Listing 1–1. *Sending Data to a Server*

```
byte buffer[] ;
while ( dataSource.hasMoreData() )
{
        buffer = dataSource.readNextChunk();
        if ( dataSource.readOK() )
        {
                try
                {
                        serverConnection.send(buffer);
                }
                catch (IOException ex)
                {
                        // handle the exception
                }

        }
        else
        {
                // something has gone wrong while reading data
        }
}
```

At first glance, there is nothing wrong with this code. We handle the case in which something goes wrong when reading data from the source, and we handle the case in which something goes wrong when sending said data to the server. So where's the problem?

The problem lies in the fact that we make one critical assumption: that the code snippet will complete in a timely fashion. Therefore, we exit the loop only when we have no more data to read and send, which might take quite a long time depending on circumstances. If this is not handled properly, the user could be stuck staring at a "transfer in progress" screen for a really, really long time. This isn't even device-dependent: if the network connection is extremely slow or unstable, you'll end up in this scenario regardless of the device you're running on.

But here's the real kicker: duration is not the main issue here. What's really bad about this code is that it locks a lot of resources (CPU time, bandwidth, memory, active connections) for the entire length of the data transfer. This might be OK for desktop computers, which have plenty of resources, but it most certainly is not OK for mobile devices. Never assume you can lock resources for a potentially long period on a mobile device.

A good way around this problem is to take any action or workload that could potentially require more than a couple of seconds to complete and split it into individual work units (this is also true for background actions or workloads). These work units can then be executed in turn with other work units, from other actions or workloads, using the same resource pool, *but not at the same time*. This helps your application keep a low resource profile and can ensure that you are able to do many things at once without running into resource shortages. Listing 1–2 shows a basic example of how this can be done.

Listing 1–2. *Sending Data to a Server the Proper Way*

```
while ( isRunning() )
{
        workListeners.jumpToFirst();
        while ( workListeners.hasMore() )
        {
                workListeners.nextListener().raiseEvent( Event.DO_WORK_UNIT )
        }
}

....

public void handleEvent(int eventType)
{
        if ( eventType == Event.DO_WORK_UNIT )
        {
                if ( dataSource.hasMoreData() )
                {
                        buffer = dataSource.readNextChunk();
                        if ( dataSource.readOK() )
                        {
                                try
                                {
                                        serverConnection.send(buffer);
                                }
                                catch (IOException ex)
                                {
                                        // handle the exception
                                }
                        }
                        else
                        {
                                // something has gone wrong while reading
                        }
                }
        }
}
```

Not only is this approach more resource-friendly, it's also more flexible. For example, you can have multiple worker threads, each processing one work unit at a time, and the DO_WORK_UNIT event can be issued from any number of sources independently.

This is extremely important for Java ME applications, as they typically run in more constrained environments than native applications, both in terms of resources and in terms of runtime flexibility. Proper defensive coding techniques usually minimize resource drain and make the application more flexible because they allow developers to handle a greater number of runtime scenarios.

Avoiding Wrong Assumptions

An erroneous assumption that is frequently made is that Java ME apps run in a single-tasking environment. This was true in the early days, but it is not the case anymore. The most obvious repercussion of this is that you can make the mistake of thinking that all of the phone's resources will be at your disposal. While this means that your application will be lightning-fast when running alone, it also means that it can be as slow as a snail when running alongside other applications. In other words, your application can appear to be inconsistent, which is not something users expect or like.

This is most dangerous when the device is running out of resources of a given type—for example, RAM. What happens then varies from device to device. For example, when I ran too many Java ME apps simultaneously on my old Nokia E50 and the phone ran out of memory, it showed a "memory full" message and immediately closed *all* running Java ME applications. Any data that wasn't saved got lost.

To avoid suffering from these problems more often than necessary, you can do one simple thing: construct your application so that it is able to reduce its resource consumption when necessary. For example, time some of your critical operations, and if they take more than a predetermined amount of time to complete, consider either dynamically reducing their complexity (e.g., fewer graphical effects for games) or informing the user that an operation is taking longer than usual and asking him to stop other background applications if possible.

The same goes for memory. For example, if you can't allocate a 2 MB buffer, try to allocate a 1 MB one and then a 512 KB one, and so forth. Make sure your code can work with buffers of any size, not just the preferred size.

The best way to keep the number of bad assumptions you make to a minimum is to be extremely pessimistic and code defensively. Always plan for the worst-case scenario and never take anything for granted, not even obvious stuff like the device having power (its battery might run out while the application is running).

Learning How to Handle Complexity

As a side-effect of defensive coding and avoiding assumptions, your application's complexity will increase. Handling complexity is thus extremely important for Java ME applications. The most common weapon employed against complexity, and the most intuitive one, is solid knowledge of object-oriented principles and techniques—for example:

- Polymorphism handles part of the complexity of deciding what methods to call based on what parameters are passed.

- Inheritance makes the relationships between data types clearer and more contained, so the complexity of understanding the data itself and how to manipulate it is partially reduced.

- The factory pattern isolates the complexity of object creation and initialization from the rest of the code.

- Interfaces allow for contract-like programming, thus compartmentalizing complexity and code in a series of black boxes.

However, if you look closely at these examples, you will notice something very important: object-oriented principles and techniques don't remove complexity, they just hide it or distribute it. Take the factory pattern: the fact that the programmer doesn't see the bulk of the complexity associated with object creation and initialization doesn't mean it's not there.

However, in many cases, complexity can be avoided elegantly. For example, consider the following scenario:

"Our application synchronizes photos and other media between the user's phone and his social networking accounts, typically in batches of hundreds of files. Files range in size from 100 KB to 200 MB, distributed more or less evenly across the range. Because of the potentially large files involved, sometimes it takes a long time before files appear either on the Web or on the device (depending on sync direction), especially when large files are involved, and users start to become worried. We want to improve this as much as possible and make the transfer seem faster from the user's point of view."

This sounds like a really complicated problem, involving caches and priority queues and other buzzwords, but in reality the solution can be very simple. The text clearly indicates that the main problem is that users *perceive* the synchronization as being slow. The easiest way around this particular scenario, and often the most effective, is to simply sort the files according to their size and start sending the smaller ones first.

The effect of this is that the user will see a lot of files being uploaded during the first moments of the sync (due to their smaller size), with the number of files uploaded per minute or per second gradually decreasing as the application reaches the larger ones.

By that time, two things have happened. Number one, the user sees that the sync does, in fact, work and is less worried about this. Number two, the user is left with the impression of a fast sync, and thus will not be as bothered by the slower sync speed toward the end.

Thus, the problem is largely solved with very little coding effort and virtually no overhead in terms of complexity. Most seemingly complicated problems can be reduced to problems that are a lot simpler and easier to solve. So, when you next feel the urge to spend an entire workweek solving a seemingly titanic problem, step back for a moment and see if you can transform it into something more manageable.

Trade-Offs Are Your Friends—Use Them Wisely

Every computer science junior knows that in the world of computers almost every resource can be traded for another resource. This principle plays a very important role in Java ME programming. Since your application is expected to run on a truckload of different devices, you should be prepared for situations where one resource is abundant while others are not, and trade off between them at runtime.

The classical example is that of CPU time vs. memory: you can solve things in less time by using more memory, or you can solve them in more time by using less memory.

Consider the following example (Listing 1–3), which can be part of any tile-based Java ME game. What the code does is change the direction an onscreen entity is facing whenever the entity is moved to a different tile in the game world. For the sake of argument, let's assume that calculating the angle also has to take into consideration the height of the tile and other factors, not just its (x,y) position.

Listing 1–3. *Changing the Direction a Game Entity Is Facing*

```
public void entityMoved(int x, int y)
{
            ...
            int angle = getAngleForTile (x, y);
            current.setFacingAngle(angle);
            ...
}

public int getAngleForTile(int x, int y)
{
        // some complex calculations involving sine and cosine here
}
```

The main problem with this code is that the CPU-heavy getAngleForTile() method will always calculate the angle for any given (x,y) pair passed as an argument. Usually this is not a concern, but when CPU resources are low, the time spent in this method might add up to something substantial. This is especially true when a lot of onscreen action is taking place, as presumably there will be a lot of entities moving around and the method will be called often.

The best way around this problem is to store the result for each (x,y) pair in a matrix, and then retrieve it from there instead of calculating it every time. Furthermore, you can use lazy initialization so you don't have to calculate all the values at once, since this might take a long time and some of the values might not even be used. What we will do is this: whenever the method is called for an (x,y) pair, we will check if the result is in the matrix. If it is, we'll retrieve it from there; if it's not, we'll calculate it, store it in the matrix, and return it to the caller. If something changes that requires the matrix to be recalculated, we'll simply create a new empty one and let that be filled again as needed.

This means that for a 200-by-200 game world, which is actually pretty large, we will need to reserve at most 160 KB of RAM for the matrix. I'm saying at most because the idea can be refined further: for example, splitting the matrix into smaller pieces, like 50×50, and keeping just the currently visible piece in memory.

We now sacrifice 160 KB of RAM in exchange for a lot of CPU time. Fair trade-off for most modern devices, but what happens if the user has a browser running in the background and it suddenly loads a very large page? Memory will become scarce, and our application might be forced to either free up some of it or be shut down.

In that case, one of the best ways to free memory would be to give up our 160 KB matrix and fall back on the CPU to calculate the facing direction for any given tile. When more memory becomes available again, we can switch back to the old approach. The code can look something like what's in Listing 1–4 (entityMoved() has been omitted for brevity):

Listing 1–4. *Changing the Direction a Game Entity Is Facing, the Proper Way*

```
boolean isInLowMemoryMode = false;
int [][] angleMatrix = new int[200][200];

public void handleEvent(int eventID, Object eventData)
{
        if ( event == Event.Environment.LOW_MEMORY )
        {
                isInLowMemoryMode = true;
                angleMatrix = null;
                ....
        }
        else if ( event == Event.Environment.HIGH_MEMORY )
        {
                isInLowMemoryMode = false;
                angleMatrix = new int[200][200];
                ...
        }
}

public int getAngleForTile(int x, int y)
{
        if ( isInLowMemoryMode )
        {
                // some cpu-heavy calculations here
        }
        else
        {
                if ( angleMatrix[x][y] == 0 )
                {
                        // some cpu-heavy calculations here
                        // store the result in angleMatrix[x][y]
                }
                return angleMatrix[x][y];

        }
}
```

Our code now changes seamlessly between using more CPU and using more RAM, depending on what events are received. You can apply this method in other parts of your application, and to other types of resources too. For example, you could use the CPU to compress data before sending it over the network, thus sacrificing CPU time and battery life in exchange for bandwidth. Or you could do the opposite and exchange bandwidth for CPU time.

If done properly, the net effect of this technique is a very flexible application resource-wise, indicated by variations of the resource consumption profile when environmental parameters change drastically.

This technique can be applied equally well to nontechnical resources, too. For example, if your application has to display a large amount of text, perhaps a long "thank you!" e-mail from one of your happy customers, you might want to consider using a slightly smaller font size than usual, thus sacrificing a bit of legibility in exchange for having a better overall picture.

Aim for a Loose and Decentralized Architecture

This is best explained with an analogy: would you prefer your car to be a tightly interconnected assembly of parts, where if your onboard computer stops working then the engine won't start, and if the engine won't start the interior lights won't go on? Or would you rather it be the way it is now, where if some parts stop working, the rest will continue to function to the best of their abilities?

My guess is you prefer the latter. The same is true for software development: You should always split your application into almost independent components, which can function on their own if necessary. To link everything together, all you have to do is use global events.

A good example of this is the code in Listing 1–4. You will notice that it reacts to the Event.Environment.LOW_MEMORY event, but that nowhere in the code is it specified where that event should come from. That's because it is a global event. You can imagine that somewhere in the code there is a module that periodically measures environmental parameters and, when it detects a significant change, it raises the appropriate event. Then, other modules can react to this event.

This technique has special importance for Java ME software development because it gives developers a very effective means of handling the huge variation in device capabilities and specifications that Java ME software has to deal with.

For example, when the device your code is running on does not support a certain feature, simply have your application ignore the corresponding events, not raise them to begin with or raise an appropriate NOT_SUPPORTED event, which can then be handled by the modules affected by it. This will allow you to alter your application's behavior in a transparent, logical, and easy to understand way, on the fly and with the kind of impact you desire (local or global).

Finally, decentralization also means that components should be able to "think for themselves," so to speak. For example, in the GUI layer, rather than having a central entity decide where each widget should be placed and how big it should be, you can have the widgets format themselves. All the "central authority" has to do is provide information, such as how much space is available in the current row. This approach can be used on all software platforms, but it's even more important for Java ME because of all the different (and small) screen sizes, UI layouts, and interaction paradigms it has to support.

Never Do On-Device What You Can Do Off-Device

The main idea behind this rule is that, rather than doing calculations on the mobile device itself, you do them beforehand and include only the *result* in the application. This can save a lot of CPU power and battery life that would otherwise go toward doing the calculations on the device at runtime.

To illustrate, please consider the example in Listing 1–5, which can be found in one form or another in many applications (especially games).

Listing 1–5. *Drawing a Sine Curve*

```
for (int x=0;x<360;x++)
{
        drawPoint(x, 199 * Math.sin( degreesToRadians(x));
}
```

We know from Listing 1–4 that we can use an array to speed things up. But there is a crucial difference between the current example and the previous one: in this example, the values in the array never change as the values of the sine function are always the same.

This means that, rather computing the array on the device, we can calculate it externally and include it explicitly in the source code, like in Listing 1–6.

Listing 1–6. *Drawing a Sine Curve with the Values of sin() Already Calculated*

```
double SIN_VALUES = { 0, 0.0174524064, 0.0348994967, ... }
for (int x=0;x<360;x++)
{
        drawPoint(x, 199 * SIN_VALUES[x] );
}
```

Now obviously the difference in CPU time between this example and the one in Listing 1–5 isn't that big overall, but for more complex scenarios, it can certainly be noticeable.

Consider the case of a sophisticated game or stock analysis application that uses neural networks to implement its AI. Training a neural network on-device can be extremely time-consuming and resource-intensive, while training it on a desktop computer and having the device use the pre-established results is cheaper, quicker, and less frustrating for the user.

The same idea can be applied to more serious stuff, such as encryption and data compression. Activities such as these can be greatly improved by calculating some values off-device and using the results. This is, of course, true for all mobile platforms, but Java ME stands to gain the most since it usually lacks the hardware support and resources necessary to do these things efficiently on its own.

Summary

After briefly examining Java ME's position in the modern mobile world, we selected an idea for our own Pro Java ME project and we discussed how nontechnical issues, such as the project's goals and source of revenue, affect its technical side.

We also discussed the primary technical limitations Java ME applications generally face, and we looked at how Pro Java ME applications differ from regular Java ME applications (code intelligence, custom frameworks, heavy use of third-party libraries, and great potential for code reuse).

Finally, we looked at some important tips for writing truly flexible and portable Java ME applications.

## Chapter 2

A Java ME Framework

There are a few more steps we have to take before we begin work on the actual application. Most of them are trivial, like setting up source control and creating an IDE project, so we will skip those entirely. However, there is one very important step we cannot skip: writing our application's framework.

The following chapter serves a dual purpose: it both goes over the basics of the framework we will be using and serves as a basis for how Java ME frameworks in general should be written.

With this in mind, our framework, though functional, will be greatly simplified in nature. The code will be kept as simple as possible, with everything that is not necessary either omitted or reduced to the bare minimum. As such, feel free to experiment with it, improve upon it, and alter it to suit your needs and your projects. Remember what we discussed in Chapter 1: never take a framework and use it as-is (the reason for this will be explained shortly).

The Importance of Using a Framework

Simply put, a good framework on top of which you can build your application considerably increases the chances that the end result will be a strong, solid, and flexible product.

For example, a Java ME application typically runs multiple threads: a UI thread, a networking thread, a data processing thread, etc. These threads need to be able to talk to one another. Furthermore, they need to do this in a way that neither stalls nor disrupts the other threads, and that minimizes overhead. A great solution for this is using an event-based system: whenever something of interest happens in one part of the application, an event is triggered, and other parts of the application that are "listening" can then respond and react to this event.

Without a framework to provide this functionality for them, these threads (or rather, the separate parts of the application that correspond to them) might implement events differently, sometimes with just the subtlest of differences, which can cause significant problems in the long run. For example, the UI part might implement events in a separate thread with an event queue, while the networking part might handle events immediately, directly, with no queue involved. Or one part of the application might use a priority-based queue while another part might use a simple queue. This can lead to race conditions, events being handled out of order, and more. In fact, given the complexity of real-life usage scenarios, the behavior of such a tangled and heterogeneous event system is best described as "undefined."

In contrast, by implementing event handling in the framework, not only can you then use a consistent event API and its associated conventions throughout the application, you also have the benefit of writing clean and focused application code; all the dirty event-related bits are handled by the framework. Furthermore, should the event system need to be overhauled or debugged, this can be done in a single central place (the framework) instead of having to do this in each part of the application separately. All of this saves considerable amounts of time, effort, and resources.

The event system is just an example, albeit a prominent one. Depending on your application's requirement, you will most likely have to add other functionalities to your framework, like dynamic resource loading or object pooling features (more on object pooling later in the book).

Another critical function of the framework is that it defines how the application's code is structured: a good framework imposes a good package structure and class hierarchy on developers, making the application's source code much more cohesive and easier to navigate.

Finally, a framework typically comes with a set of best practices and coding guidelines, which are sometimes enforced by the very nature of the framework's API, package hierarchy, and class structure. This makes the code more homogenous and easier to understand, which leads to fewer bugs and increased productivity.

Why a Custom Framework for Each Application?

A lot of companies and even individuals have a single custom-made generic framework that they use for all of their Java ME projects. In my personal opinion, this is the wrong way to go: each project should have its own, project-specific framework.

The reason for this can be summed up with just one word: overhead. For example, let's suppose we're writing a generic framework, but for a desktop platform. In this case, our event handling system will most likely be based on a priority queue, since it will be more flexible this way. A direct consequence of this decision is that, even if all our events have the same priority, the event prioritizing code still has to kick in, analyze each event, and place it in the proper place within the queue—remember, the framework is a generic one and it doesn't know that all events have the same priority. This will eat up some CPU time, but compared to the available CPU time, this overhead will be practically zero.

Now let's suppose we do the same thing within a Java ME framework. Since we're targeting considerably less powerful hardware, the event prioritizing overhead will increase. It should still be fairly low-profile by itself, but when added together with other sources of overhead, it can become significant—a compounded overhead of 5–10% or more is certainly noticeable, and the wasted resources can be better spent elsewhere. To avoid this particular source of overhead, if our application doesn't need a priority queue for events, we'll simply write an event handling system with a simple queue instead of a priority one. A direct consequence of this is that our generic framework is not so generic anymore because at least a part of it has been optimized for our particular application.

However, to truly minimize overhead, we have to apply these kinds of optimizations across the entire framework and not just to parts of it. This means that we will end up with a very slick, highly-customized, and resource-friendly backbone for our application, which will most likely be at least partially incompatible with the original framework. Furthermore, sometimes the customizations needed are so extensive that you are simply better off writing a new framework from scratch. Either way, reusing the same framework for different projects is not really a good idea for high-quality Java ME applications; if you want the best possible performance, you need a custom framework for each application.

Defining the Framework's Structure

The first step in writing a framework is to define its basic structure and clarify what parts of it go in what Java packages. Since the framework structure usually also defines the package structure of the application, we will cover that as well.

All package names start with "com.apress" in our case, but to save space, this prefix has been omitted in Table 2–1.

Table 2–1. *The Framework and Application Structure*

Package	Description
framework.objecttypes	Defines the basic object types used by the framework and the application, such as Model, Controller, View, Event, etc.
framework.common	Implementations of commonly used objects, such as the EventController; if you have many commonly used objects, it might make sense to split this package into sub-packages, according to object type.
framework.core	Implementations of core framework objects, such as the Application static class
framework.helpers	All helper and utility classes go here.
app.models	All global models (models that logically do not belong to a single module) go here—for example, the TwitterUser model.
app.module.<NAME>	Each module gets its own package.

Package	Description

`app.module.<NAME>.models`
`app.module.<NAME>.views`
`app.module.<NAME>.controllers`
`app.module.<NAME>.managers`
`app.module.<NAME>.helpers`
`app.module.<NAME>.classes.*`
	The models, views, and controllers specific to each module go into their corresponding package. The same is true for managers, helpers, and other classes.

`app.media, app.files`
`app.media.<NAME>`
`app.files.<NAME>`
	All media and other non-code files go here. For example, global media files go in the `app.media` package, while module-specific files go in the `app.media.<NAME>` package.

This is, of course, not the only way to structure a framework and the applications based on it, but this is the package layout I typically use. It allows for a clear separation of code and responsibilities, while at the same time ensuring that developers don't get lost in package names and deep package trees.

Now that we have our skeleton, it's time to put some meat on the bones. Specifically, we will populate the first three packages from the preceding table with the appropriate entities. The end result will be an extremely simple but usable framework.

We will start with the `com.apress.framework.objecttypes` package.

Basic Object Types

Most frameworks, ours included, are largely based on the Model-View-Controller paradigm, with a few modifications. This is the most flexible paradigm for Java ME development, as it allows for the high level of abstraction and flexibility that developers need to cover all their bases.

> **NOTE:** The main exceptions to this rule are game frameworks, which by their very nature require a different approach and mindset than application frameworks. For example, as games are typically very fast-paced, using events to handle communication between different parts of the code can prove to be slow and inefficient resource-wise. As such, game frameworks tend to use less flexible but more efficient means of communication, such as direct method calls between objects belonging to different areas of the application.
>
> If the subject of Java ME game writing interests you, Apress has a good selection of books that cover it.

The MVC paradigm should already be familiar to you, so instead of going deep into it, we'll just recap its basic object types.

On top of this basic design, we will add a few more object types of our own:

- *Events* define, as their name suggests, events that take place during the application's runtime.

- *Event listeners* respond to events.

- *Providers* retrieve, extract, or generate objects or data from various sources, typically external ones such as the native address book or a server.

- *Consumers* are the counterparts to providers, in that they are used for sending data or objects to external sources.

- *Managers* handle and manipulate collections of objects.

- *Models* are representations of the datatypes manipulated by the application, such as Tweets and Contacts.

- *Controllers* generally control the program flow.

- *Views* are responsible for drawing what the user sees on the screen, the forms and the UI widgets, based on the models and instructions given by controllers.

We will go over these types one by one. As mentioned previously, every class and interface discussed in this section belongs in the com.apress.framework.objecttypes package.

Before we continue, here is a quick side note. As our framework will be primarily event-based, a large portion of this chapter will be dedicated to events and event handling. Event-based development is pretty much the only paradigm that really works for Java ME applications, because with it everything is separated in discrete and individual units (events). This gives developers almost complete control over what is processed when and in what way.

Events

Events will be passed around a lot throughout the application, so it is important that they are both easy to use and clearly defined.

Thus, an event has three basic components: the event context, the event type, and the event payload. The context and the type define what kind of event has occurred and where, while the event payload provides extra information about the event, such as what object has been affected by it.

To be able to properly define events, we need two classes. One is the actual event class, shown in Listing 2–1.

Listing 2–1. *The Event Class*

```
package com.apress.framework.objecttypes;

public class Event
{
    protected int context;
    protected int type;
    protected Object payload;
```

```
    public Event(int context, int type, Object payload)
    {
        this.context = context;
        ...
    }

    public int getContext()
    {
        return this.context;
    }

    ...
}
```

The other class is a descriptor for all possible event contexts and event types. For brevity and code clarity, we will name this class EVT. It is presented in Listing 2–2.

Listing 2–2. *The EVT Class*

```
package com.apress.framework.objecttypes;
public class EVT
{
    public class CONTEXT
    {
        public static final int NONE = -1;
public static final int LOCAL = 0;
        public static final int STARTUP = 1;
        public static final int SHUTDOWN = 2;
        public static final int LOGIN_FORM = 3;
...
    }

    public class CONTACTS
    {
        public static final int ADD_CONTACT = 1;
        public static final int REMOVE_CONTACT = 2;
    }
    ...
}
```

This approach makes using events easy as pie. For example, to create an event that signals that a new contact has been added during the startup process, all we have to do is this:

```
Event someEvent = new Event( EVT.CONTEXT.STARTUP, EVT.CONTACTS.ADD_CONTACT,
contactObject );
```

Handling events is another matter altogether, and quite a more complex one, spanning many areas of the framework and of the application.

We will need event listeners to respond to them (which are up next), event controllers to dispatch events to the listeners, event controller managers to bundle together event controllers (this is done for practical reasons), and a way to have event controller managers run on their own independent threads, so as not to interfere with the rest of the application. As we go along, all of these entities will be covered in the sections dedicated to their corresponding packages.

Event Listeners

Someone has to listen for and respond to events. Event listeners do just that. All event listeners must implement the EventListener interface, defined in Listing 2–3.

Listing 2–3. *The EventListener Interface*

```
package com.apress.framework.objecttypes;

public interface EventListener
{
    public boolean handleEvent(Event event) ;
}
```

The handleEvent() method returns true if the event has been handled, false otherwise.

Providers

Providers, as the name implies, provide data and objects to the application, typically from external sources. For example, a PIMContactProvider can be used to retrieve contacts from the device's address book, while a CameraFrameProvider can be used to retrieve still frames from the device's camera.

Providers can be split into two main groups: random access and sequential ones.

Sequential providers behave like enumerations, in that they retrieve objects one by one, in order. Only one object is available at any given time, and once the next object is requested, the old one is discarded and it cannot be retrieved again. The CameraFrameProvider is a good example of a sequential provider.

Random access providers allow access to any of their objects at any given time. For example, the PIMContactProvider can provide access to any contact in the device's address book.

In our framework, all providers must implement the Provider interface shown in Listing 2–4.

Listing 2–4. *The Provider Interface*

```
package com.apress.framework.objecttypes;

public interface Provider
{
    public boolean isSequential();

    public Object retrieveCurrent();

    public void next();

    public boolean hasMore();
```

```
    public boolean jumpTo(int objectIndex);

    public int getNumberOfAvailableObjects();
}
```

Calling `retrieveCurrent()` will return the element at the current index; the current index can be changed by calling `next()` or `jumpTo()`. On sequential providers, the index can be changed only by calling `next()`.

When it is not possible to jump to a certain index or to the next index, `jumpTo()` and `next()` will return `false`.

Providers with an unknown number of objects return -1 when `getNumberOfAvailableObjects()` is called.

Calling `hasMore()` will return `true` if there are more elements after the current index, `false` otherwise.

Consumers

Consumers are the counterparts to providers. They are used to send data or objects to external sources, typically outside of the application. Like providers, they can be random and sequential, and they follow the same conventions. All consumers must implement the `Consumer` interface from Listing 2–5.

Listing 2–5. *The Consumer Interface*

```
package com.apress.framework.objecttypes;

public interface Consumer
{
    public boolean isSequential();

    public boolean next();

    public boolean store(Object object);

    public boolean jumpTo(int objectIndex);

    public int getNumberOfAvailableSlots();
}
```

Next are consumer-specific conventions.

Random access consumers store objects in the "slot" indicated by the current index. Changing the index works in the same way as it does for providers (see previous).

When `store()` is called on sequential consumers, an implicit call to `next()` is also made. Calling `store()` on random access consumers does not change the current index.

Calling `next()` on sequential consumers without storing an object first is equivalent to saying "store nothing." This may or may not fail, depending on the consumer.

Managers

Just like football managers are responsible for the careers of their players, so too our managers are responsible for specific aspects of the objects under their wings.

For example, a `ContactSyncManager` would be responsible for keeping its contacts in sync with the server, while a `ContactIntegrityManager` would be responsible for ensuring that the details of its contacts are in accordance with one another, so a contact's declared star sign matches the specified date of birth.

Managers are useful because they typically operate on the "fire and forget" principle, doing their work independently and behind the scenes. They thus compartmentalize some of the application's complexity and hide it from the rest of the code.

In order to use managers, we must be able to assign and un-assign objects to them and we should also be able to find out if a manager is responsible for a certain object. Thus, all managers must implement the `Manager` interface from Listing 2–6.

Listing 2–6. *The* Manager *Interface*

```
package com.apress.framework.objecttypes;

public interface Manager
{
    public boolean assign(Object object);

    public void unassign(Object object);

    public boolean isManaging(Object object);
}
```

It is possible for a manager to handle several types of objects, even completely unrelated ones, if it makes sense to do so. A good example of this is a manager that must ensure that all its objects, regardless of their type, occupy less than a set amount of memory.

It is also possible for one object to be handled by more than one manager.

Managers can refuse to manage objects, indicated by a `false` return value for `assign()`.

Last but not least, managers can and often do also play other roles besides their manager one. For example, they can also be providers or event listeners.

A good example of how managers can be used will be provided later in this chapter.

Models and Controllers

By their very nature, models are unique, and there is usually no common functionality associated with all of them. Thus, the template for models will look like Listing 2–7.

Listing 2–7. *The* Model *Interface*

```
package com.apress.framework.objecttypes;

public interface Model
{

}
```

All model classes will have to implement this interface, even though it is empty right now. This is done primarily for clarity in our case, but you might find out that halfway through development there are a few common features that all models share or require, for example, a checksum() method, and adding those features to the interface will then make sense.

The foregoing applies to controllers too. All controllers must implement the interface in Listing 2–8.

Listing 2–8. *The* Controller *Interface*

```
package com.apress.framework.objecttypes;

public interface Controller
{

}
```

Views

Views are the screens that the user sees when interacting with the application. Like all MVC views, our views will be used by feeding data into them, typically models or collections of models. It is then up to the views themselves to present said data to the user and to provide support for user interaction.

All views must be able to self-paint when instructed to. They must also be able to provide a reference to their parent controller and to their underlying GameCanvas. As such, views must implement the interface in Listing 2–9.

Listing 2–9. *The* View *Interface*

```
package com.apress.framework.objecttypes;

import javax.microedition.lcdui.Graphics;

public interface View
{
    public boolean refresh();

    public Controller getParentController();

    public GameCanvas getCanvas();
}
```

Many times views are little more than wrappers for the "screen" objects of the underlying GUI library. Using them still makes sense, as it makes switching GUI libraries a lot easier if this needs to be done later in the project. This aspect is a very important one to remember: views are not usually tied down to specific GUI frameworks, just to specific application screens.

We will learn more about views and how to use them in the chapter dedicated to the GUI.

After adding views, our "object types" package is now fully populated. Let's take a five-minute break and let everything sink in, before we continue with populating the "common objects" package.

Common Objects

Many objects are reused heavily throughout an application. They are typically derivatives or implementations of basic types, and they play a key role in how the framework and the applications based on it function. A prime example of this is the EventController, which we will go over shortly.

Right now we're concerned only with getting the framework running, so we will keep the number of common objects to a minimum: only two.

Let's start with the aforementioned EventController.

The EventController Class

The EventController basically acts as a traffic controller for events, dispatching them to its registered listeners. This, in EventController terminology, is called "processing events."

The code for the EventController common object is shown in Listing 2–10.

Listing 2–10. *The EventController Class*

```
package com.apress.framework.common;

import com.apress.framework.objecttypes.Controller;
import com.apress.framework.objecttypes.Event;
import com.apress.framework.objecttypes.EventListener;
import java.util.Vector;

public class EventController implements Controller
{
    protected Vector listeners = new Vector(10,10);
    protected Vector events = new Vector(10,10);

    public void registerListener(EventListener listener)
    {
        if (! listeners.contains(listener) )
        {
            listeners.addElement(listener);
        }
    }
```

```java
    public void unregisterListener(EventListener listener)
    {
        listeners.removeElement(listener);
    }

    public void queueEvent(Event event)
    {
        events.addElement(event);
    }

    public void processNextEvent()
    {
        if ( events.size() > 0 )
        {
            Event event = (Event) events.firstElement();
            events.removeElement(event);

            int listenerCount = listeners.size();
            int currentIndex;
            EventListener temp;
            for (currentIndex = 0; currentIndex < listenerCount; currentIndex++)
            {
                temp = ( (EventListener) listeners.elementAt(currentIndex));
                temp.handleEvent(event);
            }
        }
    }

    public int currentEventCount()
    {
        return events.size();
    }

    public boolean hasMoreEvents()
    {
        return events.size() > 0 ;
    }
}
```

Probably the only interesting part about this code is the existence of two different methods, queueEvent() and processNextEvent(), for handling events. Most developers tend to do both of these things in the same step, but this is wrong for two main reasons.

The first one is that you may not want to process an event at the same time that it is queued. This is often the case when CPU power is limited, for example. With this approach, you can delay event processing for later, or process events at a slower pace than usual.

The second and most important reason is threading. Consider the following example, in Listing 2–11, in which the processEvent() method does both the queuing and the processing of the event in one step. Assume that the onButtonPress() method is part of the GUI library used by the application and that handleEvent() is part of a listener registered to the EventController.

Listing 2–11. *The Wrong Way to Handle Events*

```
public void onButtonPressed(Button button)
{
        Event event = new Calculate100FactorialEvent();
        eventController.processEvent(event);
}

...

public boolean handleEvent(Event evt)
{
        if ( evnt instanceOf Calculate100FactorialEvent)
        {
                // do lots of CPU intensive stuff here
        }
        return true;
}
```

The problem with this code is that you do not know on which thread the intensive CPU stuff will run. If it will run on the main UI thread, then your application's user interface will grind to a halt in no time. Even worse, the problematic event may come from a business-critical thread, like the networking thread, in which case that one will become unresponsive and the server might log the user out or worse. Furthermore, it is possible that onButtonPressed()will run on the main UI/system event thread, perhaps by being called from the commandAction() method of a CommandListener. Depending on what goes on inside onButtonPressed(), this can potentially crash the application (for example, if a network access request is initiated and the platform attempts to ask the user for permission).

The only real solution to this problem is to have events processed on an entirely separate thread than the one you are issuing them from, or at least on a thread that you can be sure is not critical. However, it is usually not feasible to have each controller run in its own separate thread.

This is where our next common object comes in.

The EventControllerManager

The primary purpose of the EventControllerManager is to make sure that event processing for all the controllers under its supervision is done on the same thread— which is typically not the same one they were issued from. Its secondary purpose is to ensure that all controllers get roughly the same amount of CPU time.

The manager will have a makeshift queue for EventControllers. You can add controllers to the queue by calling assign(), and you can remove them from the queue by calling unassign(). When a controller is added, it is added to the back of the queue.

The manager also has a processNextEvent() method. This method must be called from the thread on which events are to be processed. You can call it from the same thread every time or from different threads; you can use an already existing thread or create a dedicated one—it's all up to you and your needs.

When the method is called, one event from the first controller in the makeshift queue will be processed. After that, the first controller will be moved to the back of the queue and the second controller will take its place, and so forth. This rotational approach provides a quick and effective way to make sure all controllers receive relatively equal attention.

As for which thread the processNextEvent() should be called from and how, that is entirely up to you and your application. The framework does provide a quick and easy solution that works great in 90% of the cases. It will be discussed in the section dedicated to the core package. However, you are not obligated to use it—feel free to design and implement your own mechanism if you want to or need to.

EventControllerManager is presented in Listing 2–12.

Listing 2–12. *The* EventControllerManager *Class*

```
package com.apress.framework.common;

import com.apress.framework.objecttypes.Manager;
import java.util.Vector;

public class EventControllerManager implements Manager
{
    public Vector controllers = new Vector(10,10);

    public boolean assign(Object object)
    {
        if ( object instanceof EventController)
        {
            if ( ! controllers.contains(object) )
            {
                controllers.addElement(object);
            }
            return true;
        }
        else
        {
            return false;
        }
    }

    public void unassign(Object object)
    {
        controllers.removeElement(object);
    }

    public boolean isManaging(Object object)
    {
        return ( controllers.indexOf(object) > -1 );
    }

    public void processNextEvent()
    {
        if ( controllers.size() > 0 )
        {
            EventController controller = (EventController) controllers.firstElement();
            controllers.removeElement(controller);
            controller.processNextEvent();
```

```
            controllers.addElement(controller);
        }
    }

    public boolean hasMoreEvents()
    {
        return currentEventCount() > 0;
    }

    public int currentEventCount()
    {
        Enumeration controllerEnum = controllers.elements();
        EventController temp = null;
        int count = 0;
        while ( controllerEnum.hasMoreElements() )
        {
            temp = (EventController) controllerEnum.nextElement() ;
            if ( temp.hasMoreEvents() )
            {
                count += temp.currentEventCount();
            }
        }
        return count;
    }
}
```

Now it's time to move on to the next package: com.apress.framework.core.

Core Objects and Classes

This package can be considered the heart of the framework, being responsible for gluing everything together and making sure that the application has access to everything it needs. We will discuss the Application class, the EventManagerThreads class, and the Bootstrap class.

The Application Class

With the foregoing in mind, the most important part of the core package is the Application class. It provides access to the main event controller, to the main event controller manager (which, by default, is *not* linked to the main event controller), to the MIDlet instance, to the display instance, and to pretty much everything else that is high-level or critical and might need to be accessible from within the application code.

A simple implementation of the Application class is presented in Listing 2–13. As you adapt the framework to the particular project you are working on, you will most likely modify this class to suit your needs.

Listing 2–13. *The Application Class*

```
package com.apress.framework.core;

import com.apress.framework.common.EventController;
import com.apress.framework.common.EventControllerManager;
```

```
import com.apress.framework.objecttypes.View;
import javax.microedition.lcdui.Display;
import javax.microedition.midlet.MIDlet;

public class Application
{
    static EventController mainEventController = new EventController();
    static EventControllerManager manager = new EventControllerManager();
    static MIDlet midlet = null ;

    protected Application()
    {
        // Do nothing
    }

    public static void showView(View view)
    {
        getDisplay().setCurrent(view.getCanvas());
        view.refresh();
    }

    public static void init(MIDlet instance)
    {
        midlet = instance;
        manager.assign(mainEventController);
    }

    public static EventController getMainEventController()
    {
        return mainEventController;
    }

    public static EventControllerManager getMainEventControllerManager()
    {
        return manager;
    }

    public static MIDlet getMIDlet()
    {
        return midlet;
    }

    public static Display getDisplay()
    {
        return Display.getDisplay(midlet);
    }
}
```

The EventManagerThreads Class

This class allows event controller managers to run in their own individual threads and at their own specific pace—we've hinted at it in the EventControllerManager section.

Using this class is dead easy. To have an event controller manager process all its underlying events from all its assigned controllers every 30 milliseconds, all you have to do is call the following:

```
EventManagerThreads.start ( someManagerInstance, 30 );
```

If you want the manager to process its events at a different interval, call `start()` again with the desired parameters.

Stopping an event controller manager from being periodically processed is equally easy:

```
EventManagerThreads.stop ( someManagerInstance );
```

The code for the `EventManagerThreads` class is shown in Listing 2–14.

Listing 2–14. *The EventManagerThreads Class*

```java
package com.apress.framework.core;

import com.apress.framework.common.EventControllerManager;
import java.util.Hashtable;

public class EventManagerThreads
{
    public static class ManagerThread implements Runnable
    {
        EventControllerManager manager = null;
        long sleepTime = 0;
        boolean run = true;

        public ManagerThread(EventControllerManager manager, long sleepTime)
        {
            this.manager = manager;
            this.sleepTime = sleepTime;
        }

        public void run()
        {
            while ( run )
            {
                int evtCount = manager.currentEventCount();
                while ( evtCount>0 )
                {
                    manager.processNextEvent();
                    evtCount--;
                }

                try
                {
                    Thread.sleep(sleepTime);
                }
                catch (InterruptedException ex)
                {
                    ex.printStackTrace();
                }
            }
        }
        public void stop()
```

```
        {
            run = false;
        }
    }

    protected static Hashtable threads = new Hashtable();

    protected EventManagerThreads()
    {
        // Do nothing
    }

    public static void start(EventControllerManager manager, long sleepTime)
    {
        stop(manager);
        ManagerThread thread = null;
        thread = new ManagerThread(manager, sleepTime);
        Thread t = new Thread(thread);
        t.start();
        threads.put(manager, thread);
    }

    public static void stop(EventControllerManager manager)
    {
        ManagerThread thread = (ManagerThread) threads.get(manager);
        if( thread != null )
        {
            thread.stop();
        }
    }
}
```

Please look at the highlighted lines in the foregoing listing. You may ask, why not simply use hasMoreEvents()? The answer is simple: as events get handled by listeners, those listeners can and often do add other events to the queues of their controllers. This can lead to situations in which your controller manager will always have more events to process, which in turn means that you will never exit the loop, which in turn means that the thread will never sleep, thus running at full speed and wasting valuable resources, especially CPU time. Our approach makes sure that only the events that are already in the queue are processed in the current time frame, while events added in the current time frame will be processed in the next one. Not handling this properly is a very frequent mistake in event-based systems.

> **NOTE:** This chapter has a sample application near the end that is great for exemplifying this issue. To see the difference between using hasMoreEvents() and using currentEventCount(), run that application using both approaches.

With this class, we finally have a functional event system. Understanding and using it can be a bit confusing at first, so let's take a few moments to examine how it functions as a whole and what you must do to get it running.

First, if you want to be able to respond to events, you have to register yourself to the appropriate event controller or controllers. If you want to register yourself as a listener to the main event controller, you should call the following:

```
Application.getMainEventController().registerListener( this )
```

Next, whenever something happens, you have to queue the appropriate event on the appropriate controller or controllers. For example, to queue an event on the main event controller, all you have to do is call the following:

```
Application.getMainEventController().queueEvent( someEvent )
```

All event controllers with the exception of local ones should be assigned to a manager. For example, to assign a controller to the main event controller manager, you must call the following:

```
Application.getMainEventControllerManager().assign( someController );
```

Lastly, you must make sure all event controller managers get the chance to periodically process their underlying events, let's say every 20 milliseconds. One easy way of doing so is by calling the following:

```
EventManagerThreads.start( someManager, 20);
```

While the approach just described is a bit more complicated than the classical "queue here, process now" one, it does allow for a greater degree of freedom and flexibility. For example, you can control which controllers are assigned to which manager, and how often each manager gets called and on what thread. So you can, if need be, assign all low-priority controllers to the same manager and have it called every five or ten seconds, thus saving CPU time. You can also easily modify the code to allow for two or more managers to run the same thread, so that all low-priority managers share the same thread, while each high-priority manager gets its own thread.

As you can probably imagine, the current code we have for this is far from perfect. CPU-intensive events can still stall the controller; there is the possibility that a very important and crucial event will be placed at the back of the queue and thus be processed too late, etc.

However, most issues that can crop up can be fixed with relative ease and with minor alterations to the code and the ideas behind it.

For example, you can create multiple event controllers and event managers, some for high priority events and some for low priority ones.

You can also split CPU-heavy events into smaller chunks, using the DO_WORK_UNIT trick from the previous chapter.

Last but not least, you can have events about events. For example, you can implement a FILL_IN_THE_BLANKS event, which takes another event as a payload, processes it in some way (modifies its payload, changes its type or context, etc.), and then puts it in circulation. It sounds complicated, but it's quite simple to do and a lot more useful than it initially looks. A basic implementation of the concept is presented in Listing 2–15.

Listing 2–15. *Events About Events*

```
Event evt = new SomeEventWithIncompleteInformation();
Event handleThis = new Event( EVT.CONTEXT.NONE, EVT.EVENTS.FILL_IN_THE_BLANKS, evt);
mainEventController.queueEvent ( handleThis ) ;

....

public void handleEvent(Event evt)
{
        if ( evt.getType() == EVT.EVENTS.EVENTS.FILL_IN_THE_BLANKS )
        {
                Event temp = (Event) evt.getPayload() ;
                if ( evt instanceOf SomeEventWithIncompleteInformation)
                {
                        completeInformation( evt );
                        mainEventController.queueEvent ( evt );
                }
        }
}
```

Before we end this discussion and continue with the book, there is one more thing I would like to mention: event handling, like all things Java ME, has no universal solution. Depending on what kind of application you are writing, you might prefer one approach over another. For example, the listener-controller paradigm is great for business applications, but it might simply be too slow for some real-time applications such as action games. In those cases, you may prefer to handle events as they occur and as close to the source as possible.

The Bootstrap Class

Flexibility and freedom is good, but you do have to make a few function calls to get everything set up. This is where our next core class, Bootstrap, comes in. It allows you to get everything up and ready to go with the minimum amount of function calls, which makes it great for quick test projects or for showing the framework to people who are unfamiliar with it. You can also add different "boot" methods to the class for different circumstances and setups—ours has just one for now. The full source code for Bootstrap is shown in Listing 2–16.

Listing 2–16. *The Bootstrap Class*

```
package com.apress.framework.core;

import com.apress.framework.common.EventControllerManager;
import javax.microedition.midlet.MIDlet;

public class Bootstrap
{
    public static void boot(MIDlet midlet, long eventManagerSleepTime)
    {
        Application.init(midlet);
        EventControllerManager main = Application.getMainEventControllerManager();
```

```
        main.assign(Application.getMainEventController());
        EventManagerThreads.start(main, eventManagerSleepTime);
    }
}
```

With the `Bootstrap` class in place, our basic framework is now complete. All that's left is to take it for a little test run, which is exactly what we'll do next.

A Simple Test Application

Once the framework is ready, the best way to get a quick feel for how it works is to write a simple test application and play around with it. This will also allow you to test for problems with the framework.

Our test application will be as basic as possible, but at the same time it will test all the important aspects of the framework: the use of controllers, events, views, and models.

The basic idea behind it is this: you have two controllers, each symbolizing a player in a PING-PONG game.

One controller responds to PING events by displaying its own view, and then it issues a PONG event.

The other controller responds to PONG events, displays its view, and then issues a PING event. The two controllers basically exchange messages back and forth continuously, while doing some processing in the middle. This simple scenario covers 90% of all the applications out there, so it is a very suitable one.

Now, before we can write the test application, we need to set up the proper events. Your EVT class should look something like the one in Listing 2–17.

Listing 2–17. *The EVT Class for Our Test Application*

```
package com.apress.framework.objecttypes;

public class EVT
{
    public class CONTEXT
    {
        public static final int TEST= 999;
        ...
    }

    public class TEST
    {
        public static final int PING=1;
        public static final int PONG=2;
    }

    ...

}
```

Now that our events are in place, we can continue with writing our application.

Let's start with the simplest class, TestModel, which can be seen in Listing 2–18. There is nothing much to say about it, as the code is self-explanatory.

Listing 2–18. *The* TestModel *Class*

```
package test;

import com.apress.framework.objecttypes.Model;

public class TestModel implements Model
{
    protected String text;

    public TestModel (String text)
    {
        this.text = text;
    }

    public String getText()
    {
        return text;
    }
}
```

Next up, we need a view capable of displaying our model. That would be TestView, shown in Listing 2–19.

Listing 2–19. *The* TestView *Class*

```
package test;

import com.apress.framework.objecttypes.Controller;
import com.apress.framework.objecttypes.View;
import javax.microedition.lcdui.Graphics;
import javax.microedition.lcdui.game.GameCanvas;

public class TestView extends GameCanvas implements View
{
    Controller controller;
    TestModel model;

    public TestView(Controller controller, TestModel model)
    {
        super(true);
        this.controller = controller;
        this.model = model;
    }

    public void paint(Graphics g)
    {
        g.setColor(255, 255, 255);
        g.fillRect(0, 0, 1000, 1000);
        g.setColor(0,0,0);
        String message = model.getText() + " received from " + controller;
        System.out.println(message);
        g.drawString(message, 10, 10, Graphics.TOP | Graphics.LEFT);
    }
```

```
public boolean refresh()
{
    repaint();
    serviceRepaints();
    return true;
}

public Controller getParentController()
{
    return controller;
}

public GameCanvas getCanvas()
{
    return this;
}

}
```

Again, the code pretty much speaks for itself. We now need to implement the Player class, which will be the bread and butter of our sample application. It is a controller that interacts with the main event controller, receiving events from it and issuing new ones in response when needed. It also creates models, attaches them to views, and displays those views whenever the proper event is received. Listing 2–20 presents its source code.

Listing 2–20. *The Player Class*

```
package test;

import com.apress.framework.core.Application;
import com.apress.framework.objecttypes.Controller;
import com.apress.framework.objecttypes.EVT;
import com.apress.framework.objecttypes.Event;
import com.apress.framework.objecttypes.EventListener;

public class Player implements Controller, EventListener
{
    private int reactsTo, responseEvent;
    private TestView testView;

    public Player(int reactsTo, int sendsOut, String saying)
    {
        this.reactsTo = reactsTo;
        this.responseEvent = sendsOut;
        TestModel model = new TestModel(saying);
        this.testView = new TestView(this,model);
    }

    public boolean handleEvent(Event event)
    {
        if ( event.getContext() == EVT.CONTEXT.TEST )
        {
            if ( event.getType() == reactsTo)
            {
                // Show the view for this controller
                Application.showView(testView);
```

```
                      // Queue the appropriate response event
                      Event evt = new Event(EVT.CONTEXT.TEST, responseEvent,this);
                      Application.getMainEventController().queueEvent(evt);

                      return true;
                  }
              }
              return false;
          }

      }
```

Last but not least, now that we have everything we need, we can implement our main TestMidlet, shown in Listing 2–21. The framework keeps everything nice and tidy.

Listing 2–21. *The* `TestMidlet` *Class*

```
package test;

import com.apress.framework.core.Application;
import com.apress.framework.core.Bootstrap;
import com.apress.framework.objecttypes.EVT;
import com.apress.framework.objecttypes.Event;
import javax.microedition.midlet.*;

public class TestMidlet extends MIDlet
{
    public void startApp()
    {
        Bootstrap.boot(this, 1500);

        Player player1 = new Player(EVT.TEST.PING, EVT.TEST.PONG, "PING!");
        Player player2 = new Player(EVT.TEST.PONG, EVT.TEST.PING, "PONG!");

        Application.getMainEventController().registerListener(player1);
        Application.getMainEventController().registerListener(player2);

        // Kick-off event
        Event evt = new Event(EVT.CONTEXT.TEST, EVT.TEST.PING, this);
        Application.getMainEventController().queueEvent(evt);

    }

    public void pauseApp() {
    }

    public void destroyApp(boolean unconditional) {
    }
}
```

And with this, our work in this chapter is done. The framework is up and running, and the sample application is ready for you to play around with, as you can see in Figure 2–1. We did a good job!

Figure 2–1. *The test application in action*

Summary

We have looked at how the framework for our Pro Java ME application functions. In the process, we have also learned how to properly structure and write Java ME application frameworks in general, as well as some of the pitfalls associated with this.

At the end of the chapter, we took our framework for a test drive by writing a small sample application based on it.

Next, we will define our application's datatypes and look at how properly defining datatypes and objects can improve a Java ME application.

## Chapter 3

Defining Our Data

In this chapter, we will cover defining data types and objects in a Java ME–friendly fashion. This step rarely receives the attention it deserves, but just as developing an application with the wrong mindset or developing it on top of the wrong framework can lead to disaster, so can using the wrong representation for your data.

The main pitfall here is the tendency to apply standard OO concepts (everything is an object, specialized objects are built on top of less specialized ones via inheritance, etc.) directly to Java ME, without consideration to the platform's peculiarities.

If you do so, you will end up with an elegant object hierarchy from an architectural point of view, but one that behaves poorly in performance-critical moments and that requires a lot of RAM. At the same time, going to the other extreme and consolidating everything in a single class (or two or three) isn't an option either, as this will lead to great performance but virtually unmaintainable code.

The sweet spot for Java ME lies somewhere in the middle: consolidate objects and data types to a high enough degree that performance issues are minimized, while still retaining enough separation between them to call the whole thing "object-oriented." This chapter aims to show how to find that sweet spot. In the process, we will also define the actual data types and entities we will use in our Twitter client.

We will concern ourselves only with global data types and entities, those that belong in the app.models package. Non-global models will be handled in their specific modules.

Why Implement the Model Interface?

You will notice that all the classes we will discuss in this chapter implement the Model interface, while all the interfaces we will discuss extend it. In other words, the Model interface is at the root of every global data type and entity within in our application. Furthermore, as we have seen in the previous chapter, the Model interface is empty. So why implement/extend it at all?

There are three main reasons for this. The first reason is that it acts as a very efficient code hint. For example, if a developer sees that class Tweet is a Model, he knows that this class should model the behavior and functionality of the associated "real-life" entity, and from the specifications he knows how exactly it should achieve this. Furthermore, when he will consider adding new functionality to the class, he will ask himself if that functionality really belongs in a Model or in some other place (like a related Controller). Finally, the information that a class extends Model can be used by code analysis/optimization tools, and by IDEs (to get a list of all models in an application, regardless of their package, one simply has to do a "Show type history" on Model).

The second reason for implementing the Model interface is that it helps in the consolidation effort. For example, you may decide (either beforehand or during development) that all models should implement a checksum() method or an isSyncedToServer() method to check if the client's local data is the same as the data on the server (extremely useful for real-time applications). Having all models implement a common interface is an elegant and effective way to achieve this.

The third reason is that the Model interface can also act as a safeguard against over-consolidation. To keep with the previous example, if inside a class it is not clear to what data the checksum() or isSyncedToServer() methods apply, or if you would conceptually need two separate checksum() methods for the same class (each method working on two different sets of data), then you have most likely over-consolidated and need to split up the problematic data types and objects until one checksum()/isSyncedToServer() method per class suffices and its scope is perfectly clear.

Making Data Types Immutable

This is a general piece of advice that can be applied to Java ME as well: whenever possible, try to make your data types immutable. For example, you should make it so that once you create a new Tweet instance, you are able only to retrieve its attributes—you cannot alter them in any way.

If you want to modify one or more of its attributes, you must create a new instance with the corresponding new set of values instead of, for example, calling setTimestamp() or setText() on the existing instance. While doing so does incur a small performance hit, if done properly, the benefits significantly outweigh the costs.

The biggest benefit of doing so is that you prevent a lot of bugs from happening by making sure you cannot alter objects by mistake, since the only way you can "alter" an object is to create a new one. Another benefit is that changes to important instance values, like the text of a Tweet, are easier to track, which in turn makes the code easier to debug. Both aspects are extremely important for large and intricate applications.

NOTE: The downside of this approach is that, if you are not careful, you might end up creating problems instead of solving them. For example, if you keep references to old and unused instances by mistake, then you not only prevent them from being garbage-collected, but you also affect your application's behavior, because "invalid" old data might get used instead of "valid" new data.

Of course, not all data types and entities can or should be immutable. Let's say you are writing a game, which features a BadGuy entity. Making it immutable is a bad idea, because a BadGuy can move() and fire() often. While good practice, creating a new instance every time one of these actions occurs will slow your game to a crawl. The same is true for other entities that change their state often, like a Scrollbar in a UI framework or a ChatRoomHistory in a chat program.

Another good example comes in the form of data types and entities that encompass large amounts of information—for example, a Level data type in the foregoing game: having to create a new instance of a level whenever a tile changes its value would be absolutely mad.

These are exceptions, however. In a typical application, with a proper plan and a proper architecture, you can probably get away with making 60–70% of the global data types and entities immutable, if not more.

This being said, let us now start with defining our objects and data types.

Defining the Tweet Data Type

This is probably the fundamental data type of the application, as its entire functionality revolves around tweets. Tweets have a body, an author, and an ID as their main attributes.

NOTE: Tweets actually have many more attributes associated with them—for example, geo-location—but for our purposes, we will stick to the three important ones just listed. Feel free to add support for the rest if you want to.

Our Tweet class will look something like Listing 3–1. As all global data types and entities, the Tweet class implements the Model interface.

Listing 3–1. *The Tweet Class*

```
package app.models;

import com.apress.framework.objecttypes.Model;

public class Tweet implements Model
{
    protected Tweet() { }
```

```
    public Tweet (String author, String body, long timestamp)
    {
        ...
    }

    public String getBody() { ... }

    public String getAuthor() { ... }

    public String getID() { ... }
}
```

As you can see, it has a protected default constructor and only setters for its fields, forcing you to initialize it with some data and making it immutable at the same time. As you add support for more attributes, it will make sense to also add additional constructors—for example, one that takes author, body, timestamp, and location as parameters. For our purposes, however, the current implementation will do just fine.

We now know how tweets will look in our code. It's now time to see how their creators, Twitter users, will be represented.

Defining the TwitterUser Data Type

Intuitively enough, users are the ones who post and read tweets. Each Twitter user has a name, a short description (or bio), an URL, and a location. Thus, the TwitterUser class looks like the one in Listing 3–2.

Listing 3–2. *The TwitterUser Class*

```
package app.models;

import com.apress.framework.objecttypes.Model;

public class TweeterUser implements Model
{

    protected TweeterUser() {  }

    public TweeterUser (String author, String body, String url, String location)
    {
        ...
    }

    public String getDescription() { ... }

    public String getName() { ... }

    public String getUrl() { ... }

    public String getLocation() { ... }
}
```

At this point, those of you who are familiar with Twitter might ask, "OK, but where are the friends, the followers, the blocked users?"

A very good question. Even though in our application overview, the Twitter user is a stand-alone entity, being able to perform actions like sending and receiving tweets, in practice, we will treat it like a simple data type and we will move all the functionality and behavior associated with it to the Twitter server entity. This actually makes some sense if you think about it: the Twitter user really cannot do anything on his own—he needs a server in order to function.

In general, if entity A depends on entity B for its functionality, it is a good idea to move that functionality from entity A to entity B, at least for Java ME. That's because this "functionality consolidation" approach usually minimizes code size, the amount of information that is passed around, and the number of method calls that are made, since most of the "action" tends to happens within a single instance of a single class.

This also leads to the situation in which 10% of the entities are taking over the functionality of the remaining 90%, which goes against a few object-oriented principles. For example, in our case, the "encapsulation of behavior" principle is broken, because although the TwitterUser retains state, all its behavior has been moved to the TwitterServer. While this is generally considered bad practice in the "civilized" OO world, Java ME is one of the few cases in which using this approach makes sense.

If applied correctly, this consolidation process will turn many of the entities in a project into simple structures in the C sense of the word, while the remaining key entities will be responsible with the bulk of the application's functionality. Out of those few entities, most of them will be written in code as interfaces or abstract classes, leaving the actual implementation to the application's modules. As such, very few members of the app.models package will be full-blown classes—in our case, none.

Now back to our application. So far we have looked at tweets and Twitter users, neither of which is really breathtaking. Let's take a look at something a bit more exciting: the Twitter server.

Defining the TwitterServer Entity

As the name implies, the TwitterServer entity corresponds to the Twitter server. Modeling it won't be as easy as modeling tweets or users, though. For one thing, it is completely outside the boundaries of our application, and so are its data and logic—we know nothing about what happens behind its closed doors. Furthermore, we ourselves can't create a new server, nor can we change the IP address or other parameters of the existing one.

What we will do is write TwitterServer as a black box that relies on the networking module to forward requests to and receive responses from the actual server. Also, in addition to the regular functionality associated with the Twitter server, like logging in and retrieving the tweets of a Timeline, the TwitterServer will take over the functionality normally associated with the TwitterUser, like posting tweets—the reason for this is discussed in the previous section.

The full code for the `TwitterServer` interface is presented in Listing 3–3, while the concrete implementation will be given in the chapter dedicated to the networking module.

Listing 3–3. *The `TwitterServer` Interface*

```
package app.models;

import com.apress.framework.objecttypes.Model;

public interface TwitterServer extends Model
{
    public boolean login(UserCredentials credentials) ;

    public TwitterUser getMyProfile();

    public TwitterUser getProfileFor(String userid);

    public Timeline getTimelineForFilter(TweetFilter filter);

    public boolean postTweet(Tweet tweet);
}
```

You can see that the code makes references to three data types that we haven't discussed so far: `UserCredentials`, `TweetFilter`, and `Timeline`. Let's examine them one by one.

Defining the UserCredentials Data Type

The `UserCredentials` class is responsible for providing to the server the credentials of the Twitter user we wish to log in.

At the time of this writing, Twitter supports three main methods of authentication if you want to access its services externally.

The first one is out-of-band authentication, which is suited only for web and desktop apps. It does not work very well for mobile apps, particularly for Java ME apps, because the user has to leave the application and enter his credentials in a browser. Furthermore, this may not work at all on some devices, as they may lack an adequate browser altogether, or the ability to open the browser from within a Java ME application. Even if it works, you can't expect the flow of the login process to be consistent across all devices (different pop-ups, confirmations, etc.). All in all, it is a bad experience for the user.

The second one is single-access tokens, which are great for single-user scenarios, since the user's credentials are "hard-coded" into the application.

The third one is xAuth, which is best suited for multi-user scenarios, like a free-for-all Twitter client similar to the one we plan to write. With xAuth, your application is authorized to work on behalf of any user, so long as the username and password provided are correct.

Obviously we would like to use xAuth for our project. However, as I am writing this, Twitter is giving xAuth privileges only on an as-needed basis—so you can't count on xAuth being available to you.

While not being able to use xAuth is sort of a roadblock for a real-life project, our learning project can do without it. If xAuth is not available, simply use single-access tokens. More details on this will be provided in the chapter related to networking.

For now, we have to make sure that Twitter has support for both xAuth and single-access tokens. Thus, our class looks like the one in Listing 3–4.

Listing 3–4. *The* `UserCredentials` *Class*

```
package app.models;

import com.apress.framework.objecttypes.Model;

public class UserCredentials implements Model
{
    protected UserCredentials() {  }

    public UserCredentials(String username, String password,
                String accessToken, String accessTokenSecret)  { ... }

    // For xAuth authentication
    public String getUsername() { ... }
    public String getPassword() { ... }

    // For token-based authentication
    public String getAccessToken() { ... }
    public String getAccessTokenSecret() { ... }
}
```

If you haven't done so already, it's time to ask yourself, "Why is this class part of the global models package?" Indeed, at first glance it feels more suited to the networking module.

The reason we're discussing credentials here instead of in the networking chapter is simple: `UserCredentials` identifies the user of the application, the person who sits on the other side of the mobile phone's screen—and he's as global an entity as it gets for a Java ME application.

A word of advice: many developers often forget that the end user is himself an entity, and a global one at that. When this happens, rather than having everything related to the user in a single package, they tend to disperse information correlated with him throughout the application's modules. However, different modules have different scopes, and most modules tend to be somewhat autonomous in nature. As a result, some of the information and functionality related to the user tends to either get lost or become overly complicated to use. This translates into code that doesn't accurately reflect the user's persona and needs, thus resulting in a poorly focused application.

Defining the TweetFilter Data Type

The TweetFilter data type will allow us to filter tweets by specific criteria. For example, we might want to get only tweets created by a certain user, or that contain a certain hashtag.

For simplicity, however, we will concern ourselves with just one criterion and filter tweets only according to the user who created them. The class is presented in Listing 3–5.

Listing 3–5. *The* TweetFilter *Class*

```
package app.models;

import com.apress.framework.objecttypes.Model;

public class TweetFilter implements Model
{
    protected TweetFilter () { }

    public TweetFilter(String userID) { ... }

    public String getUserID() { ... }
}
```

As you play with the application yourself, feel free to add more filter criteria.

Defining the Timeline Entity

The Timeline entity is a great example of how properly representing something can save time and stress and also provide great flexibility. Let's start the discussion by doing a quick recap of some of the principles behind Twitter.

Each new tweet that enters the system gets a unique ID, and all IDs are issued in chronological and alphabetical order. So, the newer the tweet, the higher its ID number is. Twitter also has two main ways of retrieving tweets: queries and timelines. Queries are very much like "give me the latest five tweets that contain the word 'JavaME,'" while timelines are a way of aggregating tweets. For example, your home timeline aggregates all the tweets from you and the people you follow, as well as some of the tweets that might be relevant to your interests.

Queries and timelines are generally accessed through different API calls, but we want to be able to unify them under a common API. As such, we will merge Twitter's queries and timelines together into our own timeline concept that works equally well for both sources, as presented here.

We will consider our timeline to be a series of chronologically ordered tweets, each tweet corresponding to the timeline's specified TweetFilter. A timeline is very similar to the integer number axis: it has a "zero-moment" tweet, from which you can go backward in time to older tweets (the equivalent of negative numbers) or forward in time to newer tweets (positive numbers). The zero-moment tweet can be considered to be the latest tweet at the moment the timeline is initialized.

To move along the timeline, you have two "cursors," one for each direction: forward and back. Each cursor moves only in its specified direction. So the "go back" cursor can move only back in time, while the "go forward" cursor can move only forward in time. Furthermore, each cursor can move only one tweet at a time. This means that in order to reach either end of the timeline, you must pass through all the tweets in that specific direction and that, regardless of how big the timeline is, you must keep track of at most two tweets at any given time—one for each cursor.

Since we want our timeline concept to cover multiple data sources, we will use the Java interface Timeline to represent it, as shown in Listing 3–6. Each corresponding data source will then be responsible for implementing this interface.

Listing 3–6. *The* Timeline *Interface*

```
package app.models;

import com.apress.framework.objecttypes.Model;

public interface Timeline extends Model
{
    public Tweet goForward();

    public Tweet goBack();
}
```

The conventions for the Timeline interface are described in the next paragraph.

The first calls to goForward() or goBack() after initialization return the zero-moment tweet, or null if no tweets match the specified filter at that time. The goBack() method will return null when it is no longer possible to go back because the oldest tweet of the timeline has been reached. The goForward() method may return null if there are no newer tweets available.

A quick side note: this is simplicity at its finest. Using just two simple methods, you can navigate in real time not only all the tweets currently in Twitter's system, but also future ones—and do so with minimal memory requirements. Furthermore, you can adapt this concept to suit pretty much every kind of continuous data source you can think of, from stock market data (which is real-time but also has a history) to search engine trends.

The timeline metaphor is also a great example of how abstract concepts in themselves can provide a lot of functionality. If you think about it, our timeline combines easy and flexible navigation with powerful data source abstraction—even though it's nothing more than an idea. It's always worth it to spend a little time and see if you can find such ideas that work well with your Java ME application's needs.

Choosing Intelligent Representations for Your Data

Most developers tend to minimize the importance of modeling their data. They typically equate this process to writing classes or interfaces with one method or field for every attribute or action of the real-life entity they are trying to model. This is fast and intuitive, and it works, but it also means that you inadvertently make your life harder in the long run, while preventing your application from reaching its full potential.

The root cause for this is the widespread notion (among developers) that data is "dumb" while code is "smart." Far from it: properly modeled data structures are oftentimes smarter than the equivalent code. I would like to take a few paragraphs to illustrate this fact by using a data structure we're all familiar with: the linked list.

Let's suppose we need a linked list that allows us quick access to both its first and last elements. There are two common ways of achieving this.

The first is to keep track of a reference to the first element of the list, for getFirst(). When getLast() is called, the code goes through all the elements in the list until the last one is reached. This is obviously slow, but it has the advantage of using only one pointer.

The second way is to have two references, one for the first element and one for the last. This is faster than the previous method, but it has the disadvantage of having to keep track of two references instead of one.

However, there is a third and smarter way of achieving our goal: we will model our list as being a circular one, by linking the last element to the first.

This small change makes a world of difference. For starters, we now have to keep track of only one reference, to the last element in the list. getLast() will return said reference, while getFirst() will simply return getLast().next(). The concept is illustrated in Figure 3–1.

Because we have only one reference to manage, the code complexity and resource consumption are as low as in the first approach. And since going from the last element to the first is virtually cost-free, the execution speed of the code is as fast as for the second approach. Furthermore, to the outside world, our circular list behaves the same way as a regular linked list.

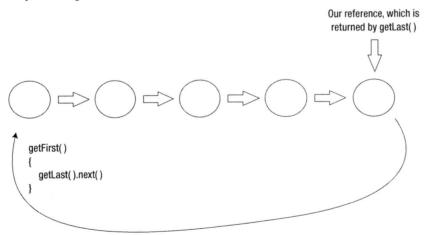

Figure 3–1. *The circular list*

By being smart about the way we defined our data and choosing a proper model, we get all the advantages of the first two methods and none of their disadvantages.

This kind of optimization can be done frequently in more complex real-life scenarios, too, though usually to a lesser extent. This means that it is often possible to make your application faster, leaner, and more flexible simply by choosing the right representation for your data and entities.

I hope this example has convinced you that modeling data and entities, and working with the resulting models, is a much more delicate and important subject than it appears at first glance. Keep this in mind and don't rush over this important step when writing your applications. This advice is especially important in the world of Java ME, where the performance and resource hit caused by the improper representation of data can be quite significant.

Summary

We have defined the global data types and entities for our project. In the process, we have also examined how to model data for Java ME applications and how choosing the right model for your data can bring significant improvements to an application.

In the next chapter, we will implement our first module for the Twitter client, the networking module, and we will also take a closer look at Java ME networking.

## Chapter 4

The Networking Module

Every client application needs a module to allow it to communicate with its associated server or servers. Our Twitter client is no different. In this chapter, we will implement our networking module, which will allow us to access Twitter's services. In the process, we will also examine some interesting aspects related to Java ME networking.

Because writing a networking module from scratch would be too time-consuming and complicated, we will instead use an already existing third-party library to handle the low-level communication with the Twitter servers. We will thus build our module around it, relying on the library to do the dirty work while exposing only high-level functionality to the rest of the application.

Setting Up and Configuring the Library

The third-party library we will use is called Twitter API ME, available from www.twapime.com. It is a cross-platform library, which at the time of this writing supports Java ME, J2SE, and Android. The source code is available under the GPL license, while the binaries can be used under LGPL. In our application, we will use the library in source-code form.

The latest version available at the time of this writing is 1.4, and this is what we will be using in this chapter. If you like, feel free to use a newer version of the library if one is available.

The first thing we need to do is download Twitter API ME. To do this, go to http://kenai.com/projects/twitterapime/downloads/directory/1.4 and download the Java ME version of the library, twitter_api_me-1.4-javame.zip.

We are mainly interested in two directories from the archive: /src and /lib . Copy the contents of /src to your project's source folder and the contents of /lib to your project's library folder.

Next, configure your IDE and environment to make sure that both the kxml and xauth-encoders libraries from the /lib folder are included in the build process (Twitter API ME depends on them, just like we depend on it) and that the Twitter API ME source code will be compiled along with your application's source code. Following that, remove the `impl.android` package and all its sub-packages to make sure the project will build without errors.

With this, the library setup is completed. However, we still need to make sure Twitter allows us access to its services. Assuming you don't have a Twitter account, create one now. Next, go to `http://dev.twitter.com/apps` and register a new Twitter application to your account. After you have registered your application, go to its details page. You will find a lot of information there that we will use in the next steps, such as the API key, your consumer key and secret, and your single-access token and token secret.

It is now time to request xAuth access. To do this, follow the instructions found at `http://dev.twitter.com/pages/xauth`. They basically ask you to send an e-mail to `api@twitter.com` with your application's description, reasons for which your application needs xAuth access, your application's consumer key, and its ID (if available). Your request will be judged, and you will usually receive a response within 24–48 hours.

> **NOTE:** At the time of this writing, xAuth is available only on a per-request basis, and not everyone will qualify for it. This might change with time, however, and xAuth might become available to everyone by default, so check for this before writing to Twitter and requesting xAuth access for your application.

In the meantime, you can use your single-access tokens to authenticate yourself. You can also use your tokens if Twitter denies your request for xAuth access for some reason. However, this means you will be able to use only your own Twitter account. Signing in as another user will not be possible. For us this will not be a problem: since we are only doing a learning project, being able to use just one user account is not a very big inconvenience.

Once you know your single-access token and secret, as well as your consumer key and secret, it's time for a quick smoke test. For this, you will need to run the MIDlet shown in Listing 4–1.

Listing 4–1. *The Smoke-Test MIDlet*

```
package test;

import com.twitterapime.rest.Credential;
import com.twitterapime.rest.UserAccountManager;
...

public class TestMidlet extends MIDlet
{
    public void startApp()
    {
        try
        {
            Token token = new Token("access_token", "access_token_secret");
            Credential c = new ("your_user_name", "consumer_key", "consumer_secret",
            token);
```

```
          UserAccountManager m = UserAccountManager.getInstance(c);
          if (m.verifyCredential())
          {
              System.out.println("Auth OK");
          }
          else
          {
              System.out.println("Auth failed");
          }
      }
      catch (Exception ex)
      {
          ex.printStackTrace();
      }
  }

  public void pauseApp() {
  }

  public void destroyApp(boolean unconditional) {
  }
}
```

The smoke-test MIDlet checks if token-based authentication works properly. To check if xAuth authentication is working for you, simply replace the lines in bold from Listing 4–1 with the following line:

```
Credential c = new Credential("user_name", "password", "consumer_key",
"consumer_secret");
```

The username and password in the foregoing example can be the username and password for any valid Twitter account.

While running either one of the two smoke-test MIDlets, you may encounter the following error, or an error similar to it:

```
javax.microedition.pki.CertificateException: Certificate was issued by an unrecognized
entity
```

This happens because the SSL certificate Twitter is using is not recognized by some older versions of the WTK emulator. Running the MIDlet on an actual device should work just fine if the device in question is reasonably recent (less than 4–5 years old) and made by a reputable company. In other words, the code will work fine on the vast majority of devices out there. However, our target device is the WTK emulator, so we will have to fix this. We can either install the missing certificate manually, which is fairly complicated, or configure Twitter API ME to use HTTP instead of HTTPS. We will choose the latter solution.

Using HTTP instead of HTTPS for authentication is extremely simple if you have access to the library's source code. All you have to do is open `UserAccountManager.java` and change the OAuth URL from `https://api.twitter.com/oauth/access_token` to `http://api.twitter.com/oauth/access_token`.

TIP: Before we proceed, I would like to share with you two important pieces of advice related to writing a networking module. While not groundbreaking, they have saved me quite a few times and they do tend to make your life easier (they have certainly made mine easier).

Working with High-Level Objects

There are many ways of writing and defining a networking module. For example, some people prefer to have the networking module be a simple conduit for data, feeding raw bytes to the rest of the application for decoding. Others prefer to have the networking module work with structured data, such as vectors and hashtables, instead of raw bytes. Others still use non-native formats such as XML and JSON, encoded in String objects.

All of these approaches, and others like them, have one big downside: they require some kind of serialization/deserialization to be done outside of the networking module. This effectively means that the networking module "bleeds through" to other modules.

There is never a good reason for this. No model, controller, or any other class outside the networking module should have methods like createFromHashtable(), createFromRawBytes(), or anything even remotely similar. The only acceptable exception to this rule is the persistence module—we will discuss why in the next chapter.

As such, a properly written networking module always consumes high-level objects and always provides high-level objects, typically models. Converting these objects to and from bytes or XML or whatever is strictly the internal job of the networking module—the rest of the application doesn't care how this happens.

Using Your Own Data Types

Most third-party libraries, Twitter API ME included, already have objects and classes that map crucial entities and data types related to their scope. For example, in the case of the Twitter API ME client library, a Tweet data type is already defined by the library. The question is, do you use these already defined data types in your application or do you implement your own?

Speaking from experience, it is always a good idea to implement and use your own data types. You should use the library-defined data types only as a buffer between the raw bytes the server sends and the data type you use in your application, which is easy to do as usually the library data types and your data types are very similar.

Doing so might involve a little more work at first, as you have to "move" the information from the library data types to your data types, but it gives you the extremely important advantage of being library-independent; this allows you to easily port your application to other platforms or to other libraries. It also allows you to model your data types and entities the way you want to use them, instead of being stuck with the library-provided representation—this alone has saved me from countless headaches.

Writing Our TwitterServer Implementation

If you remember from our previous chapter, we decided to define the Twitter server as a Java interface. It's now time to turn that interface into something concrete by building a TwitterServer implementation that is able to log in, read tweets, and post new tweets. We will also look at some useful techniques, such as using the generic timeline concept to browse data on the server (in our case, tweets) in real time and with minimal overhead, converting asynchronous requests to synchronous ones and using buffering to minimize perceived network latency and performance.

Defining the General Structure

We will start by writing a barebones version of the ServerImplementation class, shown in Listing 4–2.

Listing 4–2. *The Barebones* ServerImplementation *Class*

```
package app.module.network.models;

import app.models.Timeline;
import app.models.Tweet;
...


public class ServerImplementation implements TwitterServer {

    public boolean login(UserCredentials credentials)
    {
        throw new UnsupportedOperationException("Not supported yet.");
    }

    public TwitterUser getMyProfile()
    {
        throw new UnsupportedOperationException("Not supported yet.");
    }

    ...

}
```

As you can see, the class goes into the app.module.network package, under the models sub-package.

An interesting point: As there is no real-life code difference between a controller and regular class or a model in our framework, the distinction between them is mostly a conceptual one with the purpose of clearing things up. For example, if a new developer joins the project and sees that the networking module has no controllers, he can easily infer that the networking module is doing its job quietly and behind the scenes, merely feeding data and events to other modules. However, if he sees at least one controller in the networking module, he then knows that said module is critical and can alter the program's flow.

In our particular case, due to the nature of Twitter, our application's networking module will have no controllers at all, because nothing Twitter-related is so urgent as to require the networking module itself to alter the program's flow or interfere with it in any way.

This situation is quite different from the one found in other types of applications—for example, stock monitoring applications. In those cases, the networking module can and does control the program flow: if the client receives a STOCK_HIT_ROCK_BOTTOM message, you can be sure that the user will want to be informed of this ASAP by being taken to a dedicated screen, regardless of what the rest of the application is doing at that time. As such, it makes sense to put the logic that does this inside a controller class.

Initializing a ServerImplementation Instance

In order for the ServerImplementation class to do anything useful, we must first provide the means for it to be properly initialized.

We need three pieces of information in order to initialize a ServerImplementation instance: the consumer key, the consumer secret, and a reference to an event controller. The reason for the first two should be obvious: the consumer key and secret are what identify our application to Twitter. The event controller is needed in order to allow the instance to send notifications about important events to other parts of the application, and to be able to receive notifications from other parts of the application.

Furthermore, we should strive to make ServerImplementation as immutable as possible. Our class thus becomes the one in Listing 4–3.

Listing 4–3. *The* ServerImplementation *Class with Initialization Support*

```
public class ServerImplementation implements TwitterServer, EventListener {

    protected String consumerKey, consumerSecret;
    protected EventController eventController;

    protected ServerImplementation() { } ;

    public ServerImplementation(String consumerKey, String consumerSecret,
    EventController controller)
    {
        this.consumerKey = consumerKey;
        this.consumerSecret = consumerSecret;
        this.eventController = controller;
        controller.registerListener(this);
    }

    public boolean handleEvent(Event event)
    {
        // Empty for now
        return false;
    }

    public EventController getEventController()
    {
        return eventController;
```

```
    }

  ...
}
```

Now if, for example, we want to initialize the server implementation and attach it to the application's main event controller, all we have to do is the following:

```
ServerImplementation impl = new ServerImplementation("conKey", "conSecret",
Application.getMainEventController() );
```

Providing Login Support

After a `ServerImplementation` instance has been initialized, the most basic operation it can perform is to log in a user.

Given the fact that we have to support both username-and-password authentication and single-access tokens in a congruent manner, our login requirements are as follows: first, the application should try to log in by using a username and password combination. If this combination cannot be provided or is not valid, the application should use single-access tokens instead. If the tokens aren't provided or are invalid, the application will consider that the authentication process has failed.

If you recall from the previous chapter, we will use the `UserCredentials` data type for providing authentication information. `UserCredentials` has support for both username-and-password authentication and single-access token authentication in the same data structure. This somewhat goes against the intuitive approach of using separate data types for each means of authentication—for example, `UsernamePasswordCredentials` and `TokenCredentials`.

The reason the two are merged in a single data type is a simple one: by doing so, we can let the specialized `ServerImplementation` decide on its own which login method is best suited for any particular situation.

The importance of this is best exemplified by the following scenario (adapted from a real-life project): application X is required to authenticate the user by using his or her username and password if the connection to the server is made via HTTPS over the cellular network, or by using tokens or other encrypted credentials if the connection is made via WiFi and/or HTTP.

In this example, consider what happens if we do not provide all available credentials to the networking module in one data structure: it becomes the responsibility of other parts of the application to decide which specific credentials to provide. As per the requirements, this involves checking what types of connections are available, whether they are secure, etc. Since all of these tasks are logically part of the networking module but we do them somewhere else, we basically create "bleeding" from the networking module to other modules of the application—something we really want to avoid.

However, if we provide all available credentials in one go and say, "Take your pick," then the networking module can decide on its own which credentials to use, doing all the necessary checks internally—and in a more or less centralized fashion. This not only removes any potential "bleeding," but also helps preserve the code's structure and readability, the application's logic, and the developer's sanity (it is very frustrating and time-consuming to go hunting throughout the entire application for "that one line that does that one check").

This advice applies not only to the networking module—it is general advice. Especially with high-level operations, it is a good idea to provide all the information you have and let the specialized modules of the application decide internally what information to use and what information to discard.

We now go back to our Twitter client. Apart from the actual authentication code, there is one more thing that is needed for the login process to be properly implemented: events.

For one thing, we want to be able to trigger a login by using events. For this, we will implement support for a BEGIN_LOGIN event. We also need to generate events for when the login fails or succeeds, which is what LOGIN_FAILED and LOGIN_SUCCEEDED will do. In order to implement these events, we must first define them. Make sure that your EVT looks something like the one in Listing 4–4.

Listing 4–4. *Login Events Defined*

```
public class EVT
{
    public class CONTEXT
    {
...
        public static final int NETWORKING_MODULE = 4;
    }

    ...

    public class NETWORK
    {
        public static final int BEGIN_LOGIN=30001;
        public static final int LOGIN_FAILED=30002;
        public static final int LOGIN_SUCCEEDED=30003;
    }

}
```

It's now time for the actual implementation. First, the main login() method of ServerImplementation is shown in Listing 4–5.

Listing 4–5. *The login() Method*

```
public boolean login(UserCredentials credentials)
{
        boolean success = false ;

        // First, try to log in using username and password
        if ( credentials.getUsername()!= null && credentials.getPassword()!= null )
        {
                success = loginUsingUnPw(credentials.getUsername(),
                credentials.getPassword() );
        }
```

```
        // If that fails, try using tokens
        if ( success == false )
        {

                if ( credentials.getAccessToken() != null &&
                credentials.getAccessTokenSecret() != null )
                {
                        success = loginUsingTokens(credentials.getAccessToken(),
                        credentials.getAccessTokenSecret() );
                }
        }

        // Generate the appropriate event
        if ( success )
        {
                Event evt = new Event ( EVT.CONTEXT.NETWORKING_MODULE,
                EVT.NETWORK.LOGIN_SUCCEEDED, credentials);
                eventController.queueEvent(evt);
        }
        else
        {
                Event evt = new Event ( EVT.CONTEXT.NETWORKING_MODULE,
                EVT.NETWORK.LOGIN_FAILED, credentials);
                eventController.queueEvent(evt);
        }

        return success;
}
```

Next it is time to implement the actual login methods, loginUsingUnPw() and loginUsingTokens(). Both methods are presented in Listing 4–6. These are separated from the main login() method not only because this improves readability but also because, in the event of switching libraries, you can leave the main login logic untouched and just change the actual implementations.

Listing 4–6. *Methods loginUsingUnPw() and loginUsingTokens()*

```
protected UserAccountManager accountManager = null ;

protected boolean loginUsingUnPw(String username, String password)
{
Credential c = new Credential(username, password, this.consumerKey,
this.consumerSecret);
        UserAccountManager m = UserAccountManager.getInstance(c);
        try
        {
                if ( m.verifyCredential() )
                {
                        accountManager = m;
                        return true;
                }
                else
                {
                        return false;
                }
        }
        catch (Exception ex)
```

```
                {
                        // Error handling goes here
                        return false;
                }
        }

protected boolean loginUsingTokens(String token, String tokenSecret)
{
        Token authToken = new Token(token,tokenSecret);
        Credential c = new Credential("ignored", this.consumerKey,
        this.consumerSecret,authToken);
        UserAccountManager m = UserAccountManager.getInstance(c);
        try
        {
                if ( m.verifyCredential() )
                {
                        accountManager = m;
                        return true;
                }
                else
                {
                        return false;
                }
        }
        catch (Exception ex)
        {
                // Error handling goes here
                return false;
        }
}
```

> **NOTE:** Token-based authentication assumes that the tokens you provide are valid and *does not* actually verify them (i.e., verifyCredential() always returns true). If the tokens are in fact invalid, all calls made to the server will fail even though verifyCredential() has returned true on them. This is a library issue that will most likely be fixed in later versions.

Finally, we need to add support for the BEGIN_LOGIN event. To do this, add the code in Listing 4–7 to the handleEvent() method of ServerImplementation. The convention is that the payload for a BEGIN_LOGIN event is an object of type UserCredentials, which will be used for the actual login.

Listing 4–7. *Adding Support for the BEGIN_LOGIN Event*

```
public boolean handleEvent(Event event)
{
        ...
        if ( event.getType() == EVT.NETWORK.BEGIN_LOGIN )
        {
                login ( (UserCredentials) event.getPayload());
                return true;
        }
        ...
}
```

Now that the code's written, let's put it to the test. Listing 4–8 shows a number of possible login scenarios.

Listing 4–8. *Possible Login Scenarios*

```
// Create the ServerImplementation instance
ServerImplementation impl = new ServerImplementation("conKey", "conSecret",
Application.getMainEventController() );

// Credentials with only username and password
UserCredentials credentials1 = new UserCredentials("johndoe","123password",null,null);

// Credentials with only tokens
UserCredentials credentials2 = new UserCredentials(null,null,"token123",
"tokensecret123");

// Credentials with both username/password and tokens
UserCredentials credentials3 = new UserCredentials("johndoe","123password","token123",
"tokensecret123");

// Login by providing both username/password and tokens
impl.login(credentials3);

// Login by providing just the tokens
impl.login(credentials2);

// Log in by using events and providing just the username and password
Event event = new Event(EVT.CONTEXT.LOCAL, EVT.NETWORK.BEGIN_LOGIN, credentials1);
Application.getMainEventController().queueEvent(event);
```

As you can see, the login mechanism we have implemented is both simple to use and very flexible.

Posting Tweets

Next to logging in, the second thing users would probably like to do is post tweets of their own. With Twitter API ME, this is very easy to do. The code for the postTweet() method of our ServerImplementation is presented in Listing 4–9.

Listing 4–9. *Posting Tweets*

```
import app.models.Tweet;
...

public boolean postTweet(Tweet tweet)
    {
        com.twitterapime.search.Tweet libTweet = new com.twitterapime.search.Tweet
            (tweet.getBody());

        if ( accountManager != null )
        {
            TweetER tweeter = TweetER.getInstance(accountManager);
            try
            {
                tweeter.post(libTweet);
            }
```

```
            catch (Exception ex)
            {
                return false;
            }
            return true;
        }
        return false;
    }
```

Besides posting tweets, the foregoing code snippet serves a secondary purpose: it demonstrates one of the more annoying aspects of using third-party libraries: naming conflicts. To avoid confusion between our Tweet data type and the library's Tweet data type, we have to use the full name for the library's Tweet class, which is com.twitterapime.search.Tweet. Clashing class names are little more than a minor annoyance, but their big brothers, access modifier conflicts, can be a real pain. Access modifier conflicts happen when, for example, you want or need to override a method that is final, or you want to make public a method that is marked as private or protected. We will talk more about these issues in Chapter 11.

Retrieving Tweets

This is probably the most interesting aspect of the networking module, and the one we will spent the most time examining.

As mentioned previously, there are two major ways to retrieve tweets: tweet timelines and queries. Tweet timelines aggregate tweets from various sources (for example, tweets from all the people in your "following" list), while queries allow you to refine the tweets you receive by specifying various parameters such as tweet content, author, time, location, and more.

In our application, we want to handle both queries and tweet timelines in a unified fashion. For this we will use the timeline concept we defined in the previous chapter (which is a different concept than Twitter's timelines—please do not confuse them).

Specifically, we will implement two types of timelines (our timelines, not Twitter's), one for each source.

We will then choose the proper one based on the filter specified when calling getTimelineForFilter(). If no filter is specified, or if the filter contains a null username, then we will use the timeline corresponding to Twitter's home timeline, which is the list of tweets you see when logging into Twitter on the Web.

If a username is specified in the filter, then we will use a query to retrieve all the available tweets corresponding to the specified user. Please note that Twitter's API history is limited to a couple of days, so tweets older than that will not be available.

Listing 4–10 shows the code for ServerImplementation's getTimelineForFilter() method, which implements the selection logic already described.

Listing 4–10. *The* `getTimelineForFilter()` *Method*

```
public Timeline getTimelineForFilter(TweetFilter filter)
{
        if ( filter == null || filter.getUserID() == null )
        {
            return new TimelineHome (accountManager);
        }
        else
        {
            return new TimelineUserTweets (accountManager, filter);
        }
}
```

As we will see, each of the two timeline types referenced in the foregoing example has specific particularities when it comes to its implementation, and each will teach us important lessons. Let's start with the home timeline implementation.

TimelineHome

We will retrieve tweets from Twitter's home timeline via the `TimelineHome` class, which is based on Twitter API ME's timeline functionality.

Twitter API ME's timeline functionality is asynchronous. Each request to retrieve tweets from a timeline runs in a separate thread and has a listener attached to it, which is notified asynchronously when new tweets corresponding to the timeline are received, when the search is completed, or when it fails for some reason.

For simplicity, in our case, `TimelineHome` will be both the request issuer and the request listener, so we can handle incoming tweets in the same class instance. Thus, the declaration for `TimelineHome` is presented in Listing 4–11.

Listing 4–11. *The* `TimelineHome` *Declaration*

```
public class TimelineHome implements Timeline, SearchDeviceListener
{
...
}
```

Asynchronous retrieval is usually a great thing to have; however, in our specifications for the `Timeline` interface, retrieving tweets is a synchronous operation: `goForward()` and `goBack()` must return either the next corresponding tweet or `null` whenever they are called.

Adapting asynchronous operations to work synchronously is a pretty common task for Java ME applications that use external services since some services are, by design, at least partially asynchronous. The simplest solution, which is often also the most effective one, relies on buffers and Java's `wait()` and `notify()` methods. It works as follows.

First, in the method or class you want to work synchronously, create an object to act as a monitor—let's call this object `lock`. Then, after you issue the asynchronous request, immediately call `lock.wait()` to halt the thread.

Next, when the other thread (the one in which the request is running) or the registered listener receives a response, store the response in a buffer and call `lock.notify()`. This resumes the initial thread, which is then free to process the result now found in the buffer.

A pseudo-code version of this is presented in Listing 4–12. Please note that there are many variations possible on this idea—for example, the buffer can be passed along as a parameter, the lock can be replaced by a semaphore, etc.

Listing 4–12. *Converting Asynchronous Requests to Synchronous Ones*

```
lock = new Object();
buffer = new Buffer();

// In the issuer thread, which is synchronous
public Object getNext()
{
    issueAsyncRequest();
    lock.wait();
    result = processBuffer (buffer);
    return result;
}

// In the request thread or in the event listener
void dataReceived(data)
{
  buffer = processData(data);
  lock.notify();
}
```

Looking at the foregoing pseudo-code, you are tempted to consider the idea as being pretty easy to implement, but in practice things are rarely as simple. The following is a list of common problems you might face in real life while implementing this concept— look for them when writing your code.

First of all, you have to ensure that the buffer object is properly handled and that it cannot be overridden by other requests or method calls until it is processed or explicitly discarded. This can sometimes be very difficult, depending on the architecture used and the application's requirements. Second, you have to ensure the entire affair is thread-safe, so calling getNext() from multiple threads works as expected. Third, multiple buffer objects may be involved in some cases—be careful not to use the wrong one by mistake. Fourth, you must ensure that you do not end up deadlocking the entire application or an important thread.

Now that we know what to look out for, we can turn our attention to the TimelineHome class. Before we begin presenting the code, let's discuss in brief how it will work.

When the class is initialized, the latest tweet will be retrieved from the timeline. This will be the "origin" tweet, the reference for the entire timeline. From it, you can go either forward or back on the timeline.

To do this, we will keep track of two IDs: the ID of the oldest tweet retrieved and the ID of the newest tweet retrieved. In the beginning, both IDs are equal to the ID of the origin tweet. Then, when you call goBack() or goForward(), the appropriate next tweet for each case is retrieved from the timeline. Its ID becomes the new ID for the oldest or newest tweet, respectively.

The first calls to goBack() and goForward() will each return the origin tweet. If at any point there are no older or newer tweets available (depending on the call), the calls will return null. The origin tweet can also be null if the user has no tweets at all in the home timeline.

Now let's look at the actual code, starting with the constructor and field declarations seen in Listing 4–13.

Listing 4–13. *The Constructor and Fields for* TimelineHome

```
protected String latestID, oldestID;
protected com.twitterapime.rest.Timeline timeline;
protected Tweet resultBuffer;

protected Object lock;

protected TimelineHome() { } ;

public TimelineHome(UserAccountManager manager)
{
        lock = new Object();

        synchronized (lock)
        {
                // Create a query to get the latest tweet ID
                timeline = com.twitterapime.rest.Timeline.getInstance(manager);
                Query q = QueryComposer.count(1);
                timeline.startGetHomeTweets(q, this);

                // Wait until the request completes
                try
                {
                        lock.wait();
                }
                catch (Exception ex)
                {
                        ex.printStackTrace();
                }

                if ( resultBuffer == null )
                {
                        return;
                }

                // Retrieve the required information from the result
                // and set appropriate latest and oldest tweet IDs
                // so that the first call to goBack() and goForward()
                // return the initial tweet.
                String initialTweetID = resultBuffer.getID() ;
                latestID = String.valueOf(Long.parseLong(initialTweetID)-1);
                oldestID = String.valueOf(Long.parseLong(initialTweetID));
        }
}
```

The highlighted code does the interesting work: it sets the instance itself as the listener for startGetHomeTweets() and waits on the lock object to be notified that a response has been received and placed inside the buffer. After the lock is notified, execution of the constructor resumes and the result inside the buffer, if any, is processed.

The actual notification is done inside the tweetFound(), searchCompleted(), and searchFailed() methods, which are defined by the SearchDeviceListener interface. These methods are presented in Listing 4–14.

Listing 4–14. *TimelineHome Implementing the SearchDeviceListener Interface*

```
public void tweetFound(com.twitterapime.search.Tweet tweet)
{
        // A tweet matching the request parameters has been received. Process the tweet,
        // place it in the buffer.
        synchronized(lock)
        {
                resultBuffer = new Tweet(tweet.getString
                ( MetadataSet.TWEET_AUTHOR_USERNAME),
                tweet.getString(MetadataSet.TWEET_CONTENT),
                tweet.getString(MetadataSet.TWEET_ID));
        }
}

public void searchCompleted()
{
        // The tweet search has been completed. Notify the lock object.
        synchronized(lock)
        {
           lock.notifyAll();
        }
}

public void searchFailed(Throwable cause)
{
        // The search has failed. Set the buffer to null and print the error
        synchronized(lock)
        {
           System.out.println(cause.getMessage());
           resultBuffer = null;
           lock.notifyAll();
        }
}
```

Note that, to ensure complete thread safety, these methods should not be accessible from the outside world—that is, they should not be public. This is not hard to achieve (you could use private inner classes, for example), but it does complicate the code a bit, so for simplicity reasons we will leave the implementation as is, with these methods public.

Up next are the goForward() and goBack() methods. They are quite similar to one another and to the constructor. For this reason, we will include only the code to the goForward() method in the book (see Listing 4–15)—you can find the code for goBack() in the complete source code available from the Apress web site.

Listing 4–15. *The* `goForward()` *Method*

```
public synchronized Tweet goForward()
{
        synchronized (lock)
        {
                // Issue the query to get the next tweet
                Query q = QueryComposer.count(1);
                String currentMaxID = String.valueOf(Long.parseLong(latestID));
                q = QueryComposer.append(q, QueryComposer.sinceID(currentMaxID));
                timeline.startGetHomeTweets(q, this);

                // Wait for the result
                try
                {
                        lock.wait();
                }
                catch (Exception ex)
                {
                        ex.printStackTrace();
                }

                // Process the result, if any
                if ( resultBuffer == null )
                {
                        return null;
                }
                latestID = resultBuffer.getID() ;
                return resultBuffer;
        }
}

public synchronized Tweet goBack()
{
...
}
```

The highlighted portion of the code is extremely important: it ensures that multiple calls to goForward() or goBack() coming from different threads are executed in sequence. This means that the contents of the buffer are synchronized with the current request and thus that the implementation is thread-safe. Without the synchronized keyword, multiple calls coming from different threads would be executed in parallel and that would break the "lock and buffer" mechanism—for example, the result for a goForward() call might get processed by a goBack() call by mistake.

Now that the code is all there, let's put it to the test. The snippet in Listing 4–16 retrieves 20 tweets from the user's home timeline.

Listing 4–16. *Testing the* `TimelineHome`

```
ServerImplementation impl = new ServerImplementation("<consumerKey>",
"<consumerSecret>", Application.getMainEventController() );
UserCredentials credentials = new UserCredentials("<username>", "<password>",
"<token>", "<tokenSecret>");

if ( impl.login(credentials) )
{
```

```
Timeline t = impl.getTimelineForFilter(null);

for (int i=0;i<20;i++)
{
        Tweet twt = t.goBack() ;
        if ( twt != null )
        {
                System.out.println(">> " + twt.getID() + " : " +
                twt.getBody() );
        }
        else
        {
                System.out.println("No tweet available");
        }
}

System.out.println("Done!");
}
```

> **CAUTION:** If you are authenticating yourself directly with tokens instead of using xAuth, make sure the username and password parameters from the foregoing snippet are `null` and that the token, token secret, consumer key, and consumer secret parameters are set correctly. For xAuth, make sure that the consumer key, consumer secret, username, and password parameters are correct.

If you run the foregoing snippet and you have more than 10–15 tweets in your home timeline, you will discover that … the code doesn't work! After 10 or so tweets are retrieved, the search will fail with an error saying that the maximum socket limit has been reached.

The problem is not in our code, it's in Twitter API ME, at least in the version I'm working with, which is 1.4. The library's `com.twitterapime.rest.Timeline` class closes the active connection when no more results are available for the current search, but it doesn't close the corresponding InputStream—so basically the connection is still in use. Because of this, after a few calls to goBack() or goForward(), you'll run out of available connections.

Fear not—the problem is easily fixed if you have access to the library's source code: in the startGet() method of the recently mentioned class, just add a call to resp.getStream().close() before l.searchCompleted(). The code from Listing 4–16 should work fine after this simple modification is made.

This slight bump in the road demonstrates two very important aspects of Java ME software development. The first one is obvious: no software is perfect. While this is a general problem, Java ME suffers more from it than other platforms because its tolerance for mistakes is very low. For example, the foregoing failure would have most likely gone unnoticed were the code running on J2SE, because J2SE supports a considerably larger number of simultaneous connections.

The second aspect comes as a consequence of the first: because failure is more frequent on Java ME than on other platforms, you should *always* try to work with the source code version of the tools and libraries you want to use. This way you'll be able to easily debug and adapt them to suit your needs instead of desperately searching for workarounds and inelegant hacks. For example, I tend to ignore binary builds completely unless they're the only available option.

After getting past this small snag, our `TimelineHome` is complete and functional. It is time to move on to `TimelineUserTweets`.

TimelineUserTweets

This class is used to retrieve tweets from a specific user's history. To begin discussing it, we must first take a closer look at the implementation for `TimelineUserTweets`, specifically, at the fact that a new request is made for every call to `goForward()` or `goBack()`—so 30 calls mean 30 requests have to be made.

This is not only inefficient, it is also unfeasible in the long run: Twitter has a limit on the total number of requests any given application can make per hour, so if you `goBack()` too much and too fast, it is possible that you will run out of requests.

A very good solution to this problem, which we will implement for `TimelineUserTweets`, is buffering. It works like this: when `goBack()` is first called, we will request a batch of tweets instead of a single one, place the batch in a buffer, and return the first tweet. When the method is called the next time, the second tweet in the buffer will be returned, and so forth, until the buffer is empty, at which point a new batch will be requested. This goes on until we get an empty batch from the server, at which point it is clear that there are no more tweets to be retrieved. The same strategy applies to `goForward()`.

Buffering brings with it a huge improvement in terms of network traffic, data costs, server load, and battery life. It is an important technique for Java ME applications that rely on networking.

Moreover, its benefits are not related strictly to client-server communication. Because data from the server is stored in a buffer as it is retrieved, it can be processed before it is actually needed. A clever application can thus process the data in the buffer when CPU usage is low and halt processing when CPU usage is high. This ensures a uniform distribution of CPU load throughout the application's runtime and a smoother overall user experience, since the application has to spend less time processing data on the fly.

Going back to our application, the constructor and fields of `TimelineUserTweets` are presented in Listing 4–17.

Listing 4–17. *TimelineUserTweets Constructor and Fields*

```
public class TimelineUserTweets implements Timeline{

UserAccountManager manager;
String username;
SearchDevice search;
```

```
Tweet [] forwardBuffer ;
int forwardIndex = 0;

Tweet [] backBuffer ;
int backIndex = 0;

public static final int BUFFER_SIZE = 10 ;

public TimelineUserTweets(UserAccountManager manager, TweetFilter filter)
{
        this.username = filter.getUserID();
        this.manager = manager ;
        this.search = SearchDevice.getInstance();

        forwardBuffer = new Tweet[1];
        backBuffer = new Tweet[1];

        // Get initial tweet, if any
        Query q = QueryComposer.resultCount(1);
        q = QueryComposer.from(username);
        com.twitterapime.search.Tweet[] result;
        try
        {
                result = search.searchTweets(q);
        }
        catch (Exception ex)
        {
                ex.printStackTrace();
                return ;
        }

        // Process initial tweet
        if (result != null && result.length > 0)
        {
                com.twitterapime.search.Tweet tweet = result[0];
                Tweet requestResult = new
                Tweet(tweet.getString(MetadataSet.TWEET_AUTHOR_USERNAME),
                tweet.getString(MetadataSet.TWEET_CONTENT),
                tweet.getString(MetadataSet.TWEET_ID));
                forwardBuffer[0] = backBuffer[0] = requestResult;
        }
}
```

The code related to buffering is highlighted. As you can see, during initialization both the back and forward buffers are initialized with a single tweet—the origin tweet. You can also see that the default buffer size is 10. Feel free to experiment and increase or decrease this value to get optimum results.

However, be very careful: over-buffering is just as bad as having no buffer at all. If you retrieve 100 pieces of data from the server but you need or use only a single one, then the remaining 99 pieces become overhead. To avoid this huge waste of resources, most real-life applications use dynamic buffers, changing their size based on available resources and the task at hand.

A commonly used strategy to minimize this kind of overhead, and an effective one, is to use progressions when setting the buffer size. To exemplify this and one other point that we will discuss shortly, let's consider a new application that presents 100 messages to the user.

If the messages are sorted in the order of importance, then it is *likely* (note the emphasis) that the user will go through all of them in order, starting with the first because it is the most important. In this case, you can start with a large buffer (let's say big enough to store 30 messages) and, when that gets empty, change its size to something smaller (like 25) and so forth. The closer you get to the last piece, the higher the chance the user will stop reading messages (because they become less important), but at the same time your buffer gets smaller—so you minimize overhead in the event that the user aborts the operation.

If the messages are trivial (for example, spam), then it is *likely* the user will go through only some of them, typically the first ones. In this case, start with a very small buffer (size 5) and increase its size (to 10, 15, 20, etc.) as it gets empty. Doing so makes sense because if the user has already gone through 15 trivial messages and hasn't quit, there's a good chance he'll want to go through the next 20 too—so it's a good idea to buffer the next 20 instead of only the next 5.

There is also a third scenario: the messages are totally random and the user might choose to read any of them at any given time. In this case, using progressions makes no sense. What makes sense is to keep a buffer of the last accessed 10 or 20 messages (perhaps more). If a new message is read, it is placed in the front of the buffer and the oldest accessed message is removed. If a message that is already in the buffer is requested, it gets retrieved from the buffer and no changes are made.

As you can see, in order to function optimally, all three scenarios depend greatly on the nature of the data and on how the application and the user will process said data. This brings us to the "other point" mentioned earlier: it is important to get some real-life information on usage patterns from as many users as possible before implementing a buffering scheme. If you can't get real-life information, try to calculate or deduce the average usage pattern. In both cases, be careful: using the wrong buffering scheme for a given scenario leads to considerably less than optimal results. When in doubt, use fixed-size buffers.

Going back to `TimelineUserTweets`, we now have to implement the `goForward()` and `goBack()` methods. Again, since they are similar, we will present only the code for `goBack()`. It can be seen in Listing 4–18.

Listing 4–18. *The* `goBack()` *Method of* `TimelineUserTweets`

```
public Tweet goBack()
{
        // Current backbuffer is empty, means no more older tweets
        // are available. No need to check for more, since "end of history"
        // has been reached. We can return null.
        if ( backBuffer.length == 0 || backBuffer[0] == null )
        {
                return null;
        }

        // Check if we must get the next batch of older tweets, if any
```

```
if ( backIndex >= backBuffer.length )
{
        // Get max ID to use
        String oldestID = backBuffer[backIndex-1].getID();
        String maxID = String.valueOf(Long.parseLong(oldestID) - 1);

        // Create the query
        Query q = QueryComposer.resultCount(BUFFER_SIZE);
        q = QueryComposer.append(q, QueryComposer.from(username));
        q = QueryComposer.append(q, QueryComposer.maxID(maxID));

        try
        {
                // Run the query
                com.twitterapime.search.Tweet[] results =
                search.searchTweets(q);

                // If we have no results, it means we have reached the end
                // so we must return null. We'll also set the buffer to
                // length zero, to signal "end of history".
                if ( results == null || results.length == 0)
                {
                        backBuffer = new Tweet[0];
                        return null;
                }

                // Otherwise, process the results
                int i;
                com.twitterapime.search.Tweet tweet;
                backBuffer = new Tweet[results.length];
                for (i=0;i<results.length;i++)
                {
                        tweet = results[i];
                        backBuffer[i] = new Tweet(tweet.getString
                        ( MetadataSet.TWEET_AUTHOR_USERNAME),
                        tweet.getString(MetadataSet.TWEET_CONTENT),
                        tweet.getString(MetadataSet.TWEET_ID));
                }

                // Reset the buffer index
                backIndex = 0;
        }
        catch (Exception ex)
        {
                return null;
        }
}

// Return the next tweet in the buffer and increase the buffer index
Tweet currentTweet = backBuffer[backIndex];
backIndex++;
return currentTweet;

}
```

For convenience, all the buffering-related parts of the code have again been highlighted. As you can see, buffering in its simplest form is fairly simple and straightforward to implement: there is no reason not to use it in your applications. As an exercise, I leave it to you, the reader, to convert the TimelineHome class to use buffering.

We are now almost done with writing our networking module. The only functionality left to implement is related to retrieving user profiles. After we have covered that in the next section, we will look at some general Java ME networking best practices and the scenarios in which to apply them.

The getMyProfile() and getProfileFor() Methods

The last two remaining methods of the ServerImplementation class are getMyProfile() and getProfileFor(). The getMyProfile() method retrieves the profile for the currently logged-in user, while getProfileFor() retrieves the profile of any user, based on his or her ID or username.

The two methods are very similar to each other, and neither is particularly spectacular, so we will present only the getProfileFor() method, shown in Listing 4–19.

Listing 4–19. *The getProfileFor() Method*

```
public TwitterUser getProfileFor(String userid)
{
        try
        {
            UserAccount account = accountManager.getUserAccount(new UserAccount(userid));
            if ( account == null )
            {
                    return null;
            }
            else
            {
                    return new TwitterUser
                    (account.getString(MetadataSet.USERACCOUNT_NAME),
                            account.getString(MetadataSet.USERACCOUNT_USER_NAME),
                            account.getString(MetadataSet.USERACCOUNT_DESCRIPTION),
                            account.getString(MetadataSet.USERACCOUNT_URL),
                            account.getString(MetadataSet.USERACCOUNT_LOCATION));
            }
        }
        catch (Exception ex)
        {
                ex.printStackTrace();
                return null;
        }
}
```

Twitter API ME does the bulk of the work here, with its UserAccount class effectively serving as an intermediate between the raw data received from the server and our TwitterUser class.

Best Practices for Java ME Networking

So far in the chapter, we have concentrated on implementing a networking module based on a third-party library, in order to make the process faster and easier to understand. However, in doing so, we have overlooked a lot of best practices relevant to Java ME networking. This section of the chapter aims to compensate for this, by providing general advice pertaining to Java ME networking, as well as examples on how, where, and why to apply this advice.

Do Not Reinvent the Wheel

There are plenty of communication protocols out there, and plenty of Java ME implementations for them. Regardless of whether you prefer XML or JSON or even binary protocols, or you want to connect to Twitter or Blogger or Facebook, your back is covered, and there's no need to reinvent the wheel and write your own custom implementation or custom communication protocol. As much as possible, leave the really low-level stuff to someone else and use a readily available implementation.

This is a bit counter-intuitive considering that the essence of Java ME development is "lean and mean." From this point of view, at first glance it would appear that rolling out your own implementation is better than using an existing one: you get more specialized functionality, a smaller code size, code that is optimized for the current application, etc. You can just write a custom XML parser for your application and implement just the XML features you need and optimize them thoroughly afterward. Right?

Wrong. Even if you do manage to get the parser to work, the truth is that you have just increased the development effort by a significant number of man-hours and you have also increased the potential for bugs and poor performance. And since you're probably the only one using your parser, the only bug reports and performance issues reports you'll get are the ones from your customers, complaining that your product doesn't work as expected. Add to this the fact that your parser isn't very feature-rich, and you'll quickly see why rolling your own implementation is a losing proposition.

By contrast, dedicated third-party implementations of standard protocols are safer, feature-rich, up to date, thoroughly tested, and available for use immediately. Many people are using them, so they get plenty of feedback in terms of bugs and performance. They have dedicated teams attending to them and are under constant improvement. Sure, they may not be as "lean and mean" as a well-written and thoroughly optimized custom implementation (though, as explained previously, it is questionable whether you'll be able to write such an implementation), but when you put everything in balance, there is no real reason not to use them, save for lack of hardware resources/support.

In fact, even our third-party Twitter library does this, relying on the KXML parser for all XML-related actions. And there are many prominent products and libraries out there that do the same. If it's good for them, it's probably good for you too.

Mobile Internet Is Special

When writing your networking code, never forget that mobile Internet has different parameters than home/office Internet. It is slower, so you might want to add timestamps to your messages and allow for more lenient timeout intervals than you would for a desktop application.

Timestamps are useful for ensuring that data is processed in sequence and with the correct timeframe. For example, if you're writing a tachometer application to monitor the speed of a fleet of cars, it may happen that two readings sent one minute apart will arrive to you at the same time due to networking issues. In order to calculate the proper acceleration and speed, you must know the time at which each reading was *taken*, not the time at which it *arrived* to you. Timestamps solve this problem elegantly.

Timestamps are also useful as data integrity checks. For example, if you know that you should receive a new message for every 10 seconds of real time, and two of your consecutive messages have timestamps that are 20 seconds apart, then you can be fairly sure that a message was dropped somewhere.

In addition, timestamps are useful for real-time games or other applications that can use data interpolation. This is because timestamps allow you to use UDP instead of TCP/IP, thus improving perceived network latency. Sure, UDP can and probably will drop some messages, but since each message that does come in has a timestamp, you can just use that time information to interpolate what happened in between.

Another trait of mobile Internet is that it is generally less reliable than fixed-location Internet. As such, having checksums to ensure that you got everything right is always a good idea (checksums can sometimes even be used to reconstruct missing or garbled data). Checksums can be applied to individual messages or to a sequence of messages (to make sure you received all of them and in the correct order). Checksums can also be used as a rudimentary anti-tampering mechanism: if the algorithm for generating the checksum is unknown to third-parties, or depends on some value(s) known only by the parties involved, then any discrepancy between the message's content and its checksum indicates a potential data tampering attempt. This can serve as an extra security layer in a world in which free wireless access points are commonplace (and unsafe) and in which man-in-the-middle attacks on mobile networks (through various means) are not unheard of.

Finally, connection to the Internet from a mobile device is also considerably more expensive for the end user, so if you send a lot of data, try to compress it. This reduces not only cost, but also the time needed to transfer information, both of which will make your users happy. However, this is done at the expense of CPU time, so compressing/decompressing large amounts of data in a short amount of time isn't feasible unless the device has a very powerful CPU.

Remember the Limitations of the Devices You're Targeting

All mobile devices have networking limitations. Some limitations you are certainly aware of, like a device's maximum throughput (for example, GPRS is slower than EDGE, which is slower than 3G) and maximum number of simultaneous connections (some older devices can handle only two, while others can handle ten or more). Other limitations are more obscure, like the time it takes to initiate a new connection and low-level protocol support (there are quite a lot of devices that don't support UDP; some devices have problems with certain types of HTTPS certificates). Be aware of all these limitations and design your networking layer accordingly.

For example, if the device you're targeting does not support HTTPS, then this means that you have to encrypt and decrypt sensitive data yourself, which can be extremely CPU-intensive. It is also possible that the device you're targeting supports only certain SSL certificates—for example, only those that do not contain wildcards. This problem can be fixed on the server side—for example, by generating a new and compatible certificate—but sometimes this is simply not possible for a variety of reasons (some technical, some business-related). In this case, you are again stuck with handling encryption within the application.

The time it takes to initiate a new connection is important if you connect to a lot of IPs— for example, in a peer-to-peer application. If creating a new connection takes unusually long or if doing so has other adverse effects (for example, if it freezes the application for a second or two), then you should consider reducing either the number of connections you use (for example, by using the same connection for more than one purpose) or the frequency at which new connections are created.

Support Network Throttling and Sleep Mode

Sleep mode is extremely important for long-running applications, such as chat clients. For example, if the application has been idle for ten minutes, you can close all open connections and thus save battery life. This, of course, means that you have to re-sync with the server when the application leaves sleep mode and resumes normal operation, and this may cause a networking bottleneck, as a potentially large amount of information needs to be transferred and processed at once. It may also mean that the user does not get notified of certain events in a timely fashion (for example, if he receives a chat message and the app is in sleep mode, he will see that message only during the re-sync, which may be hours or even days away).

There are ways to compensate for these shortcomings of sleep mode. One such way is registering your application as a listener on a certain SMS port. The server can then notify the app that it needs to resume operation by sending it an SMS on the specified port. Of course, this implies that the target device has support for listening to incoming SMS messages, via either the PushRegistry or a platform-specific API. In addition, this approach will almost certainly incur significant costs in terms of the SMS messages sent, and either you or your users will have to support these costs.

Another workaround is doing periodic wake-ups. In this scenario, the application periodically wakes up from sleep mode, establishes a single connection to the server and asks if anything of interest has happened. If the answer is "yes," the app resumes normal operation and syncs with the server. If the answer is "no," the app goes back into sleep mode at once. The app can also go back into sleep mode after syncing with the server, if certain conditions are met. For example, if the user does not want to be notified of new chat messages, the app can go back to sleep until the user explicitly wakes it up.

This second approach is considerably more cost-friendly, although less battery-efficient as new connections have to be established periodically, albeit for a small period of time.

As for throttling, reducing data throughput intentionally is a good idea sometimes. For example, let's say the user is browsing through an image gallery. Even though you could retrieve 30 images per second from the server, if you limit yourself to just 20 and only download images as needed (i.e., you do not load the entire gallery beforehand), the user won't notice the difference, but you will save a lot of data traffic and a fair amount of battery life, because an active (transmitting) data connection consumes more power than an idle one.

Throttling can be applied to most data that is meant to be accessed sequentially, because many times the application is interrupted before it can get to the end of the data stream (for example, if a gallery has 10,000 images, chances are the user won't go through all of them). Large amounts of information (logs, reports, books, customer information, etc.) can be efficiently and cost-effectively transmitted to a mobile device this way, and you can also use this technique to stream media and other content.

Finally, throttling also improves the user experience. As less data has to be processed each second, the application experiences less CPU usage and thus is able to function more smoothly.

Transmitting Your Data Efficiently

You also have to be creative and practical about the way you transmit information. For example, let's say you need to transmit a slideshow to a mobile device, and each slide contains an image and one or more snippets of text. How would you approach this? Merging plain text (the snippets) and binary data (the pictures) in a single stream using a custom protocol (or any existing protocol that supports binary data) is certainly feasible. However, it's much easier and much more effective to simply use a plain-text protocol and embed an URL to the associated binary data inside the plain text.

This approach has several benefits. First, you keep the protocol simple, which makes it more easily understood by humans and more easily parsed by machines. Second, as the protocol is plain text, it is very compression-friendly. Third, because the images and text are split, you can work on them separately. For example, you could download multiple images at once, or download just the image for the slide the user is currently viewing, or ignore the images altogether and display just the text. All of these things are difficult if not impossible to pull off using a single-stream approach.

There is also the matter of what protocol to use. It should be noted that XML is not the only protocol out there! For example, I'm a fan of JSON because it's less verbose than XML, easier to implement, and just as easy to read and understand. Another good pick that most people overlook is YAML, JSON's big brother of sorts. All of these are text-based protocols, which is perfectly fine because for encapsulating binary data you can use the "embed an URL to a binary resource" approach just described.

> **NOTE:** The only reason I can think of for using a binary protocol is keeping transmission overhead at an absolute minimum. Even this is a questionable reason, as for large amounts of data, the overhead of a text-based protocol (with the exception of XML) is mostly insignificant when compared to the total amount of data transferred.

Keeping the Networking Code Light

All the networking layer should really do is establish a connection to the server, convert the data coming from the server to instances of classes specific to the client (and vice versa), and respond to networking-related events (connection down, sleep mode activated, etc.).

Everything else (issuing a high-level request for data on the server, processing the incoming data, instructing the application to go to sleep and wake up, etc.) should be done *outside* the networking module. It may be tempting to add outside logic to the networking code, most of the time because it is handy and convenient to do so, but this only ends up complicating things in the long run: the code gets messy and the logic gets scattered throughout the application.

For example, it may be tempting to add the "decide if the app needs to go to sleep" code directly to the networking layer since, after all, it's the network connections that are going to sleep. However, if later on it is decided that the app can go to sleep at the user's request or for a number of other reasons, and if it's decided that other parts of the application should react to the "going to sleep" event as well, then having that code in the networking layer will become a problem.

At that point, you can either keep the decision code in place and change it to match the new requirements (keep in mind that you are now adding non-networking logic to the networking module), or move it to a separate location (perhaps its own module) and then interface it with the remainder of the networking module. Both approaches not only are complicated, but also create the risk that something will break in what will by then be a rather complicated application.

This scenario can be easily avoided by having the networking module contain strictly networking-related code. Granted, going to sleep is network-related, but the *decision* to go to sleep has nothing to do with networking. This means that the decision code previously mentioned does not belong in the networking module to begin with, and should end up in a module of its own or in a module to which it is related (like the automation module, for example).

Be Independent

You should design your code and architecture so that neither the server nor the client relies on the other party to perform in a certain manner (as in "do this, or I will crash"). Be lenient and always assume that that something might go wrong; have a fallback option in case something does.

For example, never assume that the server will send you valid information; try to check the data received from the server before use (if it makes sense to do so and if it's possible) and notify the user of any irregularities. Also, never assume that the server will respond to your requests, since a network or power outage can happen at any time. Institute timeouts so that if you don't get a response from the server in a timely fashion, the user is informed of this and the application fails gracefully.

An offline mode is always a handy thing to have in your applications. You can use a queue to store requests and then send them to the server once the application goes back online.

Finally, design everything to be asynchronous, if possible. This minimizes the impact of network latency and outages, while providing flexibility. And, because the application doesn't have to wait for the server to respond before proceeding, it will also feel snappier for the user.

Summary

We have implemented the networking module for our Twitter client application. In the process, we have learned how to properly structure a networking module, what pitfalls to look out for, how to convert asynchronous requests to synchronous ones, and how to use buffering to improve our application's efficiency. We have also examined a few best practices related to Java ME networking and discussed their impact on real-life applications.

Next, we will write our persistence module and have a closer look at what "persistent storage" means in the world of Java ME applications.

## Chapter 5

The Persistence Module

As the name suggests, the persistence module is responsible for storing and preserving data for use at a later time and possibly in a different application session.

The most common usage scenario is keeping track of application parameters (what user is currently logged in, whether sound is enabled, etc.) across multiple sessions, but it can also be used for other tasks, such as caching large amounts of data or for long-term storage of files received from the server.

Like everything else Java ME, in order to be truly useful and flexible, a persistence module should have a well-thought-out architecture and its code should be simple and easy to use by the end developer.

In this chapter, we will discuss the most important aspects of designing and implementing a good persistence module, as well as write the actual implementation we will use for our Twitter client. We will discuss what options we have in terms of Java ME persistence and see how they compare to each other, what the components of a good persistence module are, how these components can be elegantly implemented, and more. We will also look at some persistence tips and tricks, like serializing primitive data types such as integer and long to byte arrays in an efficient manner, and at how we can elegantly serialize high-level application objects to byte arrays.

> **CAUTION:** At the time of this writing, the WTK 3.0 emulator does not preserve the RMS between sessions. As such, it is recommended that you use the WTK 2.5.2 emulator to test RMS persistence. Of course, the code works fine on real devices.

Understanding Java ME Persistence Options

In the early days of Java ME, the only option you had for persistence was to use the Record Management System (RMS). The RMS was initially very limited in size, so there wasn't much you could store in it apart from a few settings. Things have gotten a lot better with time, and on current devices the RMS can provide sufficient storage space for most applications.

After Java Specification Request (JSR) 75 came along, developers were given a second option: use the device's filesystem to store data. Back in the day, that meant access to a couple of megabytes of persistent storage, but current devices support memory cards of 8 or 16 GB, even more, so your Java ME applications can basically have access to unlimited storage. However, there is a catch: as data is stored on the filesystem, it is available for all applications to see, edit, and delete. So while you can use JSR 75 to create something akin to a very large cache or a makeshift swapfile, it's not recommended to use it for storing private information like passwords, usernames, and such. It should also be noted that not all devices out there support JSR 75. Many extremely cheap devices, especially those sold in developing countries, provide only a very basic Java ME implementation, and optional components such as JSR 75 are unavailable.

Last but certainly not least, in recent years there has been a growing shift toward the concept of storing data in the cloud. This happened because mobile Internet access has gotten cheaper and cheaper—and continues to do so. It has thus become feasible to store information remotely on a secure, central server rather than (or in addition to) on the device itself. This means that a user's settings, preferences, and critical data can be more secure and have more availability than ever. The user doesn't have to worry if his or her phone gets stolen, and he can have the same experience with the application on all his devices: he just has to authenticate himself on a new device, and all his preferences will be downloaded in a matter of seconds.

Of course, cloud-based persistence has to take into consideration the fact that not all users have Internet access on their devices (or may not be willing to allow your application to use it). In some countries, mobile Internet access is extremely expensive (almost prohibitively so) so very few people use it. In other countries, most notably in the western world, most mobile plans come with some free Internet traffic by default (in the range of 10–100 MB/month depending on the plan) and extra traffic is fairly cheap, so many people will be OK with allowing your application to access the Internet. This discrepancy means that you should do thorough research on the subject if you're targeting the international market.

These are the three main methods of providing persistence capabilities in the Java ME world. By far the most widely used method of persistence is the RMS-based one. Second to RMS-based persistence is cloud-based persistence, used by many applications ranging from IM clients to PIM suites. Finally, there are very few applications that I know of that make use of filesystem-based persistence: only a few GPS applications and a couple of larger games come to mind. It is interesting to note that an application can use multiple persistence methods. For example, data could be saved both in the RMS, for quick local access, and in the cloud, for safety and for when the user switches to a different device.

So how do you decide which persistence method is best for your application?

As a rule of thumb, whenever possible, try to limit yourself to using RMS-based persistence only, as it provides the best balance between speed, storage size, and availability. Even if you will also use other persistence mechanisms, always have RMS persistence implemented as a backup.

If you need to store large amounts of data (for example, a database), then filesystem-based persistence is usually the best option, though you should be mindful of the security and privacy implications that come with it. Filesystem-based persistence is also very useful in a variety of unconventional scenarios. For example, some devices support mounting USB flash sticks, HDDs, or even other mobile phones as external filesystems. On these devices, you can use filesystem-based persistence to create a backup of your application's data, easily transfer settings from one device to another, and more.

Cloud-based persistence should always be optional and should always be limited to storing small amounts of data (preferences, passwords, etc.) in order to minimize costs. The only exceptions to this rule are applications that are Internet-intensive by their very nature (e.g., Internet browsers, streaming clients). In these cases, you can depend on cloud-based persistence to store more information (e.g., avatar pictures, text notes), as the application will most likely generate a fair amount of traffic regardless of what persistence method is used.

Designing the Persistence Module

Designing and implementing a good persistence module takes a bit of careful thought. The best approach to work with is the top-down one: start with high-level abstractions for the RMS, filesystem, or the cloud, and work your way down to the bytes that make up your data types.

What you usually end up with is a three-tier architecture like the one in Figure 5–1.

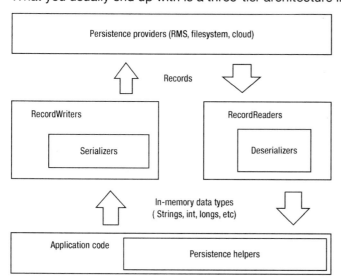

Figure 5–1. *The persistence module architecture*

Persistence providers sit at the top, feeding data in the form of records to RecordReaders and receiving data (also in the form of records) from RecordWriters.

RecordWriters and RecordReaders are what the rest of the application should use to read and write persistent data, either directly or through the use of helpers. In order to do their job, RecordWriters and RecordReaders in turn rely on Serializers and Deserializers to convert in-memory objects into stand-alone representations, and vice versa.

The rest of the module consists mostly of helpers that simplify the overall use of the persistence module and free developers from writing tedious, repetitive, and error-prone code. Though not strictly needed, they are widely used within applications because of the benefits they provide—in fact, most persistence-related operations are usually done through helpers as opposed to directly using readers, writers, and providers.

In order to better understand what all of the foregoing means, we need to examine in detail the main pieces that make up the persistence module. Let's start with persistence providers.

The Persistence Providers

As mentioned previously, providers sit at the top of the persistence pyramid. They are responsible for presenting the rest of the module with the means to store and retrieve raw persistent data. The RMS and filesystem are good examples of persistence providers, as is the networking layer (for cloud-based persistence, where applicable).

All persistence providers work with records. A record is simply a series of bytes (a byte array) identifiable by a unique index number. Persistence providers don't care what the data in each record represents or how it should be interpreted, or whether it means anything at all or it's just garbage; their job is only to retrieve, create, overwrite, and delete records.

To keep things consistent with real-life usage scenarios, each persistence provider must be "opened" before use and closed after use. Providers must also provide the means to flush the data in their cache (if any) whenever necessary.

With all the foregoing in mind, all persistence providers must implement the interface shown in Listing 5–1.

Listing 5–1. *The PersistenceProvider Interface*

```
package app.module.persistence.classes;

public interface PersistenceProvider
{
    public byte[] getRecord(int index);
    public int createRecord(byte [] data);
    public boolean overwriteRecord(int index, byte [] data);
    public boolean deleteRecord(int index);
    public boolean open();
    public void flush();
    public void close();
}
```

If you look at the `createRecord()` method, you will notice that you cannot directly specify the index of the new record. Instead, when the method is called, a new record will be created and its corresponding index returned.

This approach provides a greater level of abstraction, but at the same time it does complicate keeping track of where your information is (for example, what is the index of the record that contains the login credentials used by the current user?). A good strategy to overcome this drawback is to have the first record serve as a table of contents, keeping track of where each specific piece of information is located within the provider—we will see later how this can be done.

RecordReaders and RecordWriters

As far as providers are concerned, records are nothing more than byte arrays. This means that, in order to store and retrieve data using them, we must first give meaning to the raw bytes that make up each record.

We can achieve this easily by defining that, on a logical level, each record will represent a series of primitive values (integers, strings, etc.) serialized together according to a predefined encoding.

For example, consider the following series: the integer `123456` followed by the string "`Hello, how are you?`" followed by the Boolean "`false`". If we were to choose a simple `getBytes()`–based encoding, which simply retrieves the raw bytes that make up each primitive, the first four bytes in the resulting record would encode the integer (since a Java integer is four bytes long), the next 19 would encode the string, and the next byte after that the Boolean.

> **NOTE:** The high-level meaning behind the values is entirely up to the application. For example, a "string, string, string" record may represent a person's full name (first + middle + last name) or login credentials (username, password, and e-mail). It is up to the application to know what any given record represents and to interpret said record properly.

This encoding scheme is simple and works remarkably well in practice, so we will use it in our project. However, sometimes encoding schemes can be considerably more complex.

For example, if we were to choose to encode our data using XML, then the series must be first be serialized into an XML-valid string, something like "`<record>
<int>123456</int> <string>Hello, how are you?</string> <boolean>true</boolean>
</record>`". It is this string that must be converted to bytes and stored in the record.

Using such encoding schemes makes sense in many scenarios—for example, if your application employs a cloud-based persistence provider. In this case, since it is likely that the persistent data will also be accessed by non-Java applications (web-based clients, statistical software, etc.), storing it in a universal format like XML or JSON makes inter-application data sharing easier and safer in the long run.

As for what constitutes a primitive data type, this again varies from application to application. For example, we will consider only integers, longs, bytes, strings, and Booleans as being primitives, but other applications might consider vectors and images as being primitive data types too.

> **NOTE:** Of course, you could represent images as a series of byte primitives and retrieve said bytes one by one from the record. However, this would require a lot of time and method calls, so it is better to just consider images as stand-alone primitive data types if you need to persist them. The same is true for vectors and other more complex data types.

The raw bytes of a record are never directly manipulated by the application. Instead, the persistence module provides RecordReaders and RecordWriters to handle the decoding and encoding of primitives within a record. A reader/writer pair must exist for every encoding scheme that the application will use.

The RecordWriter interface is presented in Listing 5–2, while its concrete implementation for our project will be given later in the chapter.

Listing 5–2. *The RecordWriter Interface*

```
package app.module.persistence.classes;

public interface RecordWriter
{
    public void writeInt ( int value );
    public void writeLong ( long value );
    public void writeString ( String value );
    public void writeBoolean ( boolean value ) ;
    public void writeByte( byte value );
    public void reset();
    public byte[] getCurrentResult();
}
```

Each writer starts out with an empty record. As the writeXXX() methods are called, primitive values are added to the record, one after another. At any point, one may call getCurrentResult() to obtain a valid byte-array representation of the current record. This representation can then be passed along to a PersistenceProvider for storage. You can always reset() the writer, which will return it to its initial empty-record state.

> **TIP:** A RecordWriter is free to use any internal representation it wishes for its data (for example, a Vector of Objects or a linked list), as long as getCurrentResult() returns what is expected. Use this to your advantage and see if you can find alternate representations that save memory and/or CPU cycles.

A RecordReader does the converse process: it reads bytes from a record and turns them into primitive values. The RecordReader interface is presented in Listing 5–3, with its actual implementation also given later in the chapter.

Listing 5–3. *The RecordReader Interface*

```
package app.module.persistence.classes;

public interface RecordReader
{
    public int readInt();
    public long readLong();
    public String readString();
    public boolean readBoolean();
    public byte readByte();
}
```

To deserialize the example "Hello, how are you?" record mentioned earlier, one would have to call readInt(), readString(), and readBoolean() in sequence. Note that it is the application's responsibility to call the readXXX() methods in the right order. For example, if the application calls readInt() when the next primitive value in the record is a string, the results are undefined.

Serializers and Deserializers

RecordWriters rely on Serializers to do the actual converting of in-memory primitives to byte arrays that can be written to records. Conversely, RecordReaders use Deserializers to convert byte arrays into in-memory primitives. As with readers and writers, a serializer/deserializer pair must be provided for every encoding scheme the application will use.

Since Java ME does not have serialization support built in, we will have to implement our own, starting with the Serializer interface presented in Listing 5–4. To keep things simple, serializers will always directly return a byte-array representation of the primitives they are asked to serialize.

Listing 5–4. *The Serializer Interface*

```
package app.module.persistence.classes;

public interface Serializer
{
    public byte[] serializeByte(byte data);
    public byte[] serializeInt(int value);
    public byte[] serializeString(String value);
    public byte[] serializeLong(long value);
    public byte[] serializeBoolean(boolean value);
}
```

The Deserializer interface is presented in Listing 5–5. Since deserializers work primarily with the byte arrays that make up records, each method in the deserializer will have an offset parameter to indicate where in the byte array to start deserializing from. This is done to avoid needless memory copying operations from the record byte array to a temporary byte array used by the deserializer.

Listing 5–5. *The* Deserializer *Interface*

```
package app.module.persistence.classes;

public interface Deserializer
{
    public byte deserializeByte(byte[] data, int offset);
    public int deserializeInt(byte [] data, int offset);
    public long deserializeLong(byte [] data, int offset);
    public String deserializeString(byte[] data, int offset, int length);
    public boolean deserializeBoolean(byte[] data, int offset);
}
```

As you can see from the highlighted code, the method for deserializing strings differs a bit from the rest, because all other primitive types we use have a fixed length, while strings have variable length. As such, an extra parameter must be passed to indicate how many bytes should be deserialized into a String (this also applies to other variable-sized primitive data types, such vectors and images).

In real-life usage scenarios (within records, for example), the value of this extra parameter is encoded along with the string; however, it is *not* part of the string encoding itself. For example, the integer 5 can be encoded immediately before the string "Hello" to indicate its length. This is not needed for encodings that make it easy to determine where a string ends (XML is a good example of this).

Persistence Helpers

Each helper provides a single specific functionality, usually a high-level one, which is widely used within the application. Different applications have different helpers, according to their needs. A common role for helpers is providing easier record management and simplified serialization of high-level application objects.

Most helpers are custom-written for a specific application. Because of this, they are somehow separated from the main persistence code, in that removing them does not break the rest of the persistence module.

Implementing the Core Architecture

Next, it's time to look at how to implement serializers and deserializers, record readers, record writers, and the global RMS persistence provider, which together form the core architecture of the persistence module.

NOTE: This part of the chapter is mostly code. To save space, only the relevant bits of code are presented here, with the full source code available on the Apress web site.

Implementing Serializers and Deserializers

We have already decided that we will use a simple getBytes()–based encoding in our application. As such, our Serializer implementation will be named ByteSerializer and our Deserializer implementation will be named ByteDeserializer.

Let's look at ByteSerializer first (you can see it in Listing 5–6).

Listing 5–6. *The ByteSerializer Model*

```
package app.module.persistence.models;

import app.module.persistence.classes.Serializer;

public class ByteSerializer implements Serializer {

    public byte[] serializeInt(int value)
    {
        byte[] result = new byte[4];
        result[0] = (byte) ( value  >> 24 );
        result[1] = (byte) ( value  >> 16 );
        result[2] = (byte) ( value  >> 8 ) ;
        result[3] = (byte) (value);
        return result;
    }

    public byte[] serializeLong(long value)
    {
        byte[] result = new byte[8];
        result[0] = (byte) (value >> 56);
        result[1] = (byte) (value >> 48);
        ...
        result[7] = (byte) (value);
        return result;
    }

    public byte[] serializeString(String value)
    {
        return value.getBytes();
    }

    public byte[] serializeByte(byte data)
    {
        return new byte[] { data } ;
    }

    public byte[] serializeBoolean(boolean value) { ... }

}
```

Everything is pretty straightforward here, perhaps with the small exception of serializing integers and longs. Java ME doesn't provide a convenient getBytes() method for these data types like it does for Strings, so we have to do the conversion ourselves. We do this by using bit shifts to extract each individual byte of a long or an integer, and then place these bytes in a byte array.

For example, an integer is 32 bits wide, or 4 bytes. Shifting right 24 bits (or 3 bytes) and casting the result to a byte will give us the leftmost byte of the integer, which we then store in result[0]. Shifting right 16 bits (or 2 bytes) and casting to byte will give us the second leftmost byte of the integer, which we then store in result[1], and so forth, as shown in the highlighted portion of the code. The same process is applied to longs.

We can also extract the individual bytes by using a ByteArrayOutputStream. This is quite easy to do: simply write the integer or long to a ByteArrayOutputStream object and then call toByteArray() on it. However, using bit shifts is significantly faster and has the added advantage of incurring very little overhead.

The ByteDeserializer is up next, shown in Listing 5–7. It does the reverse process: it takes a byte array produced by a ByteSerializer and converts it into the corresponding data type.

Listing 5–7. *The ByteDeserializer Model*

```
package app.module.persistence.models;

import app.module.persistence.classes.Deserializer;

public class ByteDeserializer implements Deserializer {

    public byte deserializeByte(byte[] data, int offset)
    {
        return data[offset];
    }

    public int deserializeInt(byte[] data, int offset)
    {
            return ( (data[offset] & 0xFF) << 24 ) | ( (data[offset+1] & 0xFF)
            << 16 ) | ( (data[offset+2] & 0xFF) << 8 ) | (data[offset+3] & 0xFF );
    }

    public long deserializeLong(byte[] data, int offset)
    {
            return ( ( (long) data[offset] & 0xFF) << 56 ) | ( ( (long)
            data[offset+1] & 0xFF) << 48 ) | ... | ( (long) data[offset+7] & 0xFF );
    }

    public String deserializeString(byte[] data, int offset, int length)
    {
        return new String(data,offset,length);
    }

    public boolean deserializeBoolean(byte[] data, int offset) { ... }
}
```

As you can see from the highlighted lines, deserializing integers and longs is considerably trickier than serializing them, requiring the use of bit masks and type castings. Other than that, everything is straightforward here too.

TIP: Byte serializers and deserializers can also be used outside of the persistence module. For example, the encryption module can use them to reduce data to the lowest common denominators, bytes, before encrypting it.

Implementing RecordReaders and RecordWriters

The RecordReaders and RecordWriters interfaces will be implemented by the ByteRecordReader and ByteRecordWriter classes respectively.

ByteRecordWriter can be seen in Listing 5–8. The highlighted lines show how to serialize a string's length together with the string itself.

Listing 5–8. *The ByteRecordWriter*

```java
package app.module.persistence.models;

import app.module.persistence.classes.RecordWriter;
import java.io.ByteArrayOutputStream;
import java.io.IOException;

public class ByteRecordWriter implements RecordWriter
{
    ByteArrayOutputStream os = new ByteArrayOutputStream();
    ByteSerializer bs = new ByteSerializer();

    protected void writeRawByteArray(byte [] data)
    {
        ...
        os.write(data);
        ...

    }

    public void reset() { os.reset(); }

    public void writeString(String value)
    {
        byte [] rawStringData = bs.serializeString(value);
        writeRawByteArray( bs.serializeInt(rawStringData.length) );
        writeRawByteArray( rawStringData );
    }

    public void writeInt(int value)
    {
        writeRawByteArray( bs.serializeInt(value) );
    }

    public void writeLong(long value) { ... }
    public void writeBoolean(boolean value) { ... }
    public byte[] getCurrentResult() { return os.toByteArray(); }
    public void writeByte(byte value) { ... }

}
```

The main idea here is to treat the string's length (an integer) and the string's body (a collection of bytes) as an atomic data type and write them together. It is also very important to write the string's length first; otherwise you won't know how many bytes to read when decoding it.

The counterpart to the ByteRecordWriter is the ByteRecordReader, presented in Listing 5–9. The highlighted lines this time show how to deserialize a string that was serialized along with its length. The process is quite intuitive and simple: first we read the string's length and then we read the string's actual bytes.

Listing 5–9. *The ByteRecordReader*

```
package app.module.persistence.models;

import app.module.persistence.classes.RecordReader;

public class ByteRecordReader implements RecordReader
{
    byte [] recordData = null;
    int currentOffset = 0;
    ByteDeserializer bds = new ByteDeserializer();

    public ByteRecordReader ( byte [] data)
    {
        recordData = data;
    }

    public String readString()
    {
        int strSize = readInt();
        String result = bds.deserializeString(recordData, currentOffset, strSize);
        currentOffset += strSize;
        return result;
    }

    public int readInt()
    {
        int result = bds.deserializeInt(recordData, currentOffset);
        currentOffset += 4;
        return result;
    }

    public long readLong() { ... }
    public boolean readBoolean() { ... }
    public byte readByte() { ... }
}
```

Implementing the PersistenceProvider

Finally, the RMSPersistenceProvider shown in Listing 5–10 is a persistence provider implementation built around the RMS. In this case, we are fortunate, as the RMS API has an exact correspondent for the methods our RMSPersistenceProvider needs to implement. Because of this, our RMSPersistenceProvider is little more than a wrapper around the Java ME's RMS API.

For other providers, however, particularly cloud-based ones, things can be considerably more complicated. For example, in the case of cloud-based providers, network connections need to be established and managed, and communication with the server needs to be done via a standardized protocol as opposed to direct, native platform API calls. This complicates the code significantly and introduces a lot of potential problems, so careful thought must be given to the PersistenceProvider in such cases.

Listing 5–10. *The* RMSPersistenceProvider

```
package app.module.persistence.models;

import app.module.persistence.classes.PersistenceProvider;
import javax.microedition.rms.RecordStore;
import javax.microedition.rms.RecordStoreException;

public class RMSPersistenceProvider implements PersistenceProvider
{
    String recordStoreName;
    RecordStore rs ;

    public RMSPersistenceProvider(String recordStoreName)
    {
        this.recordStoreName = recordStoreName;
    }

    public boolean open()
    {
        ...
        rs = RecordStore.openRecordStore(recordStoreName, true);
        ...
        return true;
    }

    public byte[] getRecord(int index)
    {
        ...
        result = rs.getRecord(index);
        ...
        return result;
    }

    public boolean overwriteRecord(int index, byte[] data) { ... }
    public boolean deleteRecord(int index) { ... }
    public void close() { ... }
    public int createRecord(byte[] data) { ... }

    public void flush()
    {
        // Not needed
    }

}
```

Testing the Code

Now that everything is in place, it's time to test if everything works properly. The code in Listing 5–11 creates a new RMS persistence provider and attempts to retrieve a previously saved date (saved as a String) and timestamp (saved as a long) from one of its records. It will then output them to the console, after which it will replace them with a new date string and timestamp.

Listing 5–11. *A Quick Persistence Test*

```
// Define variables
ByteRecordReader reader;
ByteRecordWriter writer;
long timestamp = 0;
String dateString = "";

// Open the persistence provider with the "test" record store
RMSPersistenceProvider prov = new RMSPersistenceProvider("test");
prov.open();

// If there is no initial record, create one
if ( prov.getRecord(1) == null )
{
        prov.createRecord(new byte[] {0});
}
else
{       // Otherwise, read the date string and the timestamp from the existing
        // record ...
        reader = new ByteRecordReader(prov.getRecord(1));
        timestamp = reader.readLong();
        dateString = reader.readString();

        // ... and write them to the console
        System.out.println("Date: " + dateString + " Time: " + timestamp );
}

// Create a new writer
writer = new ByteRecordWriter();

// Encode the current timestamp and date string
writer.writeLong(System.currentTimeMillis());
writer.writeString( new Date().toString() );

// Save the resulting record at position one for later use
// and close the provider
prov.overwriteRecord(1, writer.getCurrentResult());
prov.close();
```

The first time you run the code, it will display nothing, as there is no initial record created. However, from the second time onward, each time you run the snippet, you should see the date string and timestamp from the previous time the snippet was run.

The persistence clearly works; but in its current state, using it in a real-life application is too convoluted and confusing. We need some helpers to make things easier.

Writing Persistence Helpers

The first helper we will write is the Table of Contents helper, or TOC for short. This is a general-purpose helper that can be used to keep track in a developer-friendly fashion of what information is stored in which record.

To put it to work, first you have to attach the TOC to a provider by calling the following:

```
TOC tableOfContents = new TOC(providerInstance) ;
```

Next, if you want to remember that the credentials for the current user are stored in record number 15, for example, all you have to do is call the following:

```
tableOfContents.addEntry("credentials",15);
```

After that, whenever you want to know where the credentials are stored, simply call the following:

```
tableOfContents.getIndexFor("credentials");
```

Deleting an entry is equally easy:

```
tableOfContents.deleteEntry("credentials");
```

The code for the TOC helper is presented in Listing 5–12, while an actual usage example will be given later on, as part of the SimplifiedPersistenceHelper. The highlighted code in Listing 5–12 exemplifies how to deserialize a complex record—in our case, the record contains the actual table of contents hashtable.

Listing 5–12. *The TOC Helper*

```
package app.module.persistence.helpers;

import app.module.persistence.classes.PersistenceProvider;
import app.module.persistence.classes.RecordReader;
...

public class TOC
{
    Hashtable TOCHashtable = new Hashtable();
    PersistenceProvider provider;
    RecordReader reader;
    RecordWriter writer;

    public TOC(PersistenceProvider provider)
    {
        this.writer = new ByteRecordWriter();
        this.provider = provider;
        provider.open();

        // Try to open the TOC. By convention, it is stored in record #1
        if ( provider.getRecord(1) == null )
        {
            return; // No TOC exists, nothing to deserialize
        }
        else
        {
            // A TOC exists, we can deserialize it
```

```
        }

        // Create a reader for record #1
        reader = new ByteRecordReader(provider.getRecord(1));

        // Read the size of the TOC
        int size = reader.readInt();

        // Read each entry in the TOC and add it to the Hashtable
        String key;
        int value;
        while (size>0)
        {
            key = reader.readString();
            value = reader.readInt();
            addEntry(key, value);
            size--;
        }
    }

    // Serialize the TOC to a byte array
    protected byte[] getCurrentTOCBytes()
    {
        String tempKey;
        int size = TOCHashtable.size();

        // Reset the writer
        writer.reset();

        // Write the size of the TOC
        writer.writeInt(size);

        // Write each entry in the TOC
        Enumeration keys = TOCHashtable.keys();
        while ( keys.hasMoreElements() )
        {
            tempKey = (String) keys.nextElement();
            writer.writeString(tempKey);
            writer.writeInt( ((Integer) TOCHashtable.get(tempKey)).intValue() );
        }

        // Return the corresponding byte array
        return writer.getCurrentResult();
    }

    public void save()
    {
        // No initial record exists. Create it.
        if ( provider.getRecord(1) == null)
        {
            provider.createRecord(new byte[] {0});
        }

        // Save the record corresponding to the TOC at index #1
        provider.overwriteRecord(1, getCurrentTOCBytes());
    }
```

```
    public void addEntry(String key, int index)
    {
        TOCHashtable.put(key, new Integer(index));
    }

    public void deleteEntry(String key)
    {
        TOCHashtable.remove(key);
    }

    public int getIndexFor(String key)
    {
        Integer result = (Integer) TOCHashtable.get(key) ;
        if ( result != null )
        {
            return result.intValue();
        }
        else
        {
            return -1;
        }
    }
}
```

Using the TOC helper does have two restrictions. First of all, in order to make sure it always gets the first record allocated to it, you must instantiate it immediately after the provider has been created, or at least before any createRecord() operations are called on the provider. Second, you must remember to call save() whenever you want the TOC to be persisted, otherwise changes to it will be lost.

The next helper we will write is tasked with serializing and deserializing high-level application objects. Its name is, appropriately enough, HighLevelSerializer. This helper will provide two methods for each high-level data type, serializeXXX() and deserializeXXX(), where XXX is the data type in question.

For example, the serializeUserCredentials() method of the helper is presented in Listing 5–13. The highlighted portion shows how to deal with fields that may be null: write a Boolean flag before each field, indicating if the field is present or not. This way, when the deserializer processes the record, it knows which fields are available for deserialization and which are not.

Also, the serializeXXX() methods append data to a currently existing writer (as opposed to returning a stand-alone byte array) to facilitate serializing multiple objects in a single record.

Listing 5–13. *Serializing* UserCredentials

```
public static void serializeUserCredentials(UserCredentials credentials, RecordWriter
writer)
{
        if ( credentials.getAccessToken() != null )
        {
                writer.writeBoolean(true);
                writer.writeString(credentials.getAccessToken());
```

```
        }
        else
        {
                writer.writeBoolean(false);
        }

        if ( credentials.getAccessTokenSecret() != null )
        {
                writer.writeBoolean(true);
                writer.writeString(credentials.getAccessTokenSecret());
        }
        else
        {
                writer.writeBoolean(false);
        }

        ...
}
```

Deserializing UserCredentials is even easier. The appropriate method is presented in Listing 5–14. You can see from the highlighted code that we attempt to deserialize only fields that are not null, which is indicated by their corresponding flags being set to true.

Like the serializeXXX(), deserialization methods work with a currently existing reader (as opposed to directly with a byte array) to facilitate deserializing multiple objects from the same record.

Listing 5–14. *Deserializing* UserCredentials

```
public UserCredentials deserializeUserCredentials(RecordReader reader)
{
        String token = null , tokenSecret = null;
        String username = null, password = null;

        if ( reader.readBoolean() )
        {
                token = reader.readString() ;
        }

        if ( reader.readBoolean() )
        {
                tokenSecret = reader.readString() ;
        }

        if ( reader.readBoolean() )
        {
                username = reader.readString() ;
        }

        if ( reader.readBoolean() )
        {
                password = reader.readString() ;
        }

        return new UserCredentials(username, password, token, tokenSecret);
}
```

The third and final helper we will write is also probably the most important one, and the one we will use the most. It is called the SimplifiedPersistenceHelper, and it uses the TOC helper to hide all the details of record index management from the rest of the application, making working with persistence a breeze.

To use it, you must first create an instance of it and attach that instance to a persistence provider, like so:

```
RMSPersistenceProvider provider = new RMSPersistenceProvider("recordStoreName");
SimplifiedPersistenceHelper helper = new SimplifiedPersistenceHelper(provider);
```

Next, if you want to store a record within the persistence provider, simply call the helper's store() method with a name under which you want to store the record and the actual record bytes as parameters, like the following example:

```
helper.store("name", writer.getCurrentResult() );
```

Retrieving a record is a piece of cake, too:

```
byte [] data = helper.getRecord("name");
```

Finally, to delete a record, all you have to do is call the following:

```
helper.delete("name");
```

The really nice part is that the helper itself is really small in size. Its entire source code is presented in Listing 5–15.

Listing 5–15. *The SimplifiedPersistenceHelper*

```java
package app.module.network.helpers;

import app.module.persistence.classes.PersistenceProvider;

public class SimplifiedPersistenceHelper
{
    PersistenceProvider provider;
    TOC toc;

    public SimplifiedPersistenceHelper(PersistenceProvider provider)
    {
        this.provider = provider;
        // Initialize the TOC imediately
        toc = new TOC(provider);
    }

    public void store(String key, byte [] data)
    {
        int index = toc.getIndexFor(key) ;
        if ( index != -1)
        {
            provider.overwriteRecord(index, data);
        }
        else
        {
            index = provider.createRecord(data);
            toc.addEntry(key, index);
        }
```

```
    }

    public byte [] getRecord(String key)
    {
        int index = toc.getIndexFor(key) ;
        if ( index != -1)
        {
            return provider.getRecord(index);
        }
        else
        {
            return null;
        }
    }

    public void delete(String key)
    {
        int index = toc.getIndexFor(key) ;
        if (  index != -1  )
        {
            provider.deleteRecord(index);
            toc.deleteEntry(key);
        }
    }

    public void close()
    {
        toc.save();
    }

}
```

Using the Module in a Real-Life Scenario

Our persistence module is now complete. To finish everything off, let's look at one final example, the one in Listing 5–16, which demonstrates how to use the module within real-life scenarios. Though the example is simple, it covers storing and retrieving both simple records (which contain only one object) and complex records (which contain multiple objects). This should give you a pretty good idea of how the persistence module is to be used in an actual application, and of how we will use it in our Twitter client.

Listing 5–16. *A Complete Usage Example for the Persistence Module*

```
// Create the provider and the SimplifiedPersistenceHelper
RMSPersistenceProvider provider = new RMSPersistenceProvider("recordStoreName");
SimplifiedPersistenceHelper helper = new SimplifiedPersistenceHelper(provider);

// Create a set of user credentials
UserCredentials creds = new UserCredentials("1", "2", null, "3");

// Serializing a single (high-level) object
ByteRecordWriter writer = new ByteRecordWriter();
HighLevelSerializer.serializeUserCredentials(creds, writer);
helper.store("credentials", writer.getCurrentResult());
```

```
// Serializing multiple objects in a single record
writer.reset(); // Reset the writer to "empty"
HighLevelSerializer.serializeUserCredentials(creds, writer);
writer.writeString("There is a string after the credentials");
helper.store("complexrecord",writer.getCurrentResult());

// Deserializing a record containing a single object
byte [] data = helper.getRecord("credentials");
ByteRecordReader reader = new ByteRecordReader(data);
UserCredentials storedCredentials =
HighLevelSerializer.deserializeUserCredentials(reader);

// Deserializing a record containing multiple objects
data = helper.getRecord("complexrecord");
reader = new ByteRecordReader(data);
storedCredentials = HighLevelSerializer.deserializeUserCredentials(reader);
String message = reader.readString();

// Don't forget to close the SimplifiedHelper after use, in order to save the TOC
helper.close();
```

As you can see, most of the details related to persistence are neatly hidden away by the helpers. Despite this, flexibility is also high: for example, each record can use a different writer and reader combination if needed and low-level record data can be directly manipulated (though this is not recommended). That being said, we can now declare our persistence module complete and ready to be used.

Taking the Module Further

As far as our project is concerned, we will leave the persistence module like it is now, as it provides a good balance between flexibility/extensibility and readability/ease of use. However, feel free to adapt the module to suit your particular needs. For example, if you will use only one type of encoding scheme in your application (which is often the case), then you can modify the code such that no explicit readers or writers must be passed as parameters—thus simplifying the code. One way this can be achieved is by creating a dedicated Record data type and adding all the serialization and deserialization code directly to it. You can also achieve the same effect without touching the main persistence code, by writing a dedicated helper.

Besides making the module simpler, you can also add project-specific functionality to it. Good examples are a priority queue to decide which data gets serialized first (this is useful in scenarios where not all the data can be serialized due to storage constraints, or in low-bandwidth situations), an "umbrella" persistence provider, which transparently works with several sub-providers for storing and retrieving data (thus providing distributed persistent storage), and a record cache (to speed up persistence operations).

Summary

We have learned how to look at Java ME persistence and what the primary means of implementing it are.

We have also learned how to structure, write, and use a persistence module—and how to handle common problems like storing data types with variable length, handling composite data types, and supporting multiple encoding schemes.

We have put that knowledge into practice by writing the persistence module for our application.

In the next chapter, we will cover what many perceive as the most important and interesting technical aspect of a Java ME application: the UI module.

## Chapter 6

The UI Module

The trickiest part of writing a mobile application, and the most rewarding in my opinion, is writing its UI module. What clearly separates Java ME from other mobile platforms is the fact that, in order to get anything useful, you must write your UI from scratch—down to the basic low-level drawing calls. The built-in UI package is simply too outdated for modern-day usage.

Writing the UI module from scratch requires knowledge of many subjects, from computational geometry to user experience analysis and interface design, so it's not an easy task. However, it does provide you with complete freedom in designing and implementing your UI in any way you see fit, and it allows you to be extremely creative. Plus, it's always a great experience to visually interact with the code you're writing—so there's also great fun to be had in this endeavor.

In this chapter, we will go over the basic principles and concepts of UI implementation and write a simple but functional UI module for our application—which you can then reuse in other applications as well. The look and feel will be very basic in order to keep the code simple and understandable, but you are free to add bells and whistles as you desire.

A good Java ME UI strikes a delicate balance between code flexibility, proper programming techniques, usability, and code complexity. It sits somewhere between SWING, which is powerful but overly verbose and resource-intensive, and the native Java ME UI, which is simple and lightning fast but way too limited for modern-day usage.

Our UI module will strive to sit exactly in the right spot. It will be written so as to provide support for any kind of widgets and containers you might wish to implement, while at the same time being fast and easy to use. For readability and simplicity purposes, no optimizations will be applied to the code. For example, the code will make heavy use of recursion. This can be greatly reduced, but at the expense of adding code complexity, which is not something we want for the purpose of this book. Ways of optimizing the code will be discussed later in the book—and applying them to the UI module is a great exercise! ☺

The UI module will also cover the basic components needed for our application: buttons, labels, input fields, horizontal-layout containers, and vertical-layout containers. Finally, its goal is to be functional, not pretty, so don't expect a state-of-the art visual experience. Nor should you expect it to be very smart about the way it does some things. I have decided to keep things simple and "dumb" so that the ideas are easier to understand; I will show you later in the book how you can make the UI module smarter.

> **NOTE:** To run the code in this chapter on the WTK 2.5.2 and earlier emulators, you need to enable touch support for them. To do this, go to `WTK_HOME_FOLDER\wtklib\devices\ DefaultColorPhone` and locate the configuration file `DefaultColorPhone.properties`. Open it, locate the `touch_screen` property and set it to `true`.

Why Create a Custom UI Module?

The reality is that, for most projects, you're better off using an off-the-shelf third-party UI library. Third-party UI libraries usually have better polish and a richer feature set than what you could come up with on your own. So why learn how to write your own?

Well, there are plenty of situations when having the know-how necessary to write a UI module comes in handy. There are plenty of projects, especially personal ones, where using a third-party library is not possible because of licensing, image, or budgetary concerns. Other times (quite often actually) you start out with a third-party UI library, but during development you will need to alter it or extend it with custom components and/or behavior. If you're targeting devices with limited resources, like older phones, then you might find that third-party libraries simply won't run well (or at all) on these devices.

Writing your own UI module is also a very educational exercise, and no matter how experienced you are, it is almost certain that going through with it will teach you at least a couple of new things. Finally, if you dedicate enough resources to it, you can even turn your UI module into a stand-alone product and make money off of it, or at least use it as a very intuitive and convincing demonstration of your skills to potential clients.

For these reasons, and many others, it pays off to know how to write your own UI module or at least to understand the basics of how UI modules function.

Understanding the Basics of Creating a UI Module

Before we get knee-deep in code, we should first look at some theoretical aspects, just so we get a better understanding of what we're going to create in this chapter. You probably already know, at least intuitively, what a widget is and what a container is, for example. What you may not know is how to define these entities the Java ME way, providing just the right amount of functionality and information to make them usable while preventing the code from becoming bloated and resource-intensive.

Widgets

The fundamental element of any UI is, conceptually, the widget. A widget is basically an abstraction for anything that the user sees on the screen and can potentially interact with. Buttons, labels, scrollbars—they are all widgets. The screen itself is a widget too, albeit a special one—more on this later.

A widget has a relative position, defined by X and Y coordinates relative to its parent, and an absolute position, relative to the screen itself. It also has a size, expressed in terms of width and height. It can respond to user interactions, such as keypresses and touch events. Widgets also have a state, which in our case can be either "focused" or "not focused," and can respond to state changes. It can also provide state information to the outside world—for example, whether it can be focused, and whether it is focused at any given time.

The widget's X and Y coordinates are always relative to its parent widget (more on that soon). Its size can be either the widget's preferred size (which it calculates itself) or a specified size set by external means. The specified size always takes priority over the preferred size.

With this in mind, the basic Widget interface is presented in Listing 6–1.

Listing 6–1. *The Basic Widget Interface*

```
package app.module.ui.models;

public interface Widget
{
    public void setX(int x);
    public void setY(int y);
    public int getX();
    public int getY();
    public int getAbsoluteX();
    public int getAbsoluteY();
    public void setContentWidth(int w);
    public int getContentWidth();
    public void setContentHeight(int h);
    public int getContentHeight();
    public int getPreferredContentHeight();
    public int getPreferredContentWidth();
    public int getTotalWidth();
    public int getTotalHeight();
    public Container getParent();
    public void setParent(Container c);
    public boolean handleKeyPressed(int key);
    public boolean handleKeyReleased(int key);
    public boolean handlePointerPressed(int x, int y);
    public boolean handlePointerDragged(int x, int y);
    public boolean handlePointerReleased(int x, int y);
    public boolean onFocus();
    public boolean onLostFocus();
    public boolean isFocusable();
    public boolean isFocused();
}
```

By far the most complicated part of this interface is the section dealing with widget size, as you can see from the highlighted code. The convention is as follows: `getPreferredContentWidth()` returns the ideal width for the widget (as calculated by the widget itself), `setContentWidth()` forces the widget's content to be of a specified width, and `getContentWidth()` returns that forced width.

Finally, `getTotalWidth()` returns the actual widget width, which is `getContentWidth()` if that's set, or `getPreferredContentWidth()` otherwise. In practice we'll mostly use `getTotalWidth()`, but sometimes you'll need the other methods too. Of course, a widget can override the convention and have any of these methods return different values—but that's not something you want to do unless absolutely necessary, as it may break your UI.

Before we continue, there are two important aspects to keep in mind. The first is knowing when to use a widget's preferred size and when to force a size on it. This is very important. For low-level widgets, such as buttons, you should always try to use a widget's preferred size. Force a smaller size only in extreme circumstances—for example, when you need to make the widget smaller in order to fit inside the parent container. Forcing a larger size on a widget is generally OK for design reasons, but this too should be avoided if possible.

The second important aspect is that a widget's size can be specified by more than width and height. For example, a widget can have paddings, margins, and borders. We will not concern ourselves with those in order to keep the code simple, but feel free to try to implement support for them as an exercise.

Now back to our interface. Since widgets exist within a Java ME application, there are also some specific methods related to this. We need to be able to retrieve a widget's absolute screen position, its clipping rectangle (the area of it which is actually visible—more on this important subject later), and its parent view. We also need to be able to paint the widget and to request a repaint when necessary. Thus, the methods in Listing 6–2 will be added to the `Widget` interface.

Listing 6–2. *Extra Methods for the* `Widget` *Interface*

```
public int getAbsoluteX();
public int getAbsoluteY();
public ClipRect getClipRect();
public void requestRepaint();
public View getParentView();
public void paint(Graphics g);
```

Containers

As stated previously, widgets can have parents. A parent is simply a widget that implements the `Container` interface, shown in Listing 6–3. Containers are very similar to collections—in fact, they are visual collections of widgets.

Listing 6–3. *The* `Container` *Interface*

```
package app.module.ui.models;

public interface Container extends Widget
```

```
{
    public boolean addWidget(Widget b);
    public boolean insertWidget(Widget b, int index);
    public int indexOf(Widget w);
    public void removeWidget(Widget b);
    public int getChildCount();
    public void focusWidget(Widget w);
    public Widget getWidget(int index);
    public void doLayout();
}
```

The highlighted method is a very important one for containers: calling it makes the container rearrange and resize its child widgets according to its layout scheme. For example, calling doLayout() on a VerticalContainer will arrange its widgets one below another in the order in which they were added, with the first added widget at the top.

At this point, you might ask what happens, for example, if the total height of the child widgets exceeds the height of the container. This is a very good question. To solve this problem, containers must implement scrolling. Thus, the methods in Listing 6–4 will be added to the Container interface.

Listing 6–4. *Container Scrolling Methods*

```
public int getXScroll();
public int getYScroll();
public void setYScroll(int scroll);
public void setXScroll(int scroll);
public boolean scrollToWidget(Widget w);
```

With scrolling, a container's visible area becomes a viewport for the actual container surface, and you can scroll the viewport to any position you like.

Containers are able to decline widgets, too. For example, a TabbedContainer may reject any widget that is not a TabContainer. The addWidget() and insertWidget() methods return false when a widget has been rejected.

The nice thing about containers is that, as they are widgets themselves, they can also have a parent. This provides for the possibility of creating complex interfaces via the matrioska effect, where containers are nested within containers that are nested within containers. Moreover, containers allow you to easily create composite widgets. For example, if you want to create a picture button, simply have the PictureButton class be a container with a picture widget and a label widget inside of it.

> **NOTE:** Keep in mind that all of this simply isn't possible with the native Java ME UI package!

It follows from the foregoing that the screen is itself a container, albeit a special one, since it doesn't have any parent per se, and its size is fixed and matches the screen resolution.

Clipping Rectangles

With container scrolling, it becomes possible that some widgets aren't entirely visible. Thus, in order to properly paint a widget, we have to determine what part of it is visible (its clipping rectangle) and clip out the rest.

This is fairly easy to do if the parent of the widget is the top-level parent, but what if the parent of the widget also has a parent of its own? For example, what if the widget's parent has a horizontal scroll that clips the widget in half horizontally, and the parent's parent has a vertical scroll that clips the widget in half vertically, like in Figure 6–1?

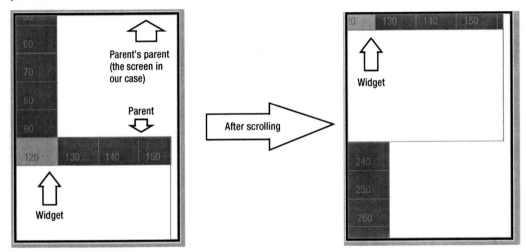

Figure 6–1. *A clipping situation*

Furthermore, what if the parent of the parent also has a parent of its own? How do you calculate the clipping rectangle then? You can see that this can get complicated really fast. However, the solution is quite simple, both conceptually and in code. It just requires a bit of clever thinking.

For starters, let's define that, initially, a widget's clipping rectangle is the same as its position and size onscreen—that is, as follows:

```
ClipRect.X = getAbsoluteX()
ClipRect.Y = getAbsoluteY()
ClipRect.Width = getTotalWidth()
ClipRect.Height = getTotalHeight()
```

Next, to get the proper clip rectangle of the widget, we must intersect its clip rectangle with the one of its parent, and then intersect the result with the clip rectangle of the parent's parent, and so on until we reach the top-level parent, which is usually the screen. Whatever the resulting intersection rectangle we have then is the actual clipping rectangle for our widget.

We have thus reduced the clipping problem to a computational geometry problem, the intersection of rectangles, which fortunately is easy to solve. But for this, we must first redefine the way in which we represent our rectangles.

Specifically, we will switch from our current approach of representing rectangles by specifying their (X,Y) coordinates and their width and height to representing rectangles by specifying the coordinates of their opposite corners, like in Figure 6–2.

Figure 6–2. *Redefining clip rectangle representations*

This seemingly minor change makes a world of difference. Consider what happens when two rectangles intersect in the new representation, like in Figure 6–3.

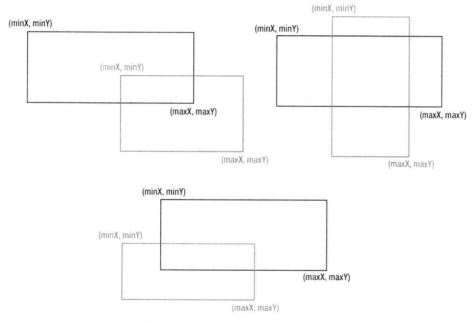

Figure 6–3. *Possible rectangle intersection scenarios*

It's obvious visually what the resulting intersection rectangles are, but computers care only about numbers. With the old representation for rectangles, it's kind of difficult and counterintuitive to *calculate* the intersection rectangle, but our new representation for rectangles makes this a walk in the park—and an intuitive one at that!

Once you play around enough with the drawings and analyze them, you will notice that in all of the cases shown in Figure 6–3, and in fact in all rectangle intersection cases, the minX of the resulting intersection rectangle is the maximum of the minX values of the source rectangles.

This is a bit of a mouthful, but writing in math is easier to understand:

```
result.minX = Max ( source1.minX, source2.minX )
```

Likewise, the maxX of the resulting rectangle is the minimum of the maxX values of the source rectangles, or the following:

```
result.maxX = Min ( source1.maxX, source2.maxX )
```

The same formulas apply for the Y coordinates, as shown here:

```
result.minY = Max ( source1.minY, source2.minY )
result.maxY = Min ( source1.maxY, source2.maxY )
```

Go ahead and try the formulas out on any two rectangles you can think of; you will find that they "magically" work!

Armed with this knowledge, we can now write our ClipRect class. The interesting parts of it are shown in Listing 6–5.

Listing 6–5. *The ClipRect Class*

```
package app.module.ui.models;

public class ClipRect
{
    ...

    public ClipRect(int minX, int minY, int maxX, int maxY)
    {
        ...
    }

    ...

    public ClipRect intersectWith(ClipRect otherRect)
    {
        ClipRect newRect = new ClipRect ( Math.max (this.minX, otherRect.getMinX()),
            Math.max (this.minY, otherRect.getMinY()),
            Math.min (this.maxX, otherRect.getMaxX()),
            Math.min (this.maxY, otherRect.getMaxY()));

        return newRect;
    }

    public boolean isVisible()
    {
        return ( this.maxX >= this.minX && this.maxY > this.minY );
    }

}
```

The highlighted portion of the code shows how to determine if a clipping rectangle is visible and/or valid. If you try to intersect two rectangles that do not overlap, then if you apply the foregoing formulas, you will get either that maxX < minX, or maxY < minY, or both. Go ahead, try it! Thus, if both of these conditions are false, the clipping rectangle is valid and thus visible.

At this point, we can write the `ClipHelper` class, which contains helper methods related to clipping. The most important parts of it are presented in Listing 6–6.

Listing 6–6. *The* `ClipHelper` *Class*

```
package app.module.ui.helpers;

import app.module.ui.models.ClipRect;
import app.module.ui.models.Widget;
import javax.microedition.lcdui.Graphics;

public class ClipHelper
{
    public static ClipRect getTargetClipRectFor(Widget w)
    {
        ClipRect result = w.getClipRect();
        Widget parent = w.getParent();
        while ( parent != null )
        {
            result = result.intersectWith(parent.getClipRect());
            parent = parent.getParent();
        }

        return result;
    }

    public static void setClipOn(Widget w, Graphics g)
    {
        ClipRect result = getTargetClipRectFor(w);
        g.setClip(result.getMinX(), result.getMinY(), result.getMaxX()-result
            .getMinX(), result.getMaxY()-result.getMinY());
    }
    ...
}
```

The highlighted portion of the code shows just how easy it is to calculate the clipping rectangle of any widget.

Clipping rectangles are commonly mishandled in Java ME UI frameworks. This is a shame, since clipping is heavily used throughout almost any UI. Using a less than optimal implementation for it can lead to complicated code and resource waste, both of which should be avoided like the plague. The solution described in this section is simple, efficient, and scalable, plus it can be made lightning fast with a few code optimizations, which we will discuss later in the book.

Clipping rectangles are also a very good example of how redefining your data structures can solve a lot of problems and make things clearer and more elegant. The presented solution is harder to figure out, more difficult to implement, and less elegant if you think in terms of (X,Y,width,height) than it is if you think in terms of (minX,minY,maxX,maxY)— don't you agree?

Views

Views are abstract representations of the application's screens. As we have seen previously in the book, the View interface does not provide many interaction capabilities on its own. This is intentional, as some views may be self-reliant and able to function on their own—for example, a ScreenSaver view. In practice, however, most concrete views implement at least one other interface, typically Container or Widget, so that the rest of the application may interact with them.

Thus, views are themselves widgets, although by their very nature they are somewhat special since they typically sit between the application's code and the platform's native code. For example, most low-level views extend the GameCanvas native class directly, which means, among other things, that views are the entry points for user interaction events such as keypresses and touch events. They also take care of low-level graphics stuff, like buffering and drawing on the screen.

Views can be made to do pretty "crazy" stuff. For example, you can implement a RemoteView class, which forwards all paint() calls to an image instead of to the screen and then sends that image over the Web to a remote server, thus allowing users to use the application anywhere in the world, in a web browser! If you think this has no real-life usage, just think about the possibilities it opens up for remote debugging and remote assistance.

Themes

Each pro Java ME application has a specific set of colors to be used for drawing, in order to ensure a consistent visual style throughout the user interface. For example, the designers might dictate that all focused widgets must have a green background, while all unfocused widgets must have a black background. To keep everything consistent, themes are used. Themes are descendents of the UITheme interface, shown in Listing 6–7.

Listing 6–7. *The UITheme Interface*

```
package app.module.ui.models;

import javax.microedition.lcdui.Font;

public interface UITheme
{
    public int getAppBgColor();
    public int getSelectedBgColor();
    public int getNotSelectedBgColor();
    public int getSelectedFgColor();
    public int getNotSelectedFgColor();
    public Font getSelectedFont();
    public Font getNotSelectedFont();
    ...
}
```

As you can see, a theme provides all the necessary colors used by the application in a consistent and global manner.

Generally, whenever a widget is created, a theme is attached to it; the widget must then use the colors specified in the theme for all drawing operations. This means that when you change the background color of a theme, for example, all widgets using that theme will then reflect the change.

Of course, you can also use multiple themes at the same time, or switch between themes at runtime; anything is possible.

Furthermore, themes can provide more than just color values: they can provide image objects to be used as icons or other UI elements, like sounds. You can even use themes to customize the speed of animated scrolling, the duration of vibrations, and pretty much everything else related to user interaction.

In our application, we will limit ourselves to just a single theme, which will specify only the colors to be used for drawing. It can be seen in Listing 6–8.

Listing 6–8. *Our AppTheme Class*

```
package app.classes;

import app.module.ui.models.UITheme;
import javax.microedition.lcdui.Font;


public class AppTheme implements UITheme
{
    public int getSelectedBgColor()
    {
        return 0x0000FF00;
    }

    public int getNotSelectedBgColor()
    {
        return 0x00888888;
    }

    ...

}
```

Finally, themes can be made smart. For example, you can create a theme class that returns different colors and media depending on the time of day. Smart themes are a great and simple way to customize and polish your applications because they're fairly easy to code and they add a lot of value to the user experience.

Handling User Interaction

User interaction is a critical part of the UI framework, so it is crucial that we get it right.

First of all, as mentioned earlier, user interaction events typically enter the application through Views. From there, they are forwarded to sub-widgets, as described next.

When a user-interaction method (handleXXXX()) is called on a widget (this includes Views and Containers), the widget should first try to forward the call to its focused sub-widget, if any, or to the sub-widget at the pointer position in the case of a touch interaction. If the sub-widget does not handle the interaction, then the widget itself should try to handle it. If neither the sub-widget nor the widget itself handles it, then the method should return false, signaling that the caller is free to try to handle the interaction.

As you can imagine, this is a very recursion-intensive process, and one you should pay close attention to. Because of the many levels of nested calls involved, forwarding an interaction event to the wrong widget, falsely signaling its handled/not handled status, or worse, not forwarding the call at all, can all lead to unpredictable consequences.

For example, in one project I worked on, which was a social network client, one of the containers wrongly calculated the widget under the pointer in some cases because it didn't take scrolling into consideration—and that resulted in the wrong widget receiving touch events. I found this out the hard way. The form I was working on at the time was a "Send message" form, and what I wanted to do was test the functionality of the Back button, which was supposed to show a pop-up saying, "Are you sure you want to discard the message?" The Back button was located below the Send button. So what I did was write a very "nice" message in the "Enter message" edit field and touch the Back button on the screen. However, since the container did not take scrolling into consideration, I will leave you to guess what button the application actually thought I was pressing and what happened next...

It is also good to remember that some widgets may want to handle certain events themselves *before* passing them over to sub-widgets, if at all. Good examples of this are touch widgets that support gestures. They might not want to forward some touch events to sub-widgets—for example, when the user does a finger swipe across the screen. Instead, they may choose to interpret this as a scroll request and handle it as such— sub-widgets receive no notice of this.

Now, the UI layer must interact with the rest of the application at some point or another. In order for this to happen, widgets need to have a way to signal when something needs to be done. This is achieved through the use of the CallbackHandler interface, shown in Listing 6–9.

Listing 6–9. *The* CallbackHandler *Interface*

```
package app.module.ui.models;

import com.apress.framework.objecttypes.Event;

public interface CallbackHandler
{
```

```
    public boolean doCallback(Event evt);
}
```

It should be pretty obvious how CallbackHandlers are used: interactive widgets have a CallbackHandler attached to them, and whenever something interesting happens, they forward the appropriate event to the handler by calling its doCallback() method.

Finally, it is worth noting that it is good to have your code provide support for widgets that don't "play nice." For example, you may need to implement an EnterPassword widget that does not relinquish focus until the proper password is entered, not even if it is explicitly instructed to do so—in effect, the user is stuck in the EnterPassword field once it is activated. This is easy to do in the widget, as all that's needed is to have the onLostFocus() method return false. However, the rest of the code, particularly the containers, must be aware that this can happen and must handle the situation accordingly. For simplicity, our UI module will not support this kind of "disobedient" behavior, but it is a good exercise in UI implementation to modify it so that it does. If you feel up for it, please do so after you finish reading this chapter.

Implementing Basic Widget Support

Now that we have our theoretical groundwork done, it's time to start writing some code. Since all the classes in the UI module are pretty big, I'll include only the important bits and pieces in the code, with the full source code available on the Apress web site.

That being said, let's start writing our UI, beginning with the BaseWidget class.

The BaseWidget Class

The BaseWidget class will serve as the basis for all other widgets. Most of it is pretty straightforward, but some aspects of it are worth going into—for starters, determining a widget's onscreen position and clip rectangle. The code for this is presented in Listing 6–10.

Listing 6–10. *Determining the Position and Clipping Rectangle of the* BaseWidget

```
package app.module.ui.models;

public abstract class BaseWidget implements Widget
{
    protected Container parent;
    protected ClipRect clipRect = new ClipRect(0,0,0,0);

    ...

    public ClipRect getClipRect()
    {
        clipRect.setMaxX(getAbsoluteX()+getTotalWidth());
        clipRect.setMaxY(getAbsoluteY()+getTotalHeight());
        clipRect.setMinX(getAbsoluteX());
        clipRect.setMinY(getAbsoluteY());
        return clipRect;
```

```
        }

        public int getAbsoluteX()
        {
            return parent.getAbsoluteX() - parent.getXScroll() + getX();
        }

        public int getAbsoluteY()
        {
            return parent.getAbsoluteY() - parent.getYScroll() + getY();
        }

        ...
}
```

I would like you to turn your attention to the highlighted code. As you can see, determining a widget's absolute position is a recursive affair. To do that, you need to get the parent's absolute position, add the widget's position relative to the parent, and then compensate for the parent's scroll, but to get the parent's absolute position you need to get *its* parent's absolute position, and so forth.

Thus, making sure every link along the recursion chain reports the correct absolute position is vital, as the absolute position will be used for painting the widget and for determining its clipping rectangle. Even small off-by-one errors are unacceptable here, as they will get compounded at each step along the way until they become noticeable and affect your application's look.

Furthermore, if calculation of a widget's absolute position takes too long, then the whole app will become slow because getting a widget's absolute position is probably the most widely used method call in the entire UI module. That's why it's important to keep everything simple in this area.

The next interesting bit of code in BaseWidget is the one concerning repaint requests. It is shown in Listing 6–11.

Listing 6–11. *Requesting a Repaint*

```
public void requestRepaint()
{
        View v = getParentView();
        if ( v != null )
        {
                getParentView().paintWidget(this);
        }
}

public View getParentView()
{
        if ( parent == null )
        {
                return null;
        }
        return parent.getParentView();
}
```

As you can see, the widget simply forwards the repaint request to its parent view, if any. It is the view's responsibility to then call the widget's paint() method with a suitable Graphics object as a parameter. Of course, retrieving a widget's parent view is done recursively as well.

The last area of interest is handling events. Since BaseWidget is the boilerplate class for all other widgets, the most common behavior must be coded in. This means that, by default, the widget should ignore all key events by returning false when the appropriate methods are called. This is so the parent container gets a chance to handle them, which is important—for example, if they are "Key up" or "Key down," they are typically responsible for navigation. Widgets that need to handle key events—for example, buttons—can simply override the appropriate methods.

Touch events are a different story. The widget will by default ignore "pointer down" and "pointer dragged" events but will respond to "pointer released" events by trying to focus the widget, as shown in Listing 6–12. This is done because the default convention in all UIs is that you touch something only if you want to interact with it or move it into focus.

Listing 6–12. *Handling "Pointer Released" Events*

```
public boolean handlePointerReleased(int x, int y)
{
        if ( isFocusable() == true && isFocused() == false )
        {
                if ( getParent() != null )
                {
                        getParent().focusWidget(this);
                }
                return true;
        }
        return false;
}
```

Before we continue, I would like to point out something very important: you should change the focus or activate an item only on "release" events, that is "key released" and "pointer released." The main reason for this is that this gives users a little wiggle room and prevents accidental actions.

For example, if you handle activation on the "pressed" event, as soon as the user touches or presses the OK button on a notification, the dialog will disappear. If, however, you handle this in the released event, then the dialog will remain visible for as long as the user keeps the key or pointer pressed. In the case of pointer events, if the user touched the button by mistake, then he can simply drag the pointer to a location outside of the button and release it there—no action will be triggered.

Finally, I would like to point out that the BaseWidget class is declared as abstract. Some methods, particularly paint(), must be explicitly implemented in its sub-classes. This serves both as a means of making sure developers implement widgets properly, by having them explicitly write all the critical methods, and as a means of documentation, by telling developers that widgets need this and that functionality implemented in order to function.

Having said that, we have now covered the most important aspects of the BaseWidget class. It's time to move on to containers.

BaseContainerWidget and BaseContainerManager

The BaseContainerWidget will serve as the basis for all the containers in the UI module. There really is nothing special about it; what it does is map all methods like addWidget(), insertWidget(), and getWidget() to a Vector instance. Apart from this, it also provides the means to set and retrieve the container scroll, but that's just about it.

It is declared as abstract, so that sub-classes must explicitly implement its two most important methods, which are paint() and doLayout().

BaseContainerManager, the direct descendent of BaseContainerWidget, is another story altogether, and it is quite an interesting one. It will serve as the intermediary class between BaseContainerWidget and the actual container implementations, providing the common-ground methods used by all concrete container implementations in our UI module.

Its functionality is not integrated in BaseContainerWidget (or vice versa) for flexibility reasons: at one point, you might decide you need to implement a container that is radically different than the rest, and then it will make sense to start with a lower common denominator than BaseContainerManager, which is exactly what BaseContainerWidget provides.

As the "Manager" part of the name suggests, BaseContainerManager is more than just a "dumb class" like the ones we have covered so far. In fact, it does quite a lot, but we'll go over only the interesting stuff.

For one thing, BaseContainerManager provides focus support by implementing general-purpose onFocus(), isFocusable(), and onLostFocus(). Out of the three, onFocus() and isFocusable() deserve special attention. Their code is shown in Listing 6–13.

Listing 6–13. *onFocus() and isFocusable()*

```
public boolean isFocusable()
{
        int i;
        for (i=0;i< getChildCount();i++)
        {
                if ( getWidget(i).isFocusable() )
                {
                        return true;
                }
        }
        return false;
}

public boolean onFocus()
{
        isFocused = false;
        if (focusedWidget == null)
        {
```

```
            for (int i = 0; i < getChildCount(); i++)
            {
                    if ( getWidget(i).isFocusable() )
                    {
                            focusedWidget = getWidget(i);
                            break;
                    }
            }
    }

    if ( focusedWidget != null && indexOf(focusedWidget) == -1 )
    {
            focusedWidget = null;
            return onFocus();
    }

    if ( focusedWidget != null )
    {
            isFocused = focusedWidget.onFocus();
            scrollToWidget(focusedWidget);
            return isFocused;
    }
    else
    {
            return false;
    }
}
```

This code is very important, and so it's important to understand it. In order determine if a container can receive focus, we must first see if any of its children can receive focus. If no children can receive focus, then the container itself cannot receive focus, as there's nothing inside it to focus. This check is done in the isFocusable() method. Please note that, as containers can be nested inside other containers, the highlighted portion of the code can be and often is recursive in nature, since getWidget() can return a Container.

The onFocus() method is slightly more complex than isFocusable(). First, it checks if there's a previously focused widget inside the container. If there is none, then it will find the first focusable widget inside the container and work with that.

Second, it checks if the focused widget, which might have been left over from the last time the container had focus, is still inside the container. This is a necessary check, as widgets can and often are removed from their parent containers—for example, when the user triggers a "delete" action. If the widget to be focused is no longer in the container, then onFocus() will attempt to focus another widget by calling itself.

Third, if we get to a point where the widget to be focused is valid (focusable and inside the container), then we call onFocus() on it, after which we scroll it into view.

This brings us to the other interesting part of the BaseContainerManager: scrolling to a specific widget. This is done in the scrollToWidget() method. The interesting bit comes from the fact that it is not enough to scroll a widget into view in the current container; you must scroll it into view *on the screen*. This is not always the same thing. For example, the currently focused widget might be visible in its parent container, but the parent container might be off-screen because of *its* parent's scroll. Thus, in effect, our currently focused widget will be invisible to the user. In order to avoid this, we must make sure that, along with scrolling the current widget into view within the current container, we also scroll the current widget into view within the current container's parent.

The code for the scrollToWidget() method is shown in Listing 6–14. For brevity, only vertical scroll is presented.

Listing 6–14. *Scrolling to a Widget*

```
public boolean scrollToWidget(Widget w)
{
        ...

        int maxScroll, neededScrollDelta;

        // Maximum allowed vertical scroll
        maxScroll = Math.max(getPreferredContentHeight() - getContentHeight(), 0);

        // Needed vertical scroll in order to bring the top side of the widget into view
        neededScrollDelta = WidgetHelper.getYDistanceBetween(w, this);

        if ( neededScrollDelta > 0 && getYScroll() + neededScrollDelta < getYScroll()
        + getTotalHeight() )
        {
                // Don't scroll if the top side of the widget is already visible
        }
        else
        {
                if ( getYScroll() + neededScrollDelta >= maxScroll   )
                {
                        // Make sure we don't overscroll
                        setYScroll(maxScroll);
                }
                else
                {
                        setYScroll(getYScroll()+neededScrollDelta);
                }
                scroll=true;
        }

        ...

        parent.scrollToWidget(w);
}
```

Let's summarize what we do here: we calculate the necessary scroll delta (with respect to the current scroll value) needed to bring the specified widget into view in the current container, and then we apply said delta to the current scroll, but only if the widget isn't already visible (in which case we do nothing) and only if the resulting scroll value isn't bigger than the maximum allowed scroll value (in which case we use that one instead). Then, as just stated, we try to scroll the widget into view in the current container's parent—please notice the recursion.

Before we can continue, a small clarification is needed: the maximum scroll value corresponds to the scroll value needed to neatly bring the bottom section of the container into view. Any scroll value larger than it will lead to unwanted whitespace at the bottom of the container viewport. You can see that the maximum scroll value is easily calculated by subtracting the content height (which is the height of the viewport) from the preferred content height (which is the height the container would need to have in order for it to be 100% visible).

Now, if you look at the highlighted code, you will see a reference to the WidgetHelper class. What is of interest to us is the getYDistanceBetween() method, which returns the distance (in onscreen pixels) between a widget and one of its ancestors. The code for this method is presented in Listing 6–15. A similar method, not presented here, exists for the X distance.

Listing 6–15. *The getYDistanceBetween() Method*

```
public static int getYDistanceBetween(Widget w, Container c)
{
        int result = 0;
        boolean found = false;
        while ( w != null )
        {
                // We have reached the desired container, we can stop.
                if ( w == c )
                {
                        found = true;
                        break;
                }

                // Add the local parent-to-child distance to the total distance
                result += w.getY();

                // Compensate for the parent scroll
                if ( w.getParent() != null )
                {
                        result -= w.getParent().getYScroll();
                }

                // Go up one level
                w = w.getParent();

        }

        if ( found )
        {
                return result;
        }
        else
        {
                return Integer.MIN_VALUE;
        }
}
```

The highlighted part of the code does the bulk of the work. It calculates the distance between the current widget and its direct parent, compensates for the parent's scroll, and then sets the parent as the current widget.

Finally, I would like to turn our attention to the paint() method and to the class constructor, both shown in Listing 6–16. These methods are interesting because they demonstrate how to use themes, as shown in the highlighted portion of the code.

Listing 6–16. *The* paint() *Method and the Constructor*

```
public BaseContainerManager(UITheme theme)
{
        this.theme = theme;
}

public void paint (Graphics g)
{
        g.setColor(theme.getAppBgColor());
        int absX = getAbsoluteX();
        int absY = getAbsoluteY();
        g.fillRect(getAbsoluteX(), getAbsoluteY(), getTotalWidth()-1,
        getTotalHeight()-1);

        Widget temp;
        for (int i=0; i < getChildCount(); i++)
        {
                temp = getWidget(i);
                if ( temp.getClipRect().isVisible() )
                {
                        temp.paint(g);
                }
        }
}
```

I would also like to point out a small but very important optimization: we paint a widget only if its clip rectangle is visible. There's no point in calling paint() and doing all the stuff that's in there, which can potentially be a lot, if none of it is going to be visible to the user.

Finally, there's one more thing I would like to cover before we move on: handling pointer events. The important lesson to be learned here is to ignore the first "pointer released" event that comes after a series of "pointer dragged" events. This is necessary because that first "released" event actually means "the user has finished dragging," not "the user wants to focus or activate the widget under the pointer"—which is what "released" events are usually used for.

This is very easy to do, as can be seen in Listing 6–17. The same approach is used in BaseContainerManager.

Listing 6–17. *Handling Pointer Events*

```
public boolean handlePointerReleased(int x, int y)
{
        if ( isDragging )
        {
                isDragging = false;
```

```
                return true;
        }
        else
        {
            ...
        }
}

public boolean handlePointerDragged(int x, int y)
{
        Widget w = getWidgetAt(x, y);
        if ( w != null )
        {
            if ( w.handlePointerDragged(x, y) )
            {
                // Do nothing
                return true;
            }
        }
        isDragging = true;
        return false;
}
```

This concludes our basic widget support. With the boilerplate classes now in place, we can move on to implementing concrete widgets.

Implementing Concrete Widgets

Having completed the basic groundwork needed for implementing widgets, we will now focus our attention on writing concrete widgets for our UI module. We will implement containers, buttons, text input fields, and labels. In doing so, we will cover concepts such as cascading events, navigation, and creating new widgets by extending an existing one.

The VerticalContainer and HorizontalContainer Classes

Most UI forms are created using a vertical layout—that is, widgets are placed one below another. This is exactly what the VerticalContainer class does. Most of the dirty work is already done for us, since VerticalContainer extends BaseContainerManager, so we can focus on the important parts.

For one thing, there's the doLayout() method, shown in Listing 6–18.

Listing 6–18. *VerticalContainer and Its doLayout() Method*

```
package app.module.ui.classes;

import app.module.ui.models.BaseContainerManager;
...

public class VerticalContainer extends BaseContainerManager
{
    ...
```

```
    protected int PADDING = 3 ;

    public void doLayout()
    {
        int currentY = 0;
        int i;
        Widget temp;

        for (i=0; i < getChildCount(); i++)
        {
            temp = getWidget(i);
            temp.setX(0);
            temp.setY(currentY);
            currentY += temp.getTotalHeight() + PADDING;
        }
    }
    requestRepaint();
}
```

The code is pretty simple: it just arranges child widgets vertically in the order in which they were added. In order to ensure that the widgets do not touch each other, a small padding is added. Having padding is important since determining where one widget ends and another begins would be difficult without it. Also, this is a very basic layout scheme, but other container implementations may employ significantly more complex layout schemes, possibly with multiple paddings and margins.

The next important part is determining the preferred size of the container. The code for this is shown in Listing 6–19.

Listing 6–19. *Determining the Preferred Size of a* `VerticalContainer`

```
public int getPreferredContentHeight()
{
        int maxH = 0;
        if ( getChildCount() > 0 )
        {
                Widget lastWidget = getWidget(getChildCount()-1);
                maxH = lastWidget.getY() + lastWidget.getTotalHeight();
        }
        return maxH;
}

public int getPreferredContentWidth()
{
        int maxW = 0;
        int tempW;
        for (int i=0;i<getChildCount();i++)
        {
                tempW = getWidget(i).getTotalWidth();
                if ( tempW > maxW )
                {
                        maxW = tempW;
                }
        }
        return maxW;
}
```

As you can see, the preferred height is equal to the position of the bottom margin of the last child (if any), while the preferred width is equal to width of the widest child widget. Because of the way the preferred content height is calculated, doLayout() must be called beforehand.

Next up, since this is a container, we should probably implement navigation support— that is, moving the focus from one widget to another. And this is where things start to get interesting, beginning with the handleKeyPressed() method shown in Listing 6–20.

Listing 6–20. *The handleKeyPressed() Method*

```
public boolean handleKeyReleased(int key)
{
        if ( getFocusedWidget().handleKeyReleased(key) )
        {
                return true;
        }
        else
        if ( GameCanvas.UP == KeyHelper.getGameAction(key) )
        {
                // Try to focus a previous widget
                int max = indexOf(getFocusedWidget());
                for (int i=max-1;i>=0;i--)
                {
                        if ( getWidget(i).isFocusable() )
                        {
                                focusWidget(getWidget(i));
                                return true;
                        }
                }
                return false;
        }
        else
        if ( GameCanvas.DOWN == KeyHelper.getGameAction(key) )
        {
                // Try to focus a previous widget
                ...
        }
        else
        {
                return false;
        }
}
```

The method rightfully assumes that, since it has been called, the container is focused and thus a focused widget exists. If you get a NullPointerException here it's because you forgot to call onFocus(), or because you tried to focus an unfocusable container.

Since this is a vertical container, we care only about presses of the UP and DOWN keys; everything else is ignored. The code showing how to handle the UP key is highlighted; the code for the DOWN key is similar, and we will not cover it here.

It's interesting to think about what happens when false is returned—for example, when there is no previous widget to focus. Returning false will signal to the parent container that it should handle the keypress.

If the keypress causes the parent container to move the focus, then onLostFocus() will be called on this container. This, in turn, will cause onLostFocus() to be called on the focused widget (which can also be a container). When all the onLostFocus() calls are done, the parent controller will call onFocus() on the new widget, which can potentially bring about another batch of cascading calls. Finally, when everything is settled down, the parent controller's handleKeyReleased() method will return true to its caller.

If the keypress is not handled by the parent, then the parent's parent will try to handle it, and everything discussed so far applies again, this time on a slightly larger scale.

> **NOTE:** As you can see, there can be a lot going on behind the scenes of a seemingly simple keypress, and many apparently unrelated parts of the code can be called to work together in unison. That's why it's crucial to get everything right everywhere, as even a minor off-by-one error can break things in a most ugly fashion due to the intricate way things are interconnected in the UI module.

Finally, let's look at how dragging can be used to scroll the container. The code for this is shown in Listing 6–21.

Listing 6–21. *The handlePointerDragged() Method*

```
public boolean handlePointerDragged(int x, int y)
{
        if ( super.handlePointerDragged(x,y) )
        {
                return true;
        }

        int deltaY = getOldY() - y ;
        setOldY(y);
        setOldX(x);

        int scroll = getYScroll() + deltaY;
        int maxScroll = Math.max(getPreferredContentHeight() - getContentHeight(), 0);
        if ( scroll >= 0 && scroll <= maxScroll )
        {
                setYScroll(scroll);
                requestRepaint();
        }
        return true;
}
```

As this is a vertical container, we care only about vertical scrolling. This is easily achieved by calculating the delta between the current Y position and the old Y position, and applying that delta to the current scroll (if the result is within limits). However, the interesting part of the code is the one highlighted. The call to super.handlePointerDragged() is crucial, because it gives sub-widgets the chance to handle the event, and most importantly because it sets the isDragging flag. Furthermore, if you decide to implement touch gestures in your application, then the best place to implement global ones is in

BaseContainerManager.handlePointerDragged(). The bottom line is if you extend BaseContainerManager, make sure your handlePointerDragged() method calls its super equivalent.

The HorizontalManager class is almost identical to the VerticalManager save for only a few differences (for example, it cares only about horizontal scroll), so we will not cover it here.

The SimpleTextButton Class

Containers are fine, but they do nothing on their own. In order to be useful, they must be populated with widgets. The most basic widget we can implement is the button. Buttons can be simple text elements or complex widgets that contain both text and images, or even other widgets. However, to keep this simple, in our UI module we will implement only a simple text button, aptly named SimpleTextButton.

A simple text button has a text, a theme, and optionally a CallbackHandler to process its events, as shown in Listing 6–22. It also has a padding for its text content, which we will hard-code to keep the code simple.

Listing 6–22. *The Basic SimpleTextButton Class*

```
package app.module.ui.classes;
...
public class SimpleTextButton extends BaseWidget
{
    protected int PADDING = 5;
    ...

    public SimpleTextButton(String text, CallbackHandler handler, UITheme theme)
    {
        this.text = text;
        this.handler = handler;
        this.theme = theme;
    }
    ...
}
```

Next comes the fun stuff: drawing the button. Its paint() method is shown in Listing 6–23.

Listing 6–23. *The paint() Method*

```
public void paint(Graphics g)
{
        ClipHelper.setClipOn(this, g);
        int bgColor = theme.getNotSelectedBgColor();
        int fgColor = theme.getNotSelectedFgColor();
        if ( isFocused() )
        {
            bgColor = theme.getSelectedBgColor();
            fgColor = theme.getSelectedFgColor();
        }

        // Draw BG
        g.setColor(bgColor);
```

```
        g.fillRoundRect(getAbsoluteX(), getAbsoluteY(), getTotalWidth(),
        getTotalHeight(), 15, 15);

        // Draw text;
        g.setColor(fgColor);
        g.setFont(theme.getSelectedFont());
        int sizeInPixels = theme.getSelectedFont().stringWidth(text);
        int posX = (getTotalWidth() - sizeInPixels) / 2;
        g.drawString(text, getAbsoluteX() + posX, getAbsoluteY()+PADDING,
        Graphics.TOP | Graphics.LEFT );

        ClipHelper.resetClip(g);
}
```

The interesting part of the code is highlighted. You can see that we set the appropriate clip on the Graphics object before drawing the button, so as not to overflow its visible area, and that we set the background and foreground colors according to the theme used and whether the button is focused.

Finally, let's see how user interactions are handled. The appropriate methods are shown in Listing 6–24.

Listing 6–24. *Handling User Interactions*

```
public boolean handleKeyReleased(int key)
{
        if ( GameCanvas.FIRE == KeyHelper.getGameAction(key) )
        {
                fireEvent();
                return true;
        }
        return false;
}

public boolean handlePointerReleased(int x, int y)
{
        super.handlePointerReleased(x,y);
        fireEvent();
        return true;
}

protected void fireEvent()
{
        if ( handler != null )
        {
                Event event = new Event(EVT.CONTEXT.UI_MODULE, EVT.UI.BUTTON_PRESSED,
                this);
                handler.doCallback(event);
        }
}
```

The code is extremely simple and no comments are needed—and yet, surprisingly, it works! In its current state, the SimpleTextButton is good enough for our purposes; however, if we wanted to make things more interesting, we could have made the button smarter by detecting whether it is pressed and change its drawing colors appropriately—feel free to do so yourself if you want to.

That's all there is to our `SimpleTextButton` class. Let's now move to something more complex, the `StringItem` class.

The StringItem Class

As the name suggests, a `StringItem` is a widget that displays text. This is extremely easy to do in its simplest form, but we want to spice things up by having the `StringItem` display only two lines of text when it is not focused, and the full text (or as much of it as it fits in the given bounds) when it is focused—in other words, the widget can dynamically change its size. Also, like the `SimpleTextButton`, the widget will trigger a `BUTTON_PRESSED` event upon activation. The methods for this are identical to the ones in `SimpleTextButton`, so they will not be presented here.

We'll start with the basic constructor for the class, as shown in Listing 6–25.

Listing 6–25. *The* `StringItem` *Constructor*

```
package app.module.ui.classes;

import app.module.ui.helpers.UITextHelper;
...

public class StringItem extends BaseWidget
{
    protected String [] linesSelected, linesNotSelected;
    ....

    public StringItem(String string, int maxLineWidth, int maxTextHeight,
    CallbackHandler handler, UITheme theme)
    {
        this.maxHeight = maxTextHeight;
        this.maxWidth = maxLineWidth;
        this.theme = theme;
         this.handler = handler;
        setText(string);
    }

    public void setText(String text)
    {
        linesSelected = UITextHelper.wrapText(text, maxWidth, maxHeight,
        theme.getSelectedFont());
        linesNotSelected = UITextHelper.wrapText(text, maxWidth,
        theme.getNotSelectedFont().getHeight() * 2, theme.getNotSelectedFont());
        ...
    }
}
```

You can see from the highlighted code that the widget keeps tracks of two sets of text lines, the one to be used when it is focused and the one to be used when it is not focused. Calculation of the `String` arrays is done by the `UITextHelper`, which can neatly reformat and clip text so that it fits within the given width and height when rendered with the specified font.

Next up are the `onFocus()` and `onLostFocus()` methods, shown in Listing 6–26.

Listing 6–26. *The* onFocus() *and* onLostFocus() *Methods*

```
public boolean onFocus()
{
        super.onFocus();
        if ( getParent() != null )
        {
                getParent().doLayout();
        }
        return true;
}

public boolean onLostFocus()
{
        super.onLostFocus();
        if ( getParent() != null )
        {
                getParent().doLayout();
        }
        return false;
}
```

The interesting parts of the methods are the doLayout() calls. These are necessary, as the size of the widget changes whenever focus changes. In fact, all dynamically sized widgets must call getParent().doLayout() whenever their size changes so that the parent container gets the chance to rearrange everything.

Determining the height of the widget is also done dynamically based on focus state, as can be seen in Listing 6–27.

Listing 6–27. *Dynamically Determining the Size of a* StringItem

```
public int getPreferredContentHeight()
{
        Font font = theme.getNotSelectedFont() ;
        String [] text = linesNotSelected;
        if ( isFocused() )
        {
                font = theme.getSelectedFont();
                text = linesSelected;
        }
        return PADDING * 2 + text.length * font.getHeight();
}
```

Drawing the widget is done dynamically too, as shown in Listing 6–28. You can see that the entire color scheme is changed based on whether the widget is focused.

Listing 6–28. *Drawing the* StringItem

```
public void paint(Graphics g)
{
        ClipHelper.setClipOn(this, g);
        int bgColor = theme.getNotSelectedBgColor();
        int fgColor = theme.getNotSelectedFgColor();
        String [] text = linesNotSelected;
        Font f = theme.getNotSelectedFont();
        if ( isFocused() )
        {
```

```
            bgColor = theme.getSelectedBgColor();
            fgColor = theme.getSelectedFgColor();
            f = theme.getSelectedFont();
            text = linesSelected;
        }

        // Draw the background
        g.setColor(bgColor);
        g.fillRect(getAbsoluteX(), getAbsoluteY(), getTotalWidth(), getTotalHeight());

        // Draw the text
        g.setColor(fgColor);
        g.setFont(f);
        int i=0;
        for (i=0;i<text.length;i++)
        {
                g.drawString(text[i], getAbsoluteX()+PADDING,
                getAbsoluteY()+PADDING+f.getHeight()*i, Graphics.TOP | Graphics.LEFT );
        }
        ClipHelper.resetClip(g);
}
```

I would like to point out at this point the very intimate relationship between paint() and getPreferredHeight(). Both methods must be speaking the same language and calculating based on the same reference numbers (font size, for example), otherwise the widget will be either too small or too large for the text it has to display.

Now that we have our SimpleTextItem, we can create an input component based on it, which the user can use to enter text.

InputStringItem

This widget will be used to get text from the user. Code-wise, it will be a combination of a StringItem and a native TextBox. Its text will be displayed as a StringItem, but when the user activates it (via touch or by pressing FIRE) it will display a native TextBox in which the user can enter text instead of triggering a BUTTON_PRESSED event. Then, when the user presses OK in the TextBox, the widget will forward a TEXT_CHANGED event to its callback handler, if any.

> **NOTE:** Normally, UI frameworks have their own custom-written input fields and do not rely on native components like the TextBox. However, writing custom input fields requires a lot of time and effort, and could very well have an entire book dedicated to it. As such, we will use the native TextBox instead.

The bulk of the work is already done for us in StringItem, so we can concentrate on implementing only the new functionality, which is displaying the TextBox and retrieving text from it.

Let's start with the basic class declaration and constructor, shown in Listing 6–29.

Listing 6–29. *InputStringItem Declaration and Constructor*

```
package app.module.ui.classes;

...

public class InputStringItem extends StringItem implements CommandListener
{
    protected CallbackHandler handler;
    protected Command CMD_OK, CMD_CANCEL;
    protected String label;
    protected TextBox textBox;
    protected View oldView;

    public InputStringItem (String label, String initialText, String OKText, String
    cancelText, int maxLineWidth, int maxTextHeight, UITheme theme)
    {
        super(initialText, maxLineWidth, maxTextHeight, theme);
        this.label = label;

        // Prepare the TextBox commands
        CMD_OK = new Command(OKText,Command.SCREEN,0 ) ;
        CMD_CANCEL = new Command (cancelText, Command.SCREEN, 1);
    }
    ...
}
```

As you can see, the InputStringItem will implement the CommandListener interface. This is done so that we may handle commands received from the TextBox.

Next up are the user event handling methods, as shown in Listing 6–30. They are very similar to the ones in SimpleTextButton, the sole exception being that we call showTextBox() instead of fireEvent(). The event will be fired only when the OK command is activated in the TextBox.

Listing 6–30. *User Event Handling Methods*

```
public boolean handleKeyReleased(int key)
{
        if ( GameCanvas.FIRE == KeyHelper.getGameAction(key) )
        {
                showTextBox();
                return true;
        }
        return false;
}

public boolean handlePointerReleased(int x, int y)
{
        super.handlePointerReleased(x,y);
        showTextBox();
        return true;
}
```

The showTextBox() method, which displays the actual TextBox, is shown in Listing 6–31.

Listing 6–31. *The showTextBox() Method*

```
public void showTextBox()
{
        Display d = Display.getDisplay(Application.getMIDlet());
        TextBox t = new TextBox(label,getText(),1024,0);
        t.addCommand(CMD_OK);
        t.addCommand(CMD_CANCEL);
        t.setCommandListener(this);
        oldView = getParentView();
        d.setCurrent(t);
}
```

The important things here are to keep track of the currently displayed View and to register this instance of InputStringItem as the command listener for the TextBox.

Finally, handling commands received from the TextBox and firing the appropriate event are shown in Listing 6–32.

Listing 6–32. *Handling Commands Received from the TextBox*

```
public void commandAction(Command c, Displayable d)
{
        if ( CMD_OK == c )
        {
                setText( ( (TextBox) d).getString() );
                if ( getParent() != null )
                {
                        getParent().doLayout();
                }
                if ( oldView != null )
                {
                                Application.showView(oldView);
                }
                fireEvent();
        }
        else
        if ( CMD_CANCEL == c)
        {
            if ( oldView != null )
            {
                Application.showView(oldView);
            }
        }
}

protected void fireEvent()
{
        if ( handler != null )
        {
                Event event = new Event(EVT.CONTEXT.UI_MODULE, EVT.UI.TEXT_CHANGED,
                this);
                handler.doCallback(event);
        }
}
```

Since the size of the widget can change depending on what text the user has entered, we call getParent().doLayout() to reformat the parent container. Also important, although it may not look like it, is the order of calls in the highlighted section of the code. If the calls were to be inversed, then the event would be handled first. If, as a consequence of handling the event, the application switches to another view, then this switch will be overridden as soon as fireEvent() completes execution, as the oldView will be displayed. By first switching the view and then handling the event, we ensure that this cannot happen.

GameCanvasView

As the name suggest, this is a view based on a GameCanvas. Hierarchically speaking, views are top-level containers. We can use this to our advantage by wrapping our GameCanvasView around a VerticalContainer—that is, we will forward most of the Container calls to the VerticalContainer and let it handle them.

In order to do this, we must first properly construct and initialize our class, as shown in Listing 6–33.

Listing 6–33. *Initializing the GameCanvasView*

```
package app.module.ui.classes;
...
public class GameCanvasView extends GameCanvas implements View, Container
{
        ...
    protected ClipRect clipRect;
    protected VerticalContainer container = null;
    protected UITheme theme;

    public GameCanvasView(boolean b, UITheme theme)
    {
        super(b);
        setFullScreenMode(true);
        clipRect = new ClipRect(0,0,getWidth(),getHeight());
        container = new VerticalContainer(theme);
        container.setParent(this);
        container.setContentHeight(getHeight());
        container.setContentWidth(getWidth());
    }
        ...
}
```

The highlighted portion of the code is where the magic happens. Basically we construct a container and configure it so that the view is its parent and that it is as big as the screen itself.

From here, we can just forward calls to the container like in Listing 6–34.

Listing 6–34. *Forwarding Calls to the Container*

```
...
public boolean addWidget(BaseWidget b)
{
        return container.addWidget(b);
}
```

```
public boolean insertWidget(BaseWidget b, int index)
{
        return container.insertWidget(b, index);
}

public void removeWidget(BaseWidget b)
{
        container.removeWidget(b);
}

public void paint (Graphics g)
{
        ...
        container.paint(g);
        ...
}
...
```

However, some calls we can't forward to the container. For example, we can't forward the view's getYScroll() to the container because that would mean the container would take its own scroll into consideration when calculating its absolute position—which obviously makes no sense. Similar reasoning applies to all methods related to the view's position and scroll. Because of this, all calls to scroll and position setters are ignored and all calls to getters return 0; in effect the view is fixed at coordinates (0,0) with no scroll. This is OK most of the time, and when you absolutely need to set the scroll on the view, then you can just call getContainer() to get the underlying container and then call setYScroll() on it. This is a bit of a hack, and if this were any platform other than Java ME, I would strongly recommend against it, but in our case the benefits in terms of code size, simplicity, and speed outweigh the cost.

Now that everything is up and running, it's time for a little test.

Testing the UI Module

Now that all our widgets are written, let's use them all together in a single test MIDlet. The code for this test MIDlet is shown in Listing 6–35.

Listing 6–35. *The Test MIDlet for the UI Module*

```
package test;

...

public class TestMidlet extends MIDlet implements CallbackHandler
{
    public boolean doCallback(Event evt)
    {
        System.out.println("EVENT " + evt.getType() + " RECEIVED FROM " +
        evt.getPayload() );
        return true;
    }

    public void startApp()
    {
```

```
        // Initialize stuff
        Application.init(this);
        UITheme theme = new AppTheme();
        GameCanvasView view = new GameCanvasView(false,theme);

        // Add some widgets
        for (int i=0; i<= 10; i++)
        {
            SimpleTextButton button = new SimpleTextButton("BUTTON #" + i, this,
            theme);

            InputStringItem inputStrItem = new InputStringItem("Enter text",
            "INPUT STRING ITEM #" + i,"Okay", "Nope", 100, 30, this, theme);

            view.addWidget(button);
            view.addWidget(inputStrItem);
        }

        // Create a horizontal container
        HorizontalContainer container = new HorizontalContainer(theme);
        container.setContentWidth(view.getWidth());

        // Add some widgets to the horizontal container
        for (int i=0; i<= 10; i++)
        {
            StringItem stringItem = new StringItem("#" + i + " This is a very very
            long string which will not fit in the small view", 77, 400, this, theme);
            container.addWidget(stringItem);
        }

        // Add the container to the main view
        view.addWidget(container);

        // Layout everything
        container.doLayout();
        view.doLayout();

        // Focus the view
        view.onFocus();

        // Display the view
        Application.showView(view);
    }
}
```

If you run this code, you'll get something that looks like Figure 6–4.

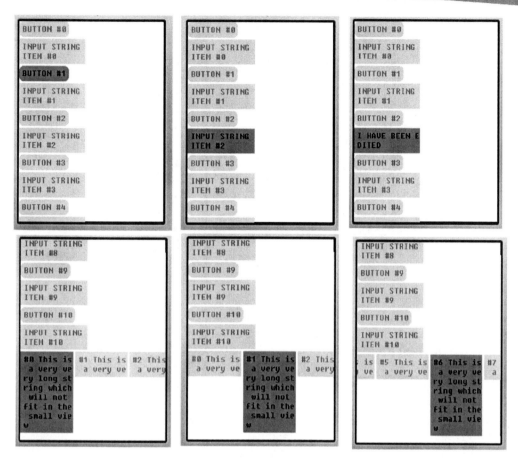

Figure 6–4. *The test application for the UI module*

Granted, it's not the prettiest application out there, but it does have all the basic elements of a modern UI: widgets, containers, support for nested containers, touch support, scrolling, and support for user interaction events. This is not bad, considering we started writing it from scratch. Of course, there are probably a few quirks here and there, and some corner cases that are not covered properly, but for all intents and purposes this is a functional and usable UI.

And this is just the beginning of the fun: now you play around with the code, create new widgets, and improve the existing ones. You could, for example, add borders and scrollbars to containers. Or you could implement check boxes and radio buttons to complement the existing array of widgets. It's up to you!

Implementing UIs on Touch-Only Devices

An increasingly common usage scenario is running your application on touch-only devices. This used to be the realm of expensive smartphones, but relatively cheap Java

ME touchscreen-only devices have gradually started to appear on the market, and their number is bound to increase as the technology gets more affordable.

What is interesting about touchscreen-only devices is that they rely on a virtual onscreen navigation area (usually containing direction keys, softkeys, and a fire/OK button) to provide compatibility with existing non-touch applications. This navigation area can be disabled most of the time (either via a property in the JAD file or from the device's menu), allowing you to break away from the classical and now somewhat antiquated Java ME user-interaction paradigm.

For example, in a typical Java ME application, one of the softkeys is usually dedicated to the "contextual menu" for the currently focused item. On a touch-only device, you can implement a click-and-hold behavior to display the contextual menu: if the user presses an item long enough (3–5 seconds), its contextual menu pops up. This feels more intuitive than the classical approach for most users, and has the advantage of being faster in many situations, as the user has to do only one action (keep the item pressed) rather than two (navigate to the desired item, press the softkey button).

You also have more freedom in the way you do the layout of your application. Classical Java ME applications, even those built using a high-quality UI framework, typically have a rectangular approach to UI layout, i.e., from any given item you can go left, right, up, or down. The reason for this is obvious: classical Java ME applications are designed to be navigated by using the joystick, which can go in only those four directions. Touch-only devices do not have this limitation; you can build your UI around any shape or layout you desire.

For example, the contextual menu discussed previously does not have to be a classical vertical menu: it can be a series of pictograms arranged in a circle. In this "circular menu" you can have item-specific commands in the upper half, and generic commands such as copy and paste in the lower half. This makes navigation not only faster, but also easier and more intuitive: users know that, if they want to paste something, the paste icon will always be in the same spot on the screen regardless of what item-specific options are in the contextual menu.

Another touch-specific feature you can implement is "drag and drop." This is especially useful when the application you are writing works with lists or tables, as the user can then easily and intuitively rearrange his data and content.

Support for finger gestures is also a very nice feature to have. This goes beyond the now-classical kinetic scrolling. For example, a swipe from right to left across the screen can signify a "go back" command, a "V" swipe across the screen could be an "OK" command, while two swipes in the form of an "X" could be the equivalent of "cancel." This makes user interaction faster, more intuitive, and more fun.

Another concept that works well with touch-only interfaces is the concept of panes. While full-fledged windows are not really feasible due to the limited screen size and resolution, panes are sometimes a perfect fit for the activity at hand. For example, in a chat program, the screen is typically divided in two areas: the upper area, where the conversation is shown, and the lower area, where the user can type in messages. By using panes, the user is free to distribute the available screen real estate as needed between the two areas simply by dragging the pane divider.

There are many more UI optimizations that you can implement on touch-only devices and that can make using your application easier and more intuitive, and set it apart from the rest of the crowd. The catch is that your application must target only touch-only devices for many of these optimizations to work. For example, the circular menu paradigm doesn't work really well with non-touch input (as is the case with classical Java ME phones or mixed touch-and-keyboard devices).

With this in mind, if your budget is tight and the range of target devices for your project contains both touch-only and mixed/non-touch devices, go for a classical UI paradigm that works well on all of them. However, if your budget allows it, it is worth considering creating a specialized UI for touch-only devices; the improved usability and image capital you will gain from it are certainly worth it.

Final Words About the UI Module

One thing you should consider before setting off to write your UI module is its granularity. For example, we chose to have scrolling and containers implemented in a single class, but for other projects, it might make sense to have two separate classes, Container (which would handle the collection of UI widgets) and Viewport (which would handle scrolling and determine the visible area of the container). Scrollbars could be built in into the Viewport, or they could be stand-alone components *attached* to the Viewport.

Determining the right granularity for your UI module is not an exact science, but there are some guidelines. First of all, think about component reuse. If scrollbars are needed only inside viewports, then you might as well have them built in. However, if you plan to use scrollbars inside other components, or as sliders, then it makes sense to have them be stand-alone.

Second, think about overhead. You could expand the granularity concept all the way to the pixel level, and have each pixel be an individual component of a larger widget, say a button, but that would slow your application to a crawl. Generally, it is best if you have at most three levels of sub-widgets. For example, a viewport can be defined as being made up of a visible container area and a scrollbar, the scrollbar is composed of two buttons (for the up and down arrows) and a sliding area, and each button component has an image inside it. However, in practice it is best if you stick to one or two levels, as anything more tends to greatly increase overhead and code complexity.

Third, and somewhat related to the last point, consider code complexity and overhead. If each of your components and sub-components is simple and straightforward, then you can afford to increase granularity. However, if by nature your widgets are complex and intricate, then each layer you add will only make things more difficult to understand and slower to run and will increase the potential for bugs. If during the design phase of the UI module, you reach a point where you are no longer 100% certain of how widgets work together, consider simplifying their functionality and their inter-connections, or reducing granularity. You can, of course, continue with having "uncertainties" and say that "you'll cross that bridge when you get to it," but in the long run this decision will always come back to haunt you.

Another thing you should consider is separating UI functionality from UI polish. This is related to compartmentalization (see ahead). For example, you may want to have a `Button` class to provide the functionality of a button, and a `ButtonRenderer` to do the actual rendering. This has obvious advantages but is not always needed, especially for custom UIs written for a single project or set of projects. It does make sense to do this; however, if you plan on writing a universal and full-featured UI framework to be used in all your projects, it most certainly makes sense if you plan to go cross-platform—for example, targeting both Java ME and Android devices (more on this later in the book).

The level of "intelligence" your UI has is also something to keep in mind. For example, a smart UI can detect when the user "flicks" a widget, and can translate this into a kinetic scrolling gesture if the widget in question can be scrolled. Or it could differentiate between focusing via keys and focusing via touch, and treat each case differently (there are some subtle differences between the two; for example, when focusing via touch, the widget in question does not need to be fully visible—the user can just scroll it into view). UI intelligence is different than application intelligence, as it is fully contained in the UI module and does not affect the rest of the application's behavior; however, it does affect the user's experience and this makes it important.

Compartmentalizing your UI module is always good. Many third-party libraries have poor or no provisions for this, and thus force you to include a lot of extra support code just so you can use that one widget or behavior you really need. This is an area where custom-made UIs can really shine, as you can design them to be as modular as you need them. The main benefit of a modular UI is that it widens the range of devices you can target, as you can include everything (polished components, smart behavior, extra features, etc.) in builds for high-end devices while keeping only the needed minimum for low-end ones. Compartmentalization is not the same as granularity. Granularity refers to how many "levels of depth" widgets have, while compartmentalization refers to how independent various aspects and features of your UI module are from one another. We will discuss how compartmentalization can be done later in the book.

Finally, but certainly not least, remember that you are writing a UI for a mobile device, where screen space is at a premium and user interaction must be as intuitive as possible. With respect to this, try to keep the UI as simple and as less cluttered as possible. For example, scrollbars don't always have to be on the screen. It is usually enough to draw them over the container when the user is scrolling and hide them at all other times—this saves the screen real estate that would otherwise be constantly dedicated to them while at the same time keeping the interface clean. It is a common mistake to approach writing mobile UIs with the same mindset with which you would approach writing a desktop UI, especially because there are many similarities between them. However, some concepts have to be adapted (like the foregoing scrollbar example) while others have to be discarded altogether (mobile devices have no place for the concept of desktop-like windows that can be dragged around the screen).

Summary

In this chapter, we have learned how to write a Java ME UI module from scratch. Some of the important aspects and the associated theoretical concepts we have discussed are clipping rectangles, nested widgets, and properly handling user interaction events such as keypresses.

In the process, we have written the UI module for our Twitter client, which features buttons, string items, editable string items, horizontal containers, vertical containers, touch support, and support for nested widgets.

In the next chapter, we will look at how to handle localization and internationalization in the context of Java ME applications.

Chapter **7**

The Localization Module

Localization, or L10n for short, is extremely important for mobile applications, as their users expect them to be as friendly and as intuitive to use as possible. Having the application running in the user's own language and with the user's own locale-specific settings is thus crucial.

At its heart, localization simply involves having separate versions of certain strings for each locale you want your application to support. These strings can be displayed directly to the user, as is the case with command names and button labels, or they can contain metadata—for example, the proper date format or currency symbol to be used for a given locale.

In this chapter, we will discuss the main options available for Java ME localization, and we will learn how to add localization support to our application from scratch, in a simple and clean way. We will also learn how to efficiently handle common localization-related tasks, such as generating and loading localization files and handling the formatting of currency, dates, and times.

Understanding the Features of a Good Localization Module

A good localization module should be flexible, simple, and intelligent. It should have a small code footprint, as well as a small resource footprint. It should be easily extensible and be written in such a way as to provide support for a multitude of possible input sources.

Localization strings are typically stored as key/value pairs, where the key is a universal identifier like "button.quit.label" and the value is the string itself. These key/value pairs can be retrieved from many sources: from the Web, from text files inside the JAR, or they can even be hard-coded within the application (by using themes, for example). Some applications combine multiple sources.

Choosing the right input source or sources is important, as each source has its pros and cons. For example, having localization hard-coded into the application as part of themes is very fast, but it has the disadvantages of being hard to update by non-programmers and of being impossible to update at runtime (via the Web, for example). Using files stored inside the application JAR is an improvement, as updating localization strings can be done easily by non-programmers and the mechanism for file-based localization can easily be extended to support web-based localization (or at least updating via the Web). Finally, web-based localization (where localization files are downloaded from the Web) is by far the most flexible approach, but it has the disadvantages of not being free and of depending on an Internet connection being available.

Another feature of a good localization module is that selecting the right locale is done transparently inside the localization module. The application code should be able to specify an optional user-preferred locale as well as a mandatory default locale, but it is up to the localization module to choose which locale to actually use. Typically the order of priorities is as follows: user specified locale, phone's current locale (which can be retrieved at runtime), and finally the application's default locale. Other than specifying the user's preferred locale and the default locale, general application code should not care about locales at all, nor should it care about what locale is actually used. All it should do is request from the localization module the value of a certain key and use that value accordingly.

A good localization module should also provide support for parameterized locale strings ("You have X e-mails"). Parameterized localization strings are extremely important, which is why it's quite amazing that most Java ME localization frameworks I've seen all have one glaring omission: they don't take into consideration the value of the parameters. Specifically, it is often the case that the template for X=0 is slightly different than the one for X=1 or X>=2. In the foregoing example, for X=0 the template would read "No new e-mails", for X=1 it would read "You have one new e-mail", and for X>=2 it would read "You have X new e-mails". If support for this isn't added in the localization module, it has to be added in the application code, which, as we have seen, is bad practice. Of course, X can also be a string (as opposed to a number), and for any localization string you can have one "general template" and as many custom templates as needed.

Understanding Native Java ME Localization

Java ME does have its own "built-in" localization and internationalization support in the form of the Mobile Internationalization API, also known as JSR 238. The Mobile Internationalization API has provisions for the most common localization-related tasks, which are the localization of strings and resources and the formatting of currency, numbers, dates, and times.

The biggest advantage of JSR 238 is, of course, its speed and resource consumption: being implemented as a native API, it is usually more efficient in these respects than non-native APIs, sometimes considerably more so.

However, JSR 238 does have two major drawbacks. First and foremost, it is not available on all devices. This means that you can rely on it only if you exclusively target devices that support it, otherwise you will have to roll your own localization support for those devices that do not support JSR 238.

Second, it is not as flexible or as powerful as a properly written custom localization implementation. For example, for JSR 238 localization and resource files must reside within the application's JAR, so there is no way to download new localization data and new resources from the Web, and parameterized localization strings are also not supported.

Because of these two drawbacks, most developers choose to roll their own implementation for a localization module. However, it should be noted that JSR 238 can be (and in fact is) a good choice if you target only JSR 238–enabled devices and if you need only the feature that JSR 238 supports and nothing else.

Adding Custom Localization Support to a Java ME Application

Now that we know what a good localization module looks like, and why utilizing JSR 238 is generally not feasible, we can begin writing our own custom localization support module.

For our application, we will implement only file-based localization (with the localization files stored inside the JAR); however, we will include support for reading localization files from generic `DataInputStreams`, so you can add web-based localization support if you want.

The first thing we need to do is to define a structure for our localization files. We want something that is both easy to parse and easy to understand, so we'll go for the generic structure shown in Listing 7–1.

Listing 7–1. *The Generic Localization File Structure*

```
<key #1>
<value #1>
<key #2>
<value #2>

# Lines starting with "#" are comment lines
# so you can use them to explain what each translation is used for, for example.
# Empty lines are also ignored.

<key #3>
<value #3>

...
```

As for the key/value pairs, they come in two forms: generic and parameter-specific. A generic key/value pair is shown in Listing 7–2.

Listing 7–2. *A Generic Key/Value Pair*

```
some.key
This is the value of "some.key", and here --> {@} <-- is the parameter

new.email
You have {@} new emails
```

The convention for keys is that they are unique and that "." is used instead of spaces to separate the pieces (or words) of each key. The convention for values is that each value can have at most one parameter and that the parameter is marked with the character sequence "{@}". The restriction for having at most one parameter is there because otherwise supporting parameter-specific keys would be extremely difficult: if your value has two parameters, and each parameter has three special cases and a generic case, then you will need to have 4×4=16 key/value pairs to cover all possible combinations, which is not feasible. If you do need to have two parameters in the same string, all you have to do is simply split that string into two smaller ones, with one parameter each.

Parameter-specific key/value pairs are almost identical to generic key/value pairs, as can be seen in Listing 7–3.

Listing 7–3. *Parameter-Specific Key/Value Pairs*

```
some.key:1
This is the value for when the parameter is 1

some.key:a string value
This is the value for when the parameter is "a string value"

new.email:0
No new emails

new.email:1
One new email
```

The only difference is that after the key name a ":" is added, followed by the parameter value to which that key/value pair pertains. This can be seen in the highlighted portion of the snippet. You will also notice that parameter-specific key/value pairs have no parameter placeholder in their values. Since the value of the parameter is known, you can directly insert it in the value instead of the placeholder. That being said, you *can* use parameter placeholders, but doing so makes little sense, except perhaps to save some space.

So how does this whole key/value thing work? Supposed we wanted to retrieve the value corresponding to the key "new.email" with a parameter of 5. The localization module will first check to see if a "new.email:5" key exists. Since none exists, it will simply use the generic "new.email" key with the appropriate parameter. Thus, it will return "You have 5 new emails". If the parameter's value would have been 0, then the localization module would have returned "No new emails" instead, corresponding to the parameter-specific "new.email:0" key.

As for the localization files themselves, they will be named after the locales they implement—for example, "en-US.bin" or "ro-RO.bin"—and they will be stored in the package app.files.L10n. The reason these files are .bin files as opposed to .txt files will be discussed shortly.

Processing Localization Files

Now that we know how to create our localization files, the next step is to load the files into our Java ME application. Unfortunately, this is easier said than done.

The reason for this is simple: Java ME doesn't have anything resembling a readLine() method, which would allow us to read the files line by line. Thus, we are forced to process the files character by character, or rather byte by byte as Java's char data type is two bytes long, and thus incompatible with either plain ASCII or UTF-8 encodings. However, while processing files byte by byte is certainly doable, it is also extremely slow (especially by Java ME standards) and can prove to be quite complicated. Fortunately, there's a far better way to solve our file-reading problem.

While Java ME doesn't have a readLine() method, its DataInputStream class does have a readUTF() method, which can read Java UTF–encoded strings. There's one catch, though: readUTF() uses a modified UTF encoding scheme (as defined in Java's specs), so using it to read regular UTF strings or plain-text files will fail. To get around this problem, we will use a little trick—namely, we will process the original translation files using a J2SE application, which will output binary files that can be read by Java ME's readUTF() method.

This is actually a lot easier than it sounds. Furthermore, it allows us to streamline and optimize the output translation files on the J2SE side—for example, by removing all comments and empty lines, thus providing an extra speed boost and decreasing overall JAR size. The J2SE application that does this is shown in Listing 7–4.

Listing 7–4. *Processing Translation Files on the J2SE Side*

```
package com.apress;

...

public class TranslationFileConverter {

    public static void main(String[] args) {
        String sourceFile = args[0];
        String destFile = args[1];
        String lineIn = "";
        try
        {
            DataInputStream in = new DataInputStream( new FileInputStream(sourceFile));
            BufferedReader br = new BufferedReader(new InputStreamReader(in));
            DataOutputStream out = new DataOutputStream(new FileOutputStream(
                            destFile));

            while ( ( lineIn = br.readLine()) != null )
            {
                // Ignore comments and empty lines
                if ( lineIn.length() == 0 || lineIn.charAt(0) == '#' )
```

```
                {
                    continue;
                }
                out.writeUTF(lineIn);
            }

            out.close();
            br.close();
        }
        catch (Exception ex)
        {
            ex.printStackTrace();
            // Do nothing
        }
    }

}
```

The highlighted lines are where the magic happens. Unlike Java ME, J2SE does have a readLine() method, which makes reading the original input files incredibly easy. Furthermore, J2SE's writeUTF() method is compatible with J2ME's readUTF() method, since they implement the same encoding standard—so that's another problem that's taken care of quite easily. In the end, all the J2SE application does is read valid lines from the original input file and write them one after another in the output file as readUTF()–compatible strings, which can easily be read from Java ME.

To use the application, all you have to do is run the following line at the command prompt:

```
java -jar TranslationFileConverter.jar C:\translations\en-US.txt C:\output\en-US.bin
```

The first parameter is the location of the original translation file, while the second parameter is the location of the output file. As a convention to help differentiate between the original files and the processed files, the processed ones will have a ".bin" extension. Finally, make sure that both directories (for the original and processed files) are valid and existing before running the application.

We'll stop here with processing translation files, but keep in mind that the entire process can be taken one step further. It's important to realize that, in the end, output files always look like Listing 7–5.

Listing 7–5. *What Translation Output Files Look Like*

```
<key 1> <value 1> <key 2> <value 2> … <key XX> <value XX>
```

This structure is extremely simple, with no newlines or special delimiters present, and with a very basic and easy to understand structure. A side effect of this is that the input files can have pretty much any format and structure, as long as that format can be translated in the end into plain key/value pairs. This means, for example, that you can change the input format for your language files to XML or JSON (or even take the translations straight from a database), that you can enhance the structure of your language files by adding preprocessing capabilities (for example, an "include" directive), that you can add dynamic elements such as "if" statements and loops, etc. As long as the output matches the structure in Listing 7–5, you're free to do anything you want.

While this degree of flexibility is usually not needed, it's great to know that it is available should the need for it arise.

Loading Localization Data on the Device

As mentioned previously, the main source for localization data will be files found within the JAR itself, but we will also provide support for loading localization data from any generic `DataInputStream`.

Before we can do this, however, we need to get the basic structure of the localization module ready. This is very simple to do, as at its core the localization module relies on the very basic key/value pair concept, which is exactly what the `Hashtable` class provides. Thus, the skeleton for the localization module will look like the code in Listing 7–6.

Listing 7–6. *The Skeleton for the Localization Module*

```
package app.module.L10n.classes;

...

public class Locale
{
    protected static Hashtable keyValuePairs = new Hashtable();

    ...
}
```

The `Locale` class will be the heart of the localization module (in fact, it will be the *entire* localization module). The keyValuePairs hashtable is what we will use to store all the key/value pairs from the localization files. Hashtables allow for quick lookup at the cost of some memory overhead. This overhead is typically acceptable and negligible. However, if you're targeting a really low-end device with extremely limited memory or if the `Hashtable` implementation of your target device is extremely memory-wasteful, then you might want to switch to using a `Vector` or even a fixed array instead. While saving memory, this will typically increase the CPU cost of lookup operations. Fortunately, these "out of memory" scenarios are quite rare, and when they do occur, the root cause tends to lie not in the localization module but in some other memory-intensive part of the application.

Now we have to get the data from the localization files into the hashtable. Just to keep our options open, we will want to load our data from an internal JAD file, from a byte array, or from an abstract `InputStream`. Loading data from a byte array might seem unnecessary, but it is often needed when the localization data is part of a larger data set— for example, when it is deserialized from a persistent record containing multiple objects. Thus, the data loading code will look like the one in Listing 7–7.

Listing 7-7. *Loading Localization Data from Various Sources*

```
public static boolean loadFromInternalFile(String internalFile)
{
        try
        {
                InputStream stream = Locale.class.getResourceAsStream(internalFile);
                if ( stream == null )
                {
                        return false;
                }
                DataInputStream in = new DataInputStream(stream);
                if ( in.available() == 0 )
                {
                        return false;
                }
                return loadFromDataInputStream(in);
        }
        catch (Exception ex)
        {
                return false;
        }
}

public static boolean loadFromByteArray(byte [] data, int offset, int length)
{
        DataInputStream in = new DataInputStream ( new ByteArrayInputStream(data,
        offset,length) );
        return loadFromDataInputStream(in);
}

public static boolean loadFromDataInputStream(DataInputStream in)
{
        String key, value;
        try
        {
                while ( true )
                {
                        key = in.readUTF();
                        value = in.readUTF();
                        keyValuePairs.put(key, value);
                }
        }
        catch (EOFException ex)
        {
                // End of file, we can stop
        }
        catch (IOException ex)
        {
                // Whoops! Read was not successful
                return false;
        }
        return true;
}
```

You can see that both the file-based and array-based methods eventually rely on
loadFromDataInputStream() to do the work. You can also see that all methods are static.

This decision was made so that the Locale class can be easily used from anywhere in the application, the importance of which will become even clearer once we actually start to use the localization functionality.

As for reading the localization data, the highlighted lines are where the magic happens. All we need to do is read key/value pairs in sequence until an EOFException is thrown (in which case the reading was successful) or an IOException is thrown (in which case something went wrong). The mechanism is simple and reliable on the Java ME side, because the original localization files were processed and verified on the J2SE side. In fact, any checks or validations should be done exclusively on the J2SE side of things.

Now that the core loading functionality is there, let's add some helper methods. We're interested in getting the device's current locale, in finding the appropriate localization file within the JAR file based solely on a locale's name, and in figuring out what localization file to load based on the user's preferred locale, the phone's locale, and the default locale. All these are covered by the code in Listing 7–8.

Listing 7–8. *Helper Methods for the Localization Module*

```java
public static String getDeviceLocale()
{
        return System.getProperty("microedition.locale");
}

public static String getLocaleFile(String locale)
{
        if ( locale == null )
        {
                return getLocaleFile(getDeviceLocale());
        }
        return "/app/files/L10n/" + locale + ".bin";
}

public static boolean loadFromFileBasedOnPreferences(String specifiedUserLocale,
String defaultLocale)
{
        // Try to load, in order, the specified user locale, the default locale,
        // and the device locale
        if ( loadFromInternalFile( getLocaleFile(specifiedUserLocale) ) ||
                loadFromInternalFile( getLocaleFile(getDeviceLocale() ) ) ||
                loadFromInternalFile( getLocaleFile(defaultLocale) ) )
        {
                return true;
        }

        // Everything has failed
        return false;
}
```

All of these are convenience methods at this point, as their underlying functionality is really, really simple. The main point of having them in the first place is long-term flexibility. For example, the resolution of locale name to file name in getLocaleFile() is extremely simple right now, but in the long run it might be changed to something more complex—for example, if the requested locale is en-UK, but that's not available, whereas en-US is, then use en-US instead.

Finally, it's time to write the methods that actually do most of the work: retrieving translation values for keys, both general and parameter-specific. Their code is presented in Listing 7–9.

Listing 7–9. *Retrieving Values for Translation Keys*

```
public static String get(String key)
{
        return (String) keyValuePairs.get(key);
}

public static String get(String key, int value)
{
        return get(key, String.valueOf(value) );
}

public static String get(String key, String parameter)
{
    // Try to read the parameter-specific key first
    String originalStr = get(key + ":" + parameter);

    // If no parameter-specific key exists then try to read the generic key
    if ( originalStr == null )
    {
        originalStr = get(key);
    }

    // No key found at all, return null
    if ( originalStr == null )
    {
        return null;
    }

    // See if a parameter placeholder exists
    int placeholderPosition = originalStr.indexOf("{@}");

    // There is no parameter placeholder, return the value as-is
    if ( placeholderPosition == -1 )
    {
        return originalStr;
    }

    // Replace the parameter placeholder with the parameter value
    // and return the resulting string
    return originalStr.substring(0, placeholderPosition) + parameter +
            originalStr.substring(placeholderPosition+3);
}
```

That's it! Our localization module is now ready for use. Let's take it for a test run.

Testing the Localization Module

To test the localization module, the first thing we need to do is create an input localization file. There are two examples at the beginning of this chapter, Listings 7–2 and 7–3, so we'll concatenate both of them into a single file and save that file to `C:\test\en-US.txt`.

After that, we'll need to process the localization file with our J2SE utility, like so:

```
java -jar TranslationFileConverter.jar C:\test\en-US.txt C:\test\en-US.bin
```

The next step is to move the resulting `en-US.bin` file to the appropriate location in the project folder, which is the sub-folder corresponding to the `app.files.L10n` package. Once this is done, we can use the localization module in our application, similar to the way shown in Listing 7–10.

Listing 7–10. *Testing the Localization Module*

```
package test;

...

public class TestMidlet extends MIDlet
{
        ...

    public void startApp()
    {
        // No user-preferred locale, default locale of en-US.
        // Localization module will try to use the phone's current
        // locale, if available, and if not it will default to en-US.
        Locale.loadFromFileBasedOnPreferences(null, "en-US");

        // Two parameter-specific localization strings
        System.out.println ( Locale.get("new.email",0) );
        System.out.println ( Locale.get("new.email",1) );

        // A generic localization string
        System.out.println ( Locale.get("new.email",9999) );

        // Parameters can also be strings
        System.out.println ( Locale.get("new.email","a couple of") );
    }
}
```

The console output will look like this:

```
No new emails
One new email
You have 9999 new emails.
You have a couple of new emails.
```

As you can see, our localization module is compact, flexible, and easy to use.

Implementing Advanced Localization Features

Translating strings from one language to another is easy; however, there's more to localization than this. For example, different locales use different date formats. As Java ME has poor support for localization, we will have to handle these ourselves.

The first thing we need to do is define a localization string that contains the proper date format, something like the snippet in Listing 7–11. We will add this to the en-US localization file.

Listing 7–11. *Defining a Date Format*

```
# Default date format
format.date
D, d/m/y
```

In this example, "d" stands for the day of the month, "m" for the month, "y" for the year, and the capital "D" stands for the day of the week. This is the convention we will use in our localization module.

Next, we need to define the days of the week, like in Listing 7–12. The "zero" day of the week will be used for unknown values (just in case something goes wrong along the way, which really shouldn't happen). Again, add these localization strings to the en-US localization file.

Listing 7–12. *Defining the Days of the Week*

```
# Week day names
weekdays.names:1
Monday

weekdays.names:2
Tuesday

...

weekdays.names:7
Sunday

weekdays.names:0
Unknown
```

The final step we need to complete is writing a date-to-string processing function in the localization module, since Java ME doesn't have one built in. Such a function, with basic support, is shown in Listing 7–13. You may enhance it as needed—for example, by adding support for month names.

Listing 7–13. *Converting Dates to Strings, According to a Given Format*

```
public static String formatDate(String dateFormat, Date date)
{
        Calendar c = Calendar.getInstance();
        c.setTime(date);
        String result;

        String day = String.valueOf(c.get(Calendar.DAY_OF_MONTH));
```

```
        result = UITextHelper.strReplace("d", day, dateFormat);

        String month = String.valueOf(c.get(Calendar.MONTH));
        result = UITextHelper.strReplace("m", month, result);

        String year = String.valueOf(c.get(Calendar.YEAR));
        result = UITextHelper.strReplace("y", year, result);

        int dayOfWeek = c.get(Calendar.DAY_OF_WEEK);
        int dayOfWeekIndex = 0;
        switch (dayOfWeek)
        {
                case Calendar.MONDAY:
                        dayOfWeekIndex = 1;
                        break;

                case Calendar.TUESDAY:
                        dayOfWeekIndex = 2;
                        break;

                ...

                case Calendar.SUNDAY:
                        dayOfWeekIndex = 7;
                        break;

                default:
                        dayOfWeekIndex = 0;
                        break;
        }
        result = UITextHelper.strReplace("D", Locale.get("weekdays.names",
        dayOfWeekIndex), result);

        return result;
}
```

The interesting thing to note here is the fact that the code relies on predefined localization strings (the weekdays.name keys) in order to function properly. This means that these "core strings" must be present in all localization files, otherwise unexpected errors might occur. The code also makes use of UITextHelper.strReplace(), which is a custom string replacement method, as Java ME doesn't have one built in.

Finally, let's put our formatDate() method to work, as shown in Listing 7–14.

Listing 7–14. *A Test of the* formatDate() *Method*

```
Date date = new Date();
String dateFormat = Locale.get("format.date");
System.out.println ( Locale.formatDate(dateFormat, date));
```

Running this code will yield a console output similar to this one:

```
Monday, 22/10/2010
```

Changing the value of the format.date key will also change the output string accordingly. By changing both format.date and weekdays.name keys, you can have the application dynamically match the expected date and time format for any given locale, without altering the actual application code.

The same idea we have used for formatting dates can be used with other aspects of the application that require locale-based formatting—for example, formatting numbers (decimal separators, thousands separators, etc.) and formatting currency. We can also use this mechanism for defining more exotic things, like locale-specific mathematical formulas (for example, the formulas for calculating taxes, which are different from country to country).

Everything in a Java ME application, from button labels to graphics files and math formulas, can be tailored to be locale-specific. As we have seen in this chapter, doing so isn't particularly difficult—it just requires a bit of creative and practical coding.

Summary

We have discussed what localization is and how localization support can be added to a Java ME application. In the process, we have examined some of the more important aspects of a good localization implementation, such as processing and optimizing localization files on the desktop before loading them onto the mobile device, implementing support for parameter-specific keys, and implementing advanced localization features, such as locale-based formatting for objects (dates, currency, etc.).

In the next chapter, we will put together everything we have learned so far and write our Twitter client application. In the process, we will discuss the best practices associated with building a complete Java ME application, such as the proper separation of UI and application logic, defining a clear event structure, and more.

## Chapter 8

Putting It All Together

So far in the book, we have looked at the various individual aspects that make up the bulk of any Java ME application. Now it's time to see how all of them come together to form a complete application.

Throughout this chapter, we'll create the basis of a fully functional Java ME Twitter client, with most of the important features implemented and the rest fairly easy to implement. As we go over the code, you will notice that the main application code base is quite small. The main reasons for this are having a good, flexible architecture and being able to depend heavily on the functionality provided by the application modules we have written so far. In fact, there is very little logic that is actually part of the application itself: most of the heavy work is done in the individual modules.

This results in an application that is fairly easy to understand and work through, portable, and compact—all of which are the most telltale signs of a Pro Java ME application.

That being said, let's get to work.

Jump-Starting the Application

Every Java ME application has to be built upon the `MIDlet` class. Ours is no different; however, we will use our `MIDlet` class only to jump-start the core application framework, associated controllers, and other classes. Thus, the `TwitterClient` MIDlet class will look like Listing 8–1.

Listing 8–1. *The TwitterClient Class*

```
public class TwitterClient extends MIDlet
{
    public void startApp()
    {
        Application.init(this);

        FlowController flowController = new FlowController();
        SettingsController settingsController = new SettingsController();
        WelcomeScreenController welcomeController = new WelcomeScreenController();
```

```
        MainScreenController mainScreenController = new MainScreenController();
        TweetsController tweetsController = new TweetsController();

        Application.getMainEventController().registerListener(tweetsController);
        Application.getMainEventController().registerListener(flowController);
        Application.getMainEventController().registerListener(settingsController);
        Application.getMainEventController().registerListener(welcomeController);
        Application.getMainEventController().registerListener(mainScreenController);

        Event start = new Event(EVT.CONTEXT.STARTUP,
        EVT.PROGRAM_FLOW.APPLICATION_START,null);
        Application.getMainEventController().queueEvent(start);

        Bootstrap.boot(this, 100);
        }


    ...
}
```

That's it. We're done with the TwitterClient class and also with the native part of our application. From now on, everything we do will be exclusively related to our application objects and our framework—no more direct native Java ME calls; they are all hidden from the main application code. This will not only make our application easier to understand and more concise, but also help in any eventual porting effort to other platforms.

Let's look a bit at what happens here. First, we initialize the framework. Then, we create instances of all the controllers we will use in our application. We will go into each of them later. Following their creation, the controllers are all added as listeners to the main event controller and an APPLICATION_START event is queued to the main event controller. Finally, the application is booted with a 100 ms interval between processing events— more than enough for our needs.

> **NOTE:** Throughout this chapter, you will see many references to the EVT class and to the events defined by it. For clarity and readability, the class will be shown in full at the end of the chapter—and only then.

Now, let's see what happens next. The key to initializing the application lies in the APPLICATION_START event. Let's see where it is handled—and how.

Implementing the FlowController

This controller is responsible for handling all major events that affect the application's flow and/or life cycle. These include the application being started up or exited, the device running out of memory or being unable to execute a critical command, etc. Of course, more than one controller can respond to these events (and more than one typically does), but the FlowController is responsible for doing the general and non-module-specific event handling.

For a concrete example, you will see that both the FlowController and the TweetsController respond to the APPLICATION_START event. However, while the TweetsController does tweet-specific stuff (like creating and initializing a ServerImplementation instance), the FlowController does more generic stuff, like loading the appropriate locale based on the user's preferences, if any.

The code for the FlowController class is shown in Listing 8–2.

Listing 8–2. *The* FlowController *Class*

```java
package app.controller;

import app.classes.Defaults;
...

public class FlowController implements Controller, EventListener
{

    public boolean handleEvent(Event event)
    {

        if (EVT.PROGRAM_FLOW.APPLICATION_START == event.getType())
        {
            // Load the user's locale, if any
            String locale = null;
            byte[] data = Defaults.persistenceHelper.getRecord(
            Defaults.DEFAULT_LOCALE_RECORD_NAME);
            if (data != null)
            {
                ByteRecordReader reader = new ByteRecordReader(data);
                locale = reader.readString();
            }
            Locale.loadFromFileBasedOnPreferences(locale, Defaults.DEFAULT_LOCALE);


            // Show the welcome form
            Event showWelcome = new Event(EVT.CONTEXT.STARTUP,
            EVT.PROGRAM_FLOW.SHOW_WELCOME_SCREEN, null);
            Application.getMainEventController().queueEvent(showWelcome);

            return true;

        } else if (EVT.PROGRAM_FLOW.APPLICATION_EXIT == event.getType())
        {
            Defaults.persistenceHelper.close();
            Application.exit();
        } else if ( EVT.PROGRAM_FLOW.INITIATE_SHUTDOWN == event.getType() )
        {
                Event shutdown = new Event(EVT.CONTEXT.SETTINGS_FORM,
                EVT.PROGRAM_FLOW.APPLICATION_PREPARE_SHUTDOWN, null);
                Application.getMainEventController().queueEvent(shutdown);

                shutdown = new Event(EVT.CONTEXT.SETTINGS_FORM,
EVT.PROGRAM_FLOW.APPLICATION_EXIT, null);
Application.getMainEventController().queueEvent(shutdown);
                return true;
        }
```

```
            return false;
        }
    }
```

You can see from the code that our FlowController currently handles only three events: APPLICATION_START, INITIATE_SHUTDOWN, and APPLICATION_EXIT, with the last two closely linked together.

In handling APPLICATION_START, we first try to see if a preferred user locale is set and, if so, we attempt to load it (even if the attempt fails, the default locale will still get loaded). Following that, we issue a SHOW_WELCOME_SCREEN event, which will result in the welcome screen (or form, if you prefer) being shown. This event is handled inside the WelcomeScreenController.

As a side note, you should always switch screens via events, and never directly. This not only allows other parts of the application to respond to the screen switching (for example, by reloading key configuration options when the settings screen is left), but also minimizes the possibility of race conditions, thread deadlocking, and various UI glitches and issues. In the case that these do happen, using events typically makes debugging easier and faster, as it becomes pretty clear what action happens where, and the code fragments themselves are usually small.

The INITIATE_SHUTDOWN event is also interesting, as what it does is set in motion a sequence of events that prepare the application for shutdown and exit. It is basically an umbrella event that helps not only shorten the code base (as you must trigger only a single event instead of two or more) but also clarify how the shutdown process works and what actions are to be performed.

Finally, I would like to point out the heavy use of the Defaults class (shown in Listing 8–3), which contains the default and hard-coded values of various application settings, such as the default locale, the name of the record that stores the preferred user locale, the default persistence helper to use, and more.

Listing 8–3. *The Defaults Class*

```
package app.classes;

...

public class Defaults {

    public static final UITheme THEME = new AppTheme();

    public static final boolean USE_SINGLE_USER_ACCESS = true ;

    public static final int TWEET_BATCH_SIZE = 1;

    public static final String DEFAULT_LOCALE = "en-US";

    public static final String DEFAULT_LOCALE_RECORD_NAME = "locale";

    public static final String DEFAULT_LOGIN_DATA_RECORD_NAME = "loginData";
```

```
public static final PersistenceProvider persistenceProvider = new
RMSPersistenceProvider("twitterclient");

public static SimplifiedPersistenceHelper persistenceHelper = new
SimplifiedPersistenceHelper(persistenceProvider);
}
```

Aside from the obvious benefit of being able to change key values in a single central location, the Defaults class also serves as a good indicator of how flexible an application is: in general, the more values are in it (which actually belong there), the more flexible the application is. For example, the first two highlighted values can be used to easily configure the application for a variety of usage and testing scenarios, by altering the login method to use and the number of tweets to retrieve per batch, while the last highlighted value can be used to change the application from using local RMS persistence to, for example, cloud-based persistence.

With this we have finished covering the FlowController. Let's now move on to the TweetsController.

Implementing the TweetsController

This controller is responsible for handling all tweet-related events and actions, such as posting tweets and retrieving tweets from the server. Let's first have a look at its source code, shown in Listing 8–4.

Listing 8–4. *The TweetsController*

```
package app.controller;

...

public class TweetsController implements Controller, EventListener {

    protected TwitterServer server = null;
    protected Timeline mainTweetTimeline = null;

    public boolean handleEvent(Event event) {
        if ( EVT.PROGRAM_FLOW.APPLICATION_START == event.getType() )
        {
            server = new ServerImplementation("<consumer-key>", "<consumer-secret>",
            Application.getMainEventController());
            return true;
        }
        else
        if ( EVT.NETWORK.LOGIN_SUCCEEDED == event.getType() )
        {
            if ( server == null )
            {
                return false;
            }
            mainTweetTimeline = server.getTimelineForFilter(null);
            return true;
        }
```

```
      else
      if ( EVT.TWEETS.REQUEST_MAIN_TWEETS_BATCH == event.getType() )
      {
          if ( mainTweetTimeline == null )
          {
              return false;
          }
          int count = 0;
          Tweet temp = null;
          while ( count < Defaults.TWEET_BATCH_SIZE )
          {
              temp = mainTweetTimeline.goBack();
              if ( temp == null )
              {
                  break;
              }
              Event evt = new Event ( EVT.CONTEXT.NETWORKING_MODULE,
              EVT.TWEETS.RECEIVED_TWEET, temp);
              Application.getMainEventController().queueEvent(evt);
              count++;
          }
          return true;
      }
      else if ( EVT.TWEETS.POST_TWEET == event.getType() )
      {
          if ( server == null )
          {
              return false;
          }
          Tweet tweet = (Tweet) event.getPayload();
          server.postTweet(tweet);
      }
      return false;
  }

}
```

As you can see, the TweetsController also responds to the APPLICATION_START event, by initializing its TwitterServer. In general, controllers that are almost surely used should initialize their underlying data structures and entities when an APPLICATION_START event is received, while controllers that may not ever be used (as is the case of controllers tied to application forms, something we will see shortly) should initialize their underlying data structures and entities only when actually needed (lazy initialization).

This typically results in a fast startup process and a fairly smooth user experience during runtime, which is especially important if your app is to run on lower-end Java ME devices. As a counter-example, imagine what would happen if all the controllers in an application would initialize themselves at startup: the startup process would take a long time (or longer than necessary, anyway), and there is a distinct possibility that the device would start to run out of resources while attempting to initialize everything at once, which would result in even worse performance or even in application crashes.

Moving on, the code also illustrates a very important principle of writing event-based applications: you should never blindly do something or initiate an action merely as a result of receiving an event. The lines in bold show some very basic checks that our code does before attempting to process events. At first glance, they are mere sanity checks, to ensure that no NullPointerExceptions can occur. While this is true, there is a "hidden" logic behind the checks. In our case, the handling of the "request tweets" event cannot proceed if the Timeline object is not initialized, which in turn is initialized when a login attempt succeeds, which in turn happens only after a successful initialization of the TweetsController during the APPLICATION_START event.

What this all means is that, in effect, you cannot request a tweet unless all the logic steps that precede this action have been carried out—issuing a "request tweets" event out of the blue does nothing. This ensures that events cannot be processed out of sequence or in inappropriate circumstances, which is vital if you plan to use events heavily in your application.

Another point of interest is the way the REQUEST_MAIN_TWEETS_BATCH event is handled. The purpose of this event is to retrieve the next batch of tweets from the server (the batch size is defined in the Defaults class). When the batch is received, instead of calling a pre-set method or returning/processing the batch directly, the code generates a RECEIVED_TWEET event for each tweet in the batch. This event can then be processed in any other controller, or even in the same controller that generated it.

The idea behind this approach is to keep everything clean and compartmentalized: you have an event for receiving tweets and one for processing them; the two are entirely independent. There is always the temptation to mix together the processing of similar or related events. For example, the separate REQUEST_PAINT and HANDLE_PAINT events might be wrongfully combined into a DO_REPAINT event in the case of a UI library. This may sound like a good idea at first, or you might not even realize that there are, in fact, two separate events that need to be implemented. However, as the application grows, you will quickly find that the HANDLE_PAINT part of the event might require processing as a result of something other than the REQUEST_PAINT part, or that receiving a DO_REPAINT event might not always result in a repaint (for example, when the widget/surface in question is not visible to the end user). As such, it is always a good idea to split monolithic events into smaller ones—without over-doing it, of course. This keeps the code base small and easier to maintain, both of which are key aspects of any good Java ME application.

This covers the TweetsController. Up next are the WelcomeScreenController and the WelcomeForm.

Implementing the WelcomeScreenController and the WelcomeForm

This form-controller combination is responsible for the way the application interacts with the user when the application is first started and the welcome screen is shown. The welcome screen also serves as the login screen for the application.

Before we continue, I would like to point out the subtle conceptual difference between a screen and a form. A screen is the totality of what the user sees, hears, and feels (via vibrations) at a certain point during an application's runtime. It is like a multimedia snapshot of the application. Of this, the form is only the UI part of the application, which contains the application widgets with which the user can interact. It may not even be the entire visual part of the screen (which happens if the application is not running in full-screen mode, for example). The difference is mostly theoretical, and in practice the two terms can be interchanged most of the time, but when designing complex applications with complex user interaction scenarios, this difference might be something to keep in mind. Of course, the denominations "screen" and "form" aren't fixed: different teams and individuals may use different terms for them.

Going back to our Twitter client, let's have a look at what the WelcomeForm source code looks like, shown in Listing 8–5.

Listing 8–5. *The WelcomeForm*

```
package app.views;

...

public class WelcomeForm extends GameCanvasView implements CallbackHandler
{

    protected InputStringItem username = null;
    protected InputStringItem password = null;
    protected SimpleTextButton login = null;

    public WelcomeForm(UITheme theme)
    {
        super(false,theme);

        // Create all the needed widgets
        username = new InputStringItem(Locale.get("username.text"), "",
        Locale.get("text.general.ok"), Locale.get("text.general.cancel"),
        getContentWidth()/2, 100, null, theme);

        password = new InputStringItem(Locale.get("username.text"), "",
        Locale.get("text.general.ok"), Locale.get("text.general.cancel"),
        getContentWidth()/2, 100, null, theme);

        login = new SimpleTextButton(Locale.get("login.button.text"), this, theme);

        // Create the form structure
        addWidget ( new Label(Locale.get("username.text") + ":",theme));
        addWidget(username);
        addWidget ( new Label(Locale.get("password.text") + ":",theme));
        addWidget(password);
        addWidget(login);

        // Lay out and focus the form
        doLayout();
        onFocus();
    }
```

```
public boolean doCallback(Event evt)
{
    if ( EVT.UI.BUTTON_PRESSED == evt.getType() )
    {
        UserCredentials credentials = null;
        if ( Defaults.USE_SINGLE_USER_ACCESS )
        {
            credentials = new UserCredentials(null,null, "<token>",
            "<token-secret>");
        }
        else
        {
            credentials = new UserCredentials(username.getText(),
            password.getText(),null,null);
        }

        Event event = new Event ( EVT.CONTEXT.LOGIN_FORM, EVT.NETWORK.BEGIN_LOGIN,
        credentials);
        Application.getMainEventController().queueEvent(event);
        return true;
    }
    return false;
}
}
```

You can see in the constructor of the class how the widgets are initialized and how the form's structure is created. This should be familiar to you from the chapter dedicated to the UI, so we won't go into it. The only thing I would like to point out are that all interface strings are localized, which should become standard practice for you if it's not already— even if the project you are working on does not specifically require localization.

The highlighted portion of the code is more interesting, however. Based on the value of USE_SINGLE_USER_ACCESS in the Defaults class, the code triggers a BEGIN_LOGIN event with either the predefined credentials or the credentials the user entered. This kind of flexibility is great for test builds or for automation of any kind, though in our case it has been done simply to be able to have a hassle-free switch between multi-user access and single-user access.

You will also notice that the class itself is pretty light code-wise. That is because all the heavy stuff gets done in the WelcomeScreenController, shown in Listing 8–6.

Listing 8–6. *The WelcomeScreenController*

```
package app.controller;

...

public class WelcomeScreenController implements Controller, EventListener {

    public static boolean firstTimeShow = true;
    public static WelcomeForm form = null;

    public boolean handleEvent(Event event)
    {
```

```
            if ( EVT.PROGRAM_FLOW.SHOW_WELCOME_SCREEN == event.getType() )
            {
                if ( firstTimeShow )
                {
                    firstTimeShow = false;
                    form = new WelcomeForm(Defaults.THEME);
                }

                // See if there's a set of stored user credentials. If there is one,
                // use that to log in directly instead of showing the welcome screen.
                    byte [] data = Defaults.
                    persistenceHelper.getRecord(Defaults.DEFAULT_LOGIN_DATA_RECORD_NAME);
                if ( data != null )
                {
                    ByteRecordReader reader = new ByteRecordReader(data);
                    UserCredentials credentials = HighLevelSerializer.
                    deserializeUserCredentials(reader);

                    Event evt = new Event ( EVT.CONTEXT.LOGIN_FORM, EVT.NETWORK
                    .BEGIN_LOGIN, credentials);
                    Application.getMainEventController().queueEvent(evt);
                }
                else
                {
                    Application.showView(form);
                    return true;
                }
            }
            else
            if ( EVT.NETWORK.LOGIN_FAILED == event.getType() )
            {
                // Error handling code goes here
                return true;
            }
            else
            if ( EVT.NETWORK.LOGIN_SUCCEEDED == event.getType() )
            {
                Event evt = new Event(EVT.CONTEXT.LOGIN_FORM,
                EVT.PROGRAM_FLOW.SHOW_MAIN_SCREEN, null);
                Application.getMainEventController().queueEvent(evt);

                // Store credentials that were used
                UserCredentials credentials = (UserCredentials) event.getPayload();
                ByteRecordWriter writer = new ByteRecordWriter();
                HighLevelSerializer.serializeUserCredentials(credentials, writer);
                Defaults.persistenceHelper.store(Defaults.DEFAULT_LOGIN_DATA_RECORD_NAME,
                writer.getCurrentResult());

                return true;
            }
        return false;
    }

}
```

There's quite a lot going on here, so let's summarize things. For starters, the actual form object is created only when the SHOW_WELCOME_SCREEN event is handled, and not before (lazy initialization, as described earlier in the chapter). Next, after the form is initialized, the code looks to see if there's a previously stored set of credentials. If one exists, it triggers a BEGIN_LOGIN event based on those; if not, then the actual WelcomeForm is displayed. The actual storing of the credentials is done in the code that handles the LOGIN_SUCCEEDED event, so every time a login is successful, the credentials on the basis of which the login was performed are saved. This is, in effect, an auto-login mechanism. You can also add support for handling failed login attempts in the branch of the code responsible for processing the LOGIN_FAILED event.

Before we continue to the next section, let's have a look at what the welcome screen will look like on the WTK emulator (shown in Figure 8–1). As you can see, the design and look are nothing fancy, but they are functional and they reflect what would be expected of the code.

Figure 8–1. *The welcome screen on the WTK emulator—the username field is focused.*

Next, let's look at what happens after the user successfully logs in.

Implementing the MainForm and MainScreenController

As the name suggests, these two classes are responsible for the user's interaction with the application's main screen. On this screen, the user is able to view tweets retrieved from the server, request a new batch of tweets, post tweets of his own, and access the settings screen.

The visual structure and layout of the MainForm is a bit more complex than that of the WelcomeForm, as can be seen in Listing 8–7 (the highlighted section).

Listing 8–7. *The* MainForm

```
package app.views;

...

import com.apress.framework.objecttypes.Event;

public class MainForm extends GameCanvasView implements CallbackHandler
{
    VerticalContainer tweetsContainer = null;

    HorizontalContainer commandButtons = null;
    InputStringItem newTweet = null;
    SimpleTextButton nextTweets = null;
    SimpleTextButton showSettingsForm = null;

    public void addTweet(Tweet tweet)
    {
        String text = tweet.getAuthor() + " : " + tweet.getBody() ;

        StringItem item = new StringItem( text , tweetsContainer.getTotalWidth()
        - 20, 100, this, Defaults.THEME );

        tweetsContainer.addWidget(item);
        tweetsContainer.doLayout();
    }

    public MainForm(UITheme theme)
    {
        super(false,theme);

        // Create the new tweet item
        newTweet = new InputStringItem(Locale.get("tweets.new.prompt"),
        Locale.get("tweets.new.prompt"), Locale.get("text.general.ok"),
        Locale.get("text.general.cancel"),
                    getContentWidth()-10, 100, this, theme);

        // Create the container for the tweets
        tweetsContainer = new VerticalContainer(theme);

        // Create the command buttons
        nextTweets = new SimpleTextButton(Locale.get("tweets.next.label"), this,
        theme);
        showSettingsForm = new SimpleTextButton(
        Locale.get("settings.form.button.label"), this, theme);
        commandButtons = new HorizontalContainer(theme);
        commandButtons.addWidget(nextTweets);
        commandButtons.addWidget(showSettingsForm);

        // Add the form elements to the form
        addWidget(newTweet);
        addWidget(tweetsContainer);
        addWidget(commandButtons);
```

```
        // Do initial layout and focus
        doLayout();
        onFocus();
    }

    public void doLayout()
    {
        commandButtons.doLayout();
        tweetsContainer.setContentHeight(getTotalHeight() -
        commandButtons.getTotalHeight() - newTweet.getTotalHeight() - 20);
        tweetsContainer.setContentWidth(getTotalWidth());
        super.doLayout();
    }

    public boolean doCallback(Event event)
    {
        if ( EVT.UI.BUTTON_PRESSED == event.getType() )
        {
            if ( nextTweets == event.getPayload() )
            {
                Event evt = new Event(EVT.CONTEXT.MAIN_FORM,
                EVT.TWEETS.REQUEST_MAIN_TWEETS_BATCH, null);
                Application.getMainEventController().queueEvent(evt);
                return true;
            }
            else
            if ( showSettingsForm == event.getPayload() )
            {
                Event evt = new Event(EVT.CONTEXT.MAIN_FORM,
                EVT.PROGRAM_FLOW.SHOW_SETTINGS_SCREEN, null);
                Application.getMainEventController().queueEvent(evt);
                return true;
            }
        }
        else if ( EVT.UI.TEXT_CHANGED == event.getType() )
        {
            // Create a new tweet with the StringItem text and post it
            Tweet tweet = new Tweet(null,newTweet.getText(),null);
            Event evt = new Event(EVT.CONTEXT.MAIN_FORM, EVT.TWEETS.POST_TWEET, tweet);
            Application.getMainEventController().queueEvent(evt);

            // Reset the StringItem text
            newTweet.setText(Locale.get("tweets.new.prompt"));
            return true;
        }
        return false;
    }
}
```

The form is made up of three areas. The first area is a single button, the "new tweet" button. The second area is a vertical container used for displaying tweets retrieved from the server. The third area is a horizontal container containing the "retrieve next tweets batch" and "go to settings form" buttons. Since the container used for displaying tweets should take up most of the screen (i.e., its size isn't fixed and depends on screen resolution), we need a custom layout for the MainForm, which is why we have overwritten the standard doLayout() method.

Please note that when the "retrieve next tweets batch" button is pressed, a REQUEST_MAIN_TWEETS_BATCH is triggered, which is handled in the TweetsController. The response(s) from the TweetsController, which comes in the form of RECEIVED_TWEET events, are handled by the MainScreenController, shown in Listing 8–8.

Listing 8–8. *The MainScreenController*

```
package app.controller;

...

public class MainScreenController implements Controller, EventListener {

    public static MainForm form = null;
    public static boolean firstTimeShow = true;

    public boolean handleEvent(Event event)
    {
        if ( EVT.PROGRAM_FLOW.SHOW_MAIN_SCREEN == event.getType() )
        {
          ...
        }
        else
        if ( EVT.TWEETS.RECEIVED_TWEET == event.getType() )
        {
            Tweet tweet = (Tweet) event.getPayload();
            form.addTweet(tweet);
        }
        return false;
    }
}
```

This listing clearly exemplifies the separation between UI code (the form class) and the underlying functionality (the controller class): the form class handles only the creation of the UI and triggering of the appropriate events when UI elements are interacted with, while the controller handles the actual application logic. In the case of the highlighted code, the form does the actual widget adding (via the addTweet() method of the MainForm class), but it is the controller that decides what tweet to add. In this regard, you can think of the form as being a kind of slave to the controller, or as an interface between the user and the controller.

The improper separation of UI and logic can be a major problem for Java ME apps. As targeting different devices can frequently lead to different UIs (or at least to device-specific UI tweaks), merging application logic with UI logic can lead to application code that is run on one device but not on another, because the UI code follows a different path on the latter.

What's even worse, sometimes application logic is wrongfully bound to UI properties. For example, viewports are common in a lot of applications, such as spreadsheet or mapping software. Determining a viewport's position based on the associated container's scroll position makes some sense, but it's fundamentally wrong because rather than binding the viewport to some application-internal variable (i.e., the calculated viewport position), you bind it to a UI widget's state. Not only might this cause code and logic "bleeding" between the UI and the core application code, but it could also transform UI bugs (in the UI library, for example) into application bugs. Consider what would happen if a bug caused the scroll position to be wrongfully reported—for example, after a resize or after switching from landscape to portrait mode; the viewport position would get affected by this too.

By keeping UI and application logic completely separated, the chances of such situations happening are greatly reduced: in the event that the UI misbehaves, the viewport position is still the same (because it's retrieved from an application-internal variable). Furthermore, in this situation and in many others, this separation makes the discrepancy between the scroll position and the actual viewport position easily traceable to a UI bug, because we know that the viewport position is always correctly calculated internally and is not affected by UI resizing or changing the layout. This considerably cuts down the time necessary to fix the UI bug itself.

> **NOTE:** If you recall from the WelcomeForm presented earlier, there is some credential-selecting logic in the handling of the BUTTON_PRESSED event on said form (i.e., in the UI), which, according to the foregoing paragraphs, should be moved to the handler method of the BEGIN_LOGIN event (i.e., to the application logic code). This is intentional, as the goal was to influence the behavior and data of the login process when it gets initiated by the login button (which is local to the WelcomeForm), and not the general behavior of the login process as triggered by the BEGIN_LOGIN event (which can come from any source).

Going back on track, the way the main application screen looks on the WTK emulator can be seen in Figure 8–2. The two snapshots reflect the screen when the "post new tweet" item is selected (first screenshot) and when a tweet is selected (second screenshot). Notice how the selected tweet is automatically expanded to full length by the StringItem class.

Figure 8–2. *The main application screen*

Now, let's look at the final form-controller pair of the application.

Implementing the SettingsScreenController and the SettingsForm

This form-controller pair is responsible for managing application settings and preferences, such as the user's locale, and for actions such as logging out a user or exiting the application.

The code for the SettingsForm can be seen in Listing 8–9.

Listing 8–9. *The SettingsForm*

```
package app.views;

...

public class SettingsForm extends GameCanvasView implements CallbackHandler
{

    SimpleTextButton switchToLanguage1 = null;
    SimpleTextButton switchToLanguage2 = null;
    SimpleTextButton goBack = null;
    SimpleTextButton exit = null;
    SimpleTextButton logout = null;

    public SettingsForm(UITheme theme)
    {
        super(false,theme);
```

```
        // Create the command buttons
        switchToLanguage1 = new SimpleTextButton(Locale.get("text.general
        .language.1"), this, theme);
        switchToLanguage2 = new SimpleTextButton(Locale.get("text.general
        .language.2"), this, theme);
        goBack = new SimpleTextButton(Locale.get("text.general.goback"), this, theme);
        exit = new SimpleTextButton(Locale.get("text.general.exit"), this, theme);
        logout = new SimpleTextButton(Locale.get("text.general.logout"), this, theme);

        addWidget(switchToLanguage1);
        addWidget(switchToLanguage2);
        addWidget(goBack);
        addWidget(exit);
        addWidget(logout);

        // Do initial layout and focus
        doLayout();
        onFocus();
    }

    public boolean doCallback(Event event)
    {
        if ( EVT.UI.BUTTON_PRESSED == event.getType() )
        {
            if ( switchToLanguage1 == event.getPayload() )
            {
                Event evt = new Event(EVT.CONTEXT.SETTINGS_FORM,
                EVT.SETTINGS.CHANGE_LANGUAGE, "en-US");
                Application.getMainEventController().queueEvent(evt);
                return true;
            }
            else
            if ( switchToLanguage2 == event.getPayload() )
            {
                Event evt = new Event(EVT.CONTEXT.SETTINGS_FORM,
                EVT.SETTINGS.CHANGE_LANGUAGE, "weird");
                Application.getMainEventController().queueEvent(evt);
                return true;
            }
            else
            if ( goBack == event.getPayload() )
            {
                Event evt = new Event(EVT.CONTEXT.SETTINGS_FORM,
                EVT.PROGRAM_FLOW.SHOW_MAIN_SCREEN, null);
                Application.getMainEventController().queueEvent(evt);
                return true;
            }
            else
            if ( logout == event.getPayload() )
            {
                Event evt = new Event(EVT.CONTEXT.SETTINGS_FORM,
                EVT.PROGRAM_FLOW.INITIATE_LOGOUT, null);
                Application.getMainEventController().queueEvent(evt);
                return true;
            }
            else
            if ( exit == event.getPayload() )
```

```
            {
                Event evt = new Event(EVT.CONTEXT.SETTINGS_FORM,
                EVT.PROGRAM_FLOW.INITIATE_SHUTDOWN, null);
                Application.getMainEventController().queueEvent(evt);
                return true;
            }
        }
        return false;
    }

}
```

The code is pretty straightforward and so are its results: you get a form with two
"change language" buttons (one for the en-US locale and one for the "weird" locale), a
"go back" button, a button for logging out the user, and a button for exiting the app.

> **NOTE:** The "weird" locale/language referenced is actually English with a funny accent (e.g.,
> "Okay" instead of "OK"), so that everyone reading the book and testing the app can understand
> it. The localization files for both locales are provided on the book's page at Apress's web site.

The SettingsScreenController class is also pretty straightforward, as can be seen in
Listing 8–10.

Listing 8–10. *The* SettingsScreenController *Class*

```
package app.controller;

...

public class SettingsScreenController implements Controller, EventListener {

    ...

    public boolean handleEvent(Event event)
    {
        if ( EVT.PROGRAM_FLOW.SHOW_SETTINGS_SCREEN == event.getType() )
        {
            ...
        }
        else
        if ( EVT.SETTINGS.CHANGE_LANGUAGE == event.getType() )
        {
            String locale = (String) event.getPayload();

            ByteRecordWriter writer = new ByteRecordWriter();
            writer.writeString(locale);
            Defaults.persistenceHelper.store(Defaults.DEFAULT_LOCALE_RECORD_NAME,
            writer.getCurrentResult());
            Locale.loadFromFileBasedOnPreferences(locale, Defaults.DEFAULT_LOCALE);
            return true;
        }
        else
        if ( EVT.SETTINGS.CLEAR_LOGIN_DATA == event.getType() )
        {
            Defaults.persistenceHelper.delete(Defaults.DEFAULT_LOGIN_DATA_RECORD_NAME);
```

```
        return true;
    }
    else
    if ( EVT.PROGRAM_FLOW.INITIATE_LOGOUT == event.getType() )
    {
        Event evt = new Event(EVT.CONTEXT.SETTINGS_FORM,
        EVT.SETTINGS.CLEAR_LOGIN_DATA, null);
        Application.getMainEventController().queueEvent(evt);

        evt = new Event(EVT.CONTEXT.SETTINGS_FORM,
        EVT.PROGRAM_FLOW.INITIATE_SHUTDOWN, null);
        Application.getMainEventController().queueEvent(evt);
        return true;
    }

    return false;
    }
}
```

The code should pretty much speak for itself at this point, so I won't go into it. Have a look at Figure 8–3 to see how the settings screen will look on the WTK emulator.

Figure 8–3. *The settings screen on the WTK emulator*

I would like to point out that the settings code has one flaw: changing the language/locale requires an application restart. That's because all the application's form fields are created inside the constructors of the forms, which are obviously called only once.

What would be needed for runtime language/locale changes is a buildFormStructure() method that rebuilds the forms when needed and that can be called as needed. Alternatively, a reloadLanguage() method could be implemented that, when called, sets the appropriate text/caption on all the widgets contained within a form.

However, implementing either method into the current application code would require significant changes to the application and UI framework structure. For example, rebuilding a form has serious implications for the user experience (for example, information about the currently focused element is lost, as are scroll offsets and potentially other important information related to UI state), while changing the text on a widget requires support from the UI framework and potentially implies a complete re-layout of the current form if the new text overflows or is significantly smaller than the original text. For this reason and for the purpose of code clarity and simplicity, these features have been omitted from the current code base and are left as an exercise for the reader.

To finish things off with our application's code, I would like to present the EVT class.

Implementing the EVT Class

The EVT class is probably the first place you should go when you want to familiarize yourself with a new project. By being basically a central repository of all the events that can happen within an application, it gives you a quick insight into how the application is supposed to run and what its critical processes are, and it also provides a great central point for branching out and exploring the source tree. All you have to do is follow the "event trail," and sooner or later you'll get to the part of the code you need to get to for debugging that weird bug or for understanding why and where that one method is used.

In the case of our Twitter client, the EVT class is shown in Listing 8–11.

Listing 8–11. *The EVT Class*

```
package com.apress.framework.objecttypes;

public class EVT
{
    public class CONTEXT
    {
        public static final int STARTUP = 1;
        public static final int LOGIN_FORM = 2;
        public static final int NETWORKING_MODULE = 3;
        public static final int UI_MODULE = 4;
        public static final int MAIN_FORM = 5;
        public static final int SETTINGS_FORM = 6;
    }

    public class PROGRAM_FLOW
    {
        public static final int SHOW_WELCOME_SCREEN = 10001;
        public static final int SHOW_MAIN_SCREEN = 10002;
        public static final int SHOW_SETTINGS_SCREEN = 10003;
        public static final int APPLICATION_START = 10004;
        public static final int APPLICATION_PREPARE_SHUTDOWN = 10005;
        public static final int APPLICATION_EXIT = 10006;
        public static final int INITIATE_SHUTDOWN = 10007;
        public static final int INITIATE_LOGOUT = 10008;
    }
```

```java
public class TWEETS
{
    public static final int REQUEST_MAIN_TWEETS_BATCH = 20001;
    public static final int RECEIVED_TWEET = 20002;
    public static final int POST_TWEET = 20003;
}

public class NETWORK
{
    public static final int BEGIN_LOGIN=30001;
    public static final int LOGIN_FAILED=30002;
    public static final int LOGIN_SUCCEEDED=30003;
}

public class UI
{
    public static final int BUTTON_PRESSED=40001;
    public static final int TEXT_CHANGED=40002;
}

public class SETTINGS
{
    public static final int CHANGE_LANGUAGE = 50001;
    public static final int CLEAR_LOGIN_DATA = 50002;
}
}
```

Please notice the naming convention. Contexts are numbered successively from 1 to infinity, while individual events use a XYYYY numbering convention, where X is unique for each context/area of the application (and has successive values from 1 to infinity), and YYYY is a unique event number within the realm of X (again with successive values). This naming scheme ensures readability, helps debugging (after a while, you sort of start to remember that 2YYYY are tweet-related events), and most importantly prevents numbering conflicts in which different events get the same event number.

Now that our Twitter client is functional, let's look at how it can be further improved.

Improving the Application

The Twitter client that we have written works and its underlying foundation is solid, but the app itself is pretty skeletal right now. Expanding it so that it can be considered a full-featured and complete application would require a lot of time, effort, and book pages, while providing marginal benefit to anyone not interested in doing a full-featured Twitter client. So while we will not go into this process in depth, we can and will take a look at some of the steps needed to reach this goal.

Improving Error Handling

Currently, error handling in our application is minimal. In order to reach "completed" status, this needs to be improved. Improving error handling should start at the core of each module (networking, UI, localization, persistence, etc.), where the native API calls are mixed with project-specific or framework-specific code and should continue until high-level errors are reached (for example, widget focusing errors in the interface).

In theory, every result of a function (especially native ones) should be checked for failure and processed accordingly, and each and every possible exception type that can be thrown in a given scenario should be caught and handled individually (i.e., the code should not rely on catch (Exception ex) as a catch-all universal safety net). So when something fails, instead of just knowing that "it failed," we should also know exactly where and why it failed, at runtime, and be able to recover from this if at all possible.

In practice, Java ME devices generally do not have enough resources for this. Catching every error type and checking every return value will result in a severe strain on CPU and RAM resources, while also increasing the code base considerably. If these checks also happen to be done in an often-run code block, the application's performance will suffer considerably. Fortunately, there are a few ways around this issue.

First of all, developers must be aware of the 80-20 rule, which in the case of error handling means that 20% of all the *possible* error-generating scenarios or blocks of code are responsible for 80% of the *actually generated* errors. If you can identify where and what that 20% is, and if you handle it properly, then you can usually get away with only minimal error handling for the remaining 80% of possible error-generating scenarios and code.

From my experience, the most common sources of errors are as follows:

- External operations, such as IO access and accessing user data on the device

- Memory allocations for large blocks of data (I have yet to see an OutOfMemory exception caused by the allocation of a single individual int or String)

- Threading/concurrency issues, typically caused by attempting to use or access a resource (either external on internal) that is either not ready for use or already in use by some other thread

- Invalid or inconsistent input data (e.g., broken HTML code, data compressed with a different algorithm than the one expected, etc.)

Second, there's the concept of *error prevention*, which is often overlooked or not properly understood. Most errors can be avoided if proper checks are employed. For example, rather than trying to bind an InputStream to a DataInputStream, reading from the DataInputStream and catching IOExceptions, you could make sure that the InputStream is not null and that it can be read from safely. You should also validate critical data and parameters to check that they won't break your code. Ensuring that you have accurate information about the runtime environment (available memory, number of running threads, number of network connections in use, etc.) and adapting your code to cope with critical changes in these parameters are equally important in some scenarios. And knowing the quirks of the device your code is running on is invaluable: if you know that a certain native function behaves improperly on the device you're running on, adapt your code to compensate (more on this in the next chapter).

The bottom line is that, rather than trying to handle errors, you should always try to prevent them from happening in the first place. You, of course, have no control over IO errors happening because of the network (or other similar scenarios), but most of the errors you'll encounter can be prevented in one way or another from within your code—especially if said errors are also generated from within your code. The advantage of error prevention over error handling should be obvious: your application becomes more robust, and it becomes easier to handle potentially delicate situations because you are aware of them ahead of time.

A third and final piece of advice is to try to bubble up your errors and centralize your error handling. If a local network access operation fails, tidy up things locally as quickly and as efficiently as you can, and then trigger an NETWORK_FAILURE event with the appropriate payload. Handle this event in a dedicated error-handling controller, and do the bulk of the error handling there (informing the user, stopping relevant threads/actions, etc.). Since many errors are handled in similar or even identical ways, having a central error-handling authority makes sense, and it also improves code readability, code flexibility, and code base size.

Increasing Functionality

Our application as it is right now provides only basic Twitter functionality—more is needed for a Pro application. This should be easy to add, as the building blocks are all there. Some of the things that might be nice to have and might be fun to implement are as follows:

- The ability to see your friends and their tweets

- Periodic auto-updating of the tweets list (every five minutes, for example)

- More information about each tweet (location, timestamp, etc.)

- Avatar pictures and more information about each friend (avatar, location, bio, etc.)

- Adding support for URL-shortening via an external service (this one might be a little bit more difficult)

- More contextual options—for example, when activating a tweet, a menu with options such as "Reply," "Retweet," and "More tweets from user" should appear.

Improving the UI Framework

Probably one of the most important parts of any Java ME application, the UI framework is, in our case, functional but very spartan. You could, of course, switch the application to a more complete UI framework, or you could attempt to improve the existing one (which is what I recommend, purely for the learning experience). Some of the things that you could try to implement are the following:

- More widgets—drop-down boxes, contextual menus, and image widgets are all good candidates.

- Support for kinetic scrolling and possibly touch gestures

- Custom fonts and text input capabilities, to replace native ones (which are inconsistent across devices)—more on this later in the book.

- More layout containers and options (such as padding, margin, lead, etc.)

- More flexibility (changing widget text at runtime, built-in support for form re-layout, etc.)

Summary

In this chapter, we have used together all the modules we have written so far. We have created a functional (although not exactly feature-complete) Twitter client. We have looked at how to separate our application into UI-related code (forms) and business-related code (controllers), how events can be used to form a complete application flow, from startup to shutdown, how they can be used to bridge the gap between the front-end UI and the back-end application code, how to implement features like auto-login and localization in real-life scenarios, and more. We have also looked at what can be done to improve the application further. A list of "to do" exercises has been suggested to the reader with respect to this.

## Chapter 9

Device Fragmentation

Device fragmentation is an age-old problem for Java ME. It stems from two main factors. First, Java ME is merely a set of specifications and APIs, which vendors are free to implement in their JVMs. However, not all vendors interpret the specifications to mean the exact same thing, which can lead to differences in the behaviors of different JVMs. These differences are usually minor or occur in corner cases, but nonetheless they do exist and can be a source of great pain for developers.

The second reason for device fragmentation is the fact that there are simply a lot of different models of Java ME phones currently in use. Java ME devices cover all price segments from the extremely cheap but low-end devices (with CLDC 1.0, MIDP 1.0, and no additional APIs—quite popular in India and Asia) to the expensive but high-end ones (Symbian devices come to mind—they typically implement the latest Java ME JSRs).

Furthermore, Java ME devices tend to be in use for a longer time than, say, iPhones, which means that you will still find 4–5 year-old devices to be quite popular in the real world, especially if said devices were high-end at the time of their launch. A consequence of this is that it is possible to find older Java ME devices with powerful hardware that do not support some of the APIs that newer but less powerful devices do.

When dealing with device fragmentation of any kind, the first goal is to adapt your application to support as many different devices as possible with a single code base (i.e., write your code to run well on as many devices as possible).

It is quite possible, especially for complex applications, that despite your best efforts custom builds for each device or class of devices you want to target will be needed, with each build adapted to the specific hardware, capabilities, and API of its intended device(s).

This has the potential of providing the best possible experience on every device, but it will make your development costs go through the roof. Because of this, you should consider this option only when you have no other choice or when your development budget has lots of zeros at the end. A midway solution, which is ideal in most cases, is to use a porting framework to automatically do the adaptation for you. This offers most of the performance (I would say 95%) of manually doing custom builds for e ach target device, but at a fraction of the cost in terms of money and development time. Porting frameworks will be covered later in the chapter.

Still, even with custom builds and porting frameworks, Java ME fragmentation is quite an ugly problem. To tackle it, we first need to compartmentalize it and split it into sub-problems. Thus, we can think of device fragmentation as having three main sub-components:

- *Hardware fragmentation*: Differences in hardware specifications (CPU, RAM, screen size, touch vs. non-touch, etc.) mean that you have to adapt your application to run on wildly different environments.

- *Capabilities fragmentation*: Not all devices support the same APIs or provide all the capabilities you need (e.g., Bluetooth file transfer, geo-location, PIM access, etc.)

- *API fragmentation*: The same API may behave differently on different devices. When this happens, the differences are typically minor and subtle, but they can cause a lot of problems for developers.

In the ideal case (if there is such a thing), you will deal with only one type of fragmentation, but usually, in the real world, you'll have to tackle all three at the same time. Also, some problems you will face will fall into more than one category.

> **NOTE:** There are a huge number of concrete fragmentation problems out there, and more appear every day. Covering them all would require not one, but several books. Furthermore, many of them and their associated solutions are highly scenario-specific. As such, in this chapter, we will cover only general advice regarding device fragmentation.

Hardware Fragmentation

This section will show you how to have your application run on devices with different hardware specifications.

CPU Power

As is the case in the desktop world, CPU power is still the main contributing factor to a device's performance. In the ideal case, all your target devices have plenty of juice and you can just code your application without thinking about the CPU cycles you burn.

However, that's rarely the case. Even if the device is fast enough, running the CPU at 100% load will decrease battery life considerably and as such isn't really an option. Furthermore, most devices you'll have to support have CPUs in the 100–300 MHz range, which pales in comparison with modern smartphones that typically start at 600 MHz.

TIP: A great way to identify potential CPU fragmentation issues early is to throttle the emulator you're working on to have ~80% of the performance of the real device(s) you'll target. This means that you'll be able to spot problems in this area even before you run your application on an actual device.

The most obvious way to deal with CPU fragmentation is to optimize your code to bring performance to an acceptable level, even on lower-end devices. This is covered in a separate chapter. Still, there are cases in which this simply cannot be done (either because the algorithms in use simply don't allow for this, or because the device is just not powerful enough). When this happens, there are a few tricks you can try.

The first thing you should try is to smooth out the CPU usage curve. What happens in a typical usage scenario is that the CPU sits idle or near-idle for 80% of the time (e.g., when the user is not interacting with the application or when he's just navigating through the menus) and goes full-out in the remaining 20% of the time (this is when CPU fragmentation becomes obvious). What you can do is use that near-idle time to prepare your application for the CPU-intensive tasks ahead.

For example, you can have a background thread that preprocesses the data and gets it ready for the actual processing your application will do. If you're writing a Yellow Pages–like application that aggregates contacts from different sources, you can have the background thread sort the aggregated contact list while the user is browsing through the menus. Then, when the user actually uses the search function, the list will already be sorted and the application will be very responsive—thus eliminating CPU fragmentation issues.

TIP: When doing background preprocessing, be careful not to use too much CPU time, as this would defeat the purpose. An easy way to make sure your preprocessing stays in the background is to split the data you'll process into smaller packets (as described in Chapter 1) and schedule those to be processed whenever the CPU usage falls below a certain threshold.

The second thing you should try is to lower all unnecessary CPU usage whenever the CPU usage level comes close to 100%. For example, if your application's UI is running at 30 FPS, consider dropping this to 20 FPS in CPU-intensive situations, or temporarily disable some fancy eye candy. If your application is designed to do a lot of computations as fast as possible (e.g., a spreadsheet program), you can throttle this (e.g., don't compute more than X cells per second).

A rarely considered cause of CPU usage is the garbage collector. By improving the way in which you create, use, and dispose of objects, you can lower your CPU usage considerably in some circumstances. For example, you could create a pool of objects and reuse those instead of creating a new object every time. More information on the garbage collector and on improving performance in this regard will be given in the next chapter.

If at this point you're still having performance problems, you should spend some time to generate a device VM profile in order to find out more about the device's behavior for VM-related operations. This profile should contain useful information related to how the device's VM works and how its inner workings impact CPU usage and performance. For example, how many threads can you start before the overhead of switching between threads becomes apparent? How much slower is synchronized code compared to non-synchronized code? How much time does the VM take to clean 100 objects? What about 10,000? What if said objects are linked? Does the object size and type matter? What about object allocation and creation—how long does that take? Does it matter if the object is a native one, such as an image, or an application-defined one?

> **NOTE:** You have to generate this profile by writing one or more sample applications to test each of the aspects you are interested in. To my knowledge, there is no ready-made application that does this. And, considering how highly empirical many of these tests are, chances are there won't be one anytime soon.

Once you have as much information about the device as possible, you can use this to adapt and optimize your application to the specific device you're having problems with. If you're using too many threads, consider consolidating related tasks into a single thread. If that synchronized section runs as slow as a snail, try reworking your program flow so that the synchronized directive isn't needed (even if this requires a bit of "hacking"). If disposing of 1,000 cross-linked objects is considerably slower than disposing of 1,000 individual objects, un-link them manually before the garbage collector gets called.

Please note that this profiling-and-adapting process is completely different from optimizing the code itself. While code optimization relies on mathematical and concrete data that is generally applicable to all devices (i.e., addition is always faster than multiplication, quick sort is faster than bubble sort, etc.), the kinds of optimizations just described are more empirical and rely on hands-on, device-specific knowledge. What works great on one device might have no impact on another, or might even make things worse. If anything, this is more voodoo than programming. Sometimes you'll spend a lot of time doing this for nothing, while other times you will strike gold early on—this unpredictability of results is why you should try this only last. Regardless, the upshot of this technique is that you'll gain a more intimate and intuitive knowledge of the device you're profiling, which can help not only improve performance but also identify bugs and other application issues. You also have to do this only once per device, as the acquired knowledge can be applied to other projects as well.

Also keep in mind that these "device adaptations" can sometimes require you to actually undo some performance optimizations you've made initially. For example, optimizing algorithms and code generally results in an increase in code size. However, on some devices, if a method's body is too large, performance is decreased considerably, because the JVM and/or CPU has to "jump" between different code sections. In this case, you must either split the method into two or more smaller ones and suffer the incurred overhead, or decrease the method size (by giving up on some of the optimizations). While in theory both options should be slower than the optimized code, in real life they are actually faster because of the way the JVM works.

Finally, you should be aware of the fact that sometimes devices underclock their CPUs to conserve battery life. They do this automatically when battery charge falls below a certain level, and there is typically no way to prevent this from happening. This means that your application can (and most likely will) perform below expectations in these situations.

By applying the tips and techniques presented in this section, you will be able to alleviate the perceived performance hit. Alternatively, you can design your application to make due with roughly 50–60% of the total CPU power available in normal circumstances. This way, when the underclock kicks in, the application will still have enough CPU cycles to run adequately. The obvious catch is that 50% of the total CPU power may not be enough for your application's needs.

RAM

The amount of available RAM is probably the second biggest cause of hardware fragmentation, next to CPU power. Having a lower amount of RAM available can cause problems in many ways. The most obvious issue is that you may simply run out of memory at runtime. Other potential problems are the garbage collector kicking in way too often (because memory gets used up faster), streaming media being interrupted by constant stuttering and buffering (because the allocated buffers are smaller), and overall slower device performance (even outside the application).

The problem is that, while some high-end devices allow Java ME applications to use tens of megabytes of RAM, low-end devices typically offer only 1–2 megabytes, sometimes considerably less. To cope with this difference, you should design and code your application defensively in terms of memory and implement a few "safety features."

Probably the first thing you should do is examine your data structures and see if any information is duplicated. All the principles that apply to database normalization also apply here; however, the one to remember is the one that states that every piece of information in your application (for example, a person's name or address) should appear once and only once within your data structures. If it appears more than once, then you should refactor your data structures by having said information present only within a single data structure, and have all other occurrences or references point to this data structure instead.

Applied globally to all the data structures within your application, this can result in significant gains in terms of free memory, especially in business-related applications, which are typically data-intensive. Keep in mind that usually it's not possible to remove all duplicate information. For example, you may have left-over duplicates because you do not have access to protected/private fields of classes (which are sometimes used to keep local copies of data, instead of references), because the inner workings of third-party libraries are usually off-limits, or because you may simply need different representations or encodings of the same data in situations in which computing these representations dynamically is not feasible. From my experience, you can usually eliminate 30–70% of all duplicates depending on the application—which can still add up to a lot of memory.

If the foregoing technique does not produce the desired results, the next thing you should attempt to do is minimize the amount of information stored in memory. Check for data fields that you do not use and simply remove them. Remove information that you can easily compute at runtime (for example, if you have a person's date of birth, you don't really need to separately keep track of his star sign, age, or other related information). Try to find alternate, more space-efficient encodings for your data (for example, use JSON instead of XML and store long strings using data compression techniques). Discard data the moment it's not needed anymore (for example, once you have converted a JSON representation of an object to an actual object, immediately discard the JSON string and everything associated with it).

If, after this, you're still short on memory, then you should try to find alternative storage space. For example, the RMS or the device's filesystem can be used as a kind of swapfile that can store objects for which there is not enough memory anymore. Typically there's a lot more storage space available on the device (via the RMS and the filesystem) than there is RAM, so this certainly makes sense if you're handling large amounts of data. Be careful, though: data stored in the RMS or on the filesystem might be accessed by other non-authorized applications or users, so don't store sensitive or personal data there.

If you decide to use alternative storage space, please keep in mind that the read/write speed can be an order or two of magnitude less than the read/write speed of in-memory operations. Because of this, you should keep an index of the information contained in the alternative storage, and this index should contain the values of the fields most commonly used for search operations. Furthermore, this index should be easily searchable, so if possible you should actually have multiple indexes, one for each commonly used field.

For example, let's consider an application that deals with lots of people records, each record containing a person's first name, last name, location, age, sex, and other information such as notes, documents, and more. Within this application, the most commonly used search criteria are a person's name and/or location. Ideally you would have two indexes in this situation. The first index would contain each person's name and a reference to the full record within the alternative storage (might be RMS record index, for example), and would be sorted according to the name field. The second index would be similar, except the name field will be replaced with the location field. Next, when looking for people with the last name "Atkinson" located in "Arizona," all the application would have to do is two binary searches, one for each field, and cross-reference the results. If done properly, this process can be extremely fast. Furthermore, it is possible to do this particular search with only one binary search operation, which speeds things up even more. Optimizing searches will be discussed in the next chapter.

If you're still running low on memory after doing all of the foregoing, it's time for drastic measures. If you're writing a client-server application, then consider offloading to the server some of the operations normally done on the client, like searching. For these operations, the client application essentially becomes a dumb terminal for the code running on the server. This can drastically reduce CPU and RAM usage on the device, at the expense of server CPU and RAM usage and network traffic. The main problem with this approach is the increase in network traffic, which typically means that the user's total cost of using the application goes up, sometimes significantly.

> **NOTE:** In client-server scenarios, sometimes memory shortage problems occur because there's no API/protocol designed with mobile devices in mind. For example, it's OK if a web service request returns a 512 KB response if said response is processed on a desktop, but if a mobile device has to receive and process a 512 KB XML string, then you're in trouble. Consider implementing a dedicated mobile API/protocol, which returns less data (for example, only the essential fields of a record; retrieving the remaining fields can be done via a separate request) and which uses a more efficient encoding (did I mention that XML isn't really suited for mobile communications?).

If you're writing a stand-alone application and not a client-server one, then you're pretty much out of luck at this point. The reality is that there is at least one scenario in which your application will simply run out of memory, no matter what. The only sensible things you can do at this point are to either move the problematic device(s) to "unsupported" status, issue a disclaimer that the application might run out of memory in some scenarios, instruct the user to close all other running apps if the problematic devices support multitasking, and finally rework the specifications so that the memory usage is lowered (this typically involves trimming down or altogether removing some features). None of these options are particularly appealing, but that's simply the way things are.

The final aspect to consider related to RAM fragmentation issues is access time. This is pretty much a moot point these days, but you should be aware that different devices have different RAM access times for a variety of reasons, ranging from hardware design (e.g., memory paging scheme and page size) to VM behavior (e.g., range checking on arrays). RAM access time usually doesn't matter that much compared to other factors (RAM size, CPU power), but you might hit the odd scenario in which it does. Should this happen, you will find a few tips in the next chapter to help you minimize its effects.

Screen

After CPU and RAM, the biggest difference between mobile devices lies in the screen. The main parameters to take into consideration are screen resolution and physical size. Constructing a high-quality mobile interface to suit your target devices is mostly a design task, so this section will be brief.

The most important thing to do is to choose a UI framework/library that supports dynamic layouts, layouts that can resize themselves to fit any given screen size and orientation. This minimizes the amount of design and programming needed to support all target devices.

Second, you should create your basic design guidelines and layout based on the lowest common denominator. That is, your reference UI should look OK on the lowest device you will target. This reference UI will then be adapted for higher-end devices to take advantage of their superior screen characteristics, not the other way around (i.e., the UI is first designed for high-end devices and then stripped down to work on low-end devices).

Third, you should always hide unneeded information and UI elements and have as little wasted space as possible. For example, scrollbars are needed only when actually scrolling. If you hide them in all other situations, you can save a few pixels, while at the same time making the design feel less cluttered. New notifications of any kind can be signaled by a small icon between the two onscreen softkey buttons (there is usually enough space between them to fit a small icon; this space would otherwise go unused). Tickers and tabs are great ways to maximize screen real estate—use them wisely, but be careful not to overdo it.

Fourth, all application functionality should be accessible via both touch and key input. This is becoming increasingly important with the proliferation of touchscreen devices. Probably the biggest problem I have seen with mixed-mode applications is that the UI elements are simply too small to be used via touch, especially when no stylus is available. Because of this, consider adding a "large UI" option in the settings screen. Also, especially for smaller UI elements, consider adding a small margin of error for touch events. For example, if the user presses the screen ten pixels outside a check box and there's no other UI element there, it's safe to consider that he intended to press the check box. There's nothing more frustrating for a user than having to exactly press a very small area of the screen with his or her finger, especially if said finger is larger than average.

Another important aspect to consider here is text input. This can be either handled inside the application or deferred to the system (i.e., display a native TextBox when the user clicks on a text field). Handling it natively has the advantage of supporting the text input methods the user is accustomed to, as well as features such as autocompletion, but it also has the major disadvantage of breaking the program flow, as being shown a native TextBox in the middle of using an application is disruptive to say the least. Handling text input within the application via a custom virtual keyboard is significantly less disruptive, but can be frustrating for some users if the keyboard is not properly designed (for example, if the keys are too small or too far apart) and is not properly positioned (i.e., instead of displacing other UI elements, it overlaps and thus hides them). Furthermore, it also means that features such as autocompletion are not available.

Choosing one method or the other depends heavily on the specific needs of the application. For entering shorts bursts of text, such as a username, password, or search criteria, the virtual keyboard approach is certainly best. For entering larger amounts of text, such as an e-mail, the native text input mechanism is better overall. You should also never mix the two input methods, as this is extremely confusing for most users.

The application should also support touch-specific extensions to common usage scenarios. For example, the user should be able to scroll both by dragging the scrollbar and by flicking whatever content needs to be scrolled (i.e., kinetic scrolling). Horizontal swipe events should also be registered as back/forward commands where applicable. Long taps should bring up the contextual menu for the selected item, if any. These fine touches enhance the user experience considerably and bridge the gap between native applications and Java ME applications.

The final aspect you should consider is the screen's number of colors. While a difference between screens supporting 65,536 colors and screens supporting 16 million colors does exist, it isn't that noticeable in practice. However, the difference between 65,536 and 4,096 colors or less is huge. Should you have to target both categories of devices, you will probably need to have separate graphics for each, optimized for their respective number of colors.

Other Hardware Considerations

There are other hardware-related factors that differentiate devices. For example, network speed varies greatly from device to device and from scenario to scenario due to a variety of reasons. As this is something completely outside your control, you cannot really fix network-related issues—but you can attempt to alleviate them.

For example, you should have the application periodically measure network throughput and inform the user if the transfer speed falls below a minimum accepted value. You should also minimize the amount of bits transferred by compressing your data and by using a mobile-friendly encoding scheme (JSON or a binary protocol such as Hessian). Finally, design your server API/protocol to return only the minimum amount of information required as a response to your requests; more information can be retrieved only if needed, via subsequent requests.

There are other tricks you can use to improve the user experience. Design your communication protocol so that you don't have to wait until the entire response is received and you can start parsing it as data is still coming in. Minimize the number of requests you make by concatenating several requests into a single, larger one, and do the same on the server side for responses. When concatenating requests and/or responses, make sure the smallest ones are first, so that processing starts as soon as possible. Try to send the data in a format that the device can directly understand (for example, don't send strings as ASCII but rather as a readUTF()-compatible byte array). Finally, try as much as possible to transfer data in the background and ahead of time.

These are good tips for all mobile platforms, but for Java ME the effects are doubled by the fact that quite often network transfer speed on Java ME devices is at least partially limited by the available CPU power. All of the foregoing tips not only minimize the amount of data transferred, but also tend to improve network-related CPU usage.

Storage space in the RMS or on the filesystem can also vary widely from device to device. If your application stores only user preferences and maybe a few things like a username and a password, this is usually not a problem. If, however, your application stores large amounts of data, such as a set of complete records or maybe documents or images received from the server, then you might run into problems. Do some research ahead of time regarding how each of your target devices stands out in this respect. For example, some devices limit your RMS record store size to a fixed value, while others allow you to use the full extent of available device storage for the RMS—this is something you need to know when working on a storage-heavy application.

Another issue of concern regarding on-device storage of any kind is security. People usually think of the filesystem as being insecure, while the RMS is fairly secure. This is not necessarily the case, in that the RMS may be very easy to get into. For example, some devices use a file on the filesystem itself to persist the RMS, which makes the RMS on those devices just as insecure as a regular file—though, to be fair, I have personally seen this on only a few cheap, no-name devices. Even if this is not the case, the RMS is still persisted to a flash chip of some sort, so it is theoretically possible to physically remove the chip and read its contents. Some devices might even encrypt data you save to the RMS (either by default or provide this option to the user), but 99% of all Java ME devices out there do not. So, to be sure, you should always encrypt extremely sensitive data yourself.

Battery life is another issue to be taken into consideration, especially for applications that are designed to be long-running (such as IM clients). Throttling the network and CPU works great to improve battery life, but there are also other tricks you can try. For example, the screen consumes a lot of power, so you may want to consider using vendor-specific APIs to dim the screen's brightness. Just as with laptops, dimming the screen even slightly can result in a noticeable increase in battery life. Not using sound or vibrations also helps increase battery life. Optimizing your code also increases battery life, as the CPU needs fewer cycles to run your application. Proper usage of sleep() and wait()/notify() methods in idle moments also noticeably increases battery life, as it allows the CPU to enter a power-saving mode.

Last but certainly not least, user input capabilities can vary widely between devices. For example, some devices do not register multiple, simultaneous key presses, so trying to move up and to the left at the same time in a video game will not work on them. Cheap touchscreen devices usually have poor accuracy and/or lack a stylus, so doing precision touch input on them is also not possible. As these issues greatly affect the user's experience, you have to take them into consideration when you design your user interface.

Capabilities Fragmentation

Devices do not differ only in terms of hardware; they also differ in terms of capabilities. Some APIs and JSRs are quite mainstream (JSR 75, for PIM and filesystem access), while others are supported on only relatively few devices (the Location API). Furthermore, even if two devices support the same capabilities, they may not support them to the same extent.

The best example of this is the Multimedia API, or MMAPI. Most modern phones support the MMAPI; however, the extent to which they support it varies widely. For example, two different devices having the same camera might support different maximum resolutions for capturing images or video. The same goes for media playback:

high-end devices support all common media types, while lower-end ones tend to support only the basic types, which usually means .wav audio files and possibly .3gp videos.

Dealing with capabilities fragmentation is a mixed affair, in that the issues are fairly easy to spot and the root cause is easily identified, but solutions usually involve some kind of compromise. To continue the foregoing MMAPI example, if the captured image resolution is lower than what the application needs, the image can be upscaled in software to match the minimum requirements, but this comes at a cost in terms of CPU usage and picture quality.

Unlike hardware fragmentation issues, you can work on capabilities-related fragmentation issues even before starting work on the actual application. The first step is to make a list of all the JSRs and APIs that are required by your application and research which of them are supported by your target devices and to what extent. If you're lucky, all your target devices support all the capabilities you require, so there's nothing further to be done here.

If you are unlucky and there are some capabilities that your target devices do not support, then the next step to take is to see if you can somehow emulate these capabilities. For example, not all devices support the location API (in fact, most Java ME devices don't). However, it is possible to ask the user what his current location is and work with that data just as if it were coming from the location API itself. If the MMAPI is not supported but JSR 75 is, which allows filesystem access, then instead of snapping a picture from within the application, the user could select a picture file that is present on the filesystem. If the Bluetooth API is not supported, then consider using the network for getting your data across: you upload your files to the server, and the other party can retrieve it from there, even if he's just three feet away.

While not particularly elegant, these workarounds are preferable to not being able to use the application. Furthermore, on devices on which the required capabilities are supported, they can even be considered extra features because they give the user more choice over what data to give to the application (e.g., even if you're in Kansas, you may want to have your application think you're in Boston).

Another common scenario involves adding support for floating-point math on CLDC 1.0 devices, or support for missing media types, such as SVG for vector graphics. These are fairly common problems, and the work has almost certainly been done before in the form of third-party libraries, so a quick Internet search should help you immensely.

It should be noted that some capabilities can't be emulated at all, such as the PIM part of JSR 75, while others can be emulated but not to a reasonable extent, such as the 3D API (you could implement it in software, but the performance would be abysmal). In these cases, you can either declare the problematic devices as unsupported, drop the capabilities altogether, or work around them (e.g., your calendar application can still work without PIM capabilities—you just won't be able to sync the app's calendar with the device's native calendar). Obviously, if the presence of a certain capability is deemed mission critical and that capability is not available natively on a certain device and cannot be emulated, then there's nothing else you can do but declare that device unsupported.

At this point, I would like to make a little detour and point out that when emulating or working around missing capabilities, you will usually end up requiring separate builds. There are tools to help you with this (which will be discussed soon), but the fact still remains that you will have to take care of and support multiple builds, and you will have to instruct the user to download the correct one for his or her device.

> **NOTE:** A commonly used technique is to configure your server to detect the phone's browser user agent and automatically deliver a build based on this. However, this technique does not work if a non-native browser is used (e.g., Opera Mini). Furthermore, the browser agent field may be spoofed and/or hidden by the browser.

The problem becomes even more complicated when a certain capability is supported in the latest firmware version but not on older firmware versions, or when capabilities are installed via add-ons (for example, sensor support for Symbian v5 devices can be added via a downloadable and completely optional package). While instructing the user to download the version for his or her specific device is common practice and fairly straightforward, instructing the user to download the appropriate version for a specific firmware is highly technical, and not many users will be able to do this.

Fortunately, in most cases, both problems can be at least partially solved via a simple yet effective trick. Instead of providing multiple public builds of your application, you provide what can be called a front-end installer application. Once on the device, this installer application can try to determine what device and firmware version it is running on, by checking environmental properties such as the `microedition.platform` system property, or by checking if specific JSR/API–related classes are present, via `getClass().forName()`. Based on this information, the correct application build is identified and the user is informed of this. He can then choose to visit the appropriate web page or directly download and install the correct build.

A front-end installer avoids the situation in which users have to deal with multiple builds, which in turn decreases the chances of users installing the wrong build and increases customer satisfaction. It also lowers the amount of support questions that you receive and improves your company's image by providing a friendly, user-centric, and easy-to-use product.

Going back on track, the final step in dealing with capabilities-related fragmentation is to make sure that all devices supporting a certain capability, either natively or through workaround/emulation, meet the minimum requirements for said capability. For example, in the case of a city guide application, the minimum requirements in terms of the Location API would be that the application knows the user's current city.

In the best-case scenario, you do not have to do anything special for this, as the minimum requirements are met by default. This is the case in the foregoing example, since even if the device does not have native GPS capabilities, the user can still manually specify his or her current city.

Opposite this are the worst-case scenarios. For example, if the city guide application requirements change from knowing the user's current city to being able to determine automatically at runtime where in the city the user is (down to street/neighborhood level), things get complicated. While difficult, if the device does not natively support the Location API, this is still possible to achieve in some scenarios.

For example, on some devices, you can retrieve the current cell ID via `System.getProperty()` (the actual property name varies, but is usually either "Cell-ID" or something like "com.X.cellid", where X is the name of the handset manufacturer). It is also helpful to know the local area code, which can be obtained similarly to the cell ID. Once you have this information, you can perform a lookup and determine the user's approximate current location.

The main problems with this approach are that obtaining the current cell information can have very stringent security requirements (on Nokia S40 devices, the app has to be signed with operator- or manufacturer-level clearance, for example) and converting this into a real-world location usually requires that you have accurate and up-to-date information regarding cellular towers—which is a daunting task in itself. Fortunately, there are open databases to help with the latter problem, such as the one available at `www.opencellid.org`. Another approach would be to use the Wireless Messaging API to listen for Cell Broadcast Service messages and retrieve the cell information from there. While this can eliminate the need for signing in most circumstances, it does require that the target device(s) support WMA, and it still requires a lookup.

We have seen the best-case and the worst-case scenarios, but things usually fall somewhere in the middle. A very common scenario involves the developers enhancing capabilities only slightly—for example, increasing Bluetooth transfer speed by compressing data or using an alternate encoding.

Finally, there are a few general tips you can follow when dealing with capabilities-related fragmentation. First and foremost, keep everything modularized and abstract. Rather than using the Location API directly, implement a location module and let all the magic happen there (it's up to the module how it retrieves the user's current location). Don't use Bluetooth file transfers directly; implement a file transfer module in which Bluetooth is the preferred option, but not the only one.

Second, and somewhat tied up to the previous tip, while defining your application requirements, try to define backup solutions for features that might not be available on all devices. For example, the backup solution for device-to-device transfer via Bluetooth might be using the network to transfer data. The benefits of having backup solutions are twofold: you minimize capabilities fragmentation problems, and you also provide users with more options to get things done.

Third, always try to keep your minimum requirements as low as possible, even if your target devices are high-end ones. This gives you the potential to target more devices later on if the application proves successful, and it also enhances the user experience on current target devices. For example, even if your Bluetooth transfer speed is 200 KB/s, design your application to work with only 100 KB/s; your app will then work properly in less than stellar scenarios, while providing top-notch performance in normal usage (since its minimum requirements are met and exceeded).

Fourth, see how others did it. This is often overlooked. It frequently happens, especially if you're a seasoned developer, that when you face a capabilities fragmentation problem you tend to implement either the first solution that comes to mind or a solution that you have used in the past, on another device. The problem with this is that Java ME devices can be wildly different and tend to have unique quirks, so chances are that there is a better solution than the one you thought of, possibly that makes uses of vendor-specific extensions or device-specific capabilities, or that the solution that worked on device X will not be as effective on the current device you're working with. Because of this, you should always research your problem thoroughly, on both generic and device-specific levels. You will probably find a better solution than the one you currently have in mind, or at least you will find a way to make your current solution even better.

Fifth, test your application in real-life circumstances. While hardware fragmentation issues or performance issues can be detected and fixed in the office, some capabilities fragmentation issues cannot. How strong and accurate is the GPS signal while you're on the move? How does Bluetooth transfer fare when in a crowded environment like a train station? How's the picture quality in low-light conditions or outdoors? The only way you can accurately test these things is if you put the application on a real device and go out into the world.

Sixth, see if there are vendor-specific APIs that might help you. Sometimes the functionality or capability that you require is not covered by standard Java ME APIs or JSRs, but it is present in vendor-specific extensions. For example, if you're writing a GPS application, chances are you'll want to keep the backlight always on. Java ME provides no mechanism for this, but most popular vendors provide the capabilities you need: Nokia has `DeviceControl.setLights()`, Samsung has `LCDLight.on()`, etc.

Seventh, if you're targeting a smartphone, check if you can use a native application to help you with your problem. For example, some Symbian devices do not allow Java ME access to the accelerometer or to the GPS chip embedded within them (or they do but in later firmware versions or by installing optional components). However, these capabilities can be accessed from within native apps.

As such, a viable though somewhat hacky solution is to create a native application that acts as a TCP/IP reachable server (running on localhost) for accelerometer and GPS data. The Java ME application then connects to the native server application via sockets and reads the data it needs. This setup is fairly contrived, but it works as a last resort.

API Inconsistencies

Out of all the fragmentation issues you're likely to encounter, API inconsistencies are the hardest ones to identify and the most annoying to fix.

API inconsistencies happen when different vendors don't interpret the Java ME standard in the same manner. This usually results in the same system call having different results on different devices, or returning different values, or even having no effect at all. Because they are system calls, developers naturally assume that they will behave in the manner that they do on other devices and that they will not fail—in other words, that they are always safe and that they always work OK. As such, they are not typically subject to examination when the application misbehaves or does not produce the expected results, so a lot of time is spent debugging and examining application code, while, in fact, the problem lies in the platform implementation. That being said, API inconsistencies should be the last thing to check for when your application misbehaves, as most of the time it is your code that does not function properly, not the platform.

API inconsistencies can be split into three subcategories:

- *Localized inconsistencies*: Usually only a single method call misbehaves, or a few tightly related functions misbehave. For example, the Graphics.translate() method does not handle translation as expected on some platforms, which tends to affect other drawing functions as well.

- *Architectural or global inconsistencies*: The standard as a whole is not properly implemented. An example of this is the fact that some phones do not call pauseApp() when they should, which can cause all sorts of unwanted side effects.

- *Open for interpretation*: The specifications do not define any clear right or wrong answer. For example, manufacturers are free to choose their own keycodes, and some devices may have keys (and their associated keycodes) that are not present on others.

Let's look over these one by one.

Localized API Inconsistencies

Localized API inconsistencies tend to be a more common occurrence on older phones, or on no-name phones, and less of an issue on newer phones (as vendors have worked out most of the kinks). Once localized API inconsistencies have been found, their fixes are usually a lot simpler compared to those required for hardware and capabilities fragmentation issues.

Performance-wise, the best fix for any API inconsistency issue is to alter either the method call parameters or the return values so that the end result matches what you would get on a well-behaved implementation. In this approach, the bulk of the work is still done natively by the platform, so the performance is still good. This is possible in most scenarios, since localized API inconsistencies and their unwanted effects tend to be subtle (e.g., off-by-one errors, precision errors, etc.) and happen only in specific corner cases. Also, sometimes it is possible to replace a problematic method by using other method calls, which eliminates the need for altering parameters or return values, thus further minimizing the impact on performance.

When either of the foregoing is not possible, the only course of action you have left is to roll your own implementation of the problematic method (either you write it yourself or use a third-party library). Obviously this usually incurs a significant performance hit and should be avoided if at all possible.

In both cases, it is best practice to create a "wrapper" for the problematic method, to both hide the complexity of the fix and minimize redundant code. For static method calls or for methods that do not care about context, it is enough to create a single-method wrapper, which can then be a stand-alone class or part of a bigger GeneralWrappers class.

For methods that do care about context, or that influence their context in some way (as is the case of the Graphics.translate() method), you have to create a wrapper for their entire context—even if you can also fix the problem via a singe-method wrapper. To keep with the translate() example, you should create a wrapper for the entire Graphics object, something like GraphicsWrapper.

The idea behind wrapping the entire context even if a single-method fix is possible is that this improves code readability and consistency (i.e., you don't use mixed wrappers and native calls in your code—you just use wrapper calls), and there's a very good chance that if something is wrong in a native method, then something is also wrong or will affect other related methods too—so you'll likely end up wrapping those also.

It is worth noting that methods that are context-aware are quite tricky to wrap properly, because of their long-lasting side effects. For example, a call to translate() influences all further drawing operations done on the Graphics object by shifting their (x,y) coordinates. If you fix a broken translate() implementation by altering the method call parameters of the native system call, then you should have nothing else to care about, as all the side effects (i.e., coordinate shifting) are handled transparently by the platform.

If, however, you fix a broken translate() by rolling your own implementation, then you have to keep track yourself of the current translation values and manually apply them to all the further drawing method calls—in other words, you have to emulate all the side effects yourself, which is what the wrapper in Listing 9–1 does.

Listing 9–1. *A Graphics Wrapper Class That Fixes a Broken translate() Method*

```
import javax.microedition.lcdui.Graphics;

public class GraphicsWrapper {

    protected Graphics graphics;
    int translateX = 0, translateY = 0;
    ...

    public GraphicsWrapper(Graphics g)
    {
        graphics = g;
    }

    public void translate(int dx, int dy)
    {
        translateX = dx;
```

```
        translateY = dy;
    }

    public void drawLine(int x1, int y1, int x2, int y2)
    {
        graphics.drawLine(translateX+x1, translateY+y1, translateX+x2, translateY+y2) ;
    }

    ...
}
```

The upshot of using wrappers is that you can actually enhance the native API. For example, there's no native way in Java ME to draw or fill polygons, but you can elegantly overcome this limitation by implementing the necessary functionality in the GraphicsWrapper class in the form of drawPoly() and fillPoly() methods. Since the rest of the code would use the wrapper and not the underlying Graphics object directly, it would look as if the platform natively supported polygons.

Probably the most annoying problems related to localized API inconsistencies are random occurrences and corner cases. What this means is that a given method call behaves properly in most circumstances, but not in all circumstances. I have seen implementations that could properly decode some PNG images but not others (transparency would be lost, for example), devices that would stop responding when a certain media file would be played, JVMs that would simply refuse to properly close certain input streams but not others (the same applies to reading from input streams), and more. This is voodoo territory once more.

For media-related random issues, what I usually do is simply recode the problematic files. This usually either fixes the problem or gives me some insight regarding what exactly triggers it (maybe it's a certain file encoding, or the media file is above a certain bitrate).

For platform-related random issues, you should first be 100% that you do everything right and by the book, and that the random or corner-case bug is indeed a bug in the implementation and not in your code. The best way to do this is to create a stand-alone simple project and try to replicate the problem there instead of in your application. Once you know for sure that the problem lies in the implementation, there are several things you can try.

First and foremost, try slight alterations to the execution context. If you have file-related problems, try moving the problematic file to another location, or try renaming it. If you have trouble reading from an URL, try removing the "www" or "http://" part of it, or if it's under your control, move the necessary content to a different URL on (preferably) a different server. If you have threading-related issues, try adding small delays in your code (or anything else that breaks the "tempo").

If that does not work, try "rephrasing" the code (i.e., try to change the order in which methods are called). This can sometimes work, even if it makes no sense. For example, I had one case in which I had to open two different input streams, one from a file and one from an URL. Opening the file first and the URL second would cause the application to crash; opening the URL first and the file second worked fine. As it turns out, the problem was a race condition in the platform implementation (the code was running on a beta JVM).

Localized API inconsistencies are annoying, but at least they affect the application only locally. As we will see next, there are inconsistencies that "operate" on the architectural level—or worse, that stem from local inconsistencies but affect the application globally.

Global API Inconsistencies

Sometimes the API inconsistencies are on a higher level than individual functions. They might be related to the MIDlet life cycle, or to the way certain optional APIs are implemented and to the life cycle of the high-level objects associated with them. For example, as mentioned previously, it is quite a common on a lot of phones that the pauseApp() method isn't called when the application is moved to the background, minimized, or paused for any reason. As some applications use this method to properly move to the stand-by state (for example, by telling the server that "I'll go away now for a while, show me as idle" in the case of a chat application), not receiving this event can cause unexpected and unpredictable results (to keep with the previous example, the mobile user might lose some IM messages or the server might disconnect the mobile client if the application is minimized for too long).

The most common way to deal with these kinds of inconsistencies is to work around them on an architectural level. For example, even though the pauseApp() method doesn't get called, most modern applications use a Canvas to display their UI, and the Canvas class provides the showNotify() and hideNotify() methods, which from my experience get called properly on 99% of the devices I've worked with. As such, while it does take a bit of work to get done properly, it is possible to move the pause/minimized detection to the application's Canvas and take the appropriate pause/minimize actions when the Canvas is hidden instead of when pauseApp() is called. The same trick of repurposing methods and callbacks can usually be applied to most inconsistencies related to the MIDlet life cycle and to the core Java ME platform itself.

Other platform-specific inconsistencies that you might find relate to the maximum number of threads you can have running (a minimum of ten is specified in JSR-185, but some devices support fewer), the number of network connections you can keep open at any given time, and more. These can be overcome by, for example, running to different tasks on the same thread or closing connections immediately after you're done with them instead of keeping them open for later use. If you follow the rules regarding flexible Java ME coding mentioned earlier in the book, you should be able to overcome these inconsistencies with relative ease.

Inconsistencies regarding how optional APIs are implemented are also fairly common. The MMAPI, for example, defines a clear life cycle for its Player objects, with five states: UNREALIZED, REALIZED, PREFETCHED, STARTED, and CLOSED. According to the specifications, you should be able to move from a higher state to a lower state (for example, from PREFETCHED to REALIZED) when needed, in order to conserve resources, and once a player has stopped playing, it should return to the PREFETCHED state, from where it can be played again.

Unfortunately, not all implementations do this right. On some devices, you cannot move from the STARTED to the PREFETCHED state (the call to deallocate(), which is responsible for this, either throws an exception or does nothing), and some devices simply do not notify registered PlayerListeners of all events (you may not get notified of VOLUME_CHANGED events if they occur in quick succession, for example).

The effects of optional API inconsistencies are also not that easily identifiable sometimes: unless you check the amount of free memory both before and after a deallocate() call, it's difficult to determine if the call actually de-allocates anything, as the specs say it should. Sometimes the only way to actually de-allocate memory from a player is to actually remove all references to the player and its associated objects, and let the GC work its magic—which requires you to manage not only Players but also DataSources, Controls, and more.

> **NOTE:** Global problems can even be related to a single method, like in the foregoing deallocate() case, but if the effect of the problem is global and affects other parts of the application, or if the solution isn't a purely local one, then you are indeed facing a global problem.

These inconsistencies, while global in scope and usually easily spotted, are somewhat harder to handle because their root causes are not so easy to pinpoint. The problem stems from the fact that JSRs or optional APIs are usually highly esoteric and serve a very specific purpose, so you need quite a bit of experience with them before you can get a feel for how things should work: to keep with the previous examples, while it is quite easy to determine that the pauseApp() method does not get called and to work around this by using showNotify()/hideNotify(), it's a bit more difficult to figure out exactly why deallocate() does nothing and what it takes to get it working properly.

Basically what you need in this case is information, and much more of it and much more specific than you would need for dealing with localized or general platform inconsistencies. As such, the first step to solving optional API inconsistencies is to thoroughly read both the standard documentation *and* the vendor-specific documentation pertaining to the API in question. Sometimes just reading through the vendor-specific documentation provides helpful hints, whether it's corner cases and the way the vendor implementation handles them, known bugs, or even usage examples or comments that highlight the way the vendor's implementation actually works. The Internet is also especially helpful here, as you're very likely to find forum topics or blog posts related to the exact specific problem you are dealing with—which is usually not covered in any book or other "official" reading material you might find available.

You can also treat these issues exactly like fragmentation issues to gather more information (this has been covered previously in the chapter); see how other devices behave and try to figure out why your target device behaves differently, run tests, and simulate various other scenarios. This is often an overlooked step, mainly because optional API inconsistencies have a very narrow scope, and developers tend to examine them in the same narrow scope.

Once you have sufficient information, it's time to fix the problem. Ideally, if you're facing a known bug, there's also a known workaround. The workaround may not always be in code. For example, you might need to re-encode your media files, ask the user to upgrade to a specific firmware version or to install an official patch, or configure his device in a certain way.

It can also be the case that there is no known workaround that applies to your scenario for whatever reason, in which case you'll have to come up with your own workaround. It has been my experience that with optional APIs you really have to get creative, which is why having as much information as possible is crucial. The API isn't releasing memory? OK, try to make more available memory from another part of the application. Having problems receiving certain event notifications? No problem—manually do a periodic check for changes.

Once you have a workaround, it's time to integrate it into your application. This usually requires adding an extra code layer to your application that sits between the API and your application code, or it requires architectural changes.

It's also quite possible that there is simply no workaround you can use, in which case you have to treat the situation exactly like you would treat an unimplementable/unavailable feature. This is hard to do psychologically if you're facing just a "small bug" in an otherwise perfectly functional API implementation, but I have seen many man-hours spent trying to overcome such "small bugs"—wasted time that could have otherwise been spent productively. That is not to say that you should give up the moment you see an API inconsistency, but if you've done your research, tried everything, and run out of ideas, then it's time to move on. On more full-blown platforms, it might be worth it to dig deeper and throw more time at the problem, because you have more possibilities to explore and more resources to work with, but Java ME is a tight platform, and there's only so much you can do with it when things don't go your way.

Inconsistencies Open for Interpretation

When the standard does not specify *exactly* how to do something, the implementations are free to make their own assumptions and decisions—which can lead to problems if not all vendors make the same assumptions and decisions.

The most eloquent example for this is keycodes. As you know, in Java ME each recognized key has a specific keycode. While it is possible to convert a given keycode to a standardized GameCanvas action (FIRE, UP, LEFT, GAME_A, GAME_B, etc.) on all implementations, the keycodes themselves are not the same among implementations, nor are they set in stone by the specification itself. Furthermore, some implementations have more keys than others and as such can generate more keycodes than others.

In fact, if you look over the platform specification or the specification of optional APIs, you will see many cases in which implementations are left to their own devices (no pun intended). A great example of this is once again the MMAPI. To quote from Sun's documentation:

The choice of functionality is left to the implementation as well. It may support media playback but not recording, some devices may support volume control while others may not, and so on.

- developers.sun.com, Oracle corporation, Qusay H. Mahmoud,
"The J2ME Mobile Media API",
`http://developers.sun.com/mobility/midp/articles/mmapioverview/`
June 2003

When this happens, you get problems ranging from minor ones, like inverted controls (for example, Sagem keycodes for left and right softkeys are exactly the same as on Sony Ericsson, except reversed), to what can be considered critical issues, like capabilities fragmentation (see the foregoing MMAPI example). From my experience, however, you will rarely hit critical issues, and those that you will hit tend to fall into the category of capabilities fragmentation issues, which have already been discussed. Most of the time, you'll hit only minor problems like the inverted key situation just described.

Fortunately, dealing with this sort of problem requires only two things. First, you have to be aware that the problem can happen. This means having general knowledge of the API and of the specifications, and knowing from the start what is considered "optional," what is "left to the implementation," and what is set in stone. Anything that is not clearly set in stone should be considered volatile by default and should be researched before use. As long as it's not set in stone, the fact that 90% of devices out there (or even 90% of devices from the same vendor) do a certain thing in the same way doesn't mean that you can assume that's the right way and hard-code that in your application.

The second thing that you will need is the actual implementation-specific values. In this respect, it's quite helpful that sometimes when the specifications don't set something in stone, they do, however, provide a way to find out what the actual implementation will behave like. For example, the media types and capabilities of the MMAPI are extremely volatile and highly implementation-specific, but the specifications do provide methods like `Manager.getSupportedContentTypes()`, which can help determine what media types are supported, even dynamically at runtime. This is not always the case, however, and some things you have to determine via experimentation (like keycodes for non-standard keys).

Once you have all the information you need, it's time to get that information into your application. You can, of course, have custom builds for each device, but a far more efficient way is to deal with these issues at runtime, by trying to determine the device vendor and family your code is running on, and using the appropriate values and/or code paths for "open to interpretation" aspects.

You can do this yourself, or you could use a third-party porting framework to do this for you. Third-party porting frameworks are a valuable tool for Java ME developers, so it's worth giving them a closer look.

Porting Frameworks

As we have seen so far in the chapter, while developing for Java ME, you will face a lot of fragmentation issues, particularly at the software level. Dealing with them manually is both time-consuming and error-prone, which is why porting frameworks exist.

A porting framework's job is mainly to help you manage fragmentation. It is a common misconception that a porting framework should hide fragmentation, and while some do indeed do this, *managing* fragmentation is a far better option.

The difference is subtle but important. In the case of hiding fragmentation, the framework takes control away from you and basically says, "Here, use this unified API for doing stuff—anything else is off-limits." You don't really have the ability to customize how the framework does stuff; you just have the ability to use the API that it provides and hope that it does what you need it to do.

A framework that manages fragmentation is different. It is built around the concept of giving you choice and freedom. While it does provide a default and standardized API, it also allows you to hook into it and use vendor- or device-specific code where you need to within your application.

Choosing a porting framework is a very important choice when doing multi-device or multi-platform development, and it will most certainly drastically influence the development process. There are, of course, business factors involved, such as price, but technical reasons should take precedence over business reasons in this respect.

You should also be aware that there are no perfect porting frameworks out there; each has its strengths and weaknesses. What you need to do is weigh each framework's technical strengths and weaknesses, and pick the one that best suits your overall goals. That being said, let's look at some of the technical aspects of porting frameworks, which you can use to evaluate and compare them.

The Preprocessor

In the desktop and server world, a preprocessor for Java is probably one of the worst ideas ever. It isn't even needed, as the platform is powerful enough to be able to do at runtime anything that the preprocessor would do at compile time.

In the Java ME world, things are quite different. Things like extremely limited reflection capabilities, restrictions on code size, capabilities and platform fragmentation, low amounts of available resources, and device quirks mean that most of the time the code has to be device-specific at compile time and that adapting it at runtime isn't an option.

As such, good porting frameworks always have a good and powerful preprocessor included. The main purpose of the preprocessor is to exclude some blocks of code (or entire files) from the build while including others. Its use is extremely similar to regular C/C++–style preprocessors, as can be seen in Listing 9–2.

Listing 9–2. *A Possible Java ME Preprocessor Code Example*

```
//#if ${device.vendor} == nokia
        import com.nokia.mid.ui.DeviceControl;
//#elseif ${device.vendor} == samsung
        import com.samsung.util.LCDLight;
//#endif


public class LCDUtils
{
....
        public static void keepBacklightOn()
        {
                //#if ${device.vendor} == nokia
                        DeviceControl.setLights(0,100);
                //#elseif ${device.vendor} == samsung
                        LCDLight.on();
                //#endif
        }
...
}
```

When passed through the preprocessor, this file would generate either a Nokia-compatible or a Samsung-compatible file, depending on the target device vendor. This means that you do not have to keep separate versions of your files for each separate vendor: you can consolidate them into a single file and have the preprocessor do the separation automatically. This makes the code clearer and the project as a whole easier to manage, thus saving an unbelievable amount of time, effort, and money.

> **TIP:** You can also use the preprocessor for more unconventional stuff, like compile-time internationalization, macros, or even stuff like multiple inheritance (which Java does not support by default). However, these are all considered hack usages even by Java ME standards and should generally be avoided.

All preprocessors are more or less equal in terms of including and excluding blocks of code, so what really differentiates them is the way in which they integrate with the rest of the framework and with external tools. For example, in the case of your preprocessor, can preprocessor directives influence the build engine (see ahead)? Can you use the preprocessor to add metadata to your code—for example, look and feel directives for the UI library (again, see ahead)? Can you use the preprocessor to run third-party tools over blocks of code or entire files?

These aspects are secondary to the preprocessor's main purpose, but they do come in handy quite often, and once you get used to them, you can't really go back.

The Device Database

A comprehensive device database is critical to any porting framework. Things like keycode values, screen resolution and size, multimedia capabilities, and supported APIs should be considered standard. The more comprehensive the database, the more information the framework has to work with and thus the higher quality the port is.

In addition, the framework should allow you to access all this information via the preprocessor and also at runtime (for example, via a dynamically generated static class). This allows you to automatically tailor your application code to match the device you're running on, something like the example in Listing 9–3.

Listing 9–3. *Runtime Device-Specific Code*

```
public void doMultipleFileUpload(File [] files, int maxSimultaneousConnections)
{
      ...
}

....

doMultipleFileUpload( someFileArray, DeviceInfo.getMaxNetworkConnections() )
```

The code in Listing 9–3 could be part of a file upload application. The DeviceInfo class, generated dynamically by the framework based on the device database, contains information pertaining to the current target device. One piece of information is the maximum number of simultaneous network connections that the device supports. The application code can then use this information at runtime to make sure it makes the most of the device's capabilities without running into problems (like opening more connections than the device supports).

The device database is also extremely useful in the project's planning phase, as it can be used to determine what devices you can target, and what features said devices will support and to what extent. Oftentimes having a quality device database is worth its weight in gold, as the time it saves in research hours can add up to something substantial.

The Build Engine

A Java ME application is made up of many different files, some of them code, some of them media resources, and some of them configuration files or miscellanea. These files then have to be bundled together in a JAR file. The responsibility of the build engine is to take the files that are needed for a specific target device, and only those files, and create the end result JAR file.

This task can prove to be more difficult than it sounds. Consider, for example, that a project might target devices with different screen resolutions, and that each screen resolution has a specific set of media files (for icons, for fonts, etc.). The build engine must include the appropriate files based on the device's specifications. The same applies for localization files, code files, configuration files, and everything else that goes into a JAR.

Furthermore, some builds will require signing or other "special touches" to be applied (to the JAD file, for example), and it is the build engine's job to handle these as well.

A good build engine can work with a comprehensive folder structure in which developers can put their files (for example, the /Screen.240x320 folder would contain resources for the 240×320 resolution, the /Vendor.Nokia folder would contain files that are needed only for Nokia builds, the /Certificates folder would contain all the necessary certificates, etc.) and also supports defining consolidation rules (for example, in the case of overlapping resources, developers should be able to specify if the /Vendor or the /Screen resources take precedence).

A good build engine should also be able to look over the code and substitute some variable names or class names for others before passing the files over to the compiler, if instructed to do so. For example, it should be able to parse a generic statement like import javax.microedition.lcdui.Canvas and substitute it with import framework.wrapper.nokia.lcdui.Canvas or with import framework.wrapper.samsung.lcdui.Canvas based on the targeted vendor. This is extremely useful when writing wrappers, but has other uses as well, like easily creating full/demo versions of applications by having two different classes, one with a nag screen and the other without.

Finally, a good build engine should be easy to integrate with a standard Java ME build tool, typically Ant.

The Abstraction API

The abstraction API is what the framework is all about. Basically, instead of calling the native platform API, you call the abstraction API instead; it then is responsible for making sure the end result matches the expected result by transparently handling fragmentation issues and inconsistencies.

The best abstraction APIs are those that mimic the native APIs themselves. Ideally, the abstraction APIs should be so easy to use that you do not have to modify your existing code at all. This can happen if the abstraction APIs exactly mimic the native APIs, and if the porting framework has vendor- or device-specific wrappers for all API classes. In conjunction with the substitution feature mentioned previously, this creates a hassle-free environment for the developer; all the porting problems are transparently handled by the framework.

A really good abstraction API not only mimics the native API, but also extends it. For example, it can add methods like drawPoly() or fillPoly() to the Graphics class in order to enhance the drawing capabilities of your application, or a generic keepBacklightOn() method to the Display class.

Multi-platform Support

This is a great feature to have, but for a strictly fragmentation-oriented framework, it is optional. Basically, this allows you to take your plain Java ME application and compile it for an entirely different platform, like Android.

This is usually done by cross-compiling the code and even translating it from one language to another, as is the case for Java ME app to iPhone app conversion, for example.

A point of concern is that different platforms have different user interaction paradigms, which need to be mitigated (for example, neither Android nor the iPhone has the concept of softkeys). As such, using a multi-platform conversion tool is really recommended only for back-end stuff or for applications that do not rely on platform-native forms and widgets and instead render their user interfaces via low-level drawing commands.

The ideal case for multi-platform support is that you just run your code through the conversion tool and it does everything on its own, resulting in a ready-to-run application for another platform. This is never the case, though, especially not for complex applications. Typically the conversion tool can do maybe up to 90–95% of the work, depending on the target platform and on the application's complexity, which means that you will still have to solve some issues yourself (memory leaks, for example). A good conversion tool will inform you of most potential problems and where in the code they might occur, so you know exactly where to look.

Utility Code and Tools

Have you noticed that Java ME has no support for big numbers? Or that its array handling capabilities are quite limited? Or that it has no XML handling capabilities to speak of? A good porting framework will have all these features as part of its "utility package," which is typically a set of stand-alone classes that you can use in your project(s) separate from the main porting framework.

External tools are also a great bonus. Cross-format converters (from XML to JSON for example), binary resource editors, configuration file editors, code obfuscators, and more are sometimes part of the porting framework complete package. As with utility classes, while these tools are not directly related to porting applications, they do make a developer's life easier.

In addition, they are typically designed with the needs of mobile/Java ME developers in mind, and are designed to be used in conjunction with the porting framework itself, and they can typically be integrated quite easily into the build process to further automate things—so they end up providing quite a bit of extra value.

UI Library

Good porting frameworks also come packaged with a quality UI library. This makes perfect sense, as the UI is typically one of the hardest things to port across devices and platforms.

You can also find stand-alone UI toolkits that support a wide range of devices; however, these offer porting support only for the UI; everything else is up to you. In addition, they do not typically come with all the goodies for porting frameworks, such as a high-quality build engine and device database. You can, of course, integrate third-party UI libraries into your framework of choice, but this can lead to unwanted side effects and bugs, and will usually void or limit your support options on the UI library side (and for good reason, since you would be basically running their code on top of a third-party software solution that they have no control over).

For this reason, it is a very good idea to stick with the UI library that comes with the porting framework. These are usually quite capable and integrate extremely well with the rest of the porting toolset.

A good UI library should do away completely with the native UI widgets and implement its own from scratch. It should also support styling via CSS or other designer-friendly means, flexible layout mechanisms for the UI (very important if you plan on targeting devices with widely different resolutions), a good selection of widgets (similar to what you would find in the desktop world), and also a good selection of eye-candy effects to add extra polish to your application.

Customer Support

Last but certainly not least, customer support is extremely important for a porting framework, both from a business *and* a technical standpoint. No matter how good the framework you will be using is, it is likely that at some point something will have to be handled manually, whether it's a new fragmentation issue or a scenario-specific problem. For example, here are a few common situations that you might encounter while developing Java ME applications:

- You might need some professional advice (e.g., on how to implement a given requirement) from people with lots of Java ME experience on both low-end and high-end devices.

- Your project's needs are very specific, and you need a lot of customization, both from a technical point of view and from a business point of view (e.g., licensing model).

- You might need to work with a company that has cross-platform experience and that can help you in porting your application to other platforms.

- You might need that extra feature added just for your project, like finding the device's coordinates based on the cell ID.

In all of these cases, customer support can make or break the project. In fact, depending on your needs, the best technical solution might not be the best solution overall for the project. When it comes to Java ME, you're usually much better off paying for development support and knowledge and a good product than you are paying for a great product with no support attached to it.

A good Java ME porting framework comes backed up with virtually unlimited support by its developer. That is, as long as you are willing to pay, the developer is willing to dedicate as much effort and time into your needs as required, and is willing to modify the framework and associated tools to suit your needs.

Code License

If possible, go for an open source or dual-license porting framework. The goal here is to be able to own, use, or modify as much of the code as possible, and to be able to share this code with others (for suggestions, reporting bugs, etc.).

Besides the obvious business implications, a closed or restrictive code license means that fewer people have knowledge of the code and of the framework itself, so fewer people are able to help you when you get in trouble. In addition to this, should the company making or supporting the product go out of business, you may run the risk of being stuck with absolutely no support and a code base that does not get updated further.

On the other hand, open source or dual-licensing means that updates are more frequent because more people can contribute, and it also provides some insurance should the parent company go out of business, since the open source community can then continue development on its own.

The difference between closed and open source is extremely important in the Java ME world. While on the desktop or on the server, you have a more or less stable environment for your code across years or even decades. In the Java ME world, changes happen so often that your code might run fine today and be broken by a firmware update tomorrow. Open source initiatives almost always react more quickly and cover more ground than closed source ones.

Cross-Development and Porting Tools

There is quite a rich selection of cross-development and porting tools available today. In this section, let's briefly look at some of them.

First off, Sun's Lightweight UI Toolkit (LWUIT) is a great UI framework that supports most of the Java ME devices in use today that meet its minimum specifications (CLDC 1.1 / MIDP 2.0). Using LWUIT, you will be able to create great-looking user interfaces and easily port them across devices. LWUIT is available under GPL (in source-code form) and under Sun's license agreement (in binary form).

Next, Enough Software's J2ME Polish is a feature-complete porting suite, offering not only a rich UI framework but also other useful features: a powerful preprocessor, serialization support, remote method invocation support, external tools, and more. It can port your Java ME application across device models and vendors as well as to the Blackberry and Android platforms. It is available under GPL and a commercial license.

Mobile Distillery's Celsius is another powerful porting tool. Like J2ME Polish, it can automatically port your Java ME application across devices, vendors, and platforms. Celsius's main focus is on efficiently porting source code and minimizing the number of device-specific builds needed for any given application. Celsius is available under a commercial license.

Last but not least is Bedrock, created by Metismo. Bedrock has a larger scope than Celsius and J2ME Polish, in that it allows you to port your Java ME application not only to mobile phones but also to a wide variety of other devices. For example, it can target Sony's PSP and Nintendo's DS, among others. Bedrock is available under a commercial license.

Summary

In this chapter, we have looked at device fragmentation. We have looked at where it comes from, into what subtypes it can be split, and how to approach each type of fragmentation issue.

We have also examined how porting frameworks can help mitigate fragmentation issues and how to compare porting frameworks from a technical standpoint.

In the following chapter, we will look at how to optimize your application's code.

Chapter 10

Optimizing Your Code

Second to device fragmentation, the most severe problem you'll encounter when writing Java ME applications is lack of CPU power. The typical Java ME device offers very limited CPU power, usually enough to comfortably run simple applications but not enough to run more complex applications, with lots of background tasks and fancy user interfaces. While this cannot be avoided, its impact on your application can be minimized by optimizing your code and your algorithms.

There is some good news and some bad news regarding this. The good news is that you can effortlessly get speed-ups of 10–20% by optimizing your code, and in some cases the speed-up can be 200% or even more, with the typical speed-up somewhere between 30% and 50%. The bad news is that you have to optimize your code manually.

Why do you have to optimize your code manually? Good question—first, because javac (the official Java compiler and the compiler you're likely using) doesn't really optimize your code. Java relies on a just-in-time compiler, which is part of the JVM, to optimize at runtime the bytecode that javac produces, and optionally convert it to native code (which is significantly faster). The JVM found on most phones does not have a just-in-time compiler. This means that the Java bytecode produced by javac is usually executed as is, without any performance optimizations whatsoever applied to it—optimizations that are usually applied by default when targeting a full-fledged JVM.

Second, because even if you do use a compiler that is capable of optimizing your bytecode at build time, it can do only so much. Sure, you will definitely get a performance boost when compared to the non-optimized bytecode produced by javac, but you can get an extra 20–30% improvement (sometimes considerably more) if you optimize the code yourself. Remember, the compiler doesn't know the device you're targeting and its peculiarities, it doesn't know what algorithm the code represents, and it doesn't know what you actually want the code to do (your intentions, so to speak). It cannot take these factors into account when optimizing your code—you can.

In this chapter, we will look at the most important code optimization techniques that apply to Java ME development, from simple ones like fast code path switching and code inlining to more advanced techniques such as math expression optimization and variable locality improvement.

We will also look at how to properly compare algorithms and what algorithms to use for searching and sorting data. Finally, we will examine important programming techniques such as object pooling (used to eliminate object creation) and dynamic programming (used to eliminate recursion).

A Crash Course in Optimizing Code

Code optimization is a delicate affair. In theory, the goal is to get the CPU to execute a given task in as little time as possible; however, in real life, limitations such as memory size and I/O speed must be taken into account, so in practice the goal is really to get the CPU to execute a given task in as little time as possible while keeping resource consumption below a certain threshold. For example, an array lookup is faster than a multiplication, so you could keep a multiplication table in memory for all possible multiplication you can do between two ints—the problem is that in real life there probably aren't enough memory cells in the world to store this table.

You can optimize code in two ways: by "rephrasing" the code and by optimizing the underlying algorithm. To rephrase the code means to convert it into an equivalent but faster form. The optimization techniques that cover this can be applied successfully to almost any code fragment, with measurable performance improvements (typically 10–30%). If platform-specific knowledge is applied, the performance improvement can be even greater.

As an example of applied platform-specific knowledge, consider that any JVM is stack-based. As such, most JVMs try to keep the top of the stack (first X elements) in the CPU registers or in the CPU cache, both of which are considerably faster than the RAM. Values further down the stack must be read from memory, thus incurring a performance hit. Knowing the value of X means that you can write your code so that you attempt to minimize the number of memory reads that the JVM needs to do, thus improving performance.

Optimizing algorithms is an entirely different beast. Here, you are not concerned with the low-level details; you instead focus on the general idea of what you want to do. For example, if your goal is to sort a list of 1,000 contacts by name, then your task would be to find a more efficient *theoretical* way of doing this, maybe by replacing your selection sort algorithm with something faster, such as quicksort. The keyword here is "theoretical": algorithm optimization is done almost exclusively on paper, and the tools of the trade are abstract notions such as the Big O notation and general programming techniques such as dynamic programming, as well as a keen sense of intuition and good logic and mathematical skills.

Furthermore, the theoretical improvements an algorithm brings may not reflect themselves in real life, for a variety of reasons. For example, the algorithm's code might be large enough to require a lot of code page changes at the hardware level, thus incurring a big performance hit. Or it may rely on slow I/O operations, or a lot of method calls (which are again slow), or on creating a lot of objects, etc. All these factors do not manifest themselves on paper, but are almost immediately visible in real life.

It should also be noted that algorithm optimizations cannot be applied in all situations (there is little you can optimize in the algorithm of summing up a list of 1,000 numbers, for example), but when you can apply them, the results are usually spectacular. Depending on the scenario, a 50% real-world improvement is very common, with 200–300% improvements often seen. Even better, if you manage to find a suitable algorithm, the performance improvements scale exponentially instead of linearly, which means that for larger sets of input data, the performance difference over the original algorithm is measured in orders of magnitude.

Optimizing code and algorithms (especially the former) does have one big disadvantage: it tends to increase code size and decrease readability, as well as introduce the potential for more bugs due to corner cases. It can also take a significant amount of time and manpower to do properly. Because of this, you should apply optimizations only to performance-critical areas of the application, which are usually easily identified by using a profiler as being the areas of code that the CPU spends the most time executing. The 80-20 rule usually applies here, so usually 80% of the CPU time is spent running 20% of the code (sometimes even less, 5% or even 1%). An improvement in these critical areas will have a huge impact on performance, while at the same time providing the best possible risk/reward (risk as measured in terms of problems) and effort/reward (effort as measured in terms of time and manpower) ratios.

Knowing when to choose one type of optimization over the other is also important. You should always choose to optimize the code rather than the algorithm if the needed performance improvement is small, such as 10–15%. For larger improvements, the best course of action would be to try and optimize the algorithm used (though, as stated, this is not always possible). If you're running short on time, you should probably go with optimizing the code (unless you know a better algorithm and are confident that you can implement it in time).

> **NOTE:** In this chapter, we will look mostly at code optimizations, due to their always-applicable nature. Algorithm optimization is a far more difficult subject (and mostly outside the scope of this book), so it will be touched only lightly.

Code optimizations work on two vectors. First, there is the direct vector, in which the code's execution speed in terms of CPU cycles is improved. This is by far the most prominent optimization vector, and the most effective one. It is also what most people have in mind when you mention "code optimization" to them.

However, there is also a secondary optimization vector, the indirect one. This vector optimizes the actual execution speed in terms of *real-life time*, not in terms of CPU cycles. This may sound a bit confusing, but consider that executing a CPU operation requires that the data needed for that operation be available too. If that data is not already in the CPU's registers, then you have to read it from the cache, from memory, or worse, via I/O operations. This takes time, time in which the CPU sits idle. Add a virtual machine on top of that, as is the case with Java ME, and suddenly you'll realize that quite a bit of CPU time is lost *not* running your application code.

With Java ME, you have little to no control over what the hardware does; however, you do have control over what the JVM does and how it does it, albeit indirectly. By minimizing the JVM's "downtime," you can increase your application's performance. You can minimize this downtime by making the JVM's life easier: use fewer variables, keep code and related data closer together, write your math expressions in a JVM-friendly way, etc. These will all be covered in this chapter.

Code Optimization Techniques

In this section, we will cover the most important code optimization techniques you can use to speed up your Java ME applications.

Fast Code Path Switching

This basic optimization applies to if...else blocks and switch statements and is most effective within loops. What you need to do is put the most common cases at the top of the block/statement, with the least common cases at the end.

Depending on the number of cases and the complexity of the conditions, the performance improvement this method brings can range from <1% (i.e., unnoticeable) to almost 100% (seen, for example, in scenarios with one or more cases, and in which the condition for each case takes longer to evaluate than it does for the actual test case to execute).

This optimization is extremely easy to implement; however, it does require a bit of profiling in order to arrange the various code paths in order of their frequency in real-life usage scenarios. In fact, it is this profiling step that is most important; if it's not carried out properly, the whole point of this optimization is lost.

Ideally, profiling is entirely theoretical: you can mathematically calculate the frequency of use for each code path and arrange them accordingly. However, most of the time code profiling has to be hands-on. In the case of hands-on profiling, you have two main options: you can either use a profiler and an emulator to see which code paths get accessed most often, or provide your testers with special-purpose debug builds that measure this.

The latter is the preferred version, as it not only saves development time but also provides more down-to-earth and unbiased results. Because each person tends to have a different usage pattern, and because each person tests the application in different conditions and on real devices, the results obtained this way are considerably more reliable than those obtained by looking at the data obtained from a single person running the application on an emulator.

Fast code path switching as a technique can be applied to any platform, mobile or otherwise; it is extremely effective for Java ME because, from my experience, if statements are one of the slowest things you can do with a mobile JVM, mostly because of the way JVMs typically work. Furthermore, this optimization can also be applied if you are using an already optimizing compiler, as the compiler has no way of knowing which case will get executed most often.

Avoid Redundancy

Try as much as possible to compute values only once (the precalculation technique presented earlier in the book is a great example) and try to avoid intermediate values. Having fewer intermediate values means having less variable allocation work to do and fewer variables to keep track of, which in turn means less work for the CPU and fewer memory/cache access operations. In addition, it also keeps the JVMs stack cleaner, which also improves performance.

This technique is usually not needed for full-blown JVMs, which can detect intermediate values and optimize the bytecode accordingly (for example, by removing the need for intermediate values altogether); however, since mobile JVMs execute the bytecode as is, this can result in a significant performance penalty, especially within loops. This is especially visible if you create or instantiate variables within loops.

Probably one of the best ways to avoid redundancy is to simplify your math operations, especially within loops. Both of these optimizations will be covered shortly.

Use Locality to Your Advantage

The concept of locality refers to how close together in memory related code and data are. As with avoiding redundancy, keeping related code and data together means the CPU and memory subsystems have to do less work to run your code.

With Java, you cannot know where in memory a certain block of code or a certain variable will be located; however, you can rewrite your code so that variables are grouped together within your expressions. This has the advantage of optimizing the JVM's stack and memory usage, which in turn leads to extra performance.

For example, consider the following expression:

```
expr1 = a * b + c * d + ... + y * z + a * z
```

You can clearly see that the variable a is used two times, at the beginning and at the start of the expression. The problem with this is that, by the time the second use of a gets evaluated, chances are a is no longer near the top of the stack, or in the CPU's cache or registers. This means that it has to be fetched from memory, which requires extra work and lost CPU cycles. However, if we group together the uses of a, like so:

```
expr1 = c * d + ... + y * z + a * z + a * b
```

then there is a very high chance that a will be read from the CPU's cache or registers, which is considerably faster. Granted, for a single access, the difference is negligible, but again, if you do this in a loop, all the small differences tend to add up.

The one thing to observe in the foregoing example is that, in order to keep both a *and* z variables together, the first sub-expression (a * b) had to be moved at the end. If we had rewritten the expression like

```
expr1 =+ a * b + a * z + c * d + ... + y * z
```

then the a variables would have been close together, but the z variables would have been far away from each other, thus negating the optimization.

Unfortunately, a side effect of this rewriting is that the meaning behind the math is sometimes made unclear; in our example, the neatness and intuitiveness of the series are lost.

Optimize Your Math

Out of all the code optimization you can perform, this has by far the largest impact. First, it is worth noting that not all operations execute with the same speed. Generally, additions are the fastest math operations a CPU can perform, followed in order by subtractions, multiplications, and divisions. Multiplications are usually at least 2–3 times slower than additions, with divisions being at least 4–5 times slower. Floating point operations are also considerably slower than integer operations. Of course, these factors depend heavily on the underlying hardware: the differences between addition and division are much less obvious on a state-of-the-art mobile CPU than they are on a low-end mobile CPU.

The first thing you need to do in optimizing math operations is to minimize the number of math operations you do. For example, consider the following expression (with which you are no doubt familiar):

```
expr2 = a * a + 2 * a * b + b * b
```

As you can see, the CPU has to do four multiplications and three additions in order to evaluate this expression. We can minimize this number by writing this expression as follows:

```
expr2 = a * ( a + b ) + b * (a + b )
```

We still have three additions to do, but only two multiplications. We can take this further, by writing the following:

```
expr2 = ( a + b ) * ( a + b )
```

It contains two additions and one multiplication—not bad. But we can take this even further, to the final form, by writing the following:

```
expr21 = a + b
expr2 = expr21 * expr21
```

In the end, we are left with one addition and one multiplication, which, when combined, take a lot less time to evaluate than the original form of the expression.

All the "math tricks" we learned in school, such as using common factors, apply here. In fact, the goal of this exercise is the same as in algebra class: to write a given expression in its simplest form. The rules, however, are a bit different: you have to keep in mind the time each operation needs in order to execute. For example, if you had to choose between three additions and a multiplication on one hand, and a division and a subtraction on the other hand, you are probably much better off with the first version.

The second trick you can use is to replace constant division by multiplication. For example, consider the following expression:

```
expr3 = someValue / 2.5
```

You can rephrase this as follows:

```
expr3 = someValue * 0.4
```

This should be much faster to evaluate, given that multiplication is faster than division. The general rule here is simple:

Instead of

```
A = B / C
```

simply do the following:

```
D = 1 / C
A = B * D
```

Of course, for this to work, you have to calculate D manually and insert the end result directly into your code.

It should be noted that this approach works with variables too, but only in some cases. For example, if the original code is

```
expr41 = a / someVariable
expr42 = b / someVariable
expr43 = c / somevariable
```

then it will certainly be faster to do the following:

```
temp = 1 / someVariable
expr41 = a * temp
expr42 = b * temp
expr43 = c * temp
```

The third and final common trick you can use is to replace floating point operations with integer operations. This can be used in a lot of cases, but the most common cases are those in which you need floating point precision during the course of a computation, but the end result is cast as an integer. For example, when drawing something on the screen, you use only integer coordinates. If you calculate the x coordinate of a drawing operation to be 2.34, the platform will start the drawing at x=2, for obvious reasons. The extra precision (i.e., the decimal part) is lost anyway, so we should try to avoid using floating point operations in the first place.

To exemplify this, let's consider the following expression, with a=1, b=2, and c=3 (all integers), and that we need to have the calculation accurate to only two decimal places, with the end result an integer (screen coordinate):

```
X = ( a * 2.31 + b * 1.53 ) * c
```

We can easily calculate that X=16.11. So, in the end, X will be evaluated to 16.

If we want to eliminate floating point operations and get the desired mid-operation precision, all we have to do is multiply the expression by 100, resulting in the following:

```
X = ( a * 231 + b * 153 ) * c
```

If we wanted three decimal places, we would have multiplied by 1,000 and so forth.

At this point, we have no more floating point operations, which should make evaluating X considerably faster than the original case. Since we multiplied by 100 initially, X will now be 1,611. If we now divide by 100, we would get a value of X=16, which is the correct result—except we used no floating point math whatsoever.

This optimization was worth it because usually three integer multiplications, an addition, and a division are faster than three floating point multiplications and a floating point addition. As a rule, the more floating point operations you need to do, the more it becomes worthwhile to convert them to integer operations.

Please note that converting from floating point to integer math has its pitfalls. For example, consider the following expression:

```
Y = ( a * 1.5 ) * 2.2
```

Let's assume for the sake of argument that we cannot alter the expression in any way (i.e., we cannot convert it to Y = a * 3.3) and that we want to convert it to integer math, while keeping a one decimal point precision. The end result must, of course, be an integer.

Your first intuitive thought would be to multiply the expression by 10, to obtain the following:

```
Y = ( a * 15 ) * 22
```

You would be wrong. If we multiply by 10, what we get is the following:

```
Y = ( a * 1.5 ) * 2.2 * 10 = ( a * 1.5 ) * 22
```

You can clearly see that inside the parentheses we still have floating point operations! To get rid of all the floating point operations, we have to multiply again by 10, to obtain the following:

```
Y = ( a * 15 ) * 220
```

This also means that, to get the final integer result, we would have to divide by 100, and not by 10!

Converting your math operations to be integer-only is a great way to improve the speed of your Java ME applications, in particular those that are computationally intensive. The speed benefits are especially visible on devices with low-end CPUs, on which the performance difference between floating point and integer-only operations can be quite significant.

Another math optimization trick, which is extremely effective, is to use bit shifts instead of math operations. For example, a << 2 is the same as a *= 2, while a >> 2 is the same as a /=2.

A great application of this trick is related to converting math to be integer-only. For example, if you want to calculate something with a precision of three decimal digits, you would normally multiply by 1,000. You can instead multiply by 1,024. This skews the calculation slightly, but the extra 24 amounts to a maximum error of just 2.4%. In exchange for this error, you get to use bit shifts instead of multiplication and division, as a * 1024 is the same as a << 10, while a / 1024 is a >> 10. In addition, if you calculate something with a precision of three decimals, but you instead use only two of them, then the error is practically insignificant.

Unroll Loops

There are many cases in which the number of iterations a loop has to go through is known beforehand. In these cases, if the number is small enough (a maximum of 10 or 15 iterations), it is worth unrolling the loop. That is, you take its original from, for example, the following:

```
for (i=0;i<4;i++)
{
        a[i] = i * i;
}
```

And you turn it into a more verbose and faster version:

```
a[0] = 0;
a[1] = 1;
a[2] = 4;
a[3] = 9;
```

This technique has several performance benefits, the most important of which are that it eliminates the jump instructions needed for the loop and the boundary conditions check, as well as the advancement instruction (e.g., i++). Furthermore, in many situations (ours included), the math inside the loop can be unrolled to a certain degree too, thus providing an even larger performance gain.

The technique is especially effective if the unrolled loop is executed many times—for example, when it is the inner loop of a nested loops structure. In cases where the loop is stand-alone, the performance benefits are usually marginal.

Inline Code

Related to loop unrolling, code inlining refers to the practice of replacing a method call with the actual body of the method. This is extremely effective for methods with small bodies, where often the call overhead is equal if not larger than the actual resources (memory, CPU time) needed to run the method.

This technique can sometimes provide an impressive performance boost for Java ME code, as some JVMs incur a lot of overhead when calling methods (older devices and JVMs tend to suffer from this the most).

The main problem of code inlining is that, unless it's done with a preprocessor or some other external tool, it can significantly add to the application's code base. This can be a problem because any change in the method's body has to be manually propagated everywhere, which is not only tiresome but also error-prone.

Furthermore, even with automatic tools, code inlining will increase your application's JAR size, and may even cause performance problems if the methods containing the inlined code become too big; however, this rarely happens.

Optimize Loop-Related Math

Many times, the value of a variable inside a loop depends on the values of the looped variable(s). This is usually a great place for code optimizations. Take, for example, the following snippet:

```
for (i=0;i<100;i++)
{
        for (j=0;j<100;j++)
        {
                someVariable = i * 10 + j * 5;
                doSomething(someVariable);
        }
}
```

Here you can clearly see that someVariable depends linearly on both the values of i and j. The code is very inefficient, calculating someVariable from scratch at every iteration, which amounts to 10,000 times.

We can optimize this in two places. First, the i * 10 part can be moved outside the loop, like so:

```
for (i=0;i<100;i++)
{
        tempI = i * 10;
        for (j=0;j<100;j++)
        {
                someVariable = tempI + j * 5;
                doSomething(someVariable);
        }
}
```

We have now saved 10,000 multiplication operations. We can save 10,000 more by noticing the sequence that j * 5 produces : 0, 5, 10, etc. In this case, we can replace j * 5 with the value of j directly, if we write the code like so:

```
for (i=0;i<100;i++)
{
        tempI = i * 10;
        for (j=0;j<500;j+=5)
        {
                someVariable = tempI + j;
                doSomething(someVariable);
        }
}
```

This trick is very useful if within the loop of a variable you use only its value multiplied by a number. However, in our case, we can do even better. Notice that, for any value of `tempI`, the sequence of values for `someVariable` is `tempI`, `tempI+5`, `tempI+10`, etc. Writing this as a recursive formula, we would get `a(i) = a(i-1) + 5`. This means that we can write our loops like so:

```
for (i=0;i<100;i++)
{
        tempI = i * 10;
        for (j=0;j<100;j++)
        {
                doSomething(tempI);
                tempI += 5;
        }
}
```

Comparing this final version to the original one, you will notice that we have reduced the number of math operations inside the inner loop from two multiplications and an addition to just an addition—quite a big improvement, considering that the inner loop runs for 10,000 iterations!

Optimizing loop-related math is frequently effective, and usually pitfall-free, but it does have the tendency of making the loop logic very hard to understand, especially if the math inside the inner loop is originally complicated. A trick I frequently use is to add the original, unoptimized version of the loop as a comment before the optimized version of the loop. I can then use this comment as a reference for debugging and for understanding the loop logic.

For Java ME, besides the obvious advantage of making the code faster, this optimization also makes the bytecode smaller in size and considerably reduces the number of variable read/writes required, which in themselves are worthy optimizations.

Keep Your Loops Conditional-Free

You should always strive to keep your critical loops conditional-free. Take, for example, the following snippet:

```
boolean multiplyByTwo = getMultiplyByTwo();
for (i=0;i<1000;i++)
{
   c[i] = a[i] + b[i];
   if ( multiplyByTwo )
   {
        c[i] += c[i]; // Replace multiplication by 2 with an addition
   }
}
```

The problem with it is that it unnecessarily checks for the `if` condition at each iteration. We can remove this bottleneck by rewriting our code so that we move the `if` outside the loop, and have a corresponding version of the loop in each of the `if`'s branches, like so:

```
boolean multiplyByTwo = getMultiplyByTwo();
if ( multiplyByTwo )
```

```
{
        for (i=0;i<1000;i++)
        {
          c[i] = a[i] + b[i];
          c[i] *= 2;
        }
}
else
{
        for (i=0;i<1000;i++)
        {
          c[i] = a[i] + b[i];
        }
}
```

This version is more verbose, but it is also considerably faster, as there are fewer operations within the loops (remember, ifs are very expensive). In addition, there are also fewer variables used, so locality is improved. Finally, you can optimize each loop independently so as to get the best performance in each case.

This technique, officially called "loop unswitching," scales well for up to two nested ifs. For more than two nested ifs, the code becomes hard to maintain and it also increases the method size considerably, which can lead to JVM or hardware performance issues.

Eliminate Special Iterations from Your Loops

It is often the case that some loops have special iterations at the beginning or at the end, or sometimes even in the middle. Take, for example, the following snippet:

```
int bIndex = 9
int cIndex = 8;
for (i=0;i<10;i++)
{
        a[i] = b[bIndex] + c[cIndex];
        bIndex = i;
        cIndex = i;

}
```

Notice that the general formula for this loop is in essence a[i] = b[i-1] + c[i-1], except for the first case, where the formula is a[0] = b[9] + c[8]. We can take advantage of this and rewrite the loop as follows:

```
a[0] = b[9] + c[8]
for (i=0;i<9;i++)
{
        a[i+1] = b[i] + c[i];
}
```

This effectively treats the first iteration separately and thus streamlines the body of the actual loop. The technique is officially known as "loop peeling."

Note that when using loop peeling, you usually have to adjust the end and/or initial conditions for the loop, as well as any array indexes that refer to the looped variable and other references to it—see the foregoing snippet for an example.

Use Loop Fission

This technique works primarily by improving locality and optimizing the JVM's stack. Consider the following loop:

```
for (i=0;i<1000;i++)
{
        a[i] = 5 + i;
        b[i] = 5 + i*2;
        ...
        z[i] = 5 + i*26;
}
```

In this case, by the time z gets processed, the other variables will most likely have to be loaded again from memory. Since this will happen on each iteration, performance will suffer. To avoid this, we will split this big loop into smaller ones, like so:

```
for (i=0;i<1000;i++)
{
        a[i] = 5 + i;
}
...
for (i=0;i<1000;i++)
{
        z[i] = 5 + i*26;
}
```

Now locality is greatly improved, and you are free to optimize each loop individually if you wish to do so.

The problem with loop fission is that its performance is highly dependent on the scenario at hand and on the target device. Generally, having a single loop is faster on most devices because loop-related overhead is minimal; however, in some scenarios (especially when lots of variables are involved, like the foregoing example), it may be faster to split a large loop into smaller ones. There is no rule for this; you just have to try it and see what works best.

Avoiding High-Level Language Features

Java is a very powerful and complex language. For example, it has features such as inheritance, method overloading, type casting, and runtime type evaluation. These features are geared toward making the lives of developers easier and making the code they write more powerful.

Unfortunately, they also incur a performance hit. For example, in the case of inheritance, whenever an object is created, the JVM has to instantiate not only the direct members of a class, but also the members of all its parent classes. Furthermore, the inheritance hierarchy and variable scope must be kept track of. This adds overhead.

In the case of method overloading, things get even more interesting as the JVM has to decide which version of a method it needs to call. It is not always possible to do this entirely at compile time, so calling an overloaded method is usually a bit slower than calling a non-overloaded one. It also complicates evaluating variable scopes quite a bit.

Type casting is also a tricky business, as it basically tells the JVM to forget everything it knows about an object and its instances, and treat it like the type you instruct it to treat it like. In addition, type casting also makes type checking at runtime mandatory, which further decreases performance.

A very surprising example for most people is that even arrays incur a performance overhead. The reason is that Java always does bounds checking on arrays, to make sure that you do not overflow (and when you do, it raises an error). This means that every time you access an array element, the JVM has to check if the element index you specified is a valid one. The performance hit because of this is small for a single sporadic access, but for lots of accesses it can add up. Because of this, whenever possible, try to use simple variables instead of arrays, especially within loops.

The list can continue, but the moral is that you should always stick to the basics in terms of language features if you can. Try to keep your inheritance tree as small as possible, try to avoid type casts and method overloading, and try not to do instanceof checks.

This eases the load on the JVM, thus making your application run faster. In addition, if you are using an optimizing compiler, it also makes it possible for the compiler to better optimize the generated bytecode.

> **TIP:** If you want the absolute best performance, try to make as many member fields and methods as possible static and final. This goes against object-oriented principles, but the performance gain can be substantial, as the JVM will have considerably less work to do. Of course, this also makes developing applications more difficult and less flexible, which in itself can degrade performance.

Stick to the Basics

Java ME does not provide a lot of utility or helper classes/objects by default, but it does provide some. We have all used Vectors and Hashtables, and even though they are less powerful than their J2SE counterparts, they do make our lives easier.

Unfortunately, as fast as they may be, using them also incurs a performance hit. Many times their use is completely warranted; however, there are many circumstances in which they can be substituted with more primitive and less elegant alternatives.

For example, Hashtables are great if you want to store key/value pairs where the key is an instance of an object, or when you need quick and efficient access to the value for any given key. Unfortunately, they also tend to require large amounts of memory, and for small data sets, their theoretical speed is offset by the overhead they incur in terms of function calls and by JVM slowness. In fact, in many cases, you are much better off using a sorted array and doing a binary search on that array.

The same is true for vectors. If you don't plan on using some of their more advanced (or convenient) features such as indexOf and dynamic resizing, stick with an old-fashioned array.

However, these optimizations make sense only if you are using these utility objects/classes in a block of code that gets executed often. For blocks of code that get executed sporadically, these optimizations don't really make sense, as the minimal performance gain they bring is greatly offset by the increase in code complexity. In addition, some JVMs have these objects implemented in native platform code, which actually makes using them better and faster than using manually written code. Because of this, some prior research must be done before choosing one approach over the other.

Avoid Unnecessary Object Creation

In the world of Java ME, creating objects is an extremely expensive operation. For one thing, there is the initial cost of creating an object: allocating memory for it, instantiating its member fields, going through its parent hierarchy, etc. Then, while the object is in use, the JVM has to keep track of all the references that point to it. Finally, when the object is destroyed, the JVM has to de-allocate the memory occupied by the object and mark it as available.

This leaves gaps of unused free memory, which can be either compacted (by moving objects around in memory so that all the free memory is a contiguous block) or left as is, in which case, future object creation operations might fail simply because there might not be a free memory block to house the data required for the new object. This is actually a problem on older and lower-end devices, which simply do not compact memory or, even worse, don't even have a proper garbage collector.

There are several ways you can avoid creating new objects. The most efficient way, from a performance point of view, is to not use objects at all. You can replace them by using plain and simple variables. For example, take the following snippet:

```
public class Person
{
        String name;
        Date dateOfBirth;
        ...

        public void savePerson(OutputStream stream)
        {
             ...
        }
}
```

It should be clear what the snippet does: it serializes a Person object to an OutputStream. However, it does this by creating at least two unnecessary objects: the dateOfBirth and the Person instance itself. Though considerably less elegant, there is a more memory-efficient way of doing the same task:

```
public class Person
{
```

```
        public static final void savePerson(String name, int yearOfBirth,
        int monthOfBirth, ... )
}
```

However, this is a very drastic solution and one that should be employed only in extreme circumstances, or in circumstances where performance is paramount. A far less drastic solution, and one that can be successfully implemented in all Java ME applications, is to use an object pool.

In its simplest form, an object pool is simply a collection of reusable objects—for example, an array of Persons. Whenever you need a new Person object, you just go through the array, take the first unused instance, and use that instead of creating a new object. This, of course, means resetting all the instance's member fields to the values you require, which might mean you need to add some extra getters/setters or a generic doInit() method to serve as a makeshift constructor. Once you find your unused instance and have initialized it with the proper parameters, you simply use it like you would a regular newly created object.

Well, almost. There are some things you must do carefully with pooled instances. For example, it is generally not a good idea to wait() on them, or use them to synchronize stuff. You also have to be careful to not use the same object for two different things at the same time. This is easier said than done, especially with more complex applications, in which object references get passed around a lot, even between different application layers/modules.

The best way to avoid this problem is to employ a simple form of reference counting. Whenever you use a shared object in a method, you increase its reference count by one at the beginning of the method code if it is passed as a parameter, or immediately after you request it from the pool. When you are done with the object, or at the end of the method, you decrease its reference count. Objects in the pool are free if and only if they have zero references.

All of the foregoing is summarized in the code found in Listing 10–1.

Listing 10–1. *Using an Object Pool*

```
public class Person
{
        public void increaseReferenceCount() { ... }
        public void decreaseReferenceCount() { ... }
        public int getReferenceCount();
        ...
        public void doInit(String name, Date dateOfBirth, ... ) { ... }
        ...
}

public class PersonPool
{
        public static final int POOL_SIZE = 30;
        protected static Person [] pool = new Person[POOL_SIZE];

        static
        {
                for (int i=0; i<POOL_SIZE; i++)
```

```
                {
                        pool[i] = new Person();
                }
        }

        public static Person getUnusedInstance()
        {
                for (int i=0; i<POOL_SIZE; i++)
                {
                        if ( pool[i].getReferenceCount == 0 )
                        {
                                return pool[i];
                        }
                }
                return new Person();
        }
}

public class SomeClass
{
        public void doSomething()
        {
                ...
                Person person = PersonPool.getUnusedInstance();
                person.increaseReferenceCount();
                person.doInit("John Doe", new Date());
                ...
                writePerson(person);
                ...
                person.decreaseReferenceCount();
                ...
        }

        public void writePerson(Person person)
        {
                person.increaseReferenceCount();
                ....
                person.decreaseReferenceCount();
        }
}
```

There are two things worth mentioning about Listing 10–1. First, if the pool cannot find an unused instance, it ultimately creates a new instance as a last resort. This acts as a fail-safe mechanism, but ideally you should define your pool size so that it comfortably handles the requirements of your application. Of course, if your object pool is too big, then you might end up wasting memory—there's always a trade-off to be made here.

The second thing worth mentioning is the use of the doInit() method for initializing the object. Pooled objects should always have barebones constructors, and all the initialization work should be done in a separate method, which can be called as needed.

Object pooling may not be extremely OO-friendly, but it does remove a lot of the performance overhead associated with creating and managing new instances, and as such can prove to be invaluable at times. It is most effective on low-end devices or on devices with unfriendly garbage collectors (for example, Blackberry devices tend to show the "hourglass" icon in the middle of the screen and completely pause the application for a few seconds, one or two usually, while the garbage collector is running).

In the hands of an experienced developer, object pooling can be a very powerful Java ME code optimization technique. However, it can also create a lot of problems if not used properly. As mentioned earlier, sharing the same object for two different purposes is the most common one, but others can arise as well. For example, if you use pooling for UI objects, then you might end up with weird visual glitches. As such, always approach object pooling carefully and make sure you work out all the details on paper (where each instance is used and how) before writing the code.

Optimize Memory Access

Sometimes you can improve your application's performance simply by changing the way you use memory. For example, rather than using arrays to store data, try using simple variables to do this (and change your usage pattern accordingly). That is, change your code from

```
expr = a[0] * b[0] + a[0] * b[1] + ... + a[1] * b[0] + a[1] * b[1] + ...
```

to

```
expr = a0 * b0 + a0 * b1 + ...
```

The main advantage of this approach is that the VM doesn't have to do bounds checking on each array element (because you use individual variables), thus improving speed. Also, depending on the code and on the VM, it may also improve the locality of data.

The main disadvantage of this method is that is makes coding difficult: in this context, it's much easier on a language level to work with arrays than it is to work with variables—as an example of this, consider that you could use a for loop to do the math for you rather than having to explicitly write it out.

Furthermore, this technique can actually hurt performance in cases where the "array" has to be passed as a parameter because passing an actual array requires a single object reference, whereas this method requires an object reference or instance for each "array" element—for this reason, use it only with data that is localized to a single method.

Another technique you can sometimes use is to simply make your arrays smaller and use more of them. For example, rather than create a 10,000 element array, create two arrays of 5,000 elements each. This is particularly effective on older devices with small memory pages, because it means that each array will fit in a single page, thus considerably reducing the number of page switches needed.

The main disadvantage of this method is that most of the time it's simply not possible to use smaller arrays, or it is possible, but doing so would incur a significant performance hit (for example, if you are inside a loop and you are forced to use an if statement to determine which of the smaller arrays you have to use). Furthermore, this technique tends to work only on very low-end devices, as the performance gains on other devices tend to be minimal.

Algorithm Optimization Techniques

In the following pages, we'll have a look at some algorithm optimization techniques. We will also look at some common algorithms that come in handy when developing Java ME applications. First, however, let's start with some basic notions about algorithm optimizations.

Broadly speaking, optimizing an algorithm means improving that algorithm so that it performs better, or replacing it with an entirely different and better one. What "better" means varies from case to case: it may mean faster performance, or lower memory usage, or lower bandwidth needed, etc. Typically the performance is of concern.

Basically what you're trying to do when optimizing an algorithm is to find a generic sequence of steps that generally performs a certain task better than your current sequence, without regard to the underlying hardware its actual implementation runs on. As such, algorithm optimization is always theoretical in nature, and it's always done on paper. In fact, if you're trying to optimize an algorithm on the computer, chances are you won't be able to do it properly as you will get biased by the actual implementation you're writing and the hardware you're running it on—both of which are extremely subjective and may not accurately represent the general case performance.

Comparing Algorithms

The question now is, how do you measure, on paper, how good an algorithm is? Keep in mind that you can't limit yourself to a specific use case and input set and you have to do this on a general level. Your measurement also has to be hardware-agnostic. So how do you do it?

Donald E. Knuth, the famous computer scientist, solved this problem by inventing the "Big O" notation. In layman's terms, here's how it works. First, you identify all the variable quantities that can affect your algorithm. For example, if you're trying to sort a list of numbers, then the size of the list is a variable quantity. If you're trying to generate all possible boy-girl pairs from a set of boys and girls, then the number of boys and the number of girls are both variable quantities. Once you have identified all variable quantities, you then express the complexity of the algorithm in terms of these variables—and these variables alone.

For example, let's say we're talking about sorting a list of n numbers with selection sort and that we want to know how good the algorithm is in terms of speed. What selection sort does is go through the list of numbers several times. At the first pass, the smallest number is found and placed first in the list. This requires that you go through all n numbers in the first pass, to find the smallest one of the lot. In the second pass, you already know that the first number in the list is in the correct position, so you need to go through only the remaining n-1 numbers to find the second smallest number. You continue the process until you get to the last number in the list, where you go through only 1 number.

The total number of steps needed is $O = n + (n-1) + (n-2) + \ldots + 1$, which is equal to $O = n * (n+1) / 2$ or $O = (n^2 + n) / 2$. Since we're talking about the general case here, we can assume that n can be a very big number, which makes O even bigger. In this case, half of O is, from a practical point of view, just as big as O (there is no real practical difference between having to do 10,000 trillion steps and just 5,000 trillion steps). This means we can simplify our formula to $O = n^2 + n$. Next, assuming n is large enough, the value of n^2 will greatly eclipse the value of n (for example, if n=1000 then n^2=100000; when compared to n^2 steps, n steps are practically irrelevant). This means that we can simplify our formula to $O = n^2$. This is our final formula, which we will write as $O(n^2)$, which is then read as "the complexity of the algorithm is n^2."

> **TIP:** To quickly find the complexity of an algorithm, just write its general complexity formula as a polynomial and then discard any constants and all but the highest-exponent terms for each variable. For example, $O = 2 * n^3 + 5 * n^2 + n + m^2 * n + m$ solves to $O(n^3+m^2*n)$. The terms $5 * n^2$, n, and m have been removed as they do not have the highest exponents for their respective variables, and the constant 2 from $2 * n^3$ has also been removed.

Alternatively, you can use the original formula for O and write $O((n^2 + n) / 2)$. This is not really correct from a theoretical point of view, but for small enough values of n this formula can yield more accurate results, especially for Java ME code, where every drop of performance matters.

Now let's assume you have two algorithms, one with $O(n^2)$ and one with $O(n*\log n)$. Which one is better? To answer this question, all you have to do is replace n with a really big number. For $n = 1000000$, the first algorithm has a "complexity" of 1,000,000,000,000, while the second one has a "complexity" of just 19,931,568. The answer should be clear.

> **NOTE:** When expressing complexity, by convention all logarithms used are base 2 logarithms.

The reason I spent the last page or so explaining these concepts is that they are crucial for Java ME development. Unlike benchmark-based measurements, algorithm complexity measurements are the same across all devices and all JVMs, and are thus a lot more relevant to how good your application really is. Where applicable, they are also much better tools in determining what the problem areas are and where improvements are needed. At the same time, they are great indicators of code-related problems that might not be visible otherwise: if your implementation of an $O(n*\log n)$ algorithm performs on par with the other guy's implementation of an $O(n^2)$ algorithm, then you can be certain you have a real problem somewhere in your code.

> **NOTE:** The complexity of some algorithms simply can't be expressed as a polynomial. This is common for adaptive and/or heuristic algorithms—for example, genetic algorithms (which start with a random solution and gradually "evolve" it until meets the problem's acceptance criteria). Unless the alternative is really considerably worse, you should avoid algorithms such as these because their execution time is entirely unpredictable.

Improving Your Algorithms

Unfortunately, unlike optimizing code, optimizing algorithms has no definite "tips and tricks" cookbook. There are no techniques that you can apply to any given algorithm and get a better algorithm as a result. Each algorithm is unique, and the process of optimizing a given algorithm is as unique as the algorithm itself.

There is, however, some good news. When working with algorithms, you'll frequently come across a couple of core operations, much like you'll frequently come across the concepts of variables and functions when working with code. These are *sorting*, *searching*, and *recursion*. In the following pages, we'll look at how you can improve your algorithms by improving these operations.

Sorting

Sorting means arranging a collection of objects in a certain order according to a given criteria. For example, you can sort people alphabetically by their names, or you can sort data packets from smallest to biggest according to their size. Sorting is a very common operation in algorithms, so it is worth it to examine more closely how sorting performance can be improved.

Unlike J2SE or J2EE, Java ME doesn't have any built-in provisions for sorting, which means that you have to roll out your own sorting algorithm and corresponding implementation. In most cases I've encountered, the algorithm used is selection sort or something similar, which, as we have seen previously, is an $O(n^2)$ algorithm. Selection sort's main strengths are its ease of implementation (it's basically two nested `for` loops) and conceptual simplicity; however, its complexity makes it unsuitable for anything other than small input sets. From a complexity point of view, a much better alternative to selection sort is quicksort, which is an $O(n*\log n)$ algorithm in general, with a worst-case scenario of $O(n^2)$. In other words, in the worst possible case, quicksort is still as good as selection sort. By using quicksort in your algorithm's implementation (instead of selection sort, for example), you can improve your application's performance considerably.

Quicksort works as follows: for a given input set, pick one of the elements to act as a pivot (typically the middle one will do just fine). Then, go through the other elements, and if they're bigger move them to the right of the pivot, while if they're smaller move them to the left of the pivot. After this is done, you will end up with two smaller input sets: one for elements smaller than the pivot and one for elements larger than the pivot, with the pivot somewhere between them. It is important to note that these smaller sets aren't necessarily sorted, or of the same size.

What you do next is apply the same steps to each of the smaller input sets, ending up with four even smaller input sets, and so forth. You do this until you're working with input sets of only one or two elements, which are either easily sorted by a simple comparison (for sets with just two elements) or already sorted (for input sets with just one element). After these smallest possible subsets are also sorted, you will find that the original input set is now sorted as well, because now for every pivot encountered along the way (including the original one) the "larger than" and "smaller than" subsets have been sorted. To better understand how this works, try it out for yourself using pen and paper.

If you have followed the foregoing description, it should be obvious that quicksort is a recursive algorithm: after you are left with a pivot and two smaller input sets, you apply quicksort to each of the smaller input sets, and so forth. You will find many implementations for quicksort; however, the quicksort implementation given in Listing 10–2 is especially well suited for Java ME, as it is an in-place implementation (meaning no additional arrays other than the original input array are created). Don't be scared by its large size. Most of it is comments that explain what is going on; the actual implementation is quite slick.

Listing 10–2. *A Java ME–Friendly Quicksort Implementation*

```java
public static void quicksort(int [] inputSet, int start, int end)
{
    int left = start;
    int right = end;
    int temp = 0;

    // First, we find the pivot value
    int pivotValue = inputSet[ (start+end)/2];

    // Then, we arrange the input set into:
    // { smaller than set, pivot, greater than set }.
    // The process for this is as follows:
    // 0: Initial left position = start; initial right position = end.
    // 1: Starting from the current left position, find a value greater than
    // the pivot.
    // We will call this value A.
    // 2: Starting from the current right position, find a value smaller than
    // the pivot.
    // We will call this value B.
    // 3: Swap A and B. Increase left position and decrease right position.
    // 4: Repeat from step 1 until the left position index is equal to or greater than
    // the right position index.

    // Next, while the left index is smaller than or equal to the right index, ....
    while (left<=right)
    {
        // ... we find a suitable A ...
        while ( inputSet[left] < pivotValue )
        {
```

```
            left++;
        }

        // ... then we find a suitable B ...
        while ( inputSet[right] > pivotValue )
        {
            right--;
        }

        // .. then, provided left <= right, ...
        if ( left <= right )
        {
            // ... we swap A and B.
            temp = inputSet[left];
            inputSet[left] = inputSet[right];
            inputSet[right] = temp;

            // Also, don't forget to increase left ...
            left++;

            // ... and decrease right. We do this so that we do not swap the same two
            // values forever.
            right--;
        }
    }

    // After the input set has been arranged, we apply quicksort on the "smaller than"
    // subset, if the set is at least two elements big.
    if ( start < right )
    {
        quicksort(inputSet,start,right);
    }

    // We then apply quicksort on the "greater than" subset, again if the set is big
    // enough.
    if ( end > left )
    {
        quicksort(inputSet,left,end);
    }
}
```

The implementation from Listing 10–2 works with numbers, but it is easily adaptable to work with any other data type. To use it, all you have to do is call the following:

```
quicksort ( inputSet, 0, inputSet.length -1 );
```

There are other efficient sorting algorithms besides quicksort—for example, merge sort and heapsort—each with its strengths and weaknesses. For example, heapsort tends to perform slightly worse overall compared to quicksort, but fares considerably better in worst-case scenarios: $O(n * \log n)$ compared to quicksort's $O(n^2)$. Depending on the task at hand and on the level of performance you need, you might want to use different algorithms for different scenarios. Still, quicksort is a very good overall solution, and you will rarely encounter any problems using it exclusively.

Searching

Searching basically means finding a certain element that matches a certain criteria, within a given input set. The most common form of searching is the linear search, where you go through all the elements of the input set until you find the one you need. This is an $O(n)$ operation. A much better alternative is the binary search, which is an $O(\log n)$ operation. Binary search works on sorted input sets only, and it is a very simple algorithm.

The idea is simple: on any given sorted input set, you look at the value in the middle of the set and compare that element against your target criteria. If it matches, you have your result. If the middle element is "greater than" your target criteria, then you do the same lookup on the interval [start,middle). If the middle element is "less than" your target criteria, then you do the same lookup on the interval (middle,end]. As you do this, your working interval becomes increasingly smaller, until eventually you reach the point where the interval has zero elements. If, at that point, you still haven't found a result, then no element in the input set matches your criteria.

Like quicksort, binary search can be implemented recursively. However, the most commonly seen implementations of it are non-recursive, like the one in Listing 10–3.

Listing 10–3. *A Binary Search Implementation*

```
public static int binarySearch(int [] inputSet, int element)
{
    int start = 0;
    int end = inputSet.length-1;
    int middleValue = 0;
    int middleIndex = 0;

    // As long as the interval has at least one element
    while ( start<=end )
    {
        // Get the index of the middle element
        middleIndex = (start+end) / 2;

        // Get the value of the middle element of the interval
        middleValue = inputSet[middleIndex];

        // And compare it to the target criteria/element
        if ( middleValue == element )
        {
            // If it matches, we have our result
            return middleIndex;
        }
        else if ( middleValue > element )
        {
            // If it is greater, use the interval (middle,end]
            end = middleIndex-1;
        }
        else
        {
            // If it is smaller, use the interval [start,middle)
            start = middleIndex+1;
        }
```

```
    }

    // Interval has zero elements, no match found
    return -1;
}
```

The foregoing method returns the index of the found element (if any), or -1 if the element has not been found. Of course, the code can be adapted to work with other data types too, not just integers.

Eliminating Unnecessary Recursion

Recursion is one of the most powerful concepts in computer science. The ability to have a method call itself gives birth to a lot of very interesting and useful programming techniques and tricks (see quicksort), and when properly understood and applied can greatly simplify code complexity (imagine implementing quicksort without recursion).

However, there are good uses for recursion and there are bad uses for it. One of the bad uses is to blindly calculate values, even if those values have been calculated before. This typically happens in formula-based recursions.

For example, consider the Fibonacci series, which is 0,1,1,2,3,5,8... In this series, every number except the first two is the sum of the previous two numbers. The general formula is $F(n) = F(n-1) + F(n-2)$. This formula can easily be implemented via recursion, as shown in Listing 10–4.

Listing 10–4. *A Recursive Fibonacci Series Implementation*

```
public static int fib(int n)
{
    if ( n < 2 )
    {
        return n;
    }
    else
    {
        return fib(n-1) + fib(n-2);
    }
}
```

The code is extremely short and simple; however, it is also overly expensive computationally. Here is the call tree it produces:

```
fib(5)
fib(4) + fib(3)
(fib(3) + fib(2)) + (fib(2) + fib(1))
((fib(2) + fib(1)) + (fib(1) + fib(0))) + ((fib(1) + fib(0)) + fib(1))
(((fib(1) + fib(0)) + fib(1)) + (fib(1) + fib(0))) + ((fib(1) + fib(0)) + fib(1))
```

You can see that fib(2) is calculated three times in the foregoing call tree. Furthermore, even if fib(0) and fib(1) are fixed-value functions and no computations are needed, they still have to be called, and this adds overhead.

Fortunately, there is a technique designed to avoid unnecessary calculations when dealing with recursion. It is called dynamic programming. Dynamic programming basically boils down to storing already calculated values for later use, instead of calculating them from scratch every time they are needed.

There are two approaches to dynamic programming. One is the top-down approach, which is exactly like recursion except with a twist: before calculating fib(n), we first check if we have calculated it before, like in Listing 10–5.

Listing 10–5. *A Top-Down Dynamic Programming Fibonacci*

```
public static int fibBuffer[] = new int [1000];

public static int fibTopDown(int n)
{
    if ( n < 2 )
    {
        return n;
    }
    else if ( fibBuffer[n] != 0 )
    {
        return fibBuffer[n];
    }
    else
    {
        fibBuffer[n] = fibTopDown(n-1) + fibTopDown(n-2);
        return fibBuffer[n];
    }
}
```

The lines in bold are where the magic happens. In this implementation, a Fibonacci value is calculated only the first time it is encountered and never after that, so the call tree becomes as follows:

```
fib(5)
fib(4) + [fib(3)]
(fib(3) + [fib(2)])
((fib(2) + fib(1)))
(((fib(1) + fib(0)) + fib(1)))
```

The calls in brackets return already calculated values instead of calculating new values from scratch. For example, when the call in bold to fib(3) is made, the value for it was already calculated as part of the fib(4) call before it. The same applies to the call in bold to fib(2): it was calculated as part of the call to fib(3) immediately before it.

The gain in using this simple technique is twofold: we do not only fewer math operations, but also fewer function calls.

The second approach to dynamic programming is the bottom-up approach. This one is more complicated, but in practice its implementations perform significantly faster. The idea is similar to mathematical induction: start at the very bottom, and then work your way up until you reach the point you want to get to. It can be thought of as being the opposite of recursion.

For example, in the case of Fibonacci numbers, we know that the first two numbers are set in stone: 0 and 1. Based on them, we can calculate the third number. Based on the third and second numbers, we can calculate the fourth, and so on. The formula is thus more like `fib(n-2) + fib(n-1) = fib(n)`. This approach has another major benefit: since at every step along the way we know the values of the previous two steps, we don't need recursion at all and we can just perform a simple array lookup. Eliminating recursion reduces overhead significantly and provides our Java ME implementation in Listing 10–6 with a very nice and noticeable performance boost.

Listing 10–6. *A Bottom-Up Fibonacci Implementation*

```
public static int fibBuffer[] = new int [1000];

public static int fibBottomUp(int n)
{
    fibBuffer[0] = 0;
    fibBuffer[1] = 1;

    int index=2;
    while (index<=n)
    {
        fibBuffer[index] = fibBuffer[index-2] + fibBuffer[index-1];
        index++;
    }
    return fibBuffer[n];
}
```

The bottom-up approach to dynamic programming is especially powerful. It eliminates unnecessary overhead in the form of extra method calls, and since it is inductive in nature, its implementation and general formula are much easier to debug than top-down dynamic programming (where you can frequently get lost in the call tree, and the general formula is much harder to verify using actual data).

On a more general level, there are many algorithms that can benefit from dynamic programming. For example, calculating the edit distance between two strings (the minimum number of changes needed to turn string A into string B) can take forever to run if implemented using recursion, yet it runs almost instantly on virtually any hardware if dynamic programming is used. This can then be used, for instance, to compensate for small typos in your application, where the user enters a person's name or address with a few characters mistyped.

The same is true for other problems, like finding the minimum distance between two nodes in a tree (for example, this can be used for optimizing routes in a GPS software) or a whole slew of decision-making problems (useful for business simulation or game AI).

In the context of Java ME, dynamic programming can be an extremely useful tool. When implemented properly, dynamic programming yields results extremely fast, which can help put the perceived performance of mobile applications on par with the perceived performance of desktop applications. For example, a desktop implementation of a dynamic programming algorithm might take just 1 ms to run, while the same implementation might take 200 ms to run on a Java ME device. While the absolute performance difference is 20,000%, there is virtually no perceived performance difference, since to the user 200 ms and 1 ms are virtually the same.

Summary

In this chapter, we have looked at how we can optimize our Java ME applications by improving both the code and the algorithms behind the code. We have examined the most commonly used code optimization techniques and how they improve application speed: optimizing math operation, fast code path switching, optimizing loops, and more. We have also examined how algorithm performance is measured and how to optimize the most commonly used algorithm operations: sorting, searching, and recursion.

In the following chapter, we will look at how you can improve your application as a whole, by refining existing features and by making the application more intuitive for the user.

## Chapter 11

Adding Fine Touches and User Interaction Improvements

By now you should have a well-structured and optimized application. This already sets you apart from most Java ME applications out there, from a technical standpoint. However, it's not enough to make your applications stand out from the user's perspective, because users do not care about what happens "under the hood."

As such, this chapter is dedicated to showing how to improve your application from a user's point of view. Besides having a good feature set (this should be a given), there are two main ways of doing so: adding fine touches to your application and improving the user's interaction with your application and with your company, thus improving the overall user experience. In the following pages, we will discuss both of these aspects.

Before we begin the discussion, it should be noted that you will most likely not be able to implement all of the suggestions presented, for technical and business reasons. Implementing everything discussed in this chapter will most likely result in a highly polished and extremely high-quality application. However, the development costs will increase significantly, so you will be able to target only the most high-end Java ME devices out there. Medium-range and low-end devices will simply not be able to handle the resource strain. Deciding which suggestions to implement and which suggestions to ignore is highly application specific. However, some guidelines are presented at the end of the chapter.

Adding Fine Touches to Your Application

One of the key aspects that separate Pro Java ME applications from regular Java ME applications are the *fine touches*—features and functionality not necessary to get the application's job done, but present nonetheless. These fine touches can be subtle—for example, having an animated border instead of a static border around the currently selected cell in a spreadsheet application (to make it easier for the user to see where edits will take place). Fine touches can also be more visible, such as having contextual help available for every selectable item in the application.

Fine touches add tremendous value to your applications. They do this not by adding major functionality (by definition) but by making the existing functionality easier and more pleasant to use. A user coming into contact with your application might not explicitly notice the fine touches you add, but will feel that your application "simply works" and that great care and much thought has been put into it.

This means not only that your users (and your customers) will continue coming back to your application, but also that you will attract more users (and more customers). Word of well-written, user-friendly, and intuitive applications gets around fast, especially in the Java ME world, where such applications tend to be few and far between.

Understanding Fine Touches

Before we can begin discussing actual fine touches, you must first get a better understanding of what they are. Though there is no textbook definition, it is safe to say that any feature or functionality characterized by the following traits can be considered a fine touch:

- *Noncritical*: A fine touch is, by definition, not critical to the operation of your Java ME application. For example, having an animated border around the currently selected cell is not necessary for the functioning of a spreadsheet application.

- *Noninvasive*: Fine touches never force or require users to adapt their usage patterns. In other words, the user should be able to use the application just the same with our without these fine touches. For example, having contextual help for each selectable item in an application can be considered a fine touch, because the user doesn't have to use this feature and can completely ignore it. On the other hand, confirmation dialogs for more-delicate operations (such as deleting items) cannot be considered a fine touch, because the user is forced to act upon them by confirming or dismissing the action.

- *Simple and intuitive*: If a feature needs explaining, it is not a fine touch.

- *Can be turned off*: This is more important than it looks, and is often forgotten. You may think that the animated border is nice, and so will a lot of users, but some of them might get distracted by it. And contextual help is great, but an experienced user might want to turn it off in order to minimize menu clutter. By being able to turn off fine touches, users get more control over their experiences.

There is a very good reason for properly understanding what a fine touch is: many features (including some of the ones discussed later in this chapter) can be implemented either as regular features or as fine touches—but they make the most impact when they are implemented as the latter. For example, in the case of a chat client or other Internet-related applications, the update functionality can be implemented in two major ways. The first is as a stand-alone feature that the user must explicitly activate (that is, a "Check for updates" option in the application's menu). The second is as a fine touch, which is done automatically by default and can be turned off by the user (that is, when the user connects to the Internet, a check for newer versions is done).

Of the two ways, the second one is usually best for several reasons: it requires no user interaction, users are notified of newer versions even if they don't check for them explicitly, and the application's menu is freed up. This results in a cleaner and seemingly more "intelligent" application, which is something users will love.

The same principle can be applied to many other aspects of your applications, resulting in applications that are simple and fun to use, while still providing all the functionality required of them. This is great for any current mobile platform, but Java ME stands to benefit the most from this because its users are generally less tech-savvy than the users of smartphone platforms, and thus they will appreciate the application's simplicity and ease of use even more. In fact, this may be users' determining criteria in choosing to use your application.

> **TIP:** When exploring fine touches, don't limit yourself to Java ME applications! In the mobile world, probably the best examples of the use of fine touches are Apple's products. Although it is usually not possible (for technical reasons) for a Java ME application to match Apple's level of fine touches, many important fine touches (Apple-related or from other platforms) can be at least partially adapted to Java ME. Researching what fine touches other platforms and their applications have to offer and adapting these fine touches to your Java ME applications is one of the best ways to increase the value of your products.

Let's now explore some of the fine touches you can add to your Java ME applications. It should be noted that this is by no means an exhaustive discussion. Instead, it covers only the most frequently used fine touches that you can implement in a Java ME application.

Adding Proper In-Application Help

For Java ME applications, *help* has traditionally meant one form accessible from the main menu, with a few instructions on it. This Spartan approach was a necessity in the early days, and it fit the simple early Java ME applications. Unfortunately, it has endured even though the applications are now considerably more complex and the hardware is now considerably more powerful. As such, adding proper in-application help is a fine touch that will differentiate you from the competition.

The most important component of a good in-application help system is a comprehensive set of help pages. Every screen in the application should have a dedicated help page associated with it, as should every concept necessary to operate the application. From each help page, you should be able to navigate to other related pages.

On each help page dedicated to an onscreen form, each control of the corresponding form should be discussed (on a separate page if the explanation is long, and otherwise in a few sentences), as should the workings of the form as a whole. Each help page should be accessible from the corresponding form's menu. As an extra, you should also have a few "Tutorial" or "Getting started" pages, to accommodate new or inexperienced users.

To make things even simpler for the user, you can implement contextual help in your application. At its simplest, an extra "Contextual help" option should be presented in the form's menu or in the widget's contextual menu. When selecting this option, the user will get information about that specific control (this can be done quite easily, for example, by opening the form's main help page and scrolling down to the section dedicated to the widget in question).

Taking the idea further, the contextual help can be customized to fit into the current usage context. For example, a help text such as "Sends a message to the selected contact" could be rewritten to "Sends a message to the selected contact (Isabel)," where *Isabel* is the name of the currently selected contact. This involves a deeper integration of the help system with the rest of the application, but is much more useful to users, because the explanations are given in context and are thus considerably easier to understand.

Then there is also the concept of learning by doing. This is covered by the tutorials and "Getting started" guide already mentioned, but we can take the concept further. An efficient way of guiding users through an application (and thus learning by doing) is the use of visual indicators. For example, let's say you have a login form with a "Username" field, a "Password" field, and a "Login" button. The first onscreen item the user has to focus attention on is the "Username" field, so a bubble with a "1" inside it should appear next to it. After the user visits this field and enters some text, the "1" bubble will disappear, and a bubble with '2" inside it will appear next to the "Password" field. After both a username and a password have been entered, a "3" bubble will appear next to the "Login" button.

This mechanism is simple and intuitive for beginner users, but more-advanced users might find this annoying or even insulting. Therefore, it's best to have this option turned off by default and to ask whether the user wants to use it, or better yet, to limit the use of this mechanism to just the tutorials.

In-application assistance has varying levels of importance, depending on the type of application you are writing and on the target market. For example, if you are writing an application that is advanced by its very nature (for example, an FTP client), you can make do with a few help pages. However, if you're writing an educational application for school children, add as much help as possible.

If you can do so, it's always a good idea to include multimedia content in your help pages. For example, if your application has a help page explaining that "while a file transfer is in progress, the file transfer icon will appear in the top-right corner of the screen," you can supplement this explanation by including the icon itself on the help page. This is not going to cost you very much in terms of resources or JAR size, because you already have the icon included in your JAR file.

Furthermore, although it's a bit of a stretch, consider also including multimedia content that explains the notions and concepts your application works with. For example, if you're developing a peer-to-peer file transfer client, consider including an image or two detailing how peer-to-peer works. This is by no means necessary, and doing so will increase your JAR file size. However, it does tend to show that great care has been given to the application—and users will appreciate this.

Adding Contextual Information

Contextual information is somewhat related to in-application assistance, in that as much helpful information as possible is presented to users so they may have a more informed interaction and thus a better user experience. Many times this information is not critical; rather, it is simply "nice to have" and shows that you pay attention to even the smallest of details.

For example, if you are writing a file manager application, the information box for the currently selected file will probably contain details such as file size, creation date, and permissions. These are generic pieces of information that apply to any file in the file system; they are not context specific. However, based on the file extension, you can detect whether the currently selected file is, say, an MP3 song. If this is the case, you could also display ID3 tag information about the file, or its duration and bitrate along with the previously mentioned generic information. This is a fine touch that most savvy users will appreciate.

Contextual information can be useful in other scenarios as well. When selecting multiple contacts in a PIM application, you could also display what details those contacts have in common—for example, that they share the same birthday or the same location. In a spreadsheet application, you could display how many cells are referenced by the current formula, or how many estimated operations are required to recalculate it. In a chat client, you could display a status history for the currently selected contact or an overview of your conversation with that person (how many messages have been exchanged, the average number of messages exchanged per hour, and so on). The list can go on.

Contextual information can be displayed either on request or automatically. Because we are in the realm of fine touches, we will concern ourselves with only contextual information that is displayed automatically. As such, we are naturally interested in two things: when to display it and how to display it.

The two go together. If there is a dedicated onscreen area for displaying contextual information, such as a ticker, you can display the contextual information as soon as the context changes. If there is no dedicated onscreen area for this, you can use the simple concept of delayed tooltips for this purpose. These tooltips appear on top of the current screen content if the application has been idle for a number of seconds—for example, when the user selects a different file and then does not touch the phone for 3–4 seconds. Delayed tooltips are also a good choice if extracting the contextual information is a more CPU-intensive operation, in which case the delay serves to minimize the performance impact of extracting the contextual information, which might be significant in the case of Java ME.

> **TIP:** Contextual information doesn't have to be all text. For example, it can be a thumbnail, a color swatch, a graph, and so on. Use whatever makes more sense in the given scenario.

Furthermore, you can make contextual information interactive. For example, a tooltip displaying a file's size in a file manager application can be used to jump to the details properties page for the file in question. This kind of interactivity can make your contextual information display very powerful, and it also tends to maximize screen real-estate use: while a static tooltip just eats up screen space, an interactive one provides functionality to the user.

Adding Proper Feedback

To help the user feel in control, user actions (no matter how small) should always be accompanied by feedback from the application. This feedback should be visible, immediate, and nonintrusive. If possible, it should also be *smooth*. For example, when navigating from one option to another in the application's menu, the background of the old option can gradually fade out, while at the same time the background of the new option can gradually fade in. This transition should be done fairly quickly, in less than 1 second, so as not to be intrusive.

Besides being aesthetically pleasing, there are practical advantages to this approach as well. The user's attention is drawn to the newly selected menu option, which serves as a helpful guideline for people with impaired vision and/or for people who are less tech-savvy (people who do not have a lot of hands-on experience with mobile phones). This is especially important if you plan to market your Java ME application to developing countries.

The application should also give the user feedback during lengthy operations, such as transferring files or processing large amounts of data. At the very least, a small hourglass icon should be displayed on the screen whenever such an operation is in progress. To further stress that a lengthy operation is in progress, the hourglass icon can also be animated if resources permit this. Finally, if you can do so, consider displaying a progress bar and an estimate indicating how long will it take for the operation to complete.

Transitioning between forms should also be accompanied by some kind of visual feedback if possible, although this is mostly an aesthetic touch. Transitions should be quick and simple, such as the "Wipe" or "Push" transitions in PowerPoint.

There are also other kinds of feedback you can use, besides visual feedback. For example, you can play a short sound clip whenever the user initiates an action or whenever the application has something to present to the user. For touch devices, you can initiate a short vibration whenever the user activates a control, to simulate the feeling of pressing a real physical button. Finally, some devices allow you to control the various light sources available (such as the LCD backlight or the breathing/notification light). You can use these to draw the user's attention to the device when in idle mode. This is especially useful if the device is not in the user's hand (for example, when it is lying on the table).

The problem with these extra means of feedback is that they tend to consume battery power. As such, they should be used with moderation. Furthermore, not all Java ME devices provide all of these extra means of feedback, so you should never count on anything other than visual feedback being available.

A very special type of feedback is feedback that comes from outside the device. For example, if you're writing a chat client (which is obviously client-server based), you may consider adding the option for users to receive transcripts of their chats by e-mail at the end of the day. Although this is by no means necessary, it helps keep your application in the spotlight and in users' attention because their interaction with it goes beyond the confines of mobile devices.

Adding Adaptive Text Capabilities

Text input on mobile phones has never been great, especially on Java ME devices. Many times text is entered in a hurry, so mistakes are plentiful even with features such as T9. As such, one great fine touch for Java ME applications is *adaptive text support*. For example, if the user has a list of contacts and searches *Dany* instead of *Danny*, a regular Java ME application will tell him that zero results have been found. End of story. A Pro Java ME application does things differently. When the original search returns no results, it asks whether the user wants to search for contacts *similar* to *Dany*, in which case our *Danny* would be found—or, better yet, the application does a *similar to Dany* search by default after the original search returns no results.

There should be no question that the second approach is better than the first. But how do we implement it? The key to this is something called the *edit distance* between two strings: the number of operations (in our case, individual character insertions, substitutions, or deletions) required to transform one string into another. For example, the edit distance between *Dany* and *Danny* is 1: you have to insert only an extra *n*. The edit distance between *Ben* and *Bob* is 2: you have to substitute *en* with *ob*. Finally, the edit distance between *Bob* and *Bo* is 1: you have to delete the final *b*.

There are many ways to calculate the edit distance between two strings, depending on the edit operations available and other factors. For our purposes, we will use the Levenshtein edit distance algorithm, which is a bottom-up dynamic programming algorithm.

The algorithm itself is quite simple. We start by calculating the minimum edit distance between S1[1...1] (the first character of the first string) and S2[1...1] (the first character of the second string), and then between S1[1...1] and S2[1...2] (the first two characters of the second string), and so forth, until we have the minimum distance between S1[1…1] and S2 as a whole. Then, we repeat the same process but with S1[1…2] instead of S1[1…1], and then with S1[1…3], and so forth, until we have the minimum distance between S1 and S2.

There are a few variations on this algorithm and quite a few possible implementations for it. The code presented in Listing 11–1 is the simplest possible one.

Listing 11–1. *Levenshtein Edit Distance Algorithm*

```
public static int editDistance(String s1, String s2) {

        int i,j;
        int sizeS1 = s1.length();
        int sizeS2 = s2.length();

        // Create the edit distance matrix
        int distances[][] = new int[sizeS1+1][sizeS2+1];

        // Initialize the matrix
        for (i=0; i<=sizeS1; i++) {
                distances[i][0] = i;
        }
        for (j=0; j<=sizeS2; j++) {
                distances[0][j] = j;
        }

        // Calculate the edit distance
        for (i=1; i<=sizeS1; i++) {
                for (j=1; j<=sizeS2; j++) {

                        if ( s1.charAt(i-1) == s2.charAt(j-1) ) {
                                // No operation required, cost stays the same
                                distances[i][j] = distances[i-1][j-1];
                        }
                        else
                        {
                                // Calculate the minimum distance based on the three
                                // operations we can do at this point:
                                distances[i][j] = Math.min (
                                        // Delete S1[i]
                                        distances[i-1][j] + 1,
                                        // Insert S2[j]
                                        Math.min ( distances[i][j-1] + 1,
                                        // Substitute S1[i] for S2[j]
                                        distances[i-1][j-1] + 1 ) );

                        }

                }
        }

        return distances[sizeS1][sizeS2];
}
```

The code in bold is where the magic happens: at each step along the way, the best possible operation (deletion, insertion, substitution) is chosen so that the edit distance between S1[1…i] and S2[1…j] is minimal.

Once we know the edit distance between two strings, we can determine whether the two *nearly match*. The definition of *near match* depends on the context. For two very short strings (*Mom* and *Dad*), an edit distance of 2 or 3 means that the user probably had something else in mind, while for longer strings an edit distance of 2 or 3 is acceptable.

Adaptive text can be used for anything from matching contacts in the address book to matching filenames in a file manager application. However, one of its more interesting applications is as a sorting filter. Rather than sorting entries alphabetically, you sort them according to their edit distance from a pattern the user enters. For example, if you're writing a dictionary of foreign-language phrases, you can ask the user to enter part of the phrase he or she is looking for, and the application will sort all the phrases in its database according to their distance to it. This works great, because many times people "kinda" remember how a phrase is written or what it sounds like, so this is usually much faster and easier for the user than it would be to go over the phrases by hand. Obviously, this makes sense only if the entered phrase is in the foreign language (for example, something the user heard on the street).

Finally, the interesting thing about adaptive text capabilities is that they can be easily ported to nontextual information. For example, the same algorithm just described (with small adaptations) can be used to calculate the edit distance between two images or between two series of numbers. This can come in handy in data processing applications.

Adding History and Auto-Complete Support

History and *auto-complete support* should be familiar to everyone reading this book, because they are both widely used in web browsers. The concepts, however, are a perfect fit for the mobile world too, and for Java ME in particular, because typing on Java ME devices is more difficult than typing on a computer keyboard.

Furthermore, they fit well not only in the context of entering e-mail addresses, web-site URLs, and search terms. You can use history to quickly get to the people you were last chatting with in a chat program, or to the dates you last viewed in a calendar/PIM application. And auto-complete can be used for more than just simple texts. For example, if you are writing an IMAP/POP e-mail client, the program application could detect addresses from well known e-mail providers (that is, someone@gmail.com or someone.else@yahoo.com) and auto-complete the necessary connection parameters. History support can also be used to implement other fine touches, such as Undo/Redo.

There are several major limitations to implementing history and auto-complete features on Java ME. The first one is that Java ME is usually extremely memory-limited, so although you can remember, for example, what object you visited last, it's usually not feasible to also remember what *state* the object was in. Therefore, it's usually best to use history-like functionality only on simple immutable objects, such as strings. Also because of limited memory, auto-complete lists are usually implemented as fixed-size LIFO (last in, first out) queues: whenever an item is added to the queue, the last item (which is the least used one in our case) is removed.

CPU limitations are also an important factor in the workings of Java ME auto-complete mechanisms. Auto-complete involves a lot of comparisons, typically between `Strings`. Therefore, if the auto-complete list is fairly large, it is usually not feasible to employ it until at least three to four characters have been entered. Small auto-complete lists can typically be used as soon as the first character is entered, but being small, their usage is limited.

Adding Intent Detection

This is a concept I have rarely seen implemented, but one that can do wonders. The main idea behind it is that people tend to do the same tasks with an application over and over again, so the application can detect this repetition and anticipate the user's intent. For example, let's say you are organizing your contacts in a chat application. You move one contact to group A, and then you move another contact and then another. At this point, when you select the fourth contact, the application could ask whether you want to move said contact to group A as well, thus anticipating your intent and saving you time.

Implementing this in practice is fairly straightforward. You simply check your *action history* to see whether the user's last couple of actions are similar—for example, say the user has set the same tags on five different photos. If those actions are similar to what the user seems to be doing currently, present that user with the option to repeat the process with respect to the current application context (that is, with respect to the currently selected photo).

There are, of course, technical difficulties related to this that you will need to overcome. For one thing, you have to add support for actions and action history. This means you will need to remember the relevant information about each action. You can do this by storing each action as a set of key/value pairs, each pair indicating a specific parameter of the performed action.

Then you need to see how similar the actions are. This means you will need to implement a comparator for each type of action, because it usually isn't enough to check whether 80 percent of the key/value pairs of two actions match. Instead, you have to look at the meaning behind each pair and at what they mean collectively. For example, if the user tags the first three photos with the tags *photo1*, *photo2*, and *photo3*, there's a good chance the fourth one will be tagged with *photo4*.

Then you will need to implement a *merger manager* for each type of action, to merge the current application context information with the context information found in the stored actions. For example, for an *edit tags* action, the merger manager should be able to create a new edit tags action with the tag information from the history and the file information (name, path) from the currently selected file.

Finally, because this is a fine touch we're discussing, you can't just ask out of the blue whether the user wants to perform an action, because that would be invasive. A nice solution is to have a small onscreen indicator show up when an intent has been detected. Then, when the user performs a long keypress on a certain key or taps the onscreen indicator, the program asks whether that user wants to perform the suggested action.

However, the main problem with intent detection is the sheer variety of possible scenarios. For example, similar actions may not always be consecutive entries in the action history list, in which case you would need to look deeper into the action history to find a match. It may also be the case that the user performed *more than one* repeat action (for example, *edit tags* followed immediately by *move to folder*), in which case the application should suggest both actions together instead of just *edit tags*. The list can go on, but the idea is that intent detection is somewhat difficult to pull off, especially in the context of Java ME applications. So why mention it in the first place? One reason and one reason only: because it is a trademark of top-of-the-line applications.

Furthermore, while full intent-detection support is nearly impossible to implement in Java ME, partial support is quite manageable. Start with analyzing some telemetry data to get a feel for what the most widely performed user actions are and add intent detection for those in the simplest possible context (for example, 80 percent of parameters match exactly, actions are repeated consecutively). Then get user feedback, and based on it either add support for more actions or fine-tune support for existing ones (for example, implement detection of nonconsecutive repeat actions, add support for parameters that almost match, and so on). Thanks to the 80-20 rule, you will be able to get a decent amount (from the user's point of view) of intent detection implemented with relatively little effort and an acceptable level of resource consumption.

Synchronizing Your Data Between Devices

In many cases, people use the same application on different devices, either because they own more than one device or because they are switching from one device to another. In these cases, it is worth adding automatic synchronization support to the application, to keep the application in sync between different devices, especially if the application itself is client-server based by nature.

Let's take, for example, the case of a chat client. When the user logs in, the application can query the server for chat messages newer than the latest chat message present on the device (that is, for messages exchanged when the application was used on another device). The number of imported messages should be user configurable, but a default of 20–30 messages is usually sufficient to give the user context, and the data traffic caused by importing them is negligible.

> **NOTE:** Synchronization via other means, such as a memory card or Bluetooth, is possible but trickier to implement properly as a fine touch because of the lack of control over the environment. For example, some devices always ask the user to confirm file system or Bluetooth access. Other devices are configured either by default or by the users themselves to leave Bluetooth on forever after it is started (you can turn it off only manually)and this would make the application needlessly drain the battery. When it's not possible to implement synchronization as a fine touch, you should try implementing it as a regular feature instead.

Regardless of the application you are writing, synchronizing everything between devices is not only unnecessary, it's also not recommended because of the monetary costs involved and the time it would take to perform the sync. You should always try to sync only the bare minimum amount of information to keep the user experience consistent between devices, and sync everything else only as needed or when the user explicitly requests it.

Synchronization support is more important than you may think. It is not yet a crucial feature, but it is one of those "I wish the app had this" features that tend to make users very happy when present and somewhat disappointed when missing. The importance of synchronization is rising as more and more people tend to own more than one mobile phone. Furthermore, it is also not a very common feature in the Java ME world, so it will make your application stand out from the crowd.

Finally, synchronization doesn't have to be strictly between mobile phones. For example, you can synchronize the phone's address book with the user's desktop calendar application or social networking accounts. This is a particularly interesting feature to have in cross-platform projects, where the desktop and mobile applications can seamlessly exchange data between them. However, make sure to implement this as a fine touch—that is, make it completely optional and do not hinge any of your application's functionality on it unless you absolutely have to.

Improving User Interaction

I mentioned in the beginning of the chapter that a good feature set is critical in order to have your application stand out, from the user's perspective. This is true, and your application should be able to do everything it advertises it can do, and it should be able to do it well. The accent here is on *do it well*, as quality is more important than quantity. Users would rather use a program with fewer features that work well all the time than a program with a slew of features that are buggy and unreliable. As such, you should always cover the core features first, and always make sure the currently implemented features work as well as possible before implementing new features. By doing so, you ensure that your application is as robust as possible and that the user's experience with your application is smooth and pleasant. Correct?

Not necessarily. Solid features aren't enough for a good user experience. The way the user interacts with these features can make or break an application regardless of how good the features are.

Unfortunately, user interaction is one of the areas that is sadly overlooked in the mobile world. That is not to say that this area is given a lot of thought in the desktop world either. However, in the desktop world, you usually have friends and Internet access to help you when you're stuck. In the case of a mobile application, you may be facing a problem somewhere alone and with no online access. In addition, as stated earlier, Java ME users tend to be less tech-savvy than smartphone users, and this subsequently increases the need for quality user interaction.

For these reasons, it is crucial that you get user interaction right, or as right as possible within the technical constraints of your Java ME application. There are basically two sides to user interaction: how the user interacts with the application itself and with its features, and how the user interacts with the company that made the application and with application-related services. The following pages cover the most important ways these two aspects can be improved in your applications. As with fine touches, the list is by no means exhaustive; it covers only the most important and generally applicable topics.

> **NOTE:** Everything discussed in the "Adding Fine Touches to Your Application" section generally counts as a user interaction improvement too.

Eliminating User Confusion

People working in the mobile industry tend to assume that their users have a higher degree of familiarity with the application at hand (and with mobile devices in general) than they do in reality. This can lead to usability issues for users, which in turn leads to frustration and lost customers.

For example, one of my favorite Java ME applications, a multinetwork IM client, actually requires several sets of credentials: one for the "main account" of the program (for logging IM sessions and more) and one for each individual IM account you want to use. When the application first starts up, it presents you with a login form for the main account, titled "Configure your IM services." This form has two fields, "Username" and "Password," labeled accordingly. Below these two fields is a list containing all your added IM accounts. Initially this list is empty, for obvious reasons. To add IM accounts, you go to the application's contextual menu and select "Add services."

The problem with this form is that it's extremely confusing for new users. Think about it: you start up the application for the first time, and all you see on the screen is a form with the title "Configure your IM services" and the two fields for entering your username and password. Many people will instinctively assume, as I initially did, that this refers to the credentials of their IM accounts, *not* to the credentials of their main account. As such, they will get frustrated when their IM account credentials are refused and will consequently remove the application from their device, possibly giving it a bad review in the process.

Ironically, the whole login process is clearly explained on the application's web page, but it's not explained in the application itself. Furthermore, it's not possible to create a main account from the application itself; you have to do this from the Web. Given all of these factors combined, I'm sure many people turned away from this application because of the confusing login/sign-up process, which is a shame because the program is otherwise really, really good. So what should the application developers have done to avoid this?

First of all, they should have included more information on the screen. For example, above the login fields, they could have placed a text box or a ticker (to conserve space) with a message clearly formulated to explain that these are the main account credentials the user has to enter, *not* the IM account(s) credentials.

Alternatively, the message in the "credentials rejected" pop-up could ask users to ensure that they have entered valid main account credentials, and not IM account credentials. Error messages should never be just "something went wrong." They should also include the most probable one or two causes for the error. Likewise, if what a user needs to do on a specific screen is reasonably ambiguous, clear instructions must be given to the user on the same screen.

Second, they should have put a button titled "Add IM services" below the login fields, separated from them by a horizontal divider. Adding IM services is one of the two main actions you can perform on the login form, and main actions should *always* be found both in the application's menu and onscreen. In addition, this also clears up a bit of the confusion regarding the "enter your credentials" fields. It is true that, given the resolution of most Java ME devices, screen real-estate is at a premium and the tendency is to move actions to the menu, but not at the expense of confusing the user.

Third, because the process deals with several accounts and account types, an in-application wizard for this would have been great. Wizards are great ways to guide users through more-complicated processes, and new or inexperienced users are especially fond of them. Sadly, very few Java ME applications seem to have wizards. Therefore, their presence can be a major plus for your application if you decide to implement them.

Fourth, they should have added some means of getting in-application help. Granted, Java ME applications are usually size-constrained, but at the very least, a link to a help page on the Web could have been added. Besides, these days you can usually spare 4–6 KB of JAR size to store critical help information directly in the application. Dynamic help (as discussed earlier) would have helped a great deal in this situation too.

Fifth, it might have been a good idea to split up more-complicated processes into several less-complex forms. For example, the "add main account credentials" and "add IM services" steps could have been organized on separate forms, with an option to navigate between them. This would have made each form better focused and would have allowed the user to concentrate on a single step at a time, without being distracted.

All these tips have the end-goal of eliminating user confusion and increasing user satisfaction. By providing visual cues and helpful messages to the user, that user then feels more in charge and more comfortable with the application, resulting in a more pleasant user experience.

Keeping the Interface Simple

Keeping the interface simple is somewhat related to eliminating user confusion but should be considered a goal in itself. As with any application platform, mobile or otherwise, the main benefit of keeping the interface simple is of course a better user experience. Simpler interfaces are more enjoyable and easier to use for most users.

Besides this, Java ME also derives two "extra" benefits from keeping the interface simple. The first benefit is that you can make better use of the screen real-estate available. If the interface is too complex, it will appear cluttered and inelegant on Java ME–class displays, even though on higher-resolution displays (such as those found in smartphones or on desktop computers), it would look great. The second benefit is that a simpler interface is considerably easier to port to other devices and platforms, and will feel more consistent across them, thus reducing fragmentation issues.

There are a few main strategies you can employ to keep your interface simple. The easiest and most natural way to do this is, as already discussed, to split up more-complex forms and operations into sub-forms and sub-operations. You can do this via wizards, via tabbed forms, or even via regular forms chained together.

Following this, or as an alternative, it is important to realize that information is layered, and that it makes no sense to have the user enter *deep* information before entering *shallow* information. For example, let's suppose that the user's phone number is an optional field during the sign-up process and that the user can (also optionally) use that number to receive notifications and recover his or her password.

The wrong way to handle this is to have all the fields (user phone number, "Receive notifications" check box, "Use number for recovering the password" check box) displayed on the sign-up form right from the start. The right way to do this is to have only a button titled "Add phone number" on the form. After the button is pressed, an inline *form within a form* is shown instead of it, containing the three fields mentioned. When the user leaves the sub-form, it is automatically hidden and replaced by an "Edit phone details" button. By doing this, you effectively ask the user for shallow information ("Do you want to enter a phone number?") before you ask for deep information ("What do you want to do with it?").

This layering approach has several advantages. The form never gets overwhelmed by input fields, as only one *section* is displayed at any given time. This means that you can actually have very complex forms (think about entering product details in an e-shop), which are at the same time easy to use and understand. In-form navigation is also improved and streamlined, as you navigate from section to section rather than from field to field by default.

Also related to the layering strategy, you should always research the most common parameters for any given operation and, if it makes sense to do so, use them as the default without asking the user to explicitly enter them. For example, if you're writing an FTP client, chances are the default port 21 will be used in most situations and that passive mode is a safe default connection mode. As such, the "connect to FTP server" form would contain only an input field for the FTP server address and an "Advanced" button. Pressing the "Advanced" button would trigger an inline sub-form to be displayed, with the input fields required to change the port number and connection mode from the default values already mentioned.

Finally, you should always present only meaningful options to the user and hide options that are not usable at that time. The most basic example that comes to mind is that there should be no "Paste" option in any menu as long as there is nothing copied. The option should not be grayed out—it should simply not be there. Things are of course different in the world of desktop-class applications that run on desktop-class displays, but in the Java ME world, it makes little sense to show an option that the user can't really use. You only end up wasting screen real-estate and creating confusion and frustration. This is especially important in feature-rich applications, which tend to have lots of potential options, of which only a few are active at any given time.

Allowing Customers to Reach You Easily

When your customers have a problem or a suggestion, they typically want to inform you of it easily and quickly. The best way to allow them to do this is to have an in-application contact form. Depending on the type of application, this can be tied in to the customer's main account (if one exists) or it can be a simple form on which the application enters the user's name, e-mail address, and the message that user wants to send to you.

In addition to this, on the contact form you can also add one or more phone numbers where customers can reach you. This is especially effective on mobile devices, because customers can simply select the number and the application will automatically initiate a call.

Depending on the type of message (bug report, suggestion, and so on), you can also ask whether the user also wants to submit meaningful application data, such as debugging logs. The application can do this automatically for the user, which will increase the chance that the problem will get solved while also showing indirectly that you care about your customers.

This kind of tight customer-relations mechanism is highly effective. It not only keeps you notified of any problems, complaints, or suggestions that users might have, but it also helps keep your customers loyal and improves your image as a software developer and as a service provider.

Of course, this implies that you have some kind of infrastructure set up to handle this communication process, and that the messages from your customers will actually get processed or responded to in a timely fashion. Enabling the customer to submit a message and then ignoring or responding late is worse than not allowing the user to submit a message in the first place.

Then there is also the question of costs, which is why I used the word *customers* instead of *users* in this section. As stated at the very beginning of the book, Java ME applications tend to generate less revenue than applications for other platforms. Therefore, especially in the case of direct sales, the cost of supporting users this way might not be worth it. However, if your budget allows it, having built-in customer support often results in a huge boost in customer satisfaction and an improved company image.

Finally, customer contact goes two ways. If it makes sense to do so, you can implement a notifications system in your application. At every startup, the application connects to your server and retrieves a kind of *message of the day*, if one exists. This message can be anything from a joke or a blog post snippet, to an important notification related to an application update or a possible server downtime.

Creating Nonmobile Versions of Your Application

There is an increasing trend in the mobile world to complement mobile applications with web-based or desktop-based versions. For example, your preferred mobile chat client may have a web-based version too, syncing chat histories, contact lists, and accounts automatically between the two.

This is a great feature to add to Java ME applications simply because it isn't a common one in the Java ME context. Such a feature can drastically increase awareness of your application and user loyalty. Many potential users may be unaware that your Java ME application exists, or that it can run on their phone. However, you may attract their interest by sporting an "integrated web and mobile experience, compatible with all phones—not just smartphones" (this is just an example).

Furthermore, a web-based version of your product means that potential users may simply stumble upon it (either completely on their own or through advertising or word of mouth), try it out on the Web, and then decide to install the mobile version on their devices. This may occur even though users were not initially looking for a mobile version of your product (chat client, e-mail client, and so on). What you are actually doing in this case is redirecting users from a high-profile and easy-to-target medium (the Web) to a low-profile and harder-to-target medium (Java ME applications), which can often be more successful than just targeting the low-profile medium in the first place.

Having nonmobile versions of your application has technical advantages too. Besides having a backup of the user's data, you can simply do some things easier on the Web or on the desktop than you can on a mobile device because of increased processing power and screen real-estate. In addition, importing data into your application might be possible only on the Web or on the desktop—for example, importing images in formats other than PNG or JPEG, or importing documents from office suites. These can be converted to an application-native format off-device, which can then be uploaded to the device via the Web, via Bluetooth, or via direct cable connection, for example.

It is also interesting to note that the nonmobile version of your application doesn't have to be feature-complete. For example, in the case of web-based applications, it is usually enough to just have some of the core features functional in order to spark the interest of potential users.

Deploying Continuous Application Updates

One of the most effective ways to keep your users loyal is to deploy small, frequent updates instead of large updates every once in a while. This is especially important for bug fixes. Many users who are frustrated with one or two bugs will not wait months for a new major release of your application that fixes the problems. Instead, they will switch to a competing application. By releasing minor releases often, even if they include only one or two bug fixes, you create the image of a dynamic and constantly updating product, while at the same time making sure your users get the fixes they want in a timely fashion.

If you do decide to go for continuous updates, you must make some preparations beforehand. For starters, make sure your distribution channels can handle the speed and strain imposed upon them by frequent updates. Make sure your server hardware and bandwidth are up to the task, and make sure that the agreements you have with third parties (application stores, mostly) have provisions to ensure that you can deploy updates quickly.

At the same time, you must make sure that you have an efficient in-application update mechanism. Because of the frequency at which it occurs, you must make sure that the update process is as seamless as possible. Ideally, users would just confirm that they want to install a new update, and the application would do the rest. For instance, the application would open a browser with the URL of the JAD file for the new version, which would in turn trigger the system to install the new version of the application.

One thing you have to be very careful of when going with the continuous update approach is the quality of each update. Make sure that what the user installs on his or her device is working properly and that it doesn't fix one bug but bring up ten new ones. Releasing updates often is not an excuse for not doing QA. This may be obvious, but it is also crucial. It takes only one faulty update version to scare users away from your application and to tarnish your reputation.

Adding Skin Support

High-quality Java ME applications are universally built with third-party UI libraries, not with the device's native UI widgets. This means that the look and feel of the application will not match the native look and feel of the device, which might be an inconvenience for some users.

To overcome this, you can create multiple *skins* (or themes) for your application, one for each device or platform, with each skin imitating the default native look of the device or platform in question. This will make users feel a lot more familiar with your application. The imitation doesn't have to be exact. It's usually enough to keep the same UI layout and just change the color theme and the graphical elements (icons, buttons, and so on), while keeping the underlying UI functionality and usage pattern intact.

An alternative to this is to keep the graphical elements intact for all builds and to bundle the application with a few built-in color themes, selecting at runtime the one that best matches the target device (if the device is in the list of known devices). This option is best if your budget is limited or if time is an issue. You can even allow users to create their own color themes, thus increasing the degree to which they can personalize their experiences.

Taking this further, you can even implement the option to download skins from the Web, just as you would download a new translation. This will keep your application fresh and will give users something to come back to every once in a while, even if they don't explicitly need to use your application.

Taking things even further, skins could also contain different UI layouts and UI-related configuration settings (for example, should the scrollbar be always visible or shown only when needed), thus creating a completely different UI experience for the user. This is not just for show, either. Many people prefer one layout over another because it simply fits better with their usage pattern, and some layouts are simply better suited for some tasks than others.

Skinning support is an important part of a great Java ME user experience. It matters for aesthetic reasons as well as functional reasons, and being able to give users control over how the application looks and feels counts a lot toward the way your application is perceived in the market. At the end of the day, users don't want a generic experience; they want something tailor-made for them. Skins are as close to this as you can get in the Java ME world.

Finally, skins can also be used to tailor your product to different classes of users. For example, an "advanced user" skin would be geared toward providing quick access to all of the application's functionality, while a "novice user" skin would be focused more on eye candy and on guiding the user through the application in easy steps, possibly even hiding potentially dangerous options altogether (for example, things like the server's IP and port number in a client-server application).

Although this sounds great, you should be aware that this level of skinning is usually achievable only through code. You can't really do this with downloadable skins without having to deal with a lot of overhead from the skinning system.

Advertising Related Products

By definition, your application will not be able to do everything users want to do with their phones. For example, your e-mail client application can take care of the users' need for e-mail but not for IM. Far from being a bad thing, this is a huge opportunity that is often neglected. To take advantage of it, all you have to do is add a "Related applications" or "Recommended apps" page somewhere in your application. On this page, you can advertise your other applications, preferably those complementary or related to the application the user is currently using. If you have no related or complementary applications of your own, advertise the applications of your partners and ask them to do the same for your products. If you have no partners, advertise freeware applications that you truly believe will suit the user's needs.

This is a win-win situation. Your users benefit from this because they learn about other applications that they may find helpful. You and your partners benefit because you get to advertise your other products directly to end users. This is a huge plus for any Java ME application developer, because Java ME lacks a central application source like Apple's App Store. Not having a central application source makes popularizing and advertising your application somewhat difficult, because you typically have to target multiple sources to reach an acceptable level of user awareness. Therefore, being able to advertise directly to potential users is a godsend.

Furthermore, you are targeting potential users who are actively curious about your other products and who have explicitly requested to see them (by visiting the "Related apps" page). Thus your chances of success are considerably higher than usual.

To make things even more tempting for users, you may even want to include special offers in your application. For example, the application could generate a dynamic coupon code that the user could then use to purchase other applications at a discount.

Deciding Which Fine Touches and Improvements to Implement

As mentioned at the beginning of this chapter, unless you're targeting only high-end Java ME devices and your budget has lots of zeros at the end, you won't be able to implement every improvement mentioned so far. As such, you will have to make some sacrifices and implement some things to the detriment of others. This section aims to serve as a small guideline for what to implement and what to leave out.

In general, you should always start with improvements that are resource-friendly, such as history, simple visual feedback, and in-application assistance. The reason for this is that you can usually have these improvements in all builds of the application, even in those for low-end devices. More resource-intensive improvements, such as adaptive text support, should be implemented last.

You should always consider what benefits of your application target users the most. For example, if your target market is primarily tech-savvy users, the choice between nice visual feedback and good contextual information should be in favor of the latter, because tech-savvy people generally value information over eye candy. However, if you are targeting beginner users, nice visual feedback is more important.

Some improvements, especially high-end ones, make sense only if the application is fairly well polished in every other respect. For example, intent detection will not benefit an application that is buggy and unreliable, or one with missing core features. In general, all the application's functionality (this includes fine touches and other improvements) should have the same overall level of quality, and more-complex functionality should be implemented only after all less-complex functionality has been implemented.

Finally, some improvements (such as adaptive text support) make the application more "lenient" toward mistakes. If the goal is an extremely user-friendly application, then these improvements are a must. The degrees to which they are implemented vary from device to device, depending on available resources and processing power, but they should be present in some form or another in all the versions of your application.

Summary

In this chapter, you have examined the most important fine touches and user interaction improvements that you can add to your application. You have learned how they improve the user's overall experience, while boosting your image and the image of your products at the same time. In the next chapter, you will take a look at Java ME application testing.

## Chapter 12

Java ME Application Testing

Testing your application is an important part of the software development process. For mobile development, particularly on the Java ME platform, proper testing of an application is almost as important as writing the application in the first place, because you have to identify not only bugs in your code but also various glitches, inconsistencies, fragmentation issues, and other problems related to the JVM and the device itself.

Viewed from up high, Java ME application testing is extremely similar to regular application testing on desktop platforms. Indeed, the same principles, best practices, and processes are applicable in both cases, and it is assumed that you are familiar with them. However, because of the nature of the platform, Java ME application testing brings with it some subtle but important differences, as well as the need to improvise and test some aspects that you simply don't need to test on a desktop platform—for example, the correct working of low-level system functions.

This chapter aims to serve as a quick guide to Java ME application testing, discussing what Java ME application testing involves and how to best approach it. I will go over the most important aspects and, where applicable, explain how these aspects are different for Java ME compared to desktop-like platforms.

Gathering Debug Information

Gathering debug information is a crucial part of the application testing process. By logging various details about the application while it is running, such as the execution time of a method call or the state of a given object, you can create a fairly good picture of what actually goes on under the hood. You can then use this information to complement the test results and the conclusions drawn based on them.

It is my opinion that gathering debug information is more important for Java ME applications than it is for desktop applications, because the problems it helps fix are more important for Java ME applications than they are for desktop applications. For example, even though your application works fine, your code can have memory leaks. On a desktop computer with gigabytes of RAM, any small memory leak will likely go unnoticed for hours or days, by which time the user will have most likely closed the program. On a Java ME device, with its limited memory, such a memory leak would cause an OutOfMemory exception a lot sooner. A good debug log can help you track the issue down and fix it.

A direct consequence of this is that debug logs for Java ME applications should be more thorough than debug logs for desktop applications. There are a lot of things that you would not always track for a desktop application but that you should always track for a Java ME application: instance counts, execution times of critical native method calls, used/free memory, performance metrics, and so on. The reason for logging so much information is simple: Java ME is considerably more unpredictable than a desktop platform, so problems can and do occur out of the blue. Moreover, sometimes they manifest themselves only sparingly and are extremely difficult to reproduce. When this happens, you'll be glad you have a complete debug log to help you out.

Let's take closer a look at the list of things you should track, mentioned in the previous paragraph. One item that stands out is tracking the execution times of native method calls. Why is that on the list? Simple: Tracking the execution times of native method calls tends to uncover platform-related bugs, and it gives you more insight into the way the platform works under the hood. For example, let's assume that similar System.arraycopy() calls usually take the same amount of time to complete, but sometimes they take considerably more. When that happens, there are two things that might be going on behind the scenes: either the JVM relocates objects in memory (compacting them) *or* there is some kind of glitch in the JVM's implementation.

Of course, this measurement alone is inconclusive, but when you combine it with information gathered from other measurements, you can get a pretty good idea about what actually happens. You can then use this knowledge to your advantage: if compacting happens, you can try to create objects in pools and arrays in larger sizes; whereas if there's a glitch going on, you can try to avoid using arraycopy() as much as possible. Either way, you'll end up with a better and smoother-running application for your efforts.

Probably one of the most important things you should keep track of in a Java ME application are network connections. At the very minimum, you should log when they are created, why they are created, and when they are actually closed. Among other things, this helps in dealing with a relatively frequent problem for Java ME applications: going over the device's maximum permitted number of simultaneous connections. In Java ME this can happen even when there are no "connection leaks" in the code. For example, some devices do not close a network connection immediately when they are requested to do so, which means that if a new connection is created too soon, you will go overboard. A good debug log can help you determine if this is the case by checking (via timestamps) whether the connections are closed immediately or after some delay.

You should also keep track, as much as possible, of the device's state. This includes device orientation, connectivity capabilities in use, other running applications, battery life, and so on. This information is invaluable in reproducing bugs that occur only in some situations (for example, only when the device is in landscape mode or when battery life is low).

One Java ME–specific thing that you should log are screen and component repaints. This is not typically needed with desktop applications, or even with smartphone platforms, because the native UI framework handles repaints automatically. However, Java ME applications tend to suffer from refresh issues (flickering, not redrawing the screen properly) because their UIs are created based on third-party frameworks, which in turn use low-level and device-specific drawing calls. As such, when a refresh bug happens, knowing when a repaint was issued, and why and when it was actually executed, helps a lot in tracking down the root cause of the bug.

For example, when you get corrupted screens when the device changes orientation, knowing when the last repaint was requested (before/after orientation change) and when it was actually executed can tell you whether the corruption happened because of bad framework code (requested before, executed after—so the refresh should have taken into consideration the new orientation) or because of a glitch in the device (requested before, executed before—the framework did not get notified in time that the orientation has changed).

Finally, it should be noted that gathering debug data can add significant overhead and resource strain on Java ME devices, which in turn can lead to poor performance ($2\times$–$5\times$ performance hits are common). To avoid this, you should always have a dedicated build for gathering debug data, separate from any other builds. Next, you should always keep data gathering to a minimum. You can do this by gathering data less often, for example every 3 seconds instead of every second.

You can also consider focusing on only a few relevant aspects at a time instead of generating a full debug log; this is quite OK when you are investigating a specific problem. All good porting frameworks have some sort of debugging support built in, so these measures should be easy to put into practice.

Performing Unit Testing

Unit testing is a great tool for testing the functional aspects of your application (the inner workings) and ensuring that new changes do not break existing functionality. The basic idea is that, for each Java class and functional subsystem of your application, you write one or more functional tests, and after each test you compare the output of the test with a previously calculated and known-to-be-correct output. If the outputs match, the test has passed. If they do not, the test has failed, typically indicating that there is a problem with your application code.

Just like J2SE has JUnit for creating and running unit tests, Java ME has tools such as JMUnit (which is even bundled with NetBeans) and J2MEUnit. Anyone familiar with JUnit should feel right at home with these. As such, the following sections focus more on the Java ME–specific aspects of unit testing.

Solving Common Unit Test–Related Problems

The main difficulty of writing Java ME unit tests lies not in writing the tests themselves or in a lack of test-writing tools; it lies in covering the differences between different devices and between real devices and emulators. It is common knowledge that some features (for example, support of various media types and SSL certificates) work on real devices but not on emulators, and vice versa. Furthermore, if you target different devices, you have to take into consideration the limitations and particularities of each device, such as screen resolution, memory size, and API support.

Overcoming this problem is not particularly difficult. The most important tool you need is a good porting framework. You can use it to create separate test builds for each different real device and for each emulator. The main idea is that if a test will not run on a given target device (for whatever reason, for example, API support), you can exclude it from the build, or replace it with an equivalent version that *will* work on the target device. You can also store build-specific information in the build configuration files—for example, different resource URLs, and different test settings and test data for different devices.

It should be noted that the goal of unit testing is not to test the application's code in a generic context, but to test it in the exact context it will run on. With this in mind, your tests and test data should always try to emulate the real-life stress of your actual application. For example, let's assume you're writing a client-server application with two communication protocol versions, a "light" one for low-end devices and a "heavy" one for high-end devices. Running the tests with "heavy" test data on a low-end device is not representative of the application. The test may fail, or the device may perform badly, but this is irrelevant for real-life scenarios because low-end devices will need to handle only "light" protocol data. Likewise, testing network-related functionality exclusively over Wi-Fi or 3G will not provide relevant information, as the application will have to function in areas with flaky signals and low-quality network connections too.

Which brings us to another important aspect of Java ME unit testing: emulating non-application-related factors, such as network connection quality, battery meter, and GPS position. This is one area where device emulators shine. All major device emulators allow you to configure these parameters easily and dynamically at runtime, usually via a handy property page, thus ensuring that you can test every possible scenario you can think of.

However, problems start to appear when you want these parameters to change according to a given script (for example, great network quality for 5 seconds, then no network for 10 seconds, then average network quality for 5) or when you need low-level control over what happens (for example, controlling the exact number of bytes read from HttpConnection and the interval between them).

The best solution for these problems is creating *mock* classes—and, once again, having a good porting framework will help you immensely. For example, in the preceding HttpConnection example, the best approach is to roll your own MockHttpConnection class, which has the same public API as the real HttpConnection, but which reads its data from a *script file* rather than from an actual HTTP connection. You can then instruct the porting framework to replace all references of HttpConnection with MockHttpConnection and, provided you have the script files ready, you're good to go.

This approach, while elegant and extremely flexible, has its pros and cons, and you have to be aware of both. On the pro side, it gives you complete control over otherwise uncontrollable aspects of the environment, and you can benefit from this control on real devices too, not just on emulators.

On the con side, you are emulating the *theoretical* behavior of the hardware/OS combination, not its actual behavior. For example, just because your MockHttpConnection test is able to process 1 MB of data per second doesn't mean that the real HttpConnection will be able to do this too. The impact of this can be minimized by making sure that the test data/script file is similar to what was observed in real-life scenarios, but you can never be 100 percent certain that your emulated behavior will match the real behavior, especially when it comes to glitches and peculiar behavior.

Also on the con side, mock classes tend to increase overhead and place added strain on the device's resources, which might in turn alter the test results and/or cause the tests to fail even though they should have passed. This is something that you will have to live with, because it is sometimes difficult to determine whether the test has failed because o your application code or because of the added strain, especially on real devices.

Gathering Quality Debug Data

Unit tests provide you with a great opportunity: gathering debug data from the various parts of your application, both when they are working independent of each other and when they are working together. By using this data, you can identify performance bottlenecks and possible problem areas throughout your application's code much more quickly and reliably than you would by gathering debug data from the actual application.

The main attraction of debug data gathered during unit testing is that it is both reflective of real-world performance (if the tests are engineered as such) and reproducible every time because of the highly controlled nature of the tests. So, for example, if the performance data gathered after a code change is worse than the performance data gathered before it, you know that the new code performs worse than the old one.

The same applies to tracking down bugs. Because the randomness factor is greatly reduced in unit tests, it becomes much easier to determine whether a certain problem is caused by a race condition, a bad algorithm, a platform glitch, or something else.

That being said, there will always be differences between debug data gathered in the laboratory and debug data gathered during real-life usage. There are many bugs, especially conjectural ones, which can be debugged in only real-life scenarios. As such, never rely exclusively on laboratory debug data, and don't assume that just because something is fixed in the laboratory tests, it's also fixed in the actual application.

Running the Tests in a Desktop Environment

In some situations, running the code in a desktop environment (as opposed to running it inside an emulator or on a real device) is desired: when you want to gather lots of telemetry data, when your script files are large or dynamically generated, when you want to integrate your tests with other tools such as debuggers and analyzers, and so on.

Fortunately, this is possible. MicroEmulator is an open source Java ME emulator written entirely in Java. It does a fairly good job of emulating the standard Java ME APIs and should be suitable for the majority of unit tests you would want to run. The main advantage of it is that, being entirely J2SE based, you can use it to mix Java ME code with J2SE native code. This is great for doing things not otherwise possible on Java ME, such as using the reflection API to tinker with your application's code without actually altering it, using J2SE native functionality to create more-powerful tests, or running J2SE-exclusive tools.

> **NOTE:** You can download the latest version of MicroEmulator from www.microemu.org.

Furthermore, because it's basically a desktop application, you can take advantage of the increased flexibility of the desktop environment. For example, you could set up your test environment so that it's accessible via remote desktop (useful when working as part of a geographically distributed team), you could make the whole testing process entirely automated, you could record detailed information about each usage session for later analysis, and so forth.

The problem with using MicroEmulator, in my opinion, is that it's essentially an emulated API on top of an emulated platform. This means that, while you can test high-level functionality and algorithms, you should never rely on it to test low-level stuff. Anything that is directly related to hardware calls (for example, networking, graphics) or OS calls (for example, graphics, life-cycle methods) should be considered as unreliable, in the sense that the resulting behavior may be radically different from the behavior of an actual device or even of a dedicated Java ME emulator.

Another problem with it is that its API set is not as rich nor as well implemented as those of a dedicated Java ME emulator. You may find that the API functionality needed to run your code or your unit tests is simply not available on MicroEmulator. If this is the case, you may consider implementing the needed API yourself or writing a feature request to the MicroEmulator team.

Performing Visual Debugging

Visual debugging simply means looking at the visual output of an application (that is, a screenshot) in order to determine whether the application's output and behavior are those expected. This is extremely relevant to Java ME because of the variety of JVMs, UI frameworks, and hardware specifications out there.

Furthermore, visual debugging is especially important for applications that involve a lot of image processing (for example, games) and for applications that deal with complex UI layouts and layout rules (for example, an HTML/CSS browser). It can help spot graphical glitches and small errors (for example, off-by-one-pixel errors) that are otherwise hard to identify in a moving, running application.

> **NOTE:** The analysis of the screenshot can be either manual (a human looks at the screenshot) or automatic (a computer compares the current screenshot with a reference one to see if they match).

Most emulators have support for manually capturing screenshots, and a few have support for capturing the entire output of the application during a whole usage session (MicroEmulator, for example, can save the session as a GIF animation). Furthermore, some SDKs (for example, BlackBerry) allow you to capture screenshots directly from attached real devices.

Visual debugging is especially powerful when combined with unit testing. One trick you can use is to run unit tests related to graphics in MicroEmulator (to take advantage of the "Save as GIF" option) and to have each test case draw a "barcode" unique to the test in the upper-left corner of the screen. The barcode would get saved along with the actual test output as a frame in the GIF animation.

Then, using a custom utility program, you can extract each individual test screenshot from the resulting GIF animation based on the barcode. This allows you to automatically get screenshots of all the tests in your test suite, no matter how many of them you have and no matter how long any given test takes to execute. This is not otherwise possible by using reasonable means (unless MicroEmulator gets a public API, accessible from test suites, to control this kind of functionality) and the technique could be adapted to work with other emulators as well.

Once you have the *per test* screenshots, you can use automatic analysis to go over them. Even with complex applications featuring hundreds of tests, it takes only a few seconds for the computer to identify differences between the reference screenshots and the current set of screenshots—something that would take a human being tens of minutes or even hours to do.

Finally, having a collection of application screenshots is also useful in getting a quick overview of how a given application looks on different devices. This is often important in finding usability issues and inconsistencies that would otherwise be hard to spot when looking at only a single device at a time.

Performing Battery Testing

Battery testing is unique to mobile devices. Often times, you need to know how much battery power your application drains, for example, for determining the estimated maximum runtime of the application, for checking the results of power optimizations added to the application's code, or simply for marketing purposes.

The easiest and most reliable way to get battery measurements is to purchase specialized power-consumption measurement devices, such as wattmeters. These devices give you reliable information regarding the device's instantaneous power consumption and overall power consumption. The downside is that run-of-the-mill wattmeters are a bit difficult to attach to a phone's power circuit, and dedicated wattmeters designed specifically for use with mobile phones tend to be expensive.

When dedicated hardware is out of the question, you can sometimes turn to using the native API to obtain battery measurements. This is a fairly common feature on smartphones. However, I have yet to see a pure Java ME device with this capability. As such, the only viable alternative to dedicated hardware measurement devices is to simply estimate the power consumption based on the battery's rated capacity and the time it takes your application to drain it. Although this requires no extra hardware and works for any Java ME device, it does, however, require patience.

The first thing you need to do is establish a few baseline cases and get the corresponding power measurements. For example, how long does it take for the device's battery to drain out when no application is running and the radio is off? How long does it take to drain the battery when no application is running but the radio is on? What about when signal strength is only 50 percent, or when Wi-Fi is enabled along with the radio? Each plausible usage scenario should be turned into a baseline measurement.

Then, you need to run your application in the same usage scenarios and compare the new measurements with the baseline ones. The difference in battery life is caused by your application's power consumption. To be realistic, you should measure power consumption for three application-usage scenarios: low usage, medium usage, and intensive usage. You should also run each scenario at least four to five times to account for varying conditions (for example, network signal).

Ideally, this would be the end of the story, but the real world is not ideal. It takes a lot of time for a phone's battery to drain. This means that someone has to "play" with the phone in a consistent manner for at least a few hours until the phone dies, and then has to repeat the same usage pattern for several more test runs. Besides being a real chore (to say the least), this is also error prone, because the differences in usage patterns between runs, even tiny ones, can skew the test results. This is even a problem for measurements taken with dedicated hardware devices. You still need to measure power consumption for at least 10–20 minutes, which is plenty of time to allow for consistent variance in usage patterns.

> **TIP:** It's not always necessary to run your application until the battery is 100 percent empty. Some devices display the remaining battery power, typically as a percentage value. In these cases, it's usually enough to cause a 5–10 percent power drain to get a realistic estimate of your application's power consumption.

One solution to this problem is to automate the process. You can do this in three ways. The first way is to simply add a *robot* class to your application, which simulates the desired usage pattern in a loop. As far as your application is concerned, it's the user issuing the commands, not the robot. This approach works, but it has some disadvantages. While your application thinks that there's a real user at the helm, your device does not. As such, power-saving features might kick in (at the very least, the screen will turn off). This can be avoided through various means, including phone settings, native API calls, and physical trickery. It should also be noted that the robot class adds some CPU usage (typically small), which in turn translates to lost battery life.

The second way involves sending commands (keypresses, touch events) to the device from a connected computer via a cable connection. These commands are usually treated in the same way as real user commands, so no power-saving measures should kick in. In addition, this gives a more accurate readout, because no extra strain gets added by the robot class. The problem with this approach is that it's not readily accessible. Depending on the manufacturer and on the chipset/firmware, there's usually quite a bit of digging and hacking involved, and the result is not always guaranteed to be successful.

The third way involves hardware modding, and though it sounds difficult, it's quite easy to do by someone who's into this kind of thing (I knew someone in college who did this), because most of the bits of hardware required are readily available. The idea is that you link some or all of the device's keys to a serial or parallel port on a PC. Signals sent to that port will be interpreted as real keypresses by the device. This works 100 percent of the time (providing the modding is properly done), and as a bonus it also provides the most realistic user simulation possible. This is by far the best solution in my opinion, although you will likely have to sacrifice a mobile phone in the process.

Finally, it should be noted that batteries lose efficiency over time. Change your battery frequently to avoid skewing your test results.

Testing the Application in a Variety of Scenarios

Testing in different scenarios is especially important considering the variety of Java ME devices out there. They come in all shapes and sizes, with all kinds of screens, and with all kinds of keyboard/keypad layouts.

Compared to desktop or web applications, mobile applications get used in a much wider variety of scenarios: one-hand usage, usage while walking, usage in sunlight, and so forth. Each of these scenarios has particularities that should be tested. For example, is it possible to operate the application with just one hand? Does the application function well in landscape mode, even with one-hand operation? Are the text and graphics large and clear enough to be understandable even when the user is not staying still? Does the color scheme used provide enough contrast to be usable in sunlight?

Then there is also the session duration factor. If the application is designed for short, frequent usage (for example, a stock market ticker application), then it is crucial that the application starts up quickly and provides as much information at a glance as possible, without the screen becoming too crowded. If the application is designed for long usage sessions it is crucial that it is not tiresome to use, neither visually nor functionally.

Always make sure that you cover every possible scenario and usage path. This is often easier said than done, especially as most test cases are designed "by ear" and overall they tend to leave untested a lot of areas of the application. The idea is to really test out every nook and cranny of your application, even if it's something so simple and logical that you don't think it's worth testing, and to do this in every single usage scenario and on every single device you need to support. Most of the errors I've encountered in real-life Java ME applications were glaring (for example, a button that is enabled when it should be disabled, a list that messes up its scroll when the device orientation changes, and so on). In contrast, I've encountered considerably fewer subtle bugs.

You should also test your application with real-life users too, not just testers who do this for a living. With this in mind, you should choose a well-diversified user base for testing, not just people who fit your target market (though obviously they should be the bulk of your guinea pig army). People of all ages and backgrounds can give you precious information about how good your application really feels, and you can get some valuable insight on how to improve or adapt your application to reach people not originally part of your target market (remember, Java ME users cover a much wider gamut than smartphone users).

A good strategy for having a well-diversified user base for testing, especially if you're writing an interesting and cool application, is to create a web page from which people interested in trying out your application can register for a closed beta test. Each person who registers should enter information such as age, profession, degree of familiarity with mobile phones, and the current phone or phones they are using. In exchange for submitting their honest opinion about your application and the occasional bug report, they get to use your application well before it reaches the market. It's a win-win situation.

Finally, covering device particularities a in your test scenarios is also important. As mentioned in the beginning of this section, Java ME devices come in various form factors, keyboard/keypad layouts, and screen sizes. Is your current application interface suitable for all devices? Do you need a custom UI layout for device X? Does device X have all the necessary keys (for example, BlackBerry devices don't have softkeys) required to operate the application comfortably and, if not, how can we improve the situation? Does the device have a full keyboard and, if so, does the application take advantage of it optimally? These are all important questions that should be examined during the testing phase.

Testing Performance Improvement and Optimization Techniques

As a Java ME developer, after a while you start to have you own "bag of dirty tricks" that you use in a variety of scenarios. These are typically optimization tricks or techniques that help make your application faster, more stable, or more flexible.

This is obviously a good thing, and this bag of tricks is what separates novice developers from experienced ones. However, a common pitfall experienced developers often fall into is blindly reusing the techniques and optimizations they have learned in the past. Just because something was effective on a device from two years ago doesn't mean it will also be effective on the device you're working with now. Similarly, something that works on a high-end device might actually make the situation worse on a low-end device.—

A very effective way to test what works and what doesn't work on a certain device is to create a special test application just for this. Basically, such an application would be just a bunch on unit tests, except instead of testing application functionality, you would test programming tricks and techniques. The result of running this automated application would be a full report detailing whether each of the tested tricks and techniques works and, if it does, what kind of performance improvements it offers.

The key to a successful test application in this context is having proper and reliable input data. Each test should be run on at least five or six widely different data sets (sometimes even more) in order to provide a conclusive overview—anything less, and the results can be considered conjectural.

Furthermore, some tests should be dynamic in nature. For example, a test dealing with threading optimizations and thread-related architecture should take into consideration the number of maximum threads each device supports, because there is a big difference between a device supporting 10 threads, one supporting 20, and one supporting only 5. (Although the requirements state that a compliant implementation should support a minimum of 10 threads, some implementations aren't compliant). The same goes for memory allocation tests and pretty much any other test that deals with variable environmental conditions.

Once you have these test results, you can use them not only to get a better picture of the device's capabilities, but also to automatically choose the most appropriate solution for it. For example, you can integrate the test results with your preprocessor, allowing it to choose the best code path for your current device. This can serve as a kind of automated application optimization process, and it can greatly reduce the time it takes to optimize your application (especially if you're looking to squeeze every last ounce of performance out of it).

Finally, it should be noted that the results of the tests aren't always translated in real-life scenarios. It's one thing to run a block of code inside a test case, and it's quite another to run in alongside other blocks of code within a real application. This being said, a properly engineered test case can make up for this deficiency by using carefully selected input data and by adding "garbage" to the environment (for example, threads that do nothing but consume resources).

Summary

In this chapter, you have examined the core areas of Java ME application testing: gathering debug information, unit testing, visual debugging, and thoroughly testing the application in all possible usage scenarios and environments. In the process, you have looked at some of the interesting aspects that Java ME brings to the table (for example, buggy JVMs, varied form factors, and different usage scenarios for different devices) and how these aspects should be covered in the testing process. In the next chapter, you will cover advanced Java ME graphics and learn a few graphical techniques useful for Java ME development.

Chapter 13

Advanced Java ME Graphics

Traditionally, graphics have never been one of Java ME's strong points. Conceived in the early days of mobile computing as we know it today, Java ME's main goal was to run on as many devices as possible, and that meant that compromises had to be made. One of those compromises was the limitation of displaying graphics by using only an extremely limited 2D API.

> **NOTE:** Although in recent years Java ME itself has also received support for 3D graphics, the vast majority of devices out there still have to make do with the very limited 2D graphics API either because their JVMs don't include 3D support or because their real-world 3D performance is abysmal. Furthermore, 3D support in Java ME is suitable only for games, and is itself quite limited.

This was fine at first, but with the advent of smartphones and their subsequent increase in popularity, Java ME applications have found themselves competing against applications that were written with much more powerful graphics APIs and that thus looked considerably better.

Fortunately, while the Java ME graphics API has remained largely unchanged for many years, Java ME devices have evolved and now have more graphics and CPU power than ever. This makes it possible to supplement the existing graphics capabilities by writing custom graphical routines and by using clever tricks and techniques that were not feasible only a few years ago. As such, amazing-looking Java ME applications are no longer a thing of the past—they are possible today.

In this chapter, you will examine some of the most important tricks and techniques related to Java ME graphics programming. Mastering them will allow you to create amazing visuals for your Java ME applications, which will instantly appeal to users and put you miles ahead of the competition.

Before we begin, it should be noted that some of the techniques presented in this chapter depend on MIDP 2.0 features, such as `Image.getRGB()`. Unfortunately, this means that they cannot be used on MIDP 1.0 devices. However, it should be noted that MIDP 1.0 devices are typically not fast enough for the job anyway.

Another important mention is related to performance. The code snippets presented in this chapter are written with clarity rather than speed in mind. As such, their performance is considerably less than optimal. By using the techniques presented in Chapter 10, the code performance can be improved considerably. In fact, optimizing these routines is probably one of the best exercises for the techniques presented in Chapter 10, as it gives you the opportunity to try out most of them.

Using Pre-rendered Graphics

Unless you're targeting really low-end devices, chances are that the maximum JAR file size for your target devices is a considerably larger number than your actual JAR file size. In other words, you usually have plenty of room to spare—so why not use it? One of the best uses for those extra available bytes is storing *pre-rendered graphics* for your application (for example, UI elements, fonts, and animation frames). This makes perfect sense; why stress your device by drawing graphics dynamically at runtime when you can simply pre-render those graphics? In addition, pre-rendered graphics are usually of a much higher quality than real-time or dynamically generated graphics, in the same way that a 3D feature film looks better than a video game.

The first things you should try to pre-render are UI elements. For fixed-sized elements, such as check boxes, you can simply render separate images for their individual states (for example, pressed, focused, checked, unchecked, disabled, checked and disabled) and then draw those images directly on the screen/canvas in the `paint()` method. This is extremely simple to do, and the results look great.

For variable-sized elements, things are a bit more complicated. The main idea here is to use a technique known as *patching*: you divide the element into two or more patches, some of which are fixed and some of which are tileable. You then assemble these patches to make up the image of your desired element in the size you want it to have. For example, let's suppose you want to draw an element that can be abstractly defined as a rounded box, such as a button or a dialog box. Figure 13–1 shows a possible patch configuration for this element.

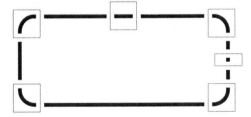

Figure 13–1. *Patch configuration for a rounded box*

You can clearly see that the four corner patches are fixed. At the same time, the other two patches, which make up the horizontal and vertical borders of the box, are tiled: they are repeated as many times as needed to cover the distance between the corners. Depending on the requirements, more patches can be added—for example, if the top and bottom borders are different or if you want the borders to follow a more intricate pattern (in which case you would alternate the corresponding pattern patches).

You can also use pre-rendered images to store UI animations that would otherwise be time-consuming or even impossible to do on the fly. This is pretty much the same technique used in sprite-based games, only in this case the animated sprite is maybe a button's background or an e-mail notification icon or a loading bar. These animations are fine details that are extremely important for Java ME applications, because they give the interface a more natural and "flowing" look, similar to the one you would find on desktops or on smartphones (for example, a button gradually "lighting up" when the cursor/pointer hovers over it instead of immediately switching to the "focused" state).

Taking this idea further, pre-rendered images are also a great way to create application themes. Changing how your UI elements look becomes a simple matter of using a different image file; no code has to be changed in the process.

There are also a lot of other small graphical elements that you can pre-render for better performance and a sleeker look. For example, in a line chart, the various segments are typically delimited with some kind of bullet. Rather than draw these bullets in real time by using low-level drawing functions (for example, fillArc()), you can pre-render them. This will not only be faster (typically), it will also look better because you can, for example, pre-render them with semitransparent pixels around the edges so that they look smoother.

Another great use for pre-rendered images is as a basis for graphical effects. As you will soon see, many graphical effects that you can implement with Java ME require two image files: a source image and a secondary image to be used as a parameter (for example, as an image mask or as a color filter). By pre-rendering these secondary images rather than generating them at runtime, you can dramatically improve the runtime performance of these graphical effects.

Even better, sometimes you can pre-render the entire output of a graphical effect, especially if the output is not dynamic in nature (for example, the output is not a frame that is part of an animation). Let's suppose you want to use image masking to create a sky-textured version of your company's logo. You can either do this at runtime, or do this at build time and store the pre-rendered masked logo in your JAR file. This is faster in terms of runtime performance, but has the obvious side-effect of increasing the JAR file size.

TIP: A good strategy is to mix dynamic and pre-rendered graphics. For example, if you're writing a sprite-based game and you need your sprites to rotate in 16 directions, consider pre-rendering eight of the needed frames and dynamically generating the remaining eight. This provides a good balance between JAR file size and runtime performance. Furthermore, if you use sprite mirroring, you need to pre-render and generate only half as many frames.

Finally, one of the best uses for pre-rendered graphics is storing fonts. Native device fonts don't usually look good. Furthermore, they can break the application's UI across devices because they tend to vary greatly in size and shape. Because of this, most high-quality Java ME applications resort to using pre-rendered bitmap fonts. However, you'll typically need several fonts for a good-looking application UI, or at least the same font in different sizes and styles (bold, italic)—so if the space is available, go for it.

The last thing I would like to discuss regarding pre-rendered graphics is the proper way to store them. Storing each graphical element in a separate file is counterproductive, both in terms of performance and in terms of occupied JAR and memory space. The best way to store pre-rendered graphics is as part of an image map. Specifically, you create one larger *parent image*, and each pre-rendered graphical element is stored as a rectangular sub-section of that image, as seen in Figure 13–2. The distances between the image map's top and left borders and the element's sub-section are known as the element's *top and left offsets*, respectively.

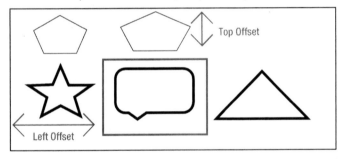

Figure 13–2. *An image map with one graphical element and its offsets highlighted*

TIP: You might be able to optimize file size by converting your PNG files to ones that use a color palette. This is helpful if your images use only a limited set of colors, but less useful for images that use a lot of colors. You should also be aware that, besides the PNG file format, which is required in the Java ME specification, all other file formats are optional. As such, when considering an alternate format (such as GIF or JPEG), make sure your target devices support it.

To render a graphical element that is part of an image map, all you have to do is calculate the drawing coordinates of the parent image *with respect to the graphical element's offsets*, clip the canvas around the onscreen coordinates you want to draw the graphical element to, and then *draw the parent image at the coordinates calculated previously.* Because we have calculated the image map's coordinates with respect to the element's offsets, the actual element will be drawn at exactly the desired position. This sounds a bit confusing when explained in words, but the pseudocode shown in Listing 13–1 will make everything clear.

Listing 13–1. *Pseudocode for Drawing an Element That Is Part of an Image Map*

```
function drawAt( Image imageMap, Graphics target, int x, int y, int elementOffsetLeft,
int elementOffsetTop, int elementWidth, int elementHeight)
{
        // Calculate the image map's target coordinates
        // with respect to the element's offsets
        imageX = x - elementOffsetLeft;
        imageY = y - elementOffsetTop;

        // Clip the canvas around the element's drawing position
        target.clip(x, y, elementWidth, elementHeight);

        // Draw the image map at the above calculated coordinates.
        // This ensures that the element itself is actually drawn at (x,y),
        // and since the canvas is clipped around the element's target
        // area, nothing else except the element will be drawn.
        target.drawImage(imageMap,imageX,imageY);
}
```

Using image maps is a very important technique for Java ME applications. It tends to be easy on resources (because fewer Image objects have to be created and managed, and fewer individual image files have to be decoded). It's also quite fast, as the vast majority of phones support clipping in hardware. In fact, if you're using a large number of graphical elements in a single drawing operation (for example, screen refresh), it's quite possible that using image maps will actually be *faster* than drawing individual images. Furthermore, high-end Java ME phones have dedicated graphics chips, which they also use for accelerating Java ME drawing operations. Because of the way these chips work, drawing different portions of the same image is almost always faster than drawing different individual images, because the graphics chip has to switch buffers (images) in the second case. The difference is unlikely to be noticeable, though.

Using Image Masking

Image masking is a technique similar to clipping. Whereas in clipping the image is "cut" according to a rectangular area, in image masking the image is cut according to a free-form mask, typically another image.

Image masking is extremely useful for a variety of purposes, ranging from stylish effects (for example, textured fonts—the image is the texture, the mask is the font) to practical, clever tricks (for example, dynamic backgrounds for nonrectangular components based on the actual shape and size of the component—in this case, the component's shape is the mask).

In addition to being quite powerful, image masking is extremely easy to implement. The trick lies in defining the mask properly. Specifically, the mask must be an image with some pixels opaque and some pixels transparent or semitransparent. The convention is that, when applied to a source image, the opaque pixels of the mask will create opaque pixels in the resulting image, while the transparent or semitransparent pixels of the mask will create transparent or semitransparent pixels in the resulting image. All we care about in the mask image is the transparency of the pixels; their actual color is irrelevant for our purposes.

Next, we know that MIDP 2.0 allows us to retrieve the individual pixels of an image via Image.getRGB(). The result will be an array of integers, with each integer in the array corresponding to a pixel of the source image. The channel data of each pixel (its Alpha, Red, Green, and Blue values) is encoded by reserving 8 bits of integer for each channel. Written in hexadecimal, the notation is 0xAARRGGBB.

With this in mind, all we need to do is take the Alpha channel of the mask image and merge it with the RGB channels of the source image. This is quite easy to do, as seen in the highlighted lines of Listing 13–2. Next, after we have the merged ARGB data, we can simply draw it on the screen or on any other Graphics object.

Listing 13–2. *Image Masking in Java ME*

```
public void drawMaskedImage(Image source, Image mask, Graphics g, int x, int y)
{
        // Reserve an array for the pixel data of each image
        int [] sourceData = new int[source.getHeight()*source.getWidth()];
        int [] maskData = new int[mask.getHeight()*mask.getWidth()];

        // Retrieve the individual pixels of each image (source, mask)
        source.getRGB(sourceData, 0, source.getWidth(), 0, 0, source.getWidth(),
        source.getHeight());
        mask.getRGB(maskData, 0, mask.getWidth(), 0, 0, mask.getWidth(),
        mask.getHeight());

        // Merge the alpha channel of the mask with the color channels of the source
        for (int i=0;i<sourceData.length;i++) {
           sourceData[i] =  (maskData[i] & 0xFF000000) |
           (sourceData[i] & 0x00FFFFFF) ;
        }

        // Draw the result
        g.drawRGB(sourceData, 0, source.getWidth(), x, y, source.getWidth(),
        source.getHeight(), true);
}
```

There is one important thing to mention: for clarity and brevity, the code in Listing 13–2 assumes that the mask and source images are of the same size. If the two images are of different sizes, either the result will look wrong or an ArrayIndexOutOfBounds exception will be raised. However, it is possible (and not that difficult) to adapt the code to work with masks and sources of different sizes. This is left as an exercise for the reader.

That's all there is to implementing image masking in Java ME! The results are quite good looking, as can be seen in Figure 13–3.

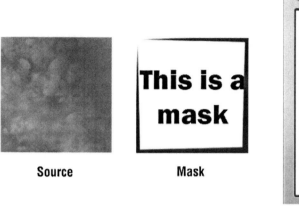

Source   **Mask**

Result

Figure 13–3. *Image masking in action*

The fun doesn't stop here, however. We can do even more with this technique. For example, the maskData array can be dynamically generated. You can use this to create all sorts of effects, from film grain or snow to animated transitions similar to PowerPoint's Checkerboard or Dissolve.

You should be aware that, while most modern MIDP 2.0 devices support transparency and alpha blending, this is not a required part of the Java ME standard. Furthermore, the number of transparency levels can vary widely among devices (from 2 levels to 256 levels). Make sure you test these two aspects on your target device before using transparency and image masking. For example, an image that makes use of the full 256 levels of transparency might look bad when displayed on a device that supports only 4 levels of transparency.

Using Image Blending Techniques

Image blending basically refers to merging two images together so that the resulting image contains color information from both images. This is similar to masking, in that two images are used to obtain a result. At the same time, it's quite different, because, unlike masking, color information from *both* images is used in the resulting image.

There are many forms of image blending, ranging from the very sophisticated (the kind of "polar bear on the beach" effects you see in Photoshop) to the simple ones (for example, alpha blending, in which two images overlap, with the top image semitransparent and enabling you to see the bottom image through it—the kind of effect you often see in 80s music videos).

This section covers only simple blending techniques. More-advanced blending techniques aren't really suitable for Java ME, because of resource constraints. Still, simple doesn't necessarily mean crude. As you will see, even with simple blending techniques, you can still get some very interesting-looking results.

First, let's look at the aforementioned alpha blending of two images. This has many applications, from smooth screen transitions (in which the top screen gradually fades to reveal the bottom one), to better and more intuitive tools to analyze data (for example, you can just overlap two visual representations of data, such as graphs or color maps, and see which areas are the same and which are different).

As a side note, this blending technique (like all simple image-blending techniques) is a per-pixel operation. That is, each pixel in the output image is dependent only on the corresponding pixels in the source images; it does not depend on neighboring pixels. This makes it easy to implement, and the code runs pretty fast, provided you do not use it on extremely large images.

By comparison, more-advanced blending techniques require you to process 2 or more pixels of each source image for every pixel of the output image. Some techniques require that you take into consideration tens of source pixels for every output pixel. This obviously makes them considerably slower and unsuitable for Java ME.

Getting back on track, the best analogy for our alpha blending effect is…mixing paint. What you do when you want to mix paint is pour two different colors in a bucket and, depending on the quantity of each color, you will get a result closer to the first color or to the second color. This is exactly what we want to do: we want our output image to reflect more of the top image or more of the bottom image, depending on the transparency level we specify.

Fortunately, there is a mathematical formula that does just this. Adapted so that all values are in the 0–255 range (so that it's easier to work with in Java ME), the formula is the one seen in Listing 13–3.

Listing 13–3. *Alpha Blending Formula*

```
Result = ( color1 * transparency + color2 * ( 255-transparency) ) / 255
```

Because each color is actually made up of four different channels (Alpha, Red, Green, and Blue), we must apply this formula to each individual channel, as in Listing 13–4.

Listing 13–4. *Per-Channel Alpha Blending Formula*

```
R.red = ( color1.red * transparency + color2.red * ( 255-transparency) ) / 255
R.green = ( color1.green * transparency + color2.green * ( 255-transparency) ) / 255
R.blue = ( color1.blue * transparency + color2.blue * ( 255-transparency) ) / 255
R.alpha = ( color1.alpha * transparency + color2.alpha * ( 255-transparency) ) / 255
```

As this is a per-pixel operation, we have to apply this formula to each individual pixel of the resulting image. The Java ME code that does this is seen in Listing 13–5, where coeff is the transparency coefficient (in the 0–255 range).

Listing 13–5. *Alpha Blending in Java ME*

```
public void drawBlendedImage(Image bottom, Image top, Graphics g,
int coeff, int x, int y)
{
        // Reserve an array for the pixel data of each image
        int [] bottomData = new int[bottom.getHeight()*bottom.getWidth()];
        int [] topData = new int[top.getHeight()*top.getWidth()];
```

```
// Retrieve the individual pixels of each image (source, mask)
bottom.getRGB(bottomData, 0, bottom.getWidth(), 0, 0, bottom.getWidth(),
bottom.getHeight());
top.getRGB(topData, 0, top.getWidth(), 0, 0, top.getWidth(), top.getHeight());

// Define the needed pixel values
int alpha1, alpha2;
int red1, red2;
int green1, green2;
int blue1, blue2;
int resultA,resultR,resultG,resultB;

// Go through all the pixels in the top and bottom images
for (int i=0;i<bottomData.length;i++) {

    // Get individual channel values for each pixel (top,bottom)
    alpha1 = (bottomData[i] & 0xFF000000) >>> 24;
    alpha2 = (topData[i] & 0xFF000000) >>> 24;
    red1 = (bottomData[i] & 0x00FF0000) >> 16;
    red2 = (topData[i] & 0x00FF0000) >> 16;
    green1 = (bottomData[i] & 0x0000FF00) >> 8;
    green2 = (topData[i] & 0x0000FF00) >> 8;
    blue1 = (bottomData[i] & 0x000000FF);
    blue2 = (topData[i] & 0x000000FF);

    // Apply the image blending formula
    resultA = ( alpha1 * coeff + alpha2 * (255 - coeff) ) / 255;
    resultR = ( red1 * coeff + red2 * (255 - coeff) ) / 255;
    resultG = ( green1 * coeff + green2 * (255 - coeff) ) / 255;
    resultB = ( blue1 * coeff + blue2 * (255 - coeff) ) / 255;

    // Create the final pixel value
    bottomData[i] = resultA << 24 | resultR << 16 | resultG << 8 | resultB ;
}

// Draw the result
g.drawRGB(bottomData, 0, bottom.getWidth(), x, y, bottom.getWidth(),
bottom.getHeight(), true);
}
```

The highlighted lines show where the magic happens. First, for each of the two source pixels, we extract the individual Alpha, Red, Green, and Blue channel values from their integer representations. This is done via classical bit masking and bit shifting. Then, we apply the formula to each channel, in order to get the resulting ARGB channel values. We then combine these values together in an integer representation of the resulting pixel. The results of running this code can be seen in Figure 13–4.

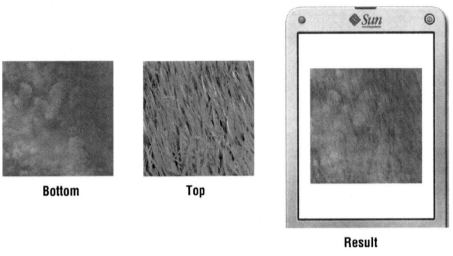

Bottom   **Top**

Result

Figure 13–4. *Semitransparent images overlapping*

The fun part about per-pixel effects is that you can just change the mixing formula to get all sorts of interesting results. For example, one very powerful blending type is Multiply Blending. The formula for this blending type, as seen in Listing 13–6, is quite simple, even simpler than the previous one.

Listing 13–6. *Multiply Blending Formula*

```
Result = ( color1 * color 2 ) / 255
```

Listing 13–7 shows the formula translated to Java ME code. The listing is extremely similar to Listing 13–5; the only real difference is the change in the blending formula, seen in the highlighted lines.

Listing 13–7. *Multiply Blending in Java ME*

```
public void drawMultipliedImage(Image firstImage, Image secondImage,
Graphics g, int x, int y)
{
        // Reserve an array for the pixel data of each image
        int [] bottomData = new int[firstImage.getHeight()*firstImage.getWidth()];
        int [] topData = new int[secondImage.getHeight()*secondImage.getWidth()];

        // Retrieve the individual pixels of each image (source, mask)
        firstImage.getRGB(bottomData, 0, firstImage.getWidth(), 0, 0,
        firstImage.getWidth(), firstImage.getHeight());
        secondImage.getRGB(topData, 0, secondImage.getWidth(), 0, 0,
        secondImage.getWidth(), secondImage.getHeight());

        // Define the needed pixel values
        int alpha1, alpha2;
        int red1, red2;
        int green1, green2;
        int blue1, blue2;
        int resultA,resultR,resultG,resultB;

        for (int i=0;i<bottomData.length;i++) {
```

```
        // Get individual channel values for each of the top and bottom images
        alpha1 = (bottomData[i] & 0xFF000000) >>> 24;
        alpha2 = (topData[i] & 0xFF000000) >>> 24;
        red1 = (bottomData[i] & 0x00FF0000) >> 16;
        red2 = (topData[i] & 0x00FF0000) >> 16;
        green1 = (bottomData[i] & 0x0000FF00) >> 8;
        green2 = (topData[i] & 0x0000FF00) >> 8;
        blue1 = (bottomData[i] & 0x000000FF);
        blue2 = (topData[i] & 0x000000FF);
        resultA = alpha1 * alpha2 / 255 ;
        resultR = red1 * red2 / 255 ;
        resultG = green1 * green2 / 255 ;
        resultB = blue1 * blue2 / 255;
        // Create the final pixel value
        bottomData[i] = resultA << 24 | resultR << 16 | resultG << 8 | resultB ;
    }

    // Draw the result
    g.drawRGB(bottomData, 0, firstImage.getWidth(), x, y, firstImage.getWidth(),
    firstImage.getHeight(), true);
}
```

So what can we do with Multiply Blending? Well, for one thing, we can apply it on the same image, which will increase its contrast and make it more vivid. This can be seen in Figure 13–5.

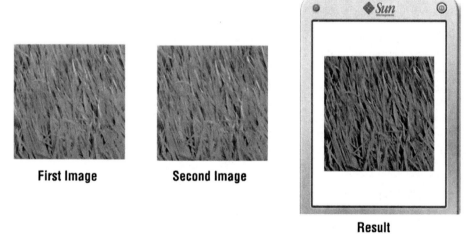

First Image   **Second Image**

Result

Figure 13–5. *Multiply Blending applied on the same image*

Or, we can apply this to an image and a gradient. This will result in a nice fade effect, as seen in Figure 13–6.

First Image   **Second Image**

Result

Figure 13–6. *Multiply Blending with an image and a gradient*

There are other blending effects you can achieve by changing the blending formula—for example, Screen Blending, whose formula is given in Listing 13–8. Screen Blending is somewhat the opposite of Multiply Blending, as it tends to result in a lighter picture with less contrast.

Listing 13–8. *Screen Blending Formula*

```
Result = 255 - ( ( (255 - color1) * (255 - color2) ) / 255 )
```

Blending techniques are a powerful tool. Used with care on UI elements, logos, and user pictures, or as part of small animations, they can add a lot of style to your applications, bridging the visual gap between smartphone UIs and Java ME UIs. They also make for a much more visually pleasing user experience than you would normally expect from Java ME applications, which will make your application stand out in the crowd. They are especially effective when applied to small images (for example, 64×64 or 32×128), because in these cases, they are typically fast enough to be used in real time without any noticeable slowdown on today's average Java ME device.

Rotating Images

Before we begin, it should be noted that this topic requires a good knowledge of mathematics (especially trigonometry) to be understood properly. However, I will do my best to explain things in the most nonmathematical way possible.

Image rotation is one of the most widely used image operations on all platforms, desktop and mobile alike. It is most commonly used in games or in multimedia applications, but has real value for business applications too. Unfortunately, standard image rotation support in Java ME is extremely limited. You can rotate images only at angles that are multiples of 90 degrees; free-angle rotation is not an option. This is a major limitation, because many times you need to rotate images at "odd" angles (that is, not multiples of 90 degrees).

For example, if you want to create a gauge widget for your application, you need to be able to draw the indicator needle at any angle. Using the standard functions available to you, there are three ways to do this: create an image for every possible angle at the expense of significantly increasing the JAR size, create fewer images but lose accuracy, or draw the gauge by using low-level functions such as drawLine() and limit yourself to a very crude and ugly-looking needle. None of these options is particularly satisfying.

As such, the best course of action is to implement your own image-rotation function, which is capable of rotating images at any angle. It may sound daunting, but this is not particularly hard to do once you understand the math involved. In fact, image rotation is quite a simple operation. Because every image is made up of individual pixels, to rotate an image, all you have to do is rotate all its pixels around the same reference point, which is usually the center of the image. You basically do the same simple operation over and over again.

The most basic thing we need in order to do this is the formula for rotating a point around the origin in a Cartesian coordinate system. The math behind this is difficult to explain in just a few paragraphs, and furthermore is outside the scope of this book (though quite an interesting read, which will give you a lot of insight into the world of 2D/3D transformations and implementing those transformations on a computer). Therefore, what we will do is just take the formula for granted. It can be seen in Listing 13–9.

Listing 13–9. *Rotating a Point Around the Origin in a Cartesian Coordinate System*

```
x' = x * cos(a) - y * sin(a)
y' = x * sin(a) + y * cos(a)
```

In the preceding formula, (x,y) are the original coordinates of the point and (x',y') are the resulting coordinates of the point after being rotated a degrees around the origin. As with most practical 2D/3D transformations, the formula is surprisingly simple.

Any image can be inscribed in a rectangle, called its *bounding box*. For an image that is not rotated, the size of the bounding box is the same as the size of the image. However, as soon as you rotate the image, you will need a bigger bounding box to contain it, as can be seen in Figure 13–7.

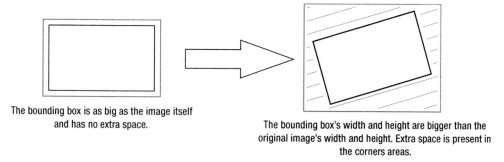

The bounding box is as big as the image itself and has no extra space.

The bounding box's width and height are bigger than the original image's width and height. Extra space is present in the corners areas.

Figure 13–7. *When rotating an image, the bounding box increases in size.*

The next thing we need to do is figure out the size of the bounding box for the rotated image. There are several ways to do this, so let's choose the one that makes the most sense (not necessarily the fastest or the most efficient).

In order to calculate the size of the bounding box, we will start with the bounding box of the original image and rotate its four corners around the origin, just as we would the image itself. We then look at the coordinates of the four resulting points, remembering the minimum and maximum x and y coordinates we encounter—so we end up with minX, maxX, minY, maxY. The difference between the maximum x coordinate and the minimum x coordinate is the width of the resulting bounding box, and the difference between the maximum y coordinate and the minimum y coordinate is the height of the resulting bounding box.

To make the mathematics simpler, we can consider one of the corners itself as being the origin of the coordinate system, rather than the more-intuitive approach of considering the center of the bounding box as being the origin of the coordinate system. This means we must calculate the coordinates only for the three remaining corners, because our initial corner has, by definition, coordinates (0,0).

The whole process is illustrated in Figure 13–8.

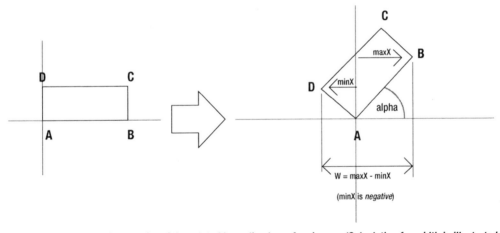

Figure 13–8. *Calculating the size of the rotated bounding box of an image. (Calculation for width is illustrated.)*

Translated into code, the result will look something like the one seen in Listing 13–10.

Listing 13–10. *Calculating the Size of the Rotated Bounding Box of an Image*

```
// Calculate rotated image size
// To do this, first assume the lower-left corner is at (0,0).
// Then, calculate the other three corners
double point1x = originalW * Math.cos(angle);
double point1y = originalW * Math.sin(angle);
double point2x = -originalH * Math.sin(angle);
double point2y = originalH * Math.cos(angle);
double point3x = originalW * Math.cos(angle) - originalH * Math.sin(angle);
double point3y = originalW * Math.sin(angle) + originalH * Math.cos(angle);
```

```
// Next find the minimum and maximum coordinate values of the corners
double minx = Math.min( 0, Math.min(point1x , Math.min(point2x , point3x)));
double miny = Math.min( 0, Math.min(point1y , Math.min(point2y , point3y)));
double maxx = Math.max( 0, Math.max(point1x , Math.max(point2x , point3x)));
double maxy = Math.max( 0, Math.max(point1y , Math.max(point2y , point3y)));

// Finally, calculate the actual width and height of the rotated image
int rotatedW = (int) Math.floor(Math.abs(maxx - minx));
int rotatedH = (int) Math.floor(Math.abs(maxy - miny));
```

Now that we know what the size of the rotated image's bounding box is, we can start "moving" the pixels from the original image to the rotated one. To do this, we will use *inverse mapping*. That is, rather than going through all the pixels of the original image and seeing where they fit in the rotated image, we will go through all the pixels of the rotated image and see what pixels of the original image, if any, correspond to them.

The reason for this is simple: regular mapping would leave holes in the rotated image. This happens because real pixels always have integer coordinates, whereas calculated pixels have real coordinates. This leads to differences between the calculated pixel coordinates and the actual pixel coordinates.

To illustrate this, let's assume that, after applying our rotation formula to a pixel in the original image, we get an x' value of 12.3. To properly map the source pixel to the rotated image, we would need it to "fill" the space between x'=11.8 and x'=12.8, so that x'=12.3 sits right in the middle. However, what actually happens when the pixel is mapped to the rotated image is that the 12.3 value gets rounded down to 12, and the space between x'=12 and x'=13 is actually filled; the 0.4 (0.2 + 0.2) difference between the calculated and actual x' values is empty space. This is illustrated in Figure 13–9.

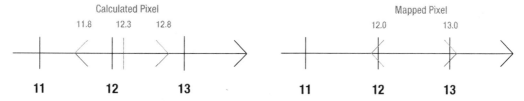

Figure 13–9. *Difference between calculated pixel coordinates and mapped pixel coordinates*

If the image had only one dimension, this would not be a problem, because the empty space would have been covered by other pixels. However, in two dimensions this leads to cases in which entire pixels in the resulting image remain uncovered, appearing as holes in the rotated image.

> **NOTE:** "Holes" are a frequent occurrence in image transformations that have formulas resulting in real coordinates (as opposed to integer ones). To avoid this issue, inverse mapping should always be used in these scenarios.

Besides using inverse mapping, there is one more thing we should do: take into consideration the center of rotation. For images, the center of rotation is the center of the image, which means that math-wise, the image center must have coordinates (0,0) in order for our rotation formulas to work.

However, Java ME assigns the (0,0) coordinates to the upper-left corner of an image. We must account for this difference in coordinate mapping by adjusting our rotation formulas accordingly. As the coordinate difference between the image center and the upper-left corner of the image is (-width/2, -height/2), the resulting adjusted formulas are the ones seen in Listing 13–11.

Listing 13–11. *Rotation Formulas, Adjusted for Mapping Differences*

```
x' = (x - width/2) * cos(a) - (y - height/2) * sin(a)
y' = (x - width/2) * sin(a) + (y - height/2)  * cos(a)
```

We now have everything we need to write our complete image rotation routine. It is shown in Listing 13–12.

Listing 13–12. *The Complete Java ME Image Rotation Routine*

```
public void drawRotatedImage(Image image, Graphics g, double angle, int x, int y)
{
        // Insert code from Listing 13-8 here.

        // Calculate the "origin" (in our case, the center) of the rotated image
        int referenceX = rotatedW / 2;
        int referenceY = rotatedH / 2;

        // Reserve an array for the pixel data of the original and rotated images
        int [] sourceData = new int[originalW * originalH];
        int [] rotatedData = new int[rotatedW * rotatedH];

        // Retrieve the pixels of the original image
        image.getRGB(sourceData, 0, originalW, 0, 0, originalW, originalH);

        // Variables to mark X,Y pixel positions in the original and rotated images
        int rotX,rotY;
        int origX, origY;

        // Variables to keep track of index positions in the RGB arrays
        int origPos, rotatedPos;

        // Process each pixel of the rotated image
        for (rotX=0;rotX<rotatedW;rotX++)
        {
                for (rotY=0;rotY<rotatedH;rotY++)
                {
                        // For the current "rotated" pixel, calculate the
                        // X coordinate of the original image pixel. Since for this
                        // operation the origin is assumed to be the center of the
                        // this reference point.
                        origX = (int) ( (rotX - referenceX) * Math.cos(angle) - (rotY
                         - referenceY) *  Math.sin(angle) + originalW / 2);
                        // Check if the resulting X value falls inside the original
                        // image or outside of it. Go to the next pixel if this is so.
                        if ( origX < 0 || origX >= originalW)
                        {
```

```
                continue;
        }
        // Calculate the Y coordinate next
        origY = (int) ( (rotY - referenceY) * Math.cos(angle) +
        (rotX -referenceX) *  Math.sin(angle) + originalH / 2);
        // Calculate the pixel's would-be position in the original
        // source array
        origPos = origY * originalW + origX ;
        // Check if the position is valid
        // Go to the next pixel if the position is not valid
        if ( origPos < 0 || origPos >= sourceData.length )
        {
                continue;
        }
        // Calculate the "rotated" pixel's positon in the rotated
        image // array
        rotatedPos = rotY * rotatedW + rotX;
        // Move the pixel data from the original array to the
        rotated // array
        rotatedData[rotatedPos] = sourceData[origPos];
        }
}
// Draw the result
g.drawRGB(rotatedData, 0, rotatedW, x, y, rotatedW, rotatedH, true);
}
```

The preceding listing may be a bit sizeable, but its workings are fairly straightforward. The more-complicated bits, such as calculating the size of the resulting rotated image, and the inverse mapping of the pixels (along with the necessary coordinate adjustments) have been explained earlier. However, I would like to draw your attention to the highlighted lines. These lines check whether the inversely mapped pixel coordinates are within the bounds of the original image. If either of the checks fails, the code skips to the next pixel of the rotated image for inverse mapping. This is needed because, as seen in Figure 13–7, some pixels in the corner of the rotated image are empty space and do not map to any pixels in the original image; trying to map them would result in an ArrayIndexOutOfBounds error.

Finally, Figure 13–10 shows our image rotation routine in action.

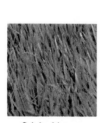

Original Image

Rotated Image

Figure 13–10. *The image rotation routine in action*

Resizing Images

Another quite common image manipulation technique is *image resizing* — that is, enlarging or shrinking an image. This is useful for a wide variety of purposes, from creating zoom effects in picture gallery applications to on-the-fly resizing of UI graphical elements.

By default, Java ME has no image resizing capabilities whatsoever. Fortunately, image resizing is extremely easy to implement, because in essence it's basically multiplying the source image with a resize factor. If the resize factor is less than 1.0, the image will be shrunk. If the factor is greater than 1.0, the image will be enlarged.

As such, the first thing we need to do is calculate the size of the resized image. This is easy to do, because we just have to multiply the original image size by the image factor. Next, we will use inverse mapping and see which pixel of the original image corresponds to each pixel of the resized image. To do this, all we have to do is *divide* the coordinates of each destination pixel by the resize factor.

The entire process is shown in Listing 13–13.

Listing 13–13. *Resizing an Image in Java ME*

```
public void drawResizedImage(Image image, Graphics g, double factor, int x, int y)
{
        // Variables to mark X,Y positions in the original and zoomed image
        int xpos,ypos;
        int origx, origy;

        // Position in the RGB array
        int origpos, zoompos;

        // Calculate zoomed image size
        int originalW = image.getWidth();
        int originalH = image.getWidth();
        int zoomW = (int) (originalW * factor);
        int zoomH = (int) (originalH * factor);

        // Reserve an array for the pixel data of the original and zoomed image
        int [] sourceData = new int[originalW * originalH];
        int [] zoomData = new int[zoomW * zoomH];

        // Retrieve the pixels of the original image
        image.getRGB(sourceData, 0, originalW, 0, 0, originalW, originalH);

        // Process each pixel of the zoomed image
        for (xpos=0;xpos<zoomW;xpos++)
        {
                for (ypos=0;ypos<zoomH;ypos++)
                {
                        // Calculate its corresponding original image pixel
                        origx = (int) (xpos / factor);
                        origy = (int) (ypos / factor);

                        // Map both pixels (original,zoomed) in the data arrays
                        origpos = origy * originalW + origx;
```

```
            zoompos = ypos * zoomW + xpos;

            // Move the pixel data from the original array to the zoomed
            // array
            zoomData[zoompos] = sourceData[origpos];
        }
    }

    // Draw the result
    g.drawRGB(zoomData, 0, zoomW, x, y, zoomW, zoomH, true);
}
```

The preceding image resizing routine can be seen in action in Figure 13–11.

Original Image

Resized Image

Figure 13–11. *Image resizing in Java ME*

Implementing Other Graphical Effects

There are many more graphical effects that you could implement. For example, you could implement a particle-based system that "explodes" a given image into many smaller chunks (or reverse-explodes the smaller chunks into a complete image).

The key to adding more graphical effects to your arsenal lies in your imagination and in the clever use of Java ME's capabilities. For example, the explosion effect just mentioned is actually quite CPU friendly, because all you do is calculate the position of each chunk and then use the source image as an image map to draw each chunk in its corresponding position.

You should also be aware that there are two types of effects you can create: those suitable for real-time use and those not suitable for real-time use. Image masking is a good example of an effect suitable for real time use, because it's simple and fast. However, should you try to implement image filters (for example, Watercolor from Photoshop), you will most likely not be able to use them in real-time scenarios. That is not to say they do not have their uses; for example, personalizing the application based on the user's own images is a very nice thing to have, and filters can go a long way toward this goal.

Implementing your own graphical effects is always a very rewarding experience. Playing with pixels is always fun, and you will get to learn a lot of things related to computer graphics, code optimization, programming techniques, and mathematics in the process. Not to mention, at the end of the day, you can use the code you've written to impress your friends, coworkers, or even your boss.

That being said, here are a few graphical effects that you may consider implementing:

- Particle-based systems, as exemplified in this section.

- Image blurring and image sharpening.

- Image anti-aliasing.

- Image skewing effects (for example, making your image appear like a trapezoid, or making it wobble like a flag).

- Image desaturation (turning colored images into black-and-white ones).

- Artistic filters, such as Watercolor and Bas Relief.

- Image morphing (seamlessly blending the contents of two images, not their pixels—for example, blending your face with that of your spouse). You should be warned: this is an extremely difficult effect to implement.

Combining Multiple Effects Together

When properly optimized, the effects presented in this chapter can be combined for even more spectacular results. For example, it is possible to create a rotated and textured version of your company's logo, in which the texture is obtained by blending two images together. This is most effective when the various parameters of the effects involved are varied (for example, the rotation angle is changed, as is the transparency coefficient of the blending operation) to create animations.

At this point, you may be wondering exactly how feasible this is. A couple of years ago, I asked myself the same question. So I set out to create a Java ME graphical effects library that was to be both fast and powerful. I was curious to see how far the Java ME platform could be pushed in this area, and I was quite pleased with how the library, called J2ME Army Knife, turned out.

The most interesting and surprising thing (for me, at least) was the level to which graphical effects could be optimized in terms of speed. For example, after I optimized the image rotation code, I was able to take a 64×64 image and rotate it almost 100 times per second on a Nokia E50. As an amusing side note, I haven't done any serious work on the library for over two years now (which is a lifetime in software development), but I still get the occasional e-mail from people saying that they're amazed with how fast the code runs and that it really shows how "state of the art" J2ME Army Knife is.

> **NOTE:** For more information on J2ME Army Knife, please visit www.j2mearmyknife.com. There you can see the library in action (live demo) and also download it. It's completely free to use in binary form, even for commercial projects, so give it a try!

Combining multiple effects together is even more feasible in nondynamic circumstances. Although a single animation frame typically has to be calculated in a maximum of 100 milliseconds in order to get a "smooth" feel, for static graphics you can use up to 500 milliseconds to do this (maybe even more, if the processing is done in a separate background thread). This means that you can either work with bigger source images, or string together more effects.

Another very powerful technique is using dynamic graphical effects in combination with image maps. For example, let's take the case of the earlier scenario in which the textured logo was rotated and animated. Rather than calculating each frame every single time, you calculate frames only the first time they are needed and then place them in an image map. Then, when the animation cycles, instead of recalculating the frames again, you use the data stored in the image map. This is extremely fast overall, but it does require quite a bit of RAM for larger images—so your mileage with this technique will vary depending on the target device.

Finally, combining graphical effects together can be done in one of two ways. Your first option is to apply each effect individually: the output of the first effect becomes the input for the second effect, and so forth. Although this is flexible, because each effect remains as a stand-alone, it also has the disadvantage of adding a lot of overhead to the overall result. For example, if two effects in the chain need to work with the individual Alpha, Red, Green, and Blue values of each pixel, then each of the two effects will have to do the extraction separately.

The second option is to create meta-effects; for example, you can combine the rotate and resize effects together. This has the advantage of eliminating a lot of unnecessary overhead, as many common calculations for both effects need to be made only once, and memory objects such as ARGB arrays can be reused. The performance improvement is particularity significant if the overhead eliminated is at the pixel level (that is, within the inner loop, where individual pixels are manipulated).

Summary

In this chapter, you have examined a couple of advanced Java ME graphical techniques: image blending, image masking, image resizing, and image rotating. You have looked at the principles behind these techniques and at their various use cases. In the next chapter, you will look at a few Java ME development stories and examine the moral behind them.

## Chapter 14

The Proper Java ME Mindset

So far in the book, we have primarily discussed the technical side of creating a Java ME application. While this is clearly the most important aspect of Java ME application development, there is another aspect that can sometimes be just as important as the technical aspect: the mindset with which you approach the development process.

In order to understand why having the proper mindset is important for Java ME development, it's important to note that every software platform out there, mobile or otherwise, tends to have a specific development methodology associated with it. This is either imposed by the platform's creators (by providing a "best practices" document and structuring the API accordingly) or tends to grow organically as the platform gains traction and evolves. Furthermore, the development methodology tends to change with time, as the platform's scope and underlying hardware technology change.

Java ME is somewhat unique in these respects. It was initially conceived to run on extremely limited devices but is now supported on (comparatively) very powerful ones too; and in practice you frequently have to support both categories of hardware at the same time. As both old and new Java ME hardware is in use today, there are no universal "best practices" you can follow, nor is there a universal development methodology; what works on old hardware may not be effective on new hardware and vice versa. There are some general tips you can take into consideration in all situations (the most important of which have been enumerated in Chapter 1), but that's about it.

Then there is the Java ME API itself, which is designed to be as simple as possible in order to be usable on as many devices as possible. This means that, in order to do more complex stuff, you frequently have to be creative and implement by yourself many features that you would take for granted on other platforms, from simple utility methods (like string matching) to complex functionality such as serialization. Deciding which of these features you need to implement in order to meet your goals (while being mindful of the project's restrictions in terms of resources and target hardware), and how to implement them, is often an art in itself—and the decisions made in this area affect the development process as a whole.

Finally, you also have to consider the type of application you are writing, as this often dictates the way you divide your available resources between the UI, flexibility, and functionality. Sometimes the UI is more important than the actual functionality, while other times it's the other way around, or the flexibility of the application (its ability to run in many different environments) is its most important trait. Making the right decision here is crucial for the success of your application.

For these reasons, having a proper mindset—a core set of principles that dictate how you approach the development of any given application—is crucial for the success of any Java ME project. These principles help you understand what Java ME as a platform can and cannot do in a given scenario, and they can help you determine what you *should* and *should not* do in a given situation.

In this chapter, we will take a look at what the proper Java ME development mindset is, and we will try to demonstrate it with a few real-life examples.

> **NOTE:** Of course, the principles described in this chapter can be applied to other platforms as well. However, they apply to other platforms to a much lesser degree than they do to Java ME; Java ME stands to gain the most from them simply because of its more constrained and less fault-tolerant nature.

Java ME Is Only As Powerful As the Devices It Runs On

It is surprising how many people tend to judge the Java ME platform separately from the underlying hardware. Sure, it feels intuitive to judge a platform based solely on its specifications, but with Java ME this is simply wrong. The reason for this is that, while Java ME itself isn't exceptionally gifted in terms of capabilities, it does have provisions for improving and extending said capabilities—and these provisions can make a world of difference.

For example, Java ME's default graphical capabilities are extremely limited by today's standards. However, as we have seen in the previous chapter, you can extend these capabilities significantly and bring Java ME to the same level as more modern platforms. The only limiting factor in this endeavor is the underlying hardware's processing power. In other words, most of the time it's not a question of whether it can be done with Java ME (it usually can be done); it's a question of whether it can be done on the hardware at hand. The same applies to many other features or capabilities that Java ME lacks or that are underdeveloped.

Also, while the device's hardware is extremely important, equally important are the optional capabilities that said device supports. This includes both optional JSRs and vendor-specific extensions, both of which can make a world of difference in deciding the feasibility of a project. Some JSRs and extensions are critical for a given project; for example, the File Connection API support is critical if you plan on writing a file manager application. Others, while not critical, greatly improve an application's performance or flexibility. For example, Nokia's UI extension has a `fillPolygon()` method, which can be used to quickly fill polygon-shaped areas of the screen. Without this extension, you would have to write your own fill routine, which would be considerably slower.

So what does this all mean? First, it means that, while Java ME is indeed a limited platform on low-end devices, it can be quite a flexible platform to develop on when you target higher-end devices and take full advantage of their potential; and that projects that are unfeasible on low-end devices can be feasible on higher-end devices. The hardware and the platform should be judged as a whole, not separately. It's important to realize this when assessing whether a project is doable, and to what degree.

Second, it means that, in order to get the most out of your target devices (or in order to level the playing field between them in terms of features), you will have to either rely a lot on third-party libraries or roll out your own code to add missing functionality and/or improve the existing one. This adds an extra layer of complexity to the development equation, and it also requires that you, as a developer, be familiar with the various third-party libraries that you will need to use and/or with the ideas and algorithms behind them. In other words, if you truly want to create the best possible application on a given target device, you have to do your research and get your hands dirty.

Third, it means that, as user's expectations regarding mobile applications in general and Java ME applications in particular increase, you can usually take advantage of the increase in the average mobile phone's computing power to meet those expectations. Of course, this requires more and more work on your part, as you have to add more and more new features and functionality to the core platform in order to keep up. Fortunately, this is alleviated by the fact that third-party tools and libraries are constantly evolving as well. Overall, this means the Java ME platform as a whole is continuously evolving.

One of my first freelance projects is a good example to illustrate the foregoing points. We were targeting only mid-level devices for this project, and a core requirement was the ability to be able to save and restore the application's state at any given time; in other words, serialization. Serialization isn't built into Java ME, so we turned our attention to some of the Java ME serialization libraries/frameworks out there. After a bit of digging, we decided to give one of the more obscure libraries a go. It wasn't the most feature-rich library, but it was simple, fast, and under active development, so we decided to go with it.

Things went well in the early stages of development. However, midway through the development process, we were required to support a very popular but low-end device. Its performance was OK for what we needed...in all respects except serialization. Whenever we needed to serialize something, the device slowed to a crawl. Using another library was out of the question at that point, as was rolling out our own serialization library. After a few experiments, we concluded that the problem was in the platform's RMS implementation: each individual write request would simply take too long. This was actually good news for us, as we feared that the low-end device was not powerful enough to handle the load.

What we ended up doing was altering the library a bit so that we buffered serialization requests to the same record and committed them only every 20 seconds or every 5–10 requests (whichever came first). This improved serialization performance tremendously and leveled the playing field in terms of perceived performance between the mid-level devices and the low-end one.

However, as more and more features were requested by the client, the low-end device started to lag behind in terms of performance. In the end, we had to cut support for the low-end device; its hardware was simply not up for the job. At the same time, the mid-level devices were behaving quite well and, aside from the occasional minor slowdown, the application ran smoothly. The application at hand was the same one on both types of devices, using the same APIs in the same way. The limiting factor in our case (and, indeed, in most cases) was clearly not the application or the platform itself, but the hardware it was running on. This is an important point to fully grasp because of its indirect implications.

The most important of these implications is the fact that the cool proof-of-concept demo you are showing off today will, in fact, be a standard feature in tomorrow's applications. This means that, as a Java ME developer, you should always experiment with new ideas, new techniques, and new projects, pushing the limits of what can be done with Java ME today, because you'll be able to put your experiments into practice on tomorrow's hardware. In other words, you should always stay ahead of the hardware curve, and thus ahead of the competition.

Another important implication of this is that, especially on long-haul projects, the application you are writing can be improved considerably over time in terms of performance and features as the "average hardware" becomes more and more powerful—and you may, in fact, be forced to do so in order to keep your application competitive. This means that you should take the application's estimated lifespan and development time into consideration when making technical decisions such as what architecture and libraries to use. If you expect your application to be around for a while, aim for freedom and flexibility. Even if this initially ends up costing you a little in terms performance, in the long run the performance loss is negligible, but the development benefits are not.

For example, about one year after the original project was finished, the client approached us again and asked me if we were interested in working on the application further; this time the "low end" of the device spectrum was represented by the original mid-level device, while the "high end" of the device spectrum consisted of a couple of newly released phones. Because of this, we ended up adding many visual effects and improving the overall user experience to keep it up to date.

A couple of months after that, the customer approached us again, and he wanted a wholly revamped UI. This meant using a different UI toolkit. Initially, the UI was somewhat intimately tied to application functionality in several key places, for performance reasons, because we did not expect the application to be under development and still active in its initial incarnation after two years, and because the initial hardware we were targeting was low-end, so we needed all the performance we could get. Because of this tight connection between UI and functionality, changing the

UI toolkit involved quite a bit of application refactoring, which could have been easily avoided had we known the application's "roadmap" from the start (this particular point is discussed in more detail later in the chapter).

Best Practices for Optimizing Your Application

When it comes to Java ME application optimizations, there are two commonly encountered schools of thought, opposite in nature, both of which are wrong, in my opinion.

The first one, most common with developers coming from the desktop world or with developers working exclusively with high-end Java ME devices, is to rarely ever optimize anything. This is wrong because you'll get either sub-optimal performance or good performance (if you're targeting high-end devices), but your competitors will have applications that either perform better or have more features, since they make better use of the available resources.

The second school of thought, most common with developers that have been in the field since the early days, is to optimize everything possible. This again is wrong because it requires a lot of developer time to do so, and many times the results are simply not worth it: the performance gain is too small, or the optimized code performs well on one device but poorly on another due to device peculiarities.

So what's the proper way to optimize a Java ME application? As discussed in the chapter dedicated to optimizations, what you should do first is profile your code and see where the most time and resources are spent. Optimize that area first, then profile again, turn your attention to the candidate area of the code, and so forth, until performance and resource consumption are acceptable. At the same time, the best optimizations are algorithm-related or architecture-related, as they tend to translate well to all devices, so these should be attempted before any code optimizations take place.

However, even when done properly, the optimization process just described doesn't always translate well to real-life scenarios. For example, you might spend a lot of time optimizing a certain set of methods, and the performance difference between the old and new code ends up being staggering on low-end devices but barely noticeable on high-end devices. Or vice versa—a 2x performance improvement isn't really noticeable on a low-end device if it improves your application's FPS from 2 frames per second to 4 frames per second; the application is still unusable. In other words, the time and resources spent on optimizing the code aren't actually reflected in the real world.

To counteract this and reach a good balance between time spent and performance gained, the best tactic is to approach optimizations incrementally. In other words, as soon as you find a problem area, rather than trying to get the best possible performance out of it, you simply try to get good performance out of it, and move on to the next area. If, after optimizing everything worth optimizing, performance still isn't good enough, you start another cycle of optimizations and further improve the already optimized code.

This works great in practice because many times code and algorithms can be optimized to about 40–50% of the maximum possible performance with relatively little effort, but the remaining 60–50% requires a lot of work. By optimizing to only about 40–50% of the maximum possible performance, you get the best bang for the buck—and, if you need to do so, you can always go back and make things even better.

The best way to internalize this concept is to think of optimizing your application as a tool, a means to an end, not as a goal unto itself. You don't optimize things just for the sake of optimization; you do it so that you may fulfill your requirements (for example, achieving acceptable performance on a specific device). As such, your approach toward application optimization should be one that maximizes the effort/reward ratio (which is something the strategy just described does) and, as soon as your goals are reached, you should *stop* optimizing. This applies to both local optimization goals (i.e., optimizing a local block of code) and overall application optimization goals.

A couple of friends and I once held an optimization contest, where we downloaded the source code of a very CPU-intensive application from the Web (a simple proof-of-concept chess engine) and tried to improve its performance as best we could in the timespan of two hours.

We all started with profiling the application, and we all identified the same critical areas for improvement. However, while another friend and I used the approach just described, and tried to optimize each critical area until we felt that we achieved an acceptable level of performance, the other two friends decided to optimize everything as best they could, in order.

After the two hours had passed, they had highly optimized about two or three critical areas of the code, while my friend and I had optimized about four or five critical areas to a "good enough" level. The end results were as expected: although their performance in the two or three critical areas they thoroughly optimized were visibly superior to what we had achieved, we had the better overall performance because we had smaller performance improvements in individual areas, but overall we managed to optimize more areas of the code. We then compared the time spent on each individual part of the code vs. the performance improvement gained, and the results showed that while their highly optimized code was 20–30% faster than ours, they had spent two or three times as much time optimizing it. In other words, they didn't have a very good return on investment.

The most interesting result of all this was noticed when we moved the code from the emulator to actual devices. One critical area actually performed noticeably better in our not-so-thoroughly optimized version than it did in the highly-optimized version of our friends'. The most probable reason for this is that, in an effort to improve CPU time, they used a lot more memory in their approach than we did, and more variables, which meant more memory reads than we used and poorer cache performance.

The lesson to be learned from this is that, in the Java ME world, optimizing code to the best possible degree isn't always a good thing. Optimize only as much as you need to, and only where you need to. If you do decide to optimize to the bone (for whatever reason), make sure you keep a copy of the unoptimized approach for reference purposes, and make sure that you test your optimization on all target devices, in order to avoid any unpleasant surprises.

Sticking to Your Priorities

As discussed previously, the resources available to the typical Java ME application are limited. Furthermore, quality standards in all respects (user interface, functionality, flexibility, etc.) have increased considerably over the years, which means that it takes more and more resources to "meet the norm" in any of the foregoing categories. Thus, Java ME developers are faced with the problem of correctly distributing the limited resources available to them between the foregoing critical areas.

First of all, it should be made clear that, unless the application you are writing is an extremely simple one, you will not be able to achieve the best possible result in all categories, so you will have to make trade-offs. For example, you may be able to give your application a stunning user interface, but in doing so you will most likely severely limit the amount of resources available for your application's actual functionality, and you will also have a hard time porting the application to lower-end devices. Or you might be able to dedicate lots of resources to the underlying functionality, at the expense of a very plain UI. Or you might choose to support a wide variety of devices, sacrificing both UI and functionality in the process.

Defining clear priorities greatly affects the way you approach your development process. For example, if you're going for flexibility and portability, then your code should be rock-solid and highly adaptable, and your application's framework should also be extremely well thought out. This involves lots of planning and thinking ahead, error checking, and error handling routines, which can add quite a bit of overhead. In addition, your development time will increase by quite a bit.

If you decide to focus on the UI aspect of your application, then choose the best-looking UI toolkit that you can find/afford and go with that. To compensate for the (most likely) high resource strain brought on by the UI, your application's functional code should be very well optimized, much more so than if you were going with a more plain-looking UI.

Or, if you try to cram as much functionality as possible into your application, you will most likely have to depend a lot on third-party libraries and on non-standard APIs. These tend to introduce a lot of portability issues and bugs that may be out of your control, so in effect the development process will be more tedious and more error-prone.

As a Java ME developer, it's critical to get your application's priorities straight in order to be able to allocate your resources efficiently. Ideally this should be done in the planning phase of the project, before you start writing any code, but it can also be done in the early development phase. Changing your priorities after that isn't really an option worth considering—you'd be probably better off writing a new application from scratch.

For example, switching to a different UI toolkit isn't always feasible or possible, for technical reasons, especially if the UI you are currently using is intimately linked to the application's functionality—or if the application's functionality is built around the capabilities and architecture of the current UI toolkit.

Deciding that you want to considerably augment the existing functionality when the code is 80% complete, while possible, will most likely introduce a lot of new bugs, performance issues, and unwanted side effects as you alter the existing code, because frequently these changes come in the form of "patches" rather than a clean implementation.

It will also involve a considerable restructuring and possibly even a complete make-over of your application's architecture, which is a nightmare scenario to encounter halfway through the development process. Adding extra functionality also frequently means that you will have to make use of or emulate non-standard APIs or bring in new third-party libraries, with all the problems these actions bring to the table.

> **NOTE:** You might get away with these on a more standardized and homogenous platform, but Java ME's constrained yet unpredictable nature makes these things considerably more difficult unless they are planned for (or provisioned for) from the very beginning.

Finally, supporting more devices than originally planned (especially ones less powerful than the ones you are currently targeting) is oftentimes simply impossible without massive reductions of features, without switching to a less intensive or less good-looking UI or without making other technical compromises and adjustments—which means that you will have to go over and seriously rewrite large parts of your code, thus increasing both development time and bug count.

I once worked as part of a team to create a simple photo-sharing application. The initial goal was simple: all that was needed was the ability to take pictures and upload them to a web-based gallery. The target devices were mid-level.

This core requirement was fairly easy to implement, so we agreed with the customer that we can and should create a snazzy interface for the application, to attract potential users. We could do this because the CPU requirements for the core application were extremely low, so the bulk of the CPU time could be dedicated to the UI.

We concentrated most of our attention on adding lots of cool UI features. For example, the upload progress bar was actually a thumbnail of the image to be uploaded. The thumbnail was initially grayscale, and it got colorized from left to right as the image content was uploaded.

So far so good, but then the customer requested that we add very simple image processing abilities to the application—for example, color effects and captioning. These features competed for CPU time with the UI itself, but there was still plenty of processing power to go around. Whenever something really intensive would need to be done, we would just display an hourglass on the screen. Our initial priorities got somewhat changed from a fancy UI to a mix of features and fancy UI. Still, it was nothing we couldn't handle. We had to do a bit of refactoring to get both the UI and the image processing features to play nice together, but nothing major. Speed did suffer a bit at this point, but not much.

Then we got the requirement for implementing image gallery capabilities. Coupled with the fancy UI, this was getting a little too much for our available processing power, so we had a discussion with the customer and agreed to have two gallery types: a very cool-looking one for high-end devices and a toned-down version for mid-range devices.

Now flexibility and portability got thrown into the mix, and things really got interesting. We had to add quite a bit of new code and alter large portions of the existing code to make sure that the application made the most of the available resources on each type of device and that it dynamically adapted its resource consumption so as not to crash. Speed suffered some more because of this, and, of course, some rather weird bugs were introduced (remember, we were doing major patching to the existing code in the process).

The icing on the cake came when the customer requested that we support lower-end phones too. We asked him what he wanted to give up: the fancy UI, the image processing capabilities, or the photo gallery feature. He said he didn't want to give up anything.

We optimized the application as best we could (it helped that the lower-end devices had lower-resolution screens, so we could get away with lower-quality graphics), but the sheer hardware requirements and our patched code base meant that the end result was nowhere near as satisfactory as we would have wanted. In the end, the customer did decide to create a special version of the application from scratch, specifically for low-end devices.

The point of this story is that a large part of the development effort on this project could have been avoided if the customer had given us the proper requirements and priorities from the beginning. It's much easier to design something from scratch (i.e., an architecture and code base that are geared equally toward UI, features, and flexibility/portability) than it is to take something designed for a specific purpose (i.e., cool UI) and then turn that something into a jack-of-all-trades.

More to the point, had we known in advance what the project's end-priorities were, the application's architecture would have been different, the development effort would have been distributed differently, we would have used different tools, and, overall, the project would have turned out better: fewer bugs, faster performance, less time spent in development, and a single application code base for all devices (instead of two code bases, one for low-end devices and one for the rest). As it was, we made the initial decisions that were best suited for our initial priorities (a fancy UI at all costs), and this ended up being costly in the long run.

> **NOTE:** Of course, this scenario of hitting a moving target is frequently encountered on all software platforms, mobile or otherwise. What makes it more problematic for Java ME is the fact that hitting a moving target tends to add "extra fat" to the application, like processing overhead and unnecessary code. While on other platforms you can even get away with sometimes obscene amounts of "fat," such is the nature of Java ME that even a little "extra fat" can lead to a "heart attack." As such, Java ME developers should spare no effort in the beginning of a project to make sure that the target is as still as possible.

Thinking Outside the Box Is Important

Java ME is not your usual platform. As we have seen thus far in the book, it has many particularities and characteristics that are mostly unique to it, so your conventional approach to application development may not apply. Because of this, it is important that developers be able to take a step back and look at the project at hand without being biased by previous development experience and development patterns; in other words, developers should be able to think outside the box, if needed.

But what does this mean, exactly? For starters, it means being aware that what has worked well in the past in similar situations may not be the best solution in the current situation. This can happen for a variety of reasons, ranging from different amounts of available resources to business reasons. As such, each situation should be approached individually, and previous solutions should be used only if they fall within the confines of the current scenario.

For example, you may be accustomed to using a certain library (either third-party or self-made) for serialization and persistence. This has worked well for you in the past in projects running on similar hardware, so naturally you decide to use it in the current project too, without giving the decision that much thought—a very common scenario.

However, in doing so, you make a lot of assumptions, many of which may not be true. You assume that the current project has the same kind of serialization needs as your old projects—what if a different serialization scheme and/or mechanism would be more suited for the current project, because the nature of the data to be serialized is different? You also assume that, just because the hardware is similar, so too is the resource distribution—what if your serialization code has to make due with only 10% of the available resources instead of the 20% it got in previous projects? Furthermore, you automatically discard any helpful but non-standard API that may be available on the current device, and that your current library doesn't make use of. The list can go on.

This "reusing of old solutions" is a common mistake for Java ME development, and stems from the fact that, on other platforms, you can indeed reuse old solutions most of the time. Even if the results are sub-optimal, they're usually still well within acceptable limits. However, in the case of Java ME, anything sub-optimal tends to be closer to "unusable" than to "good enough"—if for no other reason than that you don't make good use of the available resources and capabilities, either consuming too much or using too little.

Thus, it becomes important that you look at the current project just like it was your first one, discard any knowledge of previous projects (in our example, any knowledge of the existence of previous serialization libraries), and ask yourself what would be the best solution for what you have to do right now. If the solution you find turns out to be a library or approach that you have used in the past, then by all means go for it. If not, then start fresh. It may be hard to do this at first, because you'll usually have to start fresh on almost every project, but in the long run it becomes easier; over time, the list of approaches that you have used in the past grows, which considerably increases the chances that you'll find one among them that suits your current needs without having to come up with something new.

Thinking outside the box also means being able to come up with new and innovative solutions to your problems, if that's what is needed. Remember, just because it hasn't been done until now doesn't mean it can't be done. Even if these solutions don't turn out to be the best ones, or end up being unfeasible altogether, you can still store them for later use, and you'll most likely gain valuable experience in the process. Plus, many times the solutions you end up coming up with do turn out to be feasible, in which case you'll get to push the limits of what can be done with Java ME—and give your product and your image a boost.

Coming up with innovative solutions is not as hard as you may think. The biggest obstacle is the (completely correct) knowledge that Java ME devices are typically very limited and constrained. Thus, the first step should be to simply imagine that you're targeting a Java ME device with unlimited resources, in the sense that you will not run out of CPU power, memory, or storage space, but the APIs available to you are still the same. What would your proposed solution look like then? In fact, you should actually come up with three or four different solutions, and choose the one that sounds best to you.

After you have chosen and fleshed out the best solution, evaluate it in terms of resources and feasibility. What do you need to improve most? If it's CPU usage, see if you can optimize the algorithms or the code. If it's RAM you need, see if it's feasible to trade off CPU power for RAM, or to use persistent storage as a swap file, etc. In other words, you should try to adapt your solution to the real world, more specifically to the real-world constraints of your application. The key here is to do everything in baby steps, and focus on the critical aspects first. For example, if the expected CPU usage is very high, try to optimize the code as much as possible first, and then focus on other problem areas (such as RAM usage)—but only if you manage to get the CPU usage down to an acceptable level first.

There are two possible outcomes to this process. Either you manage to bring your solution to a usable level, in which case you can implement and test it right away, or you fall short in one or more respects, in which case you can simply store it for later (remember, what's not feasible today may very well be easily doable tomorrow as the platform and its hardware evolve), pick the second-best solution, and repeat the process.

This may sound like it's tiresome and like it will take a long, long time, but the truth is you can do most of it on paper and/or by guesstimating, and in the first phase you have to flesh out only the general solution, not implement the whole thing—in other words, you need to do only a quick feasibility test and some prototyping. This not only is fun, but also takes up far less time than you may think.

Keeping Things Simple

Most of what we have discussed so far in the book indicates that developing for Java ME is not an easy task; in fact, Java ME development has been painted as being quite a difficult endeavor. This is entirely true: developing a high-quality Java ME application is by no means a walk in the park, and complications can arise at every step of the way.

This is exactly why it's extremely important to always try to keep things simple and straightforward: no fancy tricks, no complicated algorithms and procedures, no long descriptions and convoluted requirements—just simple and clear reasoning that is easy to understand and easy to put into practice. You will hit plenty of bumps and roadblocks along the way, but keeping things simpler tends to make these unfortunate encounters rarer.

This philosophy should be applied to the project as a whole, from the start of the planning process right until the final sign-off is given by the QA team. For example, your requirements should be simple, each no more than one sentence long. Based on these requirements, your needs should also be extracted, and they should also be simple and concise. Based on these needs, you should design the simplest architecture you possibly can, and so forth.

All of the foregoing may sound obvious, but simplicity isn't always easy to find. In fact, oftentimes it's quite hard to find. The main cause for this is the fact that it's hard to formulate and identify the right problems. Many times, the problem you are facing is not the problem you are actually seeing: just like in life, your expectations, past experience, and personal point of view can alter your perception of what's actually going on.

For example, as discussed in a previous example in Chapter 1, when users complain about performance, we, as developers, naturally tend to think they are referring to code performance, when in fact what they are actually complaining about is *perceived* performance. Thus, the question is not "How can we make the application faster?" (you can optimize it), but "How can we make the application *seem* faster?" (you can optimize it, but also parallelize tasks, throttle CPU usage, change the order in which you process data, etc.). As you can see, identifying the right problem gives you more options to work with.

> **CAUTION:** Apparently similar situations can be, at their core, totally different problems, and thus they can have totally different solutions. The only way you will be able to see this is if you approach each situation individually and with an "it can be done better than it currently is" attitude.

Once you have identified the right problem, the even trickier task is identifying the right solution. Many times, simple solutions are easily looked over, because many times they are unconventional and they require thinking outside the box. A great example of this can be found at the end of Chapter 3, in the form of the linked list implementation given there: the solution is simple, but certainly not obvious.

Finally, after you have found a simple solution, the next step is to actually implement it. This, again, is trickier than it first looks, as the implementation itself also has to be simple. In this context, simple means code that is easy to write, easy to understand, and fast. Obviously, meeting three criteria at the same time isn't always possible, so if you have to make compromises, make sure you don't compromise clarity, even if this means that your code takes longer to write and to execute—you can always fine-tune these two aspects in the optimization phase.

As you might suspect, thinking outside the box is crucial to being able to keep things simple; the two go hand in hand. One project I worked on required scripting support; that is, scripts would need to be downloaded from the server and run on the device. The idea behind this was to be able to upgrade or change the application's behavior and/or feature set at runtime. The problem was that, as expected, running scripts on a Java ME device is not very fast, nor very resource-friendly.

The initial approach was to parse and run the scripts, which were in plain-text form, directly on the device, directly as is. This, of course, did not work very well: the performance was simply abysmal.

The second approach proposed was to convert the scripts into a parse tree (or abstract syntax tree) once we got them on the device. This was far better that the initial approach, but the conversion still had to be done on the device, which made the initial conversion slow. Furthermore, the language we used (a C look-alike) was pretty complex, so a full parser for it wouldn't be easy to write and execute within the confines of a Java ME device. Plus, converting a script on the device for the first time would take a really, really long time.

As such, the third approach was to do the conversion from script file to syntax tree on the server side—or at least outside of the device. This worked great, as the syntax tree was immediately usable on the device once we received it from the server. But there was still a problem here: storing the tree, going from node to node as needed, and executing each node were still not fast enough for our purposes.

Our forth and final approach solved this problem too. The syntax tree would get converted to bytecode (again, on the server side), which would be executed on a virtual machine within our Java ME application. Instead of a tree structure, we could now use a simple array to store the script's instructions, and executing the script became much faster. Furthermore, script size was considerably lowered because of this, as were the memory requirements.

Overall, we were able to create larger and more complex scripts, which downloaded faster and ran faster. The code needed to run the scripts on the actual device was also very simple, because all we had to do was go through the source array and blindly execute the bytecode present there. And, as an added bonus, the scripts could be written in any language (though only the original C variant was implemented) as long as a corresponding bytecode converter existed.

We were able to achieve this very elegant and simple solution by thinking outside the box and by identifying the core problem (and requirement) correctly. In our case, the problem was not "How can we run scripts on the device?" but rather "How can we script the device's behavior?" The difference, though subtle, is important.

Standardizing the User Experience

Like it or not, Java ME as a platform does not have a user-recognizable identity. In other words, users are unable to just look at an application and say, "Hey, this is a Java ME application!" and then proceed to use said application using a standard set of metaphors and paradigms (good examples are pressing an element for a second or two, which brings up the contextual menu on Android, or the fact that iOS applications always tend to have a kind of navigation bar at the top of the screen).

This inability stems primarily from the fact that Java ME does not have a clear and standardized set of specifications detailing how the user interface of an application should look and behave, what the platform's user experience best practices are, and what the platform's key identifiable elements that separate it from the other platforms are, as far as the user is concerned.

Without such an identity, and without clear and comprehensive user experience rules, you may end up confusing and frustrating users. For example, what you usually do these days is build your application around a high-quality UI toolkit as you see fit. This is quite easy to do, as modern UI toolkits are more or less on par with desktop UI toolkits. In the end, although you followed no platform guidelines, the application itself looks great and feels great.

The problem is that everybody does this, and, while roughly the same widgets are used across all applications, the actual user experiences are not similar at all: different applications still have different UI structures (e.g., one may be tab-based, while another may be form-based) and different subtleties (e.g., different ways to access the contextual menus, different ways to navigate from screen to screen, etc.).

This means that users have to learn how to use each application and must get accustomed to each application's interaction paradigms. Furthermore, it means that something to which the user is accustomed in one application (e.g., kinetic scrolling) may not be available in another application, and vice versa. Switching from application to application can become a bit confusing even for more advanced users; less tech-savvy ones will definitely find the experience frustrating. This being said, there are better ways to approach the user interface and user experience problem.

One alternative to the frustration just described is to try to provide a standardized experience to users, an experience to which they can relate even outside the boundaries of your application and that they will find intuitive. The first question that needs to be asked is: standardized to what? As stated previously, there are no official guidelines pertaining to this, at least not to a level relevant to today's applications: the best you'll find are some general procedures and guidelines referring to how commands map to softkeys and other such low-level stuff pertaining to the now outdated `javax.microedition.lcdui` package.

> **NOTE:** Sadly, not having a set of up-to-date user experience guidelines affects not only individual applications but also the Java ME platform as a whole, as being a "no man's land" is never a good way to increase awareness and attract users. As far as publicity is concerned, Java ME is fighting a losing battle with Android, iOS, and Blackberry—and, in my opinion, one of the main reasons it's losing is precisely the lack of a user experience standard.

Thus, the only sane and reasonable thing to do is emulate other mobile platforms. Prime candidates for this are, of course, Android and iOS. As far as the basic UI goes, as long as you use a capable UI toolkit, you should have no problems emulating said platforms: you may have to write a custom component or two and change a few things here and there, but the bulk of the work is easy-peasy, and you will get to reuse it on future projects as well.

The tricky part is emulating more advanced features of the target platform—for example, Android's drawer concept. For this, you will most likely need to write quite a few custom components—unfortunately, there is no way around this. The same goes for implementing platform-specific interaction paradigms, like the aforementioned press-for-contextual-menu: you will most likely have to get your hands dirty in order to get these implemented, though a good UI framework helps tremendously in keeping the mess to a minimum.

Next, a very interesting task is providing a standardized user experience on devices with no touchscreens and just a joystick—which is the most common scenario. Android emulation works best here, as Android's user interface, unlike iOS's, is designed to also be operated with a joystick.

Taking the concept of emulating a platform's user experience even further, you can and should also emulate the way the target platform handles errors and notifications, as well as other aspects of the user experience. For example, Android applications are, as a best practice, required to save their state so that they may be closed and restored automatically, as needed. Truly emulating the Android user experience involves at least partially implementing this behavior. For example, the last screen the user was on when the application was shut down should be shown when it gets started back up again.

There is another alternative to all of these: to emulate as closely as possible the device's native user experience, the one that the user has outside of the Java ME environment, while operating the phone's native applications. This will most likely involve writing custom versions of your application for each targeted device (as far as the UI is concerned), and will most likely require quite a bit of custom component writing and skinning. In the end, the results may not be perfect, as any skins or themes that the user has applied to the phone's native environment will not get translated to your application. However, most of the time, the results will be acceptable, and tech-savvy and less tech-savvy users alike will feel right at home with your application simply because they know how to use it from using their phone.

Finally, it should be noted that creating a custom user experience/interface with its custom tweaks to the standard formula, as described in the latter sections of Chapter 6, is still a good idea in many scenarios—for example, in the case of multimedia applications, or when it is desired to "catch the eyes" of users by sporting a radical UI, or simply for exploring new concepts and pushing the platform forward. However, for your run-of-the-mill applications (e.g., business applications), you are better off simply providing a standard and "dull" user experience, to which the user can relate instantly and intuitively.

Planning for the Worst-Case Scenario

All things considered, Java ME is not a very developer-friendly environment, and many things can and do go wrong in practice, from device fragmentation issues to insufficient resources. These concerns are more or less non-existent on other mobile platforms, so you are free to develop on them just as you would on a desktop platform; you do not have this luxury with Java ME.

As such, caution should be exercised at every step of the project. Rather than assume everything will work out fine and dive in head-first, you should adopt a more pessimistic approach and assume, by default, that things can and will go wrong.

Defensive coding is a great example of this, and the one most intuitive for developers: never assume that something will execute correctly and always handle all possible errors, no matter how unlikely. This doesn't translate to just catching all thrown exceptions, but also to checking the data you're working with for validity and consistency. Being pessimistic and cautious also means not relying on the fact that all the device's resources and capabilities will be available to you; as we have seen, this is often not the case.

Another great example comes from estimating deadlines and manpower: add an extra 20–30% to your initial estimate, just to be on the safe side. Chances are you will need at least some of the extra time and manpower provisioned, and if you don't, then you'll be able to release ahead of schedule—you win either way. If you don't provision extra time and manpower, the end result will most likely be either missed deadlines or a buggy product release.

You should also be pessimistic about your user's expectations. For example, you should never assume that your users will be satisfied with the functionality and user experience you are currently providing them, and as such you should constantly think of reasonable and feasible ways you can improve these two aspects. Even if you don't end up including these improvements in the current version of your application, a later release might see them implemented.

Furthermore, as discussed previously in the book, never assume that a user will feel familiar or at home with your application. Chances are most of them will, but at least some of them will feel confused or might not figure out how to access and use at least part of your application's functionality. This is to be expected for a platform with such a varying userbase; however, it's still a disadvantage. To minimize the negative impact this has, you should apply the tips described in Chapter 11.

Determining Your Application's Limits

When developing for Java ME, you will frequently run into difficult situations—situations to which there is no apparent good solution or to which the solution is not feasible. When you do run into these situations, it is important to be able to determine if the current course of action is worth pursuing further, if you should try a different approach because you have reached the limits of the current one, or if it's time to give up altogether.

For example, it is important to be able to determine if the current algorithm you are using for a given task can be optimized further (to meet performance requirements) or if you should just switch to a different algorithm. Unfortunately, there are no golden rules for this: your best bet is to follow your instinct and rely on your previous experience. What I usually do when I run into these situations is to simply say to myself, "I will spend one more day on this problem. If I cannot think of a way to improve the current approach, I will try something else."

This "know your limits" tip applies to all areas of Java ME development, not just to coding. For example, when deciding on the list of devices you wish to support, it is important to be able to accurately determine the lower limit in terms of specifications. What is the absolute minimum amount of CPU power your application needs? What about RAM and screen size? What about APIs?

Determining these lower limits is never an easy task. If you aim too high, you risk losing many potential users who own less powerful devices. At the same time, if you aim too low, you may end up not being able to support all the desired devices or, worse, crippling the application in order to support low-end devices. Prototyping or writing mock code works great here.

For example, let's say that you want to know if your application can run on device X with respect to CPU power. The first thing you need to do is estimate the number of calculations your application will need to do in an average second. This may sound hard, but it's just a matter of listing all the things that your application can do at any given time, estimating how many CPU cycles each of them will take, and adding up the results.

Then, you can simply create a mock application that requires roughly the same amount of CPU power to run. This mock application can be extremely simple. Often, I create one or two threads, each running an infinite loop, and I use `sleep()` and other threading mechanisms to adjust the CPU cycles they eat up. I then add a UI to the mix and simply check if the user experience while playing with the UI is smooth enough. If it is, the device is a go. If it isn't, the device gets left out.

Furthermore, in case you feel your estimates aren't accurate enough, it should be noted that many times the bulk of the CPU usage lies either in third-party libraries, in which case you can simulate real-life usage by testing the libraries with static and pre-created input data, or in a couple of critical algorithms and blocks of code, which can again be easily implemented and tested using predefined data. And, as a bonus, you can add performance metrics to your application prototype, so you can see what areas you would need to improve and by how much in order to make the project feasible.

Prototyping is a surprisingly useful tool when it comes to determining and testing all sorts of limitations. It doesn't require considerably more time to put into practice compared to simple theoretical measurements and assumptions, and tends to yield far better results because it runs real code on real hardware—and we all know how different running Java ME code on actual hardware can be from running said code on an emulator or "on paper."

Furthermore, you can use prototyping to determine not only if a given application is feasible on device X, but also what features you can add to your existing application while still keeping it usable, and what features you should remove or tone down in order to port the application to lower-end devices. In other words, prototyping and writing mock code are great tools for "juggling" with your application's features, requirements, and limitations.

One of my spare-time projects was a simple 3D ray casting engine written entirely with vanilla Java ME. The goals for this project were to learn about low-level 3D graphics and to test if 3D was feasible on Java ME without any additional API (specifically, without using JSR 184).

Obviously, before I dived into the serious math and everything, I needed to determine if the project was feasible and, if so, to what degree. In order to do this, I estimated the number of operations needed to calculate the position and size of objects on the screen (objects were, in this case, simple blocks in a rectangular grid) and the time it would take to draw these objects onto the screen, and translated this into some mock code. The mock code didn't actually do anything 3D-related; it just tried to simulate the CPU usage and the drawing operations needed. As the calculations on which the mock code was based were rough estimates, I added a 30% margin of error.

After running the mock code, it turned out that 3D was indeed a viable option for Java ME, at least for my device (at that time, a Nokia E50). So I started implementing the actual engine. As it turns out, my estimates were a little off and the actual FPS was only about 80% of what I had estimated, but this was mostly because of some unforeseen calculations that were needed (for example, compensating for the fish-eye effect).

Then, the question for me became if I could add textures to the mix. Up until that point, blocks were monochrome, so all I had to do was figure out their shape (their 2D projection) and fill it, but textures need a lot of extra computations, as I had to figure out the color of each pixel within a block's shape.

Again, I estimated the CPU time needed for this and wrote some mock code. The results were bad: texturing wasn't feasible, not for a 320x240 screen. Furthermore, the numbers were so bad that I knew I had no chance to get texturing up and running properly on that device, not to the level of performance I wanted anyway. Still, for the sake of learning, I decided to go ahead and implement texturing anyway. The end results, based on real texturing code, were almost as bad as those based on my mock code; that is to say, my estimates were correct.

Prototyping and writing mock code helped me determine that the project was feasible even before doing any 3D-related work, and later it helped me determine that adding textures would not work on my target device. As you can imagine, had I not been interested in adding it anyway, implementing texturing only to find out that the performance was abysmal would have been a major waste of time and manpower—so, from this point of view, prototyping and mock code saved the day.

Knowing your limits is also important from a business perspective. You should be realistic about your potential sales and market share. In fact, in accordance with a previous tip, you should be *pessimistic* about these aspects. Even if your application is realistically the best on the market, don't expect to corner the market or to hit the jackpot—this rarely happens.

Furthermore, it may even happen that your application doesn't gain any traction at all (or gains very little), in which case the best thing to do is to try to sell it to another company, give it away for free to users, or open-source it (you're not making any money anyway at the moment, so you have nothing to lose from this perspective, but you may gain attention and an image boost).

Summary

In this chapter, we have looked at the most important mindset rules for Java ME development, and we have demonstrated them with a couple of real-life examples.

In the next chapter, we will take a brief look at the future of Java ME and how it will stand compared to other mobile platforms.

## Chapter 15

Java ME and the Future

Up until this point in the book, you have looked at what is possible with Java ME today and at its current state of development. You have familiarized yourself with the kind of hardware you need to support, the APIs at your disposal, and the techniques best suited for developing for that hardware and APIs.

You examined the kinds of tricks and optimization needed to get the best performance out of current devices, at what users expect to find in current Java ME applications, and at how today's Java ME applications stack up against the competition in terms of functionality and user interfaces.

You have also looked at the various pitfalls that Java ME developers can encounter today, ranging from fragmentation issues to simply approaching the development process with the wrong mindset.

Now it's time to take a quick look at the future, and see what the Java ME world will look like in a few years' time. In this chapter, you will examine what the future holds for Java ME in terms of its target audience, available hardware, available APIs, development techniques, and more.

> **NOTE:** The opinions expressed within are my personal ones, but they are based on my experience with the platform and on current market trends.

Java ME Hardware Evolution

In the Java ME world, almost everything these days comes down to hardware. As many features and capabilities supported natively on other platforms are missing from Java ME's default feature set (XML support, graphics capabilities, and so on), developers have to implement these features sin Java code, which is both slower and a drain on available resources.

Furthermore, mid-level and low-end devices combined tend to dictate what kind of software you can write for any given platform, and the relatively large gap between them in Java ME's case means that developers have to walk a very thin line between underdelivering in terms of features, or overshooting in terms of requirements.

Looking at the growth that can be seen in terms of hardware performance in the past couple of years, especially the very impressive one in the low-end device segment, we can draw two very important conclusions.

The first one is that low-end devices have evolved, and still are evolving, rapidly in terms of hardware performance and are starting to catch up with mid-level devices. This is great news, as a very large part of the Java ME development effort stems from supporting these low-end devices. With their processing power increasing, developers will have to resort less and less to clever programming tricks and extreme optimizations, and they will be able to include more and more features as standard.

The second conclusion is that mid-level and high-end Java ME hardware isn't evolving at the rate it used to. Although these segments are also increasing in processing power, their growth rate isn't nearly as big as it used to be. This happens primarily because top hardware these days gets allocated to smartphones, not to feature phones.

Coupled with the rapid growth in the low-end segment, in the end this will lead to a "closing of the gap" between low-end, mid-level, and high-end Java ME devices. Differences will still exist between them, but not nearly as significant as those seen today. This is good news because Java ME will become a much more consistent platform to develop for, but also bad news because the slower growth in terms of hardware performance correlates to a slower growth in terms of innovation and new features.

That being said, processing power isn't everything. Other hardware aspects are almost as important, if not more so. For example, more and more phones today have touchscreens, which leads to more-intuitive and far more enjoyable user interfaces. Furthermore, screen sizes are constantly increasing, while support for 3D graphics is also starting to become mainstream, as is support for sensors and global positioning.

What this means is that tomorrow's Java ME applications will have much more visually pleasing and intuitive interfaces and will derive their appeal not necessarily from their processing abilities, but from the way in which users can interact with them. This trend can be observed even today, as top-notch Java ME user interfaces tend to rival those found on smartphones or on PCs, and advanced proof-of-concept applications, such as augmented reality, are starting to appear.

Also, as devices receive bigger and faster sstorage capabilities, and as they become more and more connected, Java ME applications will eventually be able to store, manipulate, and share very large amounts of data. Coupled with the growing trend of cloud computing, this will lead to Java ME applications that work together with server-based software to truly empower their users. Even offline applications will benefit greatly from this growth in storage capabilities. For example, they will be able to include more-detailed graphics and multimedia elements, and they will be able to store and work with more of the user's data.

A very important aspect of Java ME hardware evolution will be the arrival and widespread adoption of Near Field Communication (NFC) hardware. This hardware will then be used for anything from payments to business card exchange, and we will most likely see more innovative uses as the technology gains popularity. More than anything, this technology will ensure that Java ME remains a player in the mobile world in the foreseeable future, because Java ME devices with NFC capabilities will be cheap and widespread. As a side effect, more people will become aware of Java ME's potential and capabilities as they come in contact with NFC applications written for it.

Finally, as I just have hinted, there is the matter of hardware price. Hardware is constantly getting cheaper, and Java ME hardware is no exception. This will make for rapid adoption of newer hardware technologies (for example, 3D chips, touchscreens, GPS, sensors, and NFC) than even before, which in turn will lead to those technologies being quickly adopted by Java ME developers because of their widespread availability. This in turn will lead to better and more-powerful Java ME applications, with all the benefits that come from it.

The Evolution of the Java ME API

The most important thing that needs discussing here is MIDP 3.0, the successor to MIDP 2.0. MIDP 3.0 will bring with it enhanced capabilities in most areas of the Java ME platform: better graphics, UI and communications support, support for background MIDlets, MIDlet multitasking, inter-MIDlet communications, natively secure RMS stores, fewer fragmentation issues, and more.

> **NOTE:** For a full list of MIDP 3.0 enhancements, visit `http://java.sun.com/developer` `/technicalArticles/javame/midp3_enhance/`.

These enhancements are needed in order to bring the Java ME platform into the same ballpark as modern-day smartphone platforms in terms of software capabilities. Granted, smartphones will (by definition) always have better capabilities, but the fact that most of today's Java ME phones don't even support a simple thing such as multitasking (for example) means that a lot of potential users are drawn away from the platform, and it also means that the platform is starting to show its age.

MIDP 3.0 by will change all this, by providing developers with the needed tools to create competitive and modern applications. A MIDP 3.0 feature phone will not be that different at first glance compared to a smartphone. It will, for example, have multitasking support and will support widgets. (Inside an MIDP 3.0 application, widgets can be implemented quite easily by extending the `IdleItem` class, after which the application can add them to the device's idle screen by calling `Display.setIdleItem(someItem)`. Basically, `IdleItem`s are just like regular items, and can be used as such, with the distinction that they can also be added to the idle screen.) In addition, applications will be able to communicate with one another (for example, providing copy-paste support) and share functionality, and they will be able to respond to system-wide events such as incoming calls.

MIDP 3.0 will definitely be a game changer after it gets widely adopted. However, the problem is knowing when this will happen. The specifications are finalized, but there are, to my knowledge, no MIDP 3.0 devices out there at the time of this writing. There are many reasons for this, including roadmaps, licensing fees, hardware requirements, the fact that MIDP 2.0 is still quite okay for stand-alone applications running on feature phones, and pricing. There is no doubt that MIDP 3.0 devices will arrive sooner or later in order for feature phones to remain competitive (and there is clearly a demand for them, considering their market share). However, for now, we will have to wait.

The future will also see the general migration from MIDP 1.0/CLDC 1.0 to MIDP 2.0/CLDC 1.1. The former combination is still found in a wide variety of devices, especially in the developing world, but as the hardware gets cheaper and MIDP 3. 0 enters the scene, even extremely low-end devices will make the jump to MIDP 2.0.

Finally, in terms of the evolution of the Java ME optional APIs, I see no major changes. APIs for most modern capabilities already exist (for example, GPS and NFC,), so the only thing that the future will bring is their widespread adoption.

The Evolution of the Java ME Mindset and Development Philosophy

First of all, it is my belief that, as low-end, mid-level, and high-end devices continue to converge in terms of capabilities, developers will finally be able to approach all of them with a single mindset—and thus create a common development philosophy. The focus will be on elegance and simplicity. Without having to worry about the widely different environments that an application needs to support today, developers will be able to write cleaner code, better and faster.

As hardware grows more powerful, the limits of what can be done with Java ME will grow along with it, and the need for having a pessimistic and cautious approach will fade away. Fewer compromises will have to be made; you will be able to have both a good-looking and a feature-rich application.

At the same time, outside-the-box thinking and clever solutions to problems will no longer be mandatory to get an application done. Instead, they will become optional or, most likely, will become the differentiating factors between applications.

Even more emphasis than today will be placed on the user's experience, as developers will benefit from the freedom to create user interfaces that today are unfeasible even on high-end devices. This will be aided by the fact that third-party libraries and tools will also become more feature rich and will take advantage of the increase in available resources and APIs. As such, even more third-party libraries will be used than today. At the same time, the need to get your hands dirty in order to get the best possible performance on a certain device will go away: either the library will do this for you, or the target device will be powerful enough so as not to require the effort.

New mindset rules will also be introduced. For example, cloud computing and integration with the cloud will play an increasingly greater role in the Java ME world, to the point that it will become almost commonplace. This will be reflected in the developer's mindset, with one of the goals being to seamlessly blend the capabilities of the cloud with those of the device in order to get the best of both, to a much higher degree than today.

Another rule that will be introduced is that because storage space and memory are plentiful, you should always make full use of them. This will impact everything, from the quality of the graphical user interface to the amount and type of data that your applications will store and process. For example, you will be able to add full "undo" support to your application by keeping track of your data's state across an entire run. By comparison, although much better than a few years ago, developers today still have to put effort into conserving RAM and using as little storage space as possible, and applications that do have undo support are typically limited to only one or two steps.

In conclusion, Java ME development will be handled in the same way as desktop development is handled today. There will be considerably fewer optimizations needed and fewer portability tricks required, with developers relying more on native APIs and on established third-party libraries and tools. Development will be clean, simple, and elegant.

Java ME's Target Market

When they first appeared, Java ME devices were targeted toward the relatively rich (on a global scale). At that time, that meant people in the Western world. Today, Java ME devices are being replaced by smartphones in the Western world, a trend that will continue in the future. The replacement is not and will not be complete: many people will buy Java ME devices as a secondary phone or because they prefer their simplicity and their longer battery life.

As such, geographically speaking, Java ME's target market in the future will mostly be the developing world, a trend that can be observed in the present too. Many nations traditionally considered poor are undergoing an economic boom right now, which means a lot of people who couldn't previously afford a mobile phone (or could afford only extremely cheap ones, without any kind of support for third-party applications) can now purchase one. Because smartphones are too expensive for them, they are opting for feature phones running Java ME.

This, coupled with the economic boom in their countries, creates a Java ME market with great potential, just as it initially was in the Western world. For example, in Africa there are considerably more mobile phones than there are computers. So what we typically do on computers in the Western world (including banking, web surfing, games, and writing e-mails), they do on mobile phones—mobile phones that require applications for all of the previously mentioned tasks, applications that you can write and monetize.

Next, the world is much more connected now than it was when Java ME first appeared, and this trend will continue for the foreseeable future. This means that connected Java ME applications will become more and more common. Thus, a special class of applications (which are starting to gain visibility right now) are applications that are simply clients for web-based or cloud-based services—for example, clients for social networking web sites and for web-based e-mail services. These kinds of applications are a perfect match for Java ME's widespread use across the world, and they will likely grow in prominence as the hardware available to them grows in power and capabilities; they form a growing and potentially very profitable market.

Finally, when MIDP 3.0 arrives, a new market will be created for smartphone-like applications. These will be applications running on feature phones with MIDP 3.0 support and will stand somewhere between today's (comparatively limited) MIDP 2.0 applications and smartphone applications, and they will bridge the gap between feature phone functionality and smartphone functionality—for example, e-mail clients that run as idle screen applications/widgets on feature phones, or that run in the background and notify the user when a new e-mail comes in.

Java ME and Other Platforms

Java ME is the king of mobile platforms in terms of market share, and will continue to be so in the foreseeable future. However, it is no secret that, as far as money and development effort is concerned, Java ME is gradually but surely being eclipsed by smartphone platforms.

At least until the arrival of MIDP 3.0, this trend will continue. It's much easier to develop for a smartphone than it is to develop for a feature phone. Furthermore, as smartphone platforms rapidly advance and improve (Android is the prime example of this), the capabilities gap between Java ME and them will widen.

At the moment, and in the immediate future, the only thing keeping Java ME afloat is its huge market share. To leverage this, cross-platform tools have appeared, which allow developers to take their Java ME applications and automatically port them to smartphone platforms, giving developers the biggest possible market share. These tools have rapidly gained popularity and will continue to remain popular as long as market share is what's required of an application.

However, cross-platform tools that target smartphones exclusively have gained huge popularity in the past couple of years. These tools are based on web technologies (HTML, CSS, JavaScript) and have already eclipsed Java ME–based tools in terms of popularity for applications that focus on monetization. This situation will most likely continue until the widespread adoption of MIDP 3.0, at which point Java ME might also become a viable platform for monetization.

As mentioned before, MIDP 3.0 will be a game changer, allowing Java ME as a platform to significantly close the gap between it and smartphone platforms. This will make the platform attractive again for developers, at least as far as capabilities are concerned. Monetization might be a different issue, primarily because of distribution issues (it's hard to monetize an application if you can't deliver it to your users; Java ME has no central application store).

There are two main solutions to this problem: vendor-specific stores (for example, Ovi by Nokia) built into MIDP 3.0 phones and vendor-independent stores (for example,

GetJar) that users can access on their own. However, neither solution has the same elegance as a unified application store built right into the platform (for example, Android Marketplace). Still, what is lost in elegance might be won in sheer number of sales, as MIDP 3.0 devices will most likely end up being considerably more numerous than any single smartphone platform.

MIDP 3.0 will also see the resurgence of Java ME as the source platform for cross-platform application development, as the baseline low-end device for MIDP 3.0 should be about what high-end Java ME devices are today. This, augmented by the new capabilities introduced by MIDP 3.0, will make Java ME powerful enough to play in the same league as smartphone platforms.

As for the current MIDP 2.0 technology, it will be able to compete with smartphone platforms only in geographical areas where price is the most important criteria for purchasing a phone. In the Western world, virtually anyone who wants to run an application on their phone will be able to afford a smartphone as the prices for entry-level models continue to go down.

However, in geographical areas where price is the most important criteria, MIDP 2.0 still has a long life ahead of it, as it will replace both bare-bones mobile phones and MIDP 1.0 devices. In contrast, even the cheapest smartphone will be considerably more expensive than most people there will be able to afford.

Java ME Application Types

Initially, Java ME applications were little more than proofs of concept. You weren't really able to do much with them, because of their very limited platform and hardware. This continued to be the case until the MIDP 2.0 standard and devices supporting it came onto the scene.

At that point, the Java ME application scene started to boom. Most applications written were games, but a few serious applications appeared too, including calendars, calculators, and spreadsheets. Still, the selection wasn't that big, primarily because any serious number crunching required more processing power and larger screens than the devices of the day had at their disposal.

Today, Java ME has a wide assortment of applications written for it, and devices powerful enough to run them. You can find anything from games to document viewers, remote desktop clients to GPS software.

Besides these application types, as mentioned earlier, in the future Java ME will see a huge increase in applications related to social networking, banking, and cloud computing. These types of applications are all a perfect fit for Java ME's widespread nature, and because devices are becoming more and more powerful, the user's experience on them (particularly in the case of social networking) will become more and more enjoyable.

Applications relying on interaction with the real world will also grow in prominence. For example, NFC communications can be used to interface your phone with your car, your

TV set, or even your microwave oven. An appliance manufacturer will certainly target Java ME devices with NFC chips alongside any smartphone platform, simply because of their widespread use.

Applications that augment the real world will also come into play. As more Java ME devices will feature both GPS and 3D hardware, augmented-reality applications will start to appear on the market. These might be simple evolutions of existing applications (for example, a GPS application will add augmented-reality support) or as stand-alone tools (for example, a distance-measuring application or a museum guide).

MIDP 3.0 will bring with it the possibility of writing applications that are currently simply impossible to write—for example, applications that run in the background, or on a device's idle screen or that react to system-wide events. Applications will also be able to work together and share data and capabilities, in effect becoming more than the sum of their parts.

Finally, applications that interact with other computing devices will also start to appear. For example, equipped with the proper Java ME application, you will be able to use a compatible mobile phone as a game controller for your PC and console games. Prototypes of this are already available, but these are typically limited (for example, they use the phone's accelerometer capabilities as a virtual steering wheel). As devices grow in power and capabilities, the extent to which mobile phones will get used as game controllers or as enhancements to other computing devices will grow. For example, you will be able to interface your mobile phone with your car's navigation system for a point-and-drive experience: you will just take a photo of the place you want to drive to (an address, an actual photo, or a map) and the phone will automatically tell the GPS where to go.

Java ME Innovation

At this point, pretty much everything that's possible with the current state of the Java ME platform has already been done, either commercially or as a proof of concept. The only thing left to do is bring more of the proof-of-concept applications into the real world. This is happening gradually as hardware is becoming more powerful. For example, graphical processing algorithms that were unfeasible five years ago can now be run on modern-day Java ME devices, and 3D touchscreen games are no longer just wishful thinking. The same applies for GPS software, web browsers, and other categories of software that were unfeasible in the past.

And there are many other types of applications, more or less proofs of concept, that are waiting to be put in the spotlight (for example, e-banking clients and home remote-control applications). These applications are not yet ready for prime time, but their time will undoubtedly come, as living in a connected world implies that people want to do more and more things on the go.

With MIDP 2.0 devices replacing old MIDP 1.0 ones, and with the increasing number of mobile phones appearing in the developing world, the potential to truly innovate (and possibly even change lives) is there, though on a different level. For example, applications that we might regard as being useless or puerile here, such as an application that teaches young children how to read and count, are an invaluable tool in parts of the world where education is scarce. This mix of technology, innovation, and social concern can make a difference—and Java ME is the perfect platform for it.

However, real innovation will take off when MIDP 3.0 devices appear on the market, and when NFC becomes widespread. Each of these technologies provides as many innovation opportunities as the leap from MIDP 1.0 to MIDP 2.0 did.

For example, MIDP 3.0 will open the door for more-realistic games and more-powerful applications that are currently not possible (for example, applications that run in the background or as widgets). MIDP 3.0 will also open the possibility of having applications work as service providers, providing their services and capabilities to other applications.

A picture-editing application will be able to share its data in real time with a document-editing application. This will allow the document editor application to embed image files in formats that it does not natively support, but that are supported by the picture-editing application. Furthermore, this makes it possible to edit a picture in the picture-editing software and instantly see the results reflected in the document. There are many opportunities to be seized here.

As for NFC, its widespread adoption will turn mobile phones into particularly powerful tools, and Java ME phones will be like army knives: small, cheap, yet very powerful. As mentioned earlier, you will be able to use your mobile phone for anything from paying your bills to starting up your car.

There is great potential for innovation here. For example, you could potentially use your phone as a shopping assistant: you would just place you phone near a product you're interested in, and it would save that product in your "wanted" list, but it would also be able to compare it to other similar products available in the same store and provide you with detailed information about it. Or you could combine MIDP 3.0 and NFC to create really interesting social applications, such as a background-running social MIDlet that allows you to quickly exchange business cards and befriend another person on Facebook just by having the two of your touch your mobile phones together.

Java ME's Death

Though the death of Java ME will certainly happen someday (as it does to all software platforms), this event is unlikely to happen in the foreseeable future. Still, let's be pessimistic and have a look at how and why Java ME, as a platform, might die out.

The most obvious reason for this is competition from other mobile platforms, especially Android. Android has seen an unbelievable rate of adoption, and is certain to become the leading smartphone platform for the next few years. It is perceived, and for good reason, as a flexible and powerful mobile platform, and because it has no licensing fees, manufacturers have quickly adopted it.

However, Android is still a smartphone platform, and it requires the appropriate hardware: a fast CPU, lots of RAM, a big screen with touch support. These not only cost money, but also tend to eat up battery life quickly—as any smartphone user can tell you.

In contrast, Java ME is more of an application environment. Its minimum specifications are considerably lower than those of Android, which means that it can run on considerably less powerful hardware and consume considerably less power while doing so (aided by the fact that, unlike Android, the Java ME environment has to be active only when an application is running). Business reasons also come into play, as part of the premium that consumers pay for a smartphone is based on its operating system. If you deliver the same operating system on entry-level devices, you have to lower the premium, which is not something I see manufacturers doing with Android anytime soon.

All of these things mean that Java ME is far more suited for a feature phone than Android is, which is unlikely to ever change in the future. It is true that Android devices are becoming cheaper and cheaper, but Java ME will always deliver more bang for the buck in the entry-phone arena.

The second often-cited reason is that most developers are flocking to smartphone platforms. This is certainly true now, but as long as there is a market for Java ME applications (and, as we have seen, there is and there will be), there will also be Java ME developers. Furthermore, Java ME is the easiest platform to approach both in terms of cost and technology, so there will always be a stream of new developers coming toward it. MIDP 3.0 will also generate a lot of attention, because it really tremendously enhances Java ME's capabilities.

The fact that there is no money to be made in Java ME is another reason cited for the platform to die. However, that's false. There is not *as much* money to be made, but that doesn't mean that there aren't opportunities. You just have to think about your business model. As I said in the beginning of this book, Java ME applications aren't monetized by selling them to end users as smartphone applications are. You should also look further away from home for business leads, that is, in the developing world.

The final reason that could contribute to the end of Java ME is that the platform is stalling. That's somewhat true, in that its evolution in recent years has been considerably slower than the evolution of other platforms. But there *has been* an evolution. Hardware is more powerful than before, APIs are up to date and are gradually being adopted by more and more devices, and screens are getting bigger and better. What's of real concern is the gap between Java ME and other platforms. This gap is very real and currently widening, with MIDP 3.0 (which would close the gap for the most part) nowhere in sight.

However, that's not entirely true. What's missing are *devices* with MIDP 3.0 support. The standard itself is ready, and there is a reference implementation for it. Keep in mind that MIDP 3.0 is big from many points of view, so naturally companies don't want to jump head-first into it. There are many factors and implications to be considered (for one thing, implementing MIDP 3.0 will probably require extensive changes to the current generation of firmware that manufacturers use). But the jump will happen sooner or later; it's just a matter of time.

Summary

In this chapter, you have examined what the future holds for the Java ME platform in terms of hardware, software, target markets, and more. You have also looked at some of the reasons that Java ME might "die" in the foreseeable future.

Chapter 16

Final Words

At this point, we have reached the end of our journey into the world of Pro Java ME applications. As such, I would like to use these last few pages to recap what we have discussed in the book up to this point, and provide you with a few markers related to what you should do next in order to deepen your knowledge of the platform.

What we have covered in the book

We started with a simple introduction to the Java ME world: a quick overview of the platform, of the basic techniques you'll need to develop for it and of the various issues you'll encounter while doing so. As a goal, we set out to write a Java ME Twitter client using a professional development approach.

Having set our goal, we continued our journey by writing a proper framework for our application, explaining the decisions made along the way and highlighting why having a good framework for your application is paramount for its success.

Following this, we proceeded with defining the critical data structures needed for our application. We have looked at the Java ME way of handling data modeling and at how properly defined objects and data structures can ease the development process considerably and improve the application as a whole.

We then advanced by writing all our application's necessary modules: the networking module, the UI module, the persistence module and the localization module. As we did all of this, critical decisions were explained, potentially fatal mistakes were highlighted and useful advice was given.

Having completed our application, the next step on the agenda was to discuss Java ME's biggest plague: fragmentation. The common types of fragmentation were discussed and solutions for them were described.

We then delved into the equally important subject of optimizing Java ME code. Important techniques for this were explained and exemplified, as well as the reasoning and low-level workings behind them.

The next topic discussed was application improvement, by means of adding fine touches and by improving the way in which the user interacts with your application. Examples for each category were given and discussed.

After this, we explored Java ME application testing in all its forms. From basic unit testing to testing involving hardware modifications, the most pertinent Java ME application testing techniques were explained.

The second to last topic we discussed was graphics. We had a look at some very useful and interesting graphical techniques that can be used in Java ME applications today, such as image masking and image rotation.

We ended our journey with a discussion of the proper Java ME mindset. The overarching set of rules and principles that should guide the entire Java ME application development process were outlined, explained and exemplified with real-life stories.

What to research next

The first thing I would recommend is to read as much as possible on two key topics related to Java ME development: code optimizations and graphics. Both of these areas are critical for creating highly polished applications that are competitive and user friendly. They are also the main weaknesses of Java ME compared to other mobile platforms, in that you have to optimize the code yourself and you also have to implement from scratch anything but the most basic graphical operations.

Algorithms and data structures should probably be covered next. These topics are important for professional applications on any platform, but they are especially important for Java ME because using the right algorithms and data structures makes the difference between having an application that runs out of resources and/or crashes and having an application that runs smoothly along, without hiccups.

Another area you should research is that of user interface design and user interaction, particularly literature focused on UI's running on small displays. Good knowledge in this area is very important if you want to get the most out of your application. Remember, no matter how technically competent your application is, users still have to be able to use it with ease. Furthermore, this is not just a "design thing"; the knowledge you will gain researching this topic will help you better write and implement your UIs because you will better understand the principles at work behind them.

If you are not already into it, cross-platform development and application porting should also be on your list of things to look into. This is already pretty big, but will become even bigger once MIDP 3.0 devices appear on the market. In addition, even if you're only developing for Java ME, having some hands-on knowledge of how various tasks are done on other platforms and how Java ME compares to them in concrete scenarios will help your development process tremendously.

Lastly, and this may sound unusual, you should do some research into the microcomputer platforms of the '80s, such as the Commodore 64 or the ZX Spectrum. Read about them, play with some emulators, try to get a feel of what their applications were like and of how said applications were written. Java ME and these old platforms share the common spirit of doing incredible things with very limited resources, and of pushing the boundaries of the underlying platform through innovation and outside the box thinking, so researching these computers of days gone by will help you better grasp and understand the nature of Java ME software development.

In closing

The main goal of the book was to explain how to professionally approach each aspect of the Java ME development process, from the initial planning to the final fine touches. I sincerely hope that this goal was achieved and that, after reading these pages, you have gained valuable insight and information that will help you become a better Java ME developer.

I also hope that this book's approach of writing and discussing a complete Java ME application rather than working with independent snippets of code has given you a complete picture of what writing a Pro Java ME app requires, and a better understanding of how the tips and techniques presented herein can be used in real life scenarios.

Finally, I hope that you had fun reading this book, and that it has inspired you to explore, try out new things and push the limits of what's possible with the Java ME platform today.

Happy coding!

Index

G

V

W, X, Y, Z